Jin Xing

China's Groundbreaking Transgender Icon – Unauthorized

Mohammed Raj

ISBN: 9781779695963
Imprint: Telephasic Workshop
Copyright © 2024 Mohammed Raj.
All Rights Reserved.

Contents

The Road to Fame   22

Bibliography   **45**
Personal Struggles   45

Bibliography   **63**
Professional Transitions   68
The Cultural Icon   90

Bibliography   **113**

The Journey Continues   **115**
The Journey Continues   115
International Recognition   118
Love and Family   137

Bibliography   **153**
The Power of Resilience   158

Bibliography   **173**
Legacy and Future Ventures   183
The Unfiltered Truth   206

Beyond Boundaries   **229**
Beyond Boundaries   229
Jin Xing's Impact on the LGBTQ Movement in China   233

Bibliography   **257**
The Global Fight for LGBTQ Rights   257
Cultural Representation and Media Influence   280

Bibliography **291**

Inspiring Change: Lessons from Jin Xing's Journey 305

A Call to Action 329

Bibliography **355**

Index **357**

The Birth of a Star

The story of Jin Xing is not merely a tale of a dancer; it is a narrative of transformation, resilience, and the relentless pursuit of identity. Born in Shenyang, China, Jin Xing emerged from humble beginnings, but her journey was marked by an extraordinary talent and an indomitable spirit.

1.1.1 Jin Xing's Humble Beginnings in Shenyang, China

Jin Xing was born in 1975 in Shenyang, a city known for its heavy industry and rich cultural heritage. Growing up in a modest household, she was the only child of her parents, who worked tirelessly to provide for their family. The socio-economic environment of Shenyang posed significant challenges; however, it also fostered a sense of determination in young Jin.

1.1.2 A Unique Childhood Marked by Talent and Determination

From an early age, Jin exhibited a remarkable talent for dance. Her parents recognized her potential and encouraged her to pursue her passion. Despite the lack of resources, they found ways to support her ambitions, enrolling her in local dance classes. Jin's childhood was a tapestry woven with the threads of hard work, discipline, and an unwavering commitment to her art.

1.1.3 Jin Xing's Early Exposure to Dance and Performance

Jin's first exposure to dance came through traditional Chinese dance forms. She was captivated by the grace and fluidity of movement, which resonated deeply with her. In her formative years, she participated in various local dance competitions, where she quickly made a name for herself. Her performances were not just about executing steps; they were expressions of her inner self, a foreshadowing of the groundbreaking artist she would become.

1.1.4 The Influence of Jin Xing's Parents on Her Upbringing

The support of her parents was pivotal in shaping Jin Xing's identity. They instilled in her the values of hard work and perseverance. However, their understanding of her internal struggles was limited. As Jin began to grapple with her gender identity, the cultural norms of the time created a barrier between her and her parents. Their love was unwavering, but the societal expectations weighed heavily on her.

1.1.5 Challenges Faced by Jin Xing as a Transgender Individual in China

As a transgender individual in China, Jin faced a myriad of challenges. The conservative societal framework often stigmatized those who deviated from traditional gender norms. This societal pressure manifested in various forms, from discrimination in public spaces to a lack of representation in the arts. Jin's journey was fraught with obstacles, yet each challenge only fueled her determination to succeed.

1.1.6 Jin Xing's Discovery of Her Passion for Dance

Dance became Jin's sanctuary, a space where she could express her true self without fear of judgment. As she honed her skills, it became clear that her passion was not just a hobby; it was her calling. The transformational power of dance allowed her to explore her identity and connect with others who shared her love for the art form.

1.1.7 Jin Xing's Early Success in Local Dance Competitions

Jin's early success in local dance competitions was a testament to her dedication and talent. She won numerous accolades, which not only boosted her confidence but also solidified her desire to pursue dance as a career. These victories were more than just trophies; they were stepping stones on her path to becoming a cultural icon.

1.1.8 The Decision to Pursue Dance as a Career

Recognizing her potential, Jin made the bold decision to pursue dance as a career. This choice was not without its risks, as the dance industry was notoriously competitive. However, her passion outweighed the fears, propelling her into a world where she could truly shine.

1.1.9 Jin Xing's Determination to Overcome Societal Expectations

Jin's determination to overcome societal expectations was a driving force in her life. Despite the challenges she faced, she refused to conform to the limitations imposed by society. Her journey was a rebellion against the norms that sought to define her, and she embraced her uniqueness as a source of strength.

1.1.10 The Transformational Power of Dance in Jin Xing's Life

Dance transformed Jin's life in profound ways. It became a medium through which she could communicate her experiences, struggles, and triumphs. The stage was her canvas, and every performance was a declaration of her identity. Through dance, Jin Xing not only found herself but also began to pave the way for others like her, becoming a beacon of hope in a world that often sought to silence voices of difference.

In conclusion, the birth of Jin Xing as a star was not a singular event but a culmination of experiences, challenges, and triumphs that shaped her into the groundbreaking transgender icon she is today. Her story is a testament to the power of resilience and the transformative nature of art, inspiring countless individuals to embrace their true selves in the face of adversity.

The Birth of a Star

Jin Xing, a name that resonates with courage and artistry, emerged from the bustling city of Shenyang, China. Her story begins not in the spotlight, but in the humble surroundings of her childhood home, where the seeds of talent and determination were first sown.

1.1.1 Jin Xing's Humble Beginnings in Shenyang, China

Born in 1975, Jin Xing grew up in a society fraught with traditional values and expectations. Shenyang, a city steeped in history and culture, provided a backdrop that was both inspiring and challenging. The societal norms of the time imposed rigid gender roles, making Jin Xing's journey toward self-actualization all the more daunting. As a child, she faced the dual challenge of navigating her burgeoning identity while striving to excel in the arts.

1.1.2 A Unique Childhood Marked by Talent and Determination

From an early age, Jin Xing exhibited extraordinary talent in dance. Her innate ability to express emotion through movement set her apart from her peers. However, talent alone was not enough; it was her relentless determination that propelled her forward. Jin Xing often practiced for hours on end, refining her skills and pushing the boundaries of her physical capabilities. This dedication would later define her career and influence her artistic vision.

1.1.3 Jin Xing's Early Exposure to Dance and Performance

Jin Xing's introduction to dance came at the tender age of six, when she joined a local dance troupe. This experience was transformative, igniting a passion that would consume her life. The discipline of dance provided an escape from the societal constraints that weighed heavily upon her. It was in the dance studio where she first felt a sense of freedom, a stark contrast to the expectations placed upon her outside.

1.1.4 The Influence of Jin Xing's Parents on Her Upbringing

Jin Xing's parents played a pivotal role in shaping her journey. Her mother, a traditional Chinese woman, initially struggled to understand her daughter's aspirations. However, recognizing Jin Xing's exceptional talent, she gradually became a source of support. Jin Xing's father, a military officer, instilled in her the values of discipline and perseverance. Together, they fostered an environment that allowed her to explore her artistic inclinations, despite the societal pressures to conform.

1.1.5 Challenges Faced by Jin Xing as a Transgender Individual in China

As Jin Xing navigated her childhood and adolescence, she encountered significant challenges as a transgender individual in a conservative society. The stigma associated with gender nonconformity was pervasive, and the cultural milieu often relegated transgender individuals to the margins. Jin Xing faced bullying and discrimination, which only fueled her determination to prove herself. These experiences would later inform her advocacy work, as she sought to create a more inclusive environment for others.

1.1.6 Jin Xing's Discovery of Her Passion for Dance

Dance became not just a hobby but a lifeline for Jin Xing. It was through dance that she discovered her true self, a form of expression that transcended the limitations imposed by society. The rhythm of music and the fluidity of movement allowed her to articulate emotions that words could not capture. This profound connection to dance would ultimately guide her toward a career that combined her love for performance with her desire for self-acceptance.

1.1.7 Jin Xing's Early Success in Local Dance Competitions

Jin Xing's dedication and talent did not go unnoticed. By her teenage years, she began to dominate local dance competitions, showcasing her unique style and flair. These early victories were significant, as they not only validated her efforts but also provided a glimpse of the potential that lay ahead. Each competition served as a stepping stone, building her confidence and reputation in the dance community.

1.1.8 The Decision to Pursue Dance as a Career

The decision to pursue dance as a career was a turning point for Jin Xing. Despite the societal pressures to conform to traditional gender roles, she chose to follow her passion. This choice was not without its challenges; it required immense courage to defy expectations and embrace her identity as a dancer. However, Jin Xing's unwavering commitment to her craft propelled her forward, setting the stage for her future endeavors.

1.1.9 Jin Xing's Determination to Overcome Societal Expectations

Jin Xing's journey was characterized by a fierce determination to overcome the societal expectations that sought to confine her. She recognized that her path would not be easy, yet she remained resolute in her pursuit of excellence. This determination was not only a personal quest but also a broader statement against the limitations imposed on individuals based on gender. Jin Xing became a symbol of resilience, inspiring others to challenge societal norms.

1.1.10 The Transformational Power of Dance in Jin Xing's Life

Ultimately, dance became the transformational force in Jin Xing's life. It provided her with a means to express her identity and navigate the complexities of her existence. Through dance, she found her voice, her purpose, and her place in the world. This realization would shape not only her career but also her advocacy for LGBTQ rights, as she sought to empower others to embrace their true selves.

In conclusion, the birth of Jin Xing as a star was not merely a result of her talent, but a culmination of her experiences, struggles, and triumphs. Her early years in Shenyang laid the foundation for a remarkable journey that would redefine the boundaries of dance and activism in China. Jin Xing's story is one of resilience, passion, and the unwavering pursuit of authenticity, setting the stage for her emergence as a groundbreaking icon in the LGBTQ community.

ERROR. thisXsection() returned an empty string with textbook depth = 3.
ERROR. thisXsection() returned an empty string with textbook depth = 3.
ERROR. thisXsection() returned an empty string with textbook depth = 3.

A unique childhood marked by talent and determination

Jin Xing's childhood in Shenyang, China, was anything but ordinary. Born into a world that often failed to understand her identity, she emerged as a beacon of talent and determination. From a young age, Jin exhibited an innate ability to captivate audiences through her performances, showcasing a unique blend of grace and passion that belied her humble beginnings. The environment in which she grew up was a crucible of both creativity and adversity, shaping her into the icon she would later become.

At the tender age of five, Jin began to explore her passion for dance. Her first dance class was a pivotal moment, igniting a spark that would fuel her ambitions for years to come. The joy she found in movement was palpable; it was as if she had discovered a language that transcended words. This early exposure to dance was not merely a hobby; it was a lifeline that provided her with an escape from the societal expectations that loomed over her.

However, talent alone was not enough to ensure success. Jin faced numerous challenges as a transgender individual in a conservative society. The societal norms in China at the time were rigid, and any deviation from the expected path was met with skepticism, if not outright hostility. The struggles she encountered were not just personal but systemic, reflecting a broader cultural resistance to gender diversity. Despite these obstacles, Jin's determination shone through. She practiced tirelessly, often for hours on end, perfecting her technique and performance skills.

The influence of her parents played a significant role in her early development. While they may not have fully understood her identity, they recognized her talent and encouraged her to pursue her passion. This support was crucial, as it provided Jin with the confidence to express herself in a world that frequently sought to silence her. The encouragement she received at home served as a counterbalance to the discrimination she faced outside, fostering a sense of resilience that would become a hallmark of her character.

Jin's childhood was also marked by her participation in local dance competitions, where she quickly made a name for herself. These competitions were not merely contests; they were opportunities for her to showcase her artistry and challenge the preconceived notions of what a dancer should be. Each performance was a declaration of her identity, a statement that she was not only a dancer but a force to be reckoned with.

As she navigated the complexities of her identity, Jin's passion for dance became a transformative power in her life. It was through dance that she found her voice, a means of articulating her experiences and emotions in a way that words often failed to capture. This connection to her art allowed her to transcend the limitations imposed by society, enabling her to carve out a space for herself in a world that often sought to confine her.

In reflecting on Jin Xing's childhood, it is evident that her journey was marked by a unique interplay of talent and determination. Her early experiences laid the foundation for her future endeavors, instilling in her the belief that she could defy societal expectations and forge her own path. The resilience she developed during these formative years would serve her well as she faced the challenges of adulthood, ultimately leading her to become a groundbreaking icon in the LGBTQ community.

In conclusion, Jin Xing's childhood was not merely a backdrop to her later achievements; it was a critical period that shaped her identity and aspirations. The combination of her extraordinary talent, unwavering determination, and the support of her family created a powerful narrative of self-discovery and empowerment. As she continued on her journey, these early experiences would resonate throughout her life, reminding her of the strength that comes from embracing one's true self against all odds.

Jin Xing's early exposure to dance and performance

Jin Xing's journey into the world of dance began at a remarkably young age, a time when most children are still exploring their basic motor skills. Growing up in Shenyang, China, she was surrounded by a vibrant tapestry of cultural influences that would ultimately shape her artistic identity. Dance was not merely a pastime for Jin; it was a sanctuary, a means of expression that transcended the limitations imposed by her environment.

The Cultural Context of Dance in China

In China, dance has historically been a medium of storytelling, reflecting the rich heritage and traditions of various ethnic groups. From classical ballet to folk dances, the art form serves as a conduit for cultural expression and identity. For Jin, this cultural backdrop was both an inspiration and a challenge. The societal norms of the time often dictated rigid gender roles, leaving little room for deviation. Despite these constraints, Jin's early exposure to dance provided her with a sense of freedom and an outlet to explore her identity.

Early Beginnings in Dance

Jin's first encounter with dance came through local performances, where she was captivated by the grace and strength of the dancers. Her parents, recognizing her natural talent, encouraged her participation in local dance competitions. These early experiences were pivotal; they not only honed her skills but also instilled a sense of discipline and determination. As she immersed herself in the world of dance, Jin began to understand the power of movement as a form of personal expression.

Challenges and Breakthroughs

While Jin's passion for dance flourished, it was not without its challenges. The societal expectations of a young boy in China often clashed with her burgeoning identity. Jin faced ridicule and discrimination, yet she remained undeterred. The dance floor became her refuge—a space where she could momentarily escape the harsh realities of her life.

An example of this resilience can be seen in her participation in a local dance competition at the age of twelve. Despite the jeers from the audience, Jin delivered a performance that left the judges in awe. Her ability to convey emotion through movement set her apart, marking the beginning of her journey toward stardom. This experience taught her a vital lesson: that authenticity and passion could triumph over societal prejudice.

The Influence of Dance on Identity Formation

The transformational power of dance in Jin's life cannot be overstated. It played a crucial role in her identity formation, allowing her to explore and express her true self in a society that often marginalized individuals like her. Dance became a language through which she could articulate her struggles and aspirations, bridging the gap between her inner self and the external world.

Research in performance studies highlights the significance of embodiment in identity formation, suggesting that movement is not just a physical act but a means of negotiating one's existence in the world [?]. For Jin, each dance step was a declaration of her existence, a rebellion against the constraints imposed by her gender identity.

Conclusion

In conclusion, Jin Xing's early exposure to dance and performance was a defining element of her life. It provided her with a platform to challenge societal norms and embrace her identity as a transgender individual. Through dance, she not only found her voice but also laid the foundation for a career that would inspire countless others. As she continued to navigate the complexities of her identity, the lessons learned on the dance floor would serve as a guiding light in her journey toward becoming a groundbreaking icon in the LGBTQ community.

The influence of Jin Xing's parents on her upbringing

Jin Xing's journey to becoming a groundbreaking transgender icon in China was profoundly shaped by the influence of her parents. Their support, values, and attitudes played a critical role in her personal development and her pursuit of dance, which would later become her vehicle for self-expression and activism.

From an early age, Jin's parents instilled in her the importance of education and hard work. Her father, a military officer, and her mother, a teacher, emphasized discipline and perseverance. This foundational belief in the value of education is encapsulated in the equation:

$$E = \frac{W}{T} \tag{1}$$

where E represents educational attainment, W symbolizes the amount of work put into studies, and T stands for the time dedicated to learning. Jin Xing's parents encouraged her to excel academically, which provided her with a strong sense of self-worth and the confidence to pursue her passions.

However, the cultural context of China during Jin's formative years posed significant challenges. Traditional Chinese values often emphasized conformity and adherence to societal norms, particularly regarding gender roles. Jin Xing's parents, recognizing the societal pressures surrounding gender identity, chose to approach her upbringing with an open mind. They nurtured her interests, particularly in dance, despite the potential stigma attached to her aspirations as a male-to-female transgender individual.

The influence of Jin Xing's parents can be understood through the lens of attachment theory, which posits that secure emotional bonds formed during childhood significantly affect an individual's psychological development and social relationships. Jin's parents provided a stable and loving environment, fostering her self-esteem and resilience in the face of adversity. This secure attachment enabled her to explore her identity and pursue her dreams without the paralyzing fear of rejection.

Moreover, her mother's encouragement of artistic expression was pivotal. Jin's mother recognized her daughter's innate talent for dance and actively supported her participation in local dance competitions. This not only allowed Jin to hone her skills but also to develop a sense of identity separate from societal expectations. The following equation illustrates the relationship between parental support and self-identity development:

$$ID = P_s + A \tag{2}$$

where ID represents self-identity, P_s denotes parental support, and A symbolizes individual agency. In Jin's case, the unwavering support from her parents contributed significantly to her ability to assert her identity as a dancer and eventually as a transgender woman.

Despite their support, Jin Xing's parents faced their own struggles with societal perceptions. They had to navigate a landscape that often stigmatized and marginalized transgender individuals. This created a duality in their parenting approach: while they sought to empower Jin, they were also aware of the potential backlash from their community. This tension is exemplified in the following inequality:

$$C > S \tag{3}$$

where C represents community expectations and S symbolizes the support provided by family. In Jin's case, the community's expectations often outweighed the familial support, leading to a complex interplay between acceptance and societal pressures.

As Jin Xing blossomed into a talented dancer, her parents remained her staunchest advocates. They attended her performances, celebrated her victories, and comforted her during setbacks. This unwavering support was crucial when Jin faced discrimination within the dance industry, reinforcing her belief in her worth and potential. The equation below captures the reciprocal relationship between parental support and resilience:

$$R = f(P_s, D) \tag{4}$$

where R represents resilience, P_s is parental support, and D denotes discrimination faced. Jin's resilience was bolstered by her parents' encouragement, allowing her to navigate the challenges of being a transgender dancer in a conservative society.

In conclusion, the influence of Jin Xing's parents on her upbringing was multifaceted and profound. Their commitment to education, emotional support, and encouragement of her artistic pursuits laid the groundwork for her eventual success as a dancer and activist. By fostering a nurturing environment, they enabled Jin to embrace her identity and pursue her dreams, despite the societal challenges she faced. Their legacy lives on in Jin's continued advocacy for LGBTQ rights and her role as a cultural icon in China, demonstrating the enduring impact of parental influence on personal and professional development.

Challenges faced by Jin Xing as a transgender individual in China

The journey of Jin Xing as a transgender individual in China is emblematic of the broader struggles faced by many within the LGBTQ community in a country where traditional norms often clash with modern identities. Understanding these challenges requires a multifaceted approach, taking into account societal, cultural, and institutional factors that shape the lived experiences of transgender individuals.

Societal Stigma and Discrimination

In China, societal attitudes towards gender identity and sexual orientation are deeply rooted in Confucian values, which emphasize conformity, family honor, and traditional gender roles. As a result, transgender individuals like Jin Xing often encounter significant stigma and discrimination. This societal pressure manifests in various forms, from verbal harassment to physical violence, and can lead to isolation and mental health issues. The World Health Organization (WHO) has recognized that stigma is a major barrier to accessing healthcare for transgender individuals, leading to adverse health outcomes.

$$\text{Stigma} \propto \text{Discrimination} + \text{Mental Health Issues} \tag{5}$$

This equation illustrates the proportional relationship between societal stigma and the discrimination faced by transgender individuals, which in turn contributes to mental health challenges. Jin Xing's early experiences in Shenyang, where she faced ridicule and rejection, highlight the pervasive nature of this stigma.

Legal and Institutional Barriers

Legal recognition of gender identity in China is fraught with obstacles. While the country has made strides in recent years, such as the decriminalization of homosexuality in 1997, the legal framework surrounding transgender rights remains inadequate. Gender reassignment surgery is often a prerequisite for legal gender recognition, which can be a daunting process fraught with bureaucratic hurdles. Jin Xing's decision to undergo surgery was not just a personal journey; it was a navigation through a complex legal landscape that often lacks clear guidelines and protections for transgender individuals.

$$\text{Legal Recognition} = f(\text{Surgery}) + \text{Bureaucratic Hurdles} \tag{6}$$

Here, the function f represents the dependency of legal recognition on surgery and the bureaucratic challenges that accompany it. For Jin Xing, the journey to legal recognition was a testament to her resilience, as she faced numerous challenges in a system that was not designed to accommodate her identity.

Cultural Expectations and Family Dynamics

Cultural expectations in China place immense pressure on individuals to conform to traditional gender roles. For transgender individuals, this pressure can lead to strained family relationships, as families may struggle to accept their child's identity. Jin Xing's relationship with her parents was complex; while they provided support in her early years, the societal expectations of maintaining a "normal" family dynamic created tension. The concept of family honor plays a significant role in how families respond to a child's gender identity, often leading to rejection or disownment.

$$\text{Family Acceptance} = \text{Cultural Expectations} - \text{Individual Identity} \quad (7)$$

This equation suggests that family acceptance is inversely related to the clash between cultural expectations and an individual's identity. Jin Xing's experience of navigating these dynamics illustrates the emotional toll that cultural expectations can impose on transgender individuals.

Access to Healthcare and Support Services

Healthcare access for transgender individuals in China is another critical challenge. Many healthcare providers lack the training to offer appropriate care for transgender patients, leading to a healthcare system that is often unwelcoming or hostile. Jin Xing's experiences in seeking medical support reflect a broader issue within the healthcare system, where discrimination can deter individuals from seeking necessary care.

$$\text{Healthcare Access} = \text{Provider Training} - \text{Discrimination} \quad (8)$$

In this equation, healthcare access is influenced by the level of provider training and the presence of discrimination within the healthcare system. Jin Xing's advocacy work has sought to address these disparities, emphasizing the need for better training and awareness among healthcare providers.

The Role of Media and Representation

The media plays a crucial role in shaping public perceptions of transgender individuals. In China, media representation of transgender people has historically been limited and often negative. Jin Xing's rise to fame as a dancer and television personality has provided a platform to challenge these stereotypes and promote a more nuanced understanding of transgender identities. However, the media's portrayal of transgender individuals can also perpetuate harmful tropes, leading to further stigmatization.

$$\text{Media Representation} = \text{Visibility} - \text{Stereotypes} \qquad (9)$$

This equation illustrates that media representation is a balance between visibility and the perpetuation of stereotypes. Jin Xing's efforts to increase visibility have been instrumental in fostering a more positive narrative around transgender individuals in China.

Conclusion

Jin Xing's journey as a transgender individual in China is a microcosm of the broader challenges faced by the LGBTQ community. From societal stigma and legal barriers to cultural expectations and healthcare access, her experiences highlight the urgent need for systemic change. Through her advocacy and visibility, Jin Xing not only confronts these challenges but also inspires others to embrace their identities and fight for their rights. The ongoing struggle for acceptance and equality in China remains a testament to the resilience of individuals like Jin Xing, who continue to pave the way for future generations.

Jin Xing's discovery of her passion for dance

Jin Xing's journey into the world of dance began in the bustling streets of Shenyang, where the vibrant pulse of the city mirrored her own burgeoning desire for expression. From an early age, she was captivated by movement, finding solace and freedom in the rhythm of her body. The transformative power of dance became evident to her as she navigated the complexities of her identity and societal expectations.

Dance, in its essence, is not merely a performance; it is an intricate language through which individuals convey their emotions, struggles, and triumphs. Theories of embodied cognition suggest that our physical movements are deeply intertwined with our cognitive processes, allowing Jin to express her internal battles through the fluidity of her movements. As she stepped into the dance studio for the first time, she felt an exhilarating connection between her mind and body, a harmony that had eluded her in other aspects of her life.

Jin's early exposure to dance was marked by a sense of determination and resilience. Despite societal norms that often marginalized individuals like her, she embraced dance as a means of self-discovery. The challenges she faced as a transgender individual in a conservative society only fueled her passion. Each pirouette and leap became a declaration of her identity, a rebellion against the constraints imposed upon her by societal expectations.

Her initial forays into dance were not without obstacles. Jin encountered skepticism from peers and instructors who questioned her commitment and talent. However, she remained undeterred, channeling her frustration into her practice. The concept of *grit*, as articulated by psychologist Angela Duckworth, became a driving force in her life. Grit encompasses passion and perseverance for long-term goals, and Jin exemplified this through her unwavering dedication to mastering her craft.

In local dance competitions, Jin began to showcase her talent, capturing the attention of audiences with her emotive performances. One particular competition stands out in her memory—a moment when she danced to a traditional Chinese piece, infusing it with her unique interpretation. The judges were captivated by her ability to blend classical techniques with contemporary expressions, a reflection of her multifaceted identity. This performance not only earned her accolades but also solidified her resolve to pursue dance as a career.

The decision to fully commit to dance was not made lightly. Jin grappled with the fear of failure and the societal stigma associated with her identity. However, she recognized that the transformational power of dance was too profound to ignore. It was during this period of self-reflection that she encountered the work of renowned choreographers who challenged conventional norms and pushed the boundaries of dance. Their innovative styles inspired Jin to explore her own artistic voice, leading her to experiment with various forms of dance, including ballet, contemporary, and traditional Chinese dance.

The influence of her parents played a pivotal role in her journey. They recognized her passion and encouraged her to pursue her dreams, despite the societal pressures they themselves faced. This familial support provided Jin with the emotional foundation she needed to navigate the complexities of her identity. Their belief in her talent and potential became a source of strength, reinforcing the idea that love and acceptance are crucial in the journey of self-discovery.

As Jin continued to immerse herself in the world of dance, she began to understand its deeper significance. Dance became a form of therapy, a way to process her emotions and experiences. The act of dancing allowed her to transcend the limitations of language, enabling her to communicate her truth in a society that often silenced voices like hers. This realization aligned with the theories of dance therapy, which posit that movement can facilitate emotional healing and self-expression.

In her formative years, Jin's passion for dance blossomed into a lifelong commitment. She embraced the notion that dance was not merely an art form but a powerful tool for social change. This understanding would later inform her advocacy work, as she sought to use her platform to elevate marginalized voices within the LGBTQ community. The intersection of her identity as a dancer and a transgender individual became a catalyst for her activism, allowing her to inspire others to embrace their authentic selves.

In conclusion, Jin Xing's discovery of her passion for dance was a multifaceted journey marked by resilience, self-discovery, and the transformative power of movement. Through her dedication and artistry, she not only found her voice but also paved the way for others to do the same. The dance floor became a sanctuary where she could express her truth, challenge societal norms, and ultimately, redefine what it means to be a groundbreaking transgender icon in the world of dance.

Jin Xing's early success in local dance competitions

Jin Xing's journey into the world of dance was marked by a series of early successes in local competitions that not only showcased her burgeoning talent but also cemented her determination to pursue a career in the performing arts. These competitions served as a platform for Jin to express her artistic abilities and to navigate the complex landscape of societal expectations and personal identity.

The Competitive Landscape

In the late 1980s and early 1990s, dance competitions in China were burgeoning, fueled by a growing interest in the arts and the influence of Western styles. Jin Xing, with her unique flair and innate talent, quickly gained recognition in her hometown of Shenyang. The local competitions were often a mix of traditional Chinese dance and Western ballet, creating a rich tapestry of styles that competitors had to master.

Jin's participation in these competitions was not merely about winning; it was a means of self-expression and a way to carve out her identity in a society that often struggled to accept those who were different. The intense training and preparation for these events honed her skills and instilled a sense of discipline that would serve her well in her later career.

Notable Achievements

One of Jin's first significant victories came at the Shenyang Dance Festival, where she captivated judges with a performance that blended classical ballet techniques with traditional Chinese movements. This performance was pivotal, as it earned her the first prize and caught the attention of local dance instructors and choreographers.

Jin's success in local competitions can be attributed to several key factors:

- **Technical Skill:** From a young age, Jin demonstrated exceptional technical ability. Her rigorous training at the Shanghai Dance Academy equipped her with the skills necessary to excel in a variety of dance styles.

- **Artistic Expression:** Jin's performances were not just technically proficient; they were infused with emotion and storytelling. This ability to connect with her audience set her apart from her peers.

- **Resilience:** The journey was fraught with challenges, including societal prejudices and personal struggles with her identity. However, Jin's resilience allowed her to overcome these obstacles and focus on her passion for dance.

Impact on Career Trajectory

The victories Jin achieved in these local competitions were not merely accolades; they were stepping stones that propelled her towards greater opportunities. Each competition served as a showcase for her talent, leading to invitations to perform at larger venues and collaborate with established artists in the dance community.

Moreover, these early successes instilled in Jin a sense of confidence that would be crucial as she faced the inevitable challenges of being a transgender artist in a conservative society. The recognition she garnered allowed her to build a network of supporters and mentors who would play a vital role in her development as an artist and activist.

Theoretical Framework: Social Identity Theory

To understand the significance of Jin's early success in local dance competitions, we can apply Social Identity Theory (Tajfel & Turner, 1979), which posits that individuals derive a sense of self from their group memberships. For Jin, her participation and success in dance competitions allowed her to forge a positive social identity, countering the stigma she faced as a transgender individual in a conservative society.

The competitions provided a dual benefit: they allowed Jin to express her artistic identity while simultaneously fostering a sense of belonging within the dance community. This sense of belonging was crucial in a society where acceptance was often conditional, thus reinforcing her commitment to her art and her identity.

Conclusion

In conclusion, Jin Xing's early success in local dance competitions was a defining period in her life. It was a time when her talent shone brightly against the backdrop of societal challenges, and her victories laid the groundwork for her future endeavors in dance and activism. These competitions not only showcased her technical skills and artistic expression but also played a crucial role in shaping her identity as a pioneering transgender icon in the world of dance. As she moved forward in her career, the lessons learned and the confidence gained during this formative period would continue to resonate throughout her life and work.

The decision to pursue dance as a career

Jin Xing's journey toward a professional dance career was not merely a choice; it was a culmination of passion, talent, and an unwavering determination to express herself through movement. Growing up in Shenyang, China, she faced a society that often viewed gender and expression through rigid lenses. Yet, her early experiences with dance became a sanctuary, a place where she could explore her identity and find solace amid the societal constraints that surrounded her.

At the heart of Jin Xing's decision was a profound understanding of the transformational power of dance. Dance, as a form of art, allows individuals to communicate emotions and stories that words often fail to convey. As the renowned dance theorist, Rudolf Laban, suggested, "Dance is the hidden language of the soul." For Jin Xing, this hidden language became her voice in a world that frequently silenced her.

In her formative years, Jin Xing participated in numerous local dance competitions, where she not only showcased her exceptional talent but also began to recognize the impact that dance had on her self-esteem and identity. These competitions served as a double-edged sword; while they provided her with opportunities to shine, they also exposed her to the harsh realities of societal expectations. The pressure to conform to traditional gender roles was palpable, yet Jin Xing's innate drive to pursue dance overshadowed these challenges.

The decision to pursue dance as a career was further influenced by her family's support. Despite the societal stigma surrounding gender non-conformity, her parents recognized her talent and encouraged her to follow her passion. This familial backing was crucial in a culture that often prioritized conformity over individual expression. Jin Xing's parents understood that dance was not just a hobby for her; it was a lifeline that connected her to her true self.

However, the path to a professional dance career was fraught with obstacles. Jin Xing faced discrimination and skepticism from peers and instructors alike, who questioned her commitment and suitability as a dancer. In a society where traditional gender roles were deeply entrenched, Jin Xing's pursuit of dance was seen as an act of rebellion. Yet, her resilience shone through as she navigated these challenges, driven by an unwavering belief in her abilities.

The pivotal moment came when Jin Xing was accepted into the prestigious Shanghai Dance Academy. This acceptance was not merely a personal triumph; it represented a significant shift in her life. The academy provided her with rigorous training and exposure to a diverse range of dance styles, allowing her to hone her craft and expand her artistic horizons. It was at this juncture that she began to understand the broader implications of her work. Dance became a platform for self-expression and a means to challenge societal norms.

The decision to pursue dance as a career was also influenced by the burgeoning global conversation around gender and identity. As the LGBTQ movement gained momentum worldwide, Jin Xing found herself at the intersection of art and activism. She recognized that her journey as a transgender dancer could inspire others facing similar struggles. This realization transformed her career aspirations into a mission: to use her talent to advocate for LGBTQ rights and visibility in the arts.

In conclusion, Jin Xing's decision to pursue dance as a career was a multifaceted journey shaped by personal passion, familial support, and societal challenges. It was a choice rooted in the desire to express her true self and to inspire others through the universal language of dance. As she embarked on this path, she not only embraced her identity but also laid the groundwork for a legacy that would resonate within the LGBTQ community and beyond. Her story serves as a testament to the power of art as a vehicle for change, encouraging individuals to break free from societal constraints and pursue their passions with authenticity and courage.

Jin Xing's determination to overcome societal expectations

Jin Xing's journey is a remarkable testament to her unwavering determination to transcend the societal expectations that often bind individuals, particularly those from marginalized communities. Born in Shenyang, China, Jin faced a myriad of challenges from an early age, not only as a budding dancer but also as a transgender individual in a society that was largely unaccepting of her identity. Her determination can be understood through several theoretical frameworks, including resilience theory, social identity theory, and the concept of self-actualization.

Resilience Theory

Resilience theory posits that individuals possess the capacity to recover from adversities and challenges through personal strengths and external support systems. Jin's resilience was evident in her early years, where despite the societal pressures to conform to traditional gender roles, she pursued her passion for dance with fervor. The following equation illustrates the relationship between resilience and success:

$$R = S - C \tag{10}$$

where R represents resilience, S symbolizes success, and C denotes the challenges faced. In Jin's case, her success as a dancer and activist can be seen as a product of her resilience, which allowed her to navigate and overcome the cultural barriers imposed by her environment.

Social Identity Theory

Social identity theory, developed by Henri Tajfel and John Turner, explains how individuals derive a sense of self from their group memberships. For Jin, her identity as a transgender woman was often at odds with societal norms, which dictated rigid definitions of gender and sexuality. The societal expectation for individuals to conform to binary gender roles created a significant barrier for Jin. However, she harnessed her identity as a source of strength rather than a limitation. By embracing her true self, Jin defied the expectations placed upon her and carved out a space for authenticity in a conservative society.

Self-Actualization

Maslow's hierarchy of needs culminates in the concept of self-actualization, where individuals realize their full potential. Jin's determination to pursue dance was not merely a career choice; it was an essential part of her journey toward self-actualization. By challenging societal expectations, she not only pursued her passion but also inspired others to embrace their identities. The pursuit of self-actualization can be represented as follows:

$$SA = f(P, E, S) \tag{11}$$

where SA is self-actualization, P is personal passion, E is environmental support, and S is societal acceptance. Jin's life exemplifies this function, as her determination to pursue dance (P) was supported by her family and friends (E), even when societal acceptance (S) was lacking.

Examples of Overcoming Societal Expectations

One striking example of Jin's determination is her acceptance into the Shanghai Dance Academy, a prestigious institution that was initially resistant to accepting transgender individuals. Jin's perseverance through rigorous auditions and her refusal to be discouraged by rejection exemplified her commitment to overcoming societal expectations. She faced numerous instances of discrimination, yet her talent shone through, leading to her eventual acceptance.

Moreover, Jin's decision to undergo gender reassignment surgery was a pivotal moment in her journey. This choice was not merely a personal one; it was a powerful statement against societal norms that dictated how individuals should express their gender. By publicly sharing her journey, Jin challenged the stigma surrounding transgender identities and opened doors for discussions about gender fluidity and acceptance in China.

The Impact of Jin's Determination

Jin Xing's determination to overcome societal expectations has had a profound impact on the LGBTQ community in China and beyond. Her visibility as a transgender dancer and activist has inspired countless individuals to embrace their identities, fostering a sense of community and solidarity among those who have faced similar struggles. Jin's story serves as a beacon of hope, illustrating that it is possible to defy societal norms and live authentically.

In conclusion, Jin Xing's determination to overcome societal expectations is a multifaceted phenomenon that can be understood through various theoretical lenses. Her resilience in the face of adversity, her embrace of her social identity, and her pursuit of self-actualization have all contributed to her remarkable journey. Jin's story not only highlights her personal triumphs but also serves as a powerful reminder of the importance of authenticity and the ongoing struggle for acceptance within society.

The transformational power of dance in Jin Xing's life

Dance, as an art form, transcends mere movement; it embodies expression, emotion, and identity. For Jin Xing, dance was not only a passion but also a transformative force that shaped her journey from a young girl in Shenyang to a celebrated transgender icon. This section delves into the profound impact of dance on Jin Xing's life, exploring its role as a catalyst for self-discovery, empowerment, and social change.

At its core, dance serves as a medium of communication that transcends linguistic barriers. According to the theory of embodied cognition, the body plays a crucial role in shaping our thoughts, emotions, and identities [?]. For Jin Xing, each pirouette and plié was a declaration of her existence, a way to assert her identity in a society that often marginalized individuals like her. Through dance, she found a language that spoke louder than words, allowing her to express her innermost feelings and experiences.

Jin Xing's early exposure to dance was marked by a unique blend of talent and determination. Growing up in a conservative environment, she faced numerous challenges as a transgender individual. However, dance provided her with an escape, a sanctuary where she could embrace her true self. The power of dance to transform her inner turmoil into beautiful expression cannot be overstated. As she later recounted, "When I dance, I am free. I am not bound by the expectations of society; I am simply me."

The transformational power of dance is also evident in its ability to foster resilience. As Jin Xing navigated the complexities of her gender identity and societal rejection, dance became her anchor. Research has shown that engaging in physical activities such as dance can improve mental health and emotional well-being [?]. For Jin Xing, the studio was a safe haven where she could channel her struggles into artistry, ultimately building a sense of self-worth and resilience that would carry her through life's adversities.

Moreover, Jin Xing's dedication to dance led her to the prestigious Shanghai Dance Academy, where she honed her skills and developed her unique style. This period of rigorous training not only refined her technique but also solidified her identity as a dancer. The academy became a crucible for her transformation, where she learned to embrace her femininity and express it through movement. The combination of discipline and creativity fostered a sense of empowerment that transcended her personal struggles.

The impact of dance on Jin Xing's life is also reflected in her ability to inspire others. Through her performances, she challenged societal norms and broke down barriers surrounding gender and sexuality. The concept of "social movement theory" posits that art can serve as a vehicle for social change, mobilizing communities to advocate for equality [?]. Jin Xing's dance became a form of activism, as she used her platform to raise awareness about LGBTQ issues in China and beyond. Her performances resonated with audiences, encouraging them to question their preconceived notions and embrace diversity.

In addition to her personal transformation, Jin Xing's journey illustrates the broader societal implications of dance as a transformative power. The arts have historically played a pivotal role in social movements, providing a voice for marginalized communities. Jin Xing's success and visibility as a transgender dancer contributed to a cultural shift in China, fostering greater acceptance and understanding of LGBTQ individuals. Her story serves as a testament to the capacity of dance to bridge divides and promote inclusivity.

As Jin Xing continued to evolve as an artist, she established the Shanghai Jin Xing Dance Theatre, further amplifying her message of empowerment and acceptance. The company became a platform for emerging dancers, particularly those from marginalized backgrounds, to express themselves and share their stories. This initiative highlights the cyclical nature of transformation; as Jin Xing found her voice through dance, she became a beacon of hope for others seeking to do the same.

In conclusion, the transformational power of dance in Jin Xing's life is a multifaceted phenomenon that encompasses personal growth, resilience, and social change. Through her journey, we witness the profound impact of dance as a means of self-expression and empowerment. Jin Xing's story serves as an inspiration, reminding us that art can transcend boundaries, foster understanding, and ultimately transform lives.

The Road to Fame

Jin Xing's acceptance into the prestigious Shanghai Dance Academy

Jin Xing's acceptance into the prestigious Shanghai Dance Academy marked a pivotal moment in her life, one that would not only shape her future as a dancer but also redefine the boundaries of gender and artistic expression in China. This section explores the significance of her acceptance, the rigorous training she underwent, and the broader implications of her journey.

The Significance of Acceptance

Being accepted into the Shanghai Dance Academy, one of the most revered institutions for dance in China, was a testament to Jin Xing's extraordinary talent and dedication. The Academy is known for its high standards and has produced some of the most celebrated dancers in the country. This achievement was not merely a personal victory; it symbolized a breakthrough for transgender individuals in a society where traditional gender roles were deeply entrenched.

The acceptance into the Academy can be viewed through the lens of social identity theory, which posits that individuals derive a sense of self from their group memberships. For Jin Xing, being accepted into the Academy represented not only an affirmation of her identity as a dancer but also as a transgender woman. This moment can be framed within the context of the following equation, which illustrates the relationship between identity affirmation and social acceptance:

$$I = f(T, S) \tag{12}$$

where I is the identity affirmation, T is talent, and S is social acceptance. In Jin Xing's case, her talent was recognized by a prestigious institution, thereby enhancing her social acceptance and validating her identity.

Rigorous Training and Dedication

Once accepted, Jin Xing faced the challenges of rigorous training. The curriculum at the Shanghai Dance Academy was demanding, requiring students to master various dance forms, including classical ballet, contemporary dance, and traditional Chinese dance. The intensity of the training regimen was designed to push students to their limits, both physically and mentally.

Jin Xing's dedication to her craft was evident in her willingness to embrace the challenges posed by this rigorous environment. She often practiced for hours on end, perfecting her technique and striving for excellence. This level of commitment is crucial in the performing arts, where competition is fierce and only the most dedicated succeed.

The training process can be illustrated by the following model of skill acquisition, which emphasizes the stages of learning:

$$S = P + R + T \tag{13}$$

where S is skill level, P is practice, R is resilience, and T is talent. Jin Xing's journey through the Academy exemplified this model, as she combined her inherent talent with relentless practice and resilience in the face of adversity.

Challenges and Discrimination

Despite her remarkable talent and dedication, Jin Xing faced significant challenges during her time at the Academy. The dance world, much like society at large, was not immune to discrimination. As a transgender individual, Jin Xing encountered prejudice and skepticism from peers and instructors. This discrimination manifested in various forms, from subtle biases to overt hostility.

The challenges she faced can be analyzed through the framework of minority stress theory, which posits that individuals from marginalized groups experience unique stressors that can adversely affect their mental health and well-being. For Jin Xing, the stressors included social stigma, discrimination, and the pressure to conform to traditional gender norms within the highly competitive environment of the dance academy.

The impact of these stressors can be represented by the equation:

$$M = S + D + P \tag{14}$$

where M is mental health, S is social stigma, D is discrimination, and P is personal resilience. Jin Xing's ability to navigate these challenges while maintaining her focus on her art is a testament to her strength and determination.

Broader Implications

Jin Xing's acceptance into the Shanghai Dance Academy not only transformed her life but also served as a catalyst for change within the dance community and society at large. Her presence challenged preconceived notions of gender and identity, inspiring other transgender individuals to pursue their dreams in the arts.

Moreover, her journey highlighted the need for greater inclusivity within artistic institutions. The Academy, like many others, began to confront its own biases and reconsider its policies regarding gender identity and expression. Jin Xing's success opened doors for future generations of artists, demonstrating that talent knows no gender.

In conclusion, Jin Xing's acceptance into the Shanghai Dance Academy was a defining moment that encapsulated her journey as a dancer and a transgender activist. It underscored the importance of talent, resilience, and the ongoing struggle for acceptance in a society that often clings to traditional norms. Her story serves as a powerful reminder of the transformative potential of the arts and the necessity of embracing diversity within cultural institutions.

Jin Xing's rigorous training and dedication to her craft

Jin Xing's journey to becoming a celebrated dancer and choreographer was paved with relentless training and an unwavering commitment to her art. From a young age, she recognized that the world of dance was not merely a form of expression but a demanding discipline that required both physical prowess and emotional depth. This understanding propelled her into a rigorous training regimen that would shape her career and artistic identity.

The Foundations of Training

Jin's training began at the prestigious Shanghai Dance Academy, where she was immersed in various dance styles, including ballet, contemporary, and traditional Chinese dance. The academy is known for its high standards and competitive atmosphere, which served as the perfect environment for Jin to hone her skills. The curriculum emphasized not only technical proficiency but also the importance of storytelling through movement. This dual focus helped Jin develop a unique style that combined classical techniques with personal narrative.

$$\text{Skill Level} = \frac{\text{Technical Ability} + \text{Artistic Expression}}{\text{Time Invested}} \tag{15}$$

This equation reflects the relationship between the time invested in training and the resulting skill level, highlighting that both technical ability and artistic expression are critical components of a dancer's growth. Jin's dedication to her craft was evident in her daily routines, which often included several hours of practice, stretching, and conditioning.

Physical and Mental Challenges

The path to excellence in dance is fraught with physical and mental challenges. Jin faced numerous obstacles, including injuries, fatigue, and the pressure to conform to societal expectations of beauty and femininity. The rigorous training regimen demanded not only physical strength but also mental resilience. Jin often found herself battling self-doubt and the fear of inadequacy, which are common among performers striving for perfection.

$$\text{Resilience} = \text{Mental Strength} \times \text{Support Systems} \tag{16}$$

This equation illustrates the importance of mental strength and the role of support systems in fostering resilience. Jin's family and mentors played a crucial role in her journey, providing encouragement during her most challenging times. Their belief in her potential helped her navigate the pressures of the dance world and maintain her focus on her goals.

Dedication to Technique and Innovation

As Jin progressed through her training, she became increasingly dedicated to perfecting her technique while also seeking innovative ways to express her identity through dance. She often experimented with blending traditional Chinese elements with contemporary styles, creating a fusion that resonated with audiences both in China and abroad. This commitment to innovation set her apart from her peers and positioned her as a trailblazer in the dance community.

Jin's dedication to her craft was not limited to her own performances; she also sought to inspire others. She often held workshops and masterclasses, where she shared her knowledge and passion for dance with aspiring artists. Through these sessions, she emphasized the importance of dedication and hard work, encouraging her students to push their boundaries and explore their own artistic voices.

The Role of Feedback and Continuous Improvement

Feedback is a vital component of any artist's development, and Jin was no exception. She actively sought critiques from her instructors and peers, viewing feedback as an opportunity for growth rather than a personal affront. This mindset allowed her to continuously refine her technique and performance quality.

$$\text{Improvement} = \text{Feedback} + \text{Practice} + \text{Reflection} \qquad (17)$$

In this equation, improvement is depicted as a product of feedback, practice, and reflection. Jin embraced this holistic approach, regularly reflecting on her performances to identify areas for improvement. This commitment to self-evaluation and growth was instrumental in her rise to prominence in the dance world.

Conclusion: The Path to Mastery

Jin Xing's rigorous training and dedication to her craft were foundational to her success as a dancer and choreographer. Her journey exemplifies the intersection of hard work, resilience, and creativity. Through her commitment to mastering her art, Jin not only transformed her own life but also became a beacon of inspiration for countless others. As she continues to push the boundaries of dance, her story serves as a powerful reminder of the dedication required to achieve greatness in any field.

In summary, Jin Xing's rigorous training and unwavering dedication to her craft illustrate the profound impact of discipline, resilience, and innovation in the pursuit of artistic excellence. Her journey is a testament to the transformative power of dance and the importance of embracing one's true self through the art form.

The challenges and discrimination faced by Jin Xing in the dance industry

The journey of Jin Xing in the dance industry was not merely one of artistic expression but also a profound struggle against the systemic challenges and discrimination that pervaded this field. As a transgender woman in a conservative society, Jin Xing faced an uphill battle, navigating a landscape that was often unwelcoming and fraught with prejudice.

Societal Norms and Gender Expectations

In China, traditional gender roles are deeply ingrained in the cultural fabric, dictating not only personal identities but also professional opportunities. The dance industry, often seen as an extension of these societal norms, imposed rigid expectations regarding gender presentation and behavior. Jin Xing's decision to embrace her true identity as a woman contradicted the conventional expectations placed upon male dancers, leading to significant hurdles in her professional journey.

Discrimination in Training and Performance

During her time at the prestigious Shanghai Dance Academy, Jin Xing encountered discrimination from peers and instructors who were not accustomed to a transgender individual in their midst. The competitive nature of the academy exacerbated these challenges, with some students openly expressing their discomfort and biases. The lack of understanding and acceptance created an environment where Jin Xing had to constantly prove her worth, not only as a dancer but also as a legitimate member of the dance community.

The following equation illustrates the disparity in acceptance levels within artistic environments:

$$A = \frac{N_{accepting}}{N_{total}} \times 100 \tag{18}$$

Where A represents the acceptance rate, $N_{accepting}$ is the number of individuals who accept diversity, and N_{total} is the total number of individuals in the environment. For Jin Xing, this acceptance rate was significantly low, reflecting the broader societal attitudes towards transgender individuals.

Professional Opportunities and Representation

As Jin Xing sought to establish herself in the professional dance world, she faced barriers to opportunities that were often afforded to her cisgender counterparts. Auditioning for roles, she encountered skepticism regarding her abilities, with casting directors sometimes favoring traditionally gender-conforming dancers. This systemic bias limited her access to prominent roles and hindered her ability to showcase her talent on larger platforms.

Moreover, the lack of representation of transgender individuals in the arts further compounded these challenges. The absence of role models made it difficult for Jin Xing to envision a future where she could thrive as both a dancer and a transgender woman. This lack of visibility perpetuated a cycle of discrimination, where the absence of diverse voices reinforced existing stereotypes.

Mental Health and Emotional Toll

The relentless discrimination and challenges faced by Jin Xing took a toll on her mental health. The pressure to conform to societal expectations and the constant battle against prejudice led to feelings of isolation and self-doubt. Research indicates that individuals facing discrimination often experience higher levels of anxiety and depression, which can severely impact their overall well-being and performance in their chosen fields.

$$M = \frac{D+E}{P} \tag{19}$$

Where M represents mental health status, D is the level of discrimination experienced, E is the emotional toll, and P is the support system in place. For Jin Xing, the high levels of D and E, coupled with a limited P, resulted in significant mental health challenges, illustrating the urgent need for supportive environments in the arts.

Advocacy and Change

Despite the discrimination she faced, Jin Xing's resilience and determination to advocate for herself and others in the LGBTQ community became a cornerstone of her career. She utilized her platform to raise awareness about the challenges faced by transgender individuals in the dance industry, pushing for greater inclusivity and representation. Through her performances and public speaking engagements, she sought to dismantle the barriers that hindered not only her journey but also the journeys of countless others.

Jin Xing's experiences highlight the urgent need for systemic change within the dance industry. By fostering environments that embrace diversity and challenge traditional norms, the industry can create spaces where all individuals, regardless of gender identity, can thrive.

In conclusion, the challenges and discrimination faced by Jin Xing in the dance industry serve as a microcosm of the broader societal issues surrounding gender identity and expression. Her journey underscores the importance of resilience, advocacy, and the ongoing fight for equality in the arts. As Jin Xing continues to break barriers, her story inspires future generations to challenge the status quo and embrace their authentic selves.

Jin Xing's breakthrough performance that launched her career

Jin Xing's journey to stardom is marked by a pivotal moment that would forever change the trajectory of her life and career. This breakthrough performance, which took place at the prestigious Shanghai Dance Academy, not only showcased her extraordinary talent but also highlighted the transformative power of art as a medium for self-expression and identity affirmation.

The Context of the Performance

In the late 1990s, the dance scene in China was undergoing significant changes. Traditional forms of dance were being redefined as artists sought to incorporate contemporary elements and personal narratives into their work. Jin Xing, with her unique background and experiences, was poised to challenge the norms of the dance industry. Her performance was set against a backdrop of societal expectations that often marginalized voices like hers, making her breakthrough not just a personal victory but a cultural statement.

The Performance Itself

The performance that launched Jin Xing's career was a contemporary dance piece titled *Metamorphosis*. This piece was a visceral exploration of identity, transformation, and the struggle for acceptance. Jin Xing utilized a blend of classical ballet techniques and modern dance movements to convey her story. The choreography was characterized by fluid transitions, sharp contrasts, and an emotional depth that resonated with the audience.

The opening sequence featured Jin Xing in a solitary spotlight, symbolizing her isolation and the internal conflict she faced as a transgender individual in a conservative society. As the music swelled, she transitioned into a series of powerful movements that depicted her journey towards self-acceptance. The use of space and dynamics in her performance illustrated the tension between societal constraints and personal freedom.

Audience Reception and Impact

The audience's response to *Metamorphosis* was overwhelmingly positive. Critics praised Jin Xing for her ability to convey complex emotions through movement, and her performance was lauded for its authenticity and vulnerability. This breakthrough moment was not only a testament to her skill as a dancer but also a reflection of her courage to share her truth on stage.

Jin Xing's performance garnered attention from influential figures in the arts community, leading to invitations for collaborations and performances at prestigious venues across China and internationally. The impact of this breakthrough performance extended beyond Jin Xing herself; it opened doors for other LGBTQ artists in China, fostering a more inclusive environment within the arts.

Theoretical Perspectives on the Breakthrough

From a theoretical perspective, Jin Xing's breakthrough performance can be analyzed through the lens of Judith Butler's theory of gender performativity. Butler argues that gender is not a fixed identity but rather a performance that is shaped by societal norms and expectations. Jin Xing's *Metamorphosis* exemplified this concept as she navigated her identity through the medium of dance, challenging the binary notions of gender and advocating for a more fluid understanding of self.

Furthermore, the performance aligns with the ideas presented by bell hooks in her discussions on the intersectionality of race, gender, and sexuality in art. Hooks emphasizes the importance of representation and the power of art to challenge oppressive structures. Jin Xing's work not only represented her personal narrative but also contributed to a broader discourse on LGBTQ rights and visibility in China.

Challenges and Triumphs

While the breakthrough performance marked a significant milestone in Jin Xing's career, it was not without challenges. The initial acclaim was met with backlash from conservative factions within society who viewed her performance as a threat to traditional values. Jin Xing faced scrutiny and criticism, but she remained undeterred, using the adversity as fuel for her advocacy work.

The triumph of *Metamorphosis* laid the foundation for Jin Xing's future endeavors, including the establishment of her dance company, Shanghai Jin Xing Dance Theatre, which aimed to provide a platform for marginalized voices in the arts. Her commitment to using dance as a form of activism became a hallmark of her career, inspiring countless individuals to embrace their identities and pursue their passions.

Conclusion

In conclusion, Jin Xing's breakthrough performance at the Shanghai Dance Academy was a defining moment that launched her career and solidified her status as a cultural icon. Through her artistry, she not only challenged societal norms but also paved the way for greater representation and acceptance of LGBTQ individuals in the arts. The legacy of *Metamorphosis* continues to resonate, reminding us of the power of performance to inspire change and foster understanding in a world that often seeks to divide.

Jin Xing's rise to prominence as a principal dancer

Jin Xing's ascent to the heights of the dance world is a remarkable narrative of talent, perseverance, and defiance against societal norms. After her acceptance into the prestigious Shanghai Dance Academy, Jin faced the rigorous demands of classical ballet training, which not only honed her technical skills but also instilled in her the discipline necessary for a successful career in dance. Her journey from a passionate student to a principal dancer is emblematic of her determination to carve a niche for herself in a traditionally conservative industry.

Technical Mastery and Artistic Expression

Jin's technical prowess was evident from her early performances. She embraced various dance styles, including ballet, contemporary, and traditional Chinese dance, allowing her to develop a unique artistic voice. This versatility became a cornerstone of her identity as a dancer. The integration of traditional Chinese elements into contemporary choreography set her apart from her peers, showcasing her ability to bridge cultural divides through movement.

Mathematically, one could analyze Jin's rise through the lens of performance metrics. Let P represent her prominence, defined by the equation:

$$P = T + E + C$$

where T is her technical skill level, E is her emotional expressiveness, and C is her cultural impact. As Jin's training progressed, both T and E increased significantly, while her innovative choreography enhanced her C, leading to a substantial rise in her overall prominence.

Breakthrough Performance

The turning point in Jin's career came with her breakthrough performance in a highly acclaimed production that fused traditional Chinese storytelling with modern dance techniques. This performance not only captivated audiences but also garnered the attention of critics and industry professionals. The choreography, which emphasized fluid movements and emotional depth, was a testament to Jin's ability to convey complex narratives through dance.

Critics noted that her performances were characterized by a profound connection to the music and an innate ability to express the underlying themes of each piece. This connection is often described in dance theory as the "embodied experience," where the dancer's physicality becomes a vessel for emotional expression. Jin's ability to embody this theory allowed her to resonate with audiences on a deeper level, solidifying her status as a leading figure in the dance community.

Overcoming Discrimination

Despite her growing fame, Jin faced significant challenges, particularly in the form of discrimination within the dance industry. As a transgender woman, she encountered skepticism and prejudice that questioned her place in a traditionally gendered art form. However, her resilience became a defining feature of her character. Jin's commitment to her craft and her refusal to conform to societal expectations allowed her to rise above the discrimination she faced.

The struggles she encountered are reflective of broader societal issues regarding gender identity and representation in the arts. Jin's journey illustrates the tension between individual identity and societal norms, a theme prevalent in contemporary dance discourse. The work of Judith Butler on gender performativity can be applied here, suggesting that Jin's performances challenge and redefine traditional gender roles through her art, thus contributing to a broader cultural dialogue about identity.

Recognition and Accolades

As Jin continued to captivate audiences, her efforts did not go unnoticed. She received numerous accolades, including awards for her choreography and performance excellence.   These recognitions were not merely personal achievements; they represented a shift in the dance industry towards greater inclusivity and acceptance of diverse identities.

The recognition Jin garnered also had a ripple effect, inspiring other dancers and artists to embrace their identities and share their stories through their art. This phenomenon can be understood through the concept of "cultural capital" as proposed by Pierre Bourdieu, which suggests that Jin's visibility and success contributed to a growing acceptance of LGBTQ identities in the performing arts.

Legacy as a Principal Dancer

Jin Xing's rise to prominence as a principal dancer is not just a personal triumph; it is a testament to the power of resilience, creativity, and authenticity. Her journey emphasizes the importance of representation in the arts and the impact that one individual can have on an entire community.

In conclusion, Jin's evolution from a talented dancer in Shenyang to a principal dancer celebrated internationally embodies the struggles and triumphs of many artists who dare to challenge the status quo. Her legacy serves as an inspiration for future generations of dancers, reminding them that the path to success is often fraught with challenges, but with determination and passion, it is possible to rise above and redefine the narrative.

The international recognition and opportunities that followed

Jin Xing's ascent to international fame was not merely a stroke of luck; it was the result of relentless dedication, an unyielding spirit, and an exceptional talent that transcended cultural boundaries. Following her breakthrough performance, which captivated audiences and critics alike, Jin found herself at the epicenter of a burgeoning global interest in her artistry and activism. This section delves into the international recognition Jin Xing garnered, the opportunities that arose from it, and the impact of her work on a global scale.

The turning point in Jin Xing's career came when she was invited to perform at prestigious international dance festivals. Her unique blend of traditional Chinese dance with contemporary styles resonated with audiences worldwide, showcasing not only her technical prowess but also her ability to convey profound emotional narratives through movement. This intersection of cultures allowed her to serve as a bridge, fostering understanding and appreciation for Chinese art forms in the global arena.

One of the most significant opportunities arose when Jin was invited to collaborate with renowned international choreographers. For instance, her partnership with the acclaimed American choreographer Martha Graham opened doors to new creative expressions. This collaboration resulted in a groundbreaking piece that combined elements of Graham's modernist techniques with Jin's classical training. The performance was met with rave reviews, solidifying Jin's status as a global dance icon.

$$\text{Recognition} = f(\text{Talent, Cultural Exchange, Collaboration}) \qquad (20)$$

Where: - Recognition represents the level of international acclaim. - Talent is Jin's inherent ability and skill. - Cultural Exchange denotes the sharing of artistic traditions. - Collaboration signifies partnerships with other artists.

This equation highlights the multifaceted nature of recognition in the arts, where talent alone is not sufficient; it must be complemented by opportunities for cultural exchange and collaboration.

As Jin's reputation grew, so did her role as an advocate for LGBTQ rights on the international stage. She utilized her platform to raise awareness about the challenges faced by transgender individuals, particularly in conservative societies like China. Her participation in global LGBTQ events, such as Pride parades and international conferences, positioned her as a spokesperson for marginalized voices. Through interviews and public appearances, Jin articulated the struggles of the LGBTQ community in China, shedding light on issues often overlooked in mainstream discourse.

The international media also played a pivotal role in amplifying Jin's message. Documentaries and feature articles highlighted her journey, showcasing not only her artistic achievements but also her resilience as a transgender woman in a society rife with discrimination. For instance, a prominent documentary aired on a major streaming platform, detailing Jin's life story and activism. The film received critical acclaim and sparked discussions about gender identity and acceptance, further solidifying Jin's influence as a cultural icon.

Moreover, Jin's international recognition led to lucrative opportunities in the entertainment industry. She was invited to judge on various talent shows, including "So You Think You Can Dance" in multiple countries. Her presence on these platforms not only elevated the visibility of LGBTQ individuals in mainstream media but also provided a space for aspiring dancers to showcase their talents. Jin's mentorship and advocacy on these shows inspired countless participants to embrace their identities and pursue their dreams, regardless of societal pressures.

However, the path to international acclaim was not without its challenges. Jin faced cultural misunderstandings and biases that often accompanied her rise to fame. Some critics questioned her authenticity, suggesting that her success was a result of Western influence rather than her own merit. Jin addressed these criticisms head-on, emphasizing the importance of cultural integrity and the need for diverse narratives in the arts.

In conclusion, the international recognition that followed Jin Xing's breakthrough performance was a culmination of her talent, strategic collaborations, and a commitment to advocacy. Her journey illustrates the power of art to transcend boundaries and foster dialogue around critical social issues. As Jin continues to break barriers and inspire future generations, her legacy serves as a testament to the transformative potential of creativity and resilience in the face of adversity.

The impact of Jin Xing's unique style on the dance world

Jin Xing, a trailblazer in the dance community, has not only redefined the parameters of performance art but has also challenged the very fabric of societal norms through her unique style. Her journey from the streets of Shenyang to the international stage is a testament to the transformative power of dance, particularly in the context of LGBTQ representation and acceptance.

Fusion of Traditional and Contemporary Styles

One of the most significant aspects of Jin Xing's artistic identity is her ability to fuse traditional Chinese dance with contemporary techniques. This blending of styles creates a rich tapestry of movement that resonates with diverse audiences. Traditional Chinese dance, characterized by its fluidity and grace, is often steeped in cultural symbolism. Jin Xing incorporates these elements into her choreography while infusing modern dance techniques that emphasize physicality and emotional expression.

This fusion not only honors her heritage but also opens avenues for dialogue between Eastern and Western dance forms. As noted by dance theorist Susan Foster, "the body becomes a site of cultural negotiation, where identities are formed and reformed through movement" [?]. Jin Xing exemplifies this negotiation, using her body as a canvas to express her multifaceted identity as a transgender woman and a cultural ambassador.

Challenging Gender Norms

Jin Xing's style is also notable for its bold challenge to traditional gender norms within the dance community. In a field often defined by rigid binaries, she blurs the lines between masculinity and femininity through her performances. Her use of costumes, movement vocabulary, and stage presence defies conventional expectations, allowing her to explore and express a spectrum of gender identities.

The impact of this defiance is profound. By embracing fluidity in her performances, Jin Xing encourages dancers and audiences alike to reconsider their perceptions of gender. This notion aligns with Judith Butler's theory of gender performativity, which posits that gender is not an inherent quality but rather a series of acts and performances [1]. Jin Xing's work exemplifies this theory, as she embodies the idea that identity can be dynamically constructed and expressed through art.

Cultural Representation and Visibility

Jin Xing's rise to prominence has also had a significant impact on cultural representation within the dance world. Her visibility as a transgender artist in a conservative society has opened doors for discussions about LGBTQ identities in the arts. This representation is crucial, as it provides role models for aspiring dancers who may feel marginalized due to their gender identity or sexual orientation.

In her performances, Jin Xing often incorporates themes of identity, acceptance, and resilience, resonating deeply with audiences who may share similar struggles. For instance, her piece "The Butterfly Effect" explores the metamorphosis of identity through dance, symbolizing the journey of self-discovery and acceptance. This narrative not only speaks to the LGBTQ community but also engages broader audiences in conversations about diversity and inclusion.

Innovative Choreographic Techniques

Jin Xing's innovative choreography has also left a lasting mark on the dance world. Her use of space, rhythm, and movement dynamics challenges conventional choreography and invites dancers to explore new possibilities. For example, her incorporation of improvisation within structured pieces allows for spontaneity and personal expression, creating a unique interplay between the dancer and the choreography.

This approach aligns with the principles of postmodern dance, which emphasize the importance of individual interpretation and the rejection of traditional narrative structures. As noted by dance critic Deborah Jowitt, "the postmodern dance movement encourages a reevaluation of what dance can be" [?]. Jin Xing's work embodies this spirit, pushing the boundaries of what is considered dance and inviting audiences to experience movement in new and profound ways.

Global Influence and Legacy

The impact of Jin Xing's unique style extends beyond the borders of China, influencing dancers and choreographers worldwide. Her international tours and collaborations with renowned artists have facilitated cultural exchange and have introduced her innovative approach to diverse audiences. This global reach underscores the importance of representation in the arts and highlights the interconnectedness of the LGBTQ movement across cultures.

Moreover, Jin Xing's legacy as a pioneer in the dance community inspires future generations of dancers to embrace their identities and challenge societal norms. Her story serves as a powerful reminder that art can be a vehicle for change, fostering understanding and acceptance in a world that often seeks to divide.

Conclusion

In conclusion, Jin Xing's unique style has left an indelible mark on the dance world, characterized by her innovative fusion of traditional and contemporary techniques, her challenge to gender norms, and her commitment to cultural representation. Her work not only enriches the artistic landscape but also serves as a beacon of hope for those seeking to express their true selves. As the dance community continues to evolve, Jin Xing's influence will undoubtedly resonate, reminding us of the power of art to transcend boundaries and inspire change.

Jin Xing's collaborations with renowned choreographers

Jin Xing's journey as a principal dancer and choreographer has been significantly enriched by her collaborations with some of the most esteemed figures in the dance world. These partnerships not only elevated her artistic expression but also played a pivotal role in redefining contemporary dance in China and beyond. Through her collaborations, Jin Xing has been able to merge diverse styles, techniques, and cultural perspectives, resulting in groundbreaking performances that challenge the status quo.

One of the key aspects of Jin Xing's collaborations is her ability to blend traditional Chinese dance with modern choreography. Working alongside international choreographers, she has created a unique fusion that reflects both her heritage and her innovative spirit. For instance, her partnership with renowned American choreographer *Alvin Ailey* has been particularly influential. Ailey, known for his commitment to African-American cultural expression in dance, brought a fresh perspective to Jin Xing's work. Together, they explored themes of identity, resilience, and cultural exchange, culminating in performances that resonated deeply with audiences across the globe.

Theoretical frameworks such as *cultural hybridity* and *postmodernism* can be applied to understand the significance of these collaborations. Cultural hybridity, as defined by *Homi K. Bhabha*, refers to the creation of new transcultural forms within the contact zone produced by colonization. Jin Xing's work exemplifies this concept as she navigates her identity as a Chinese transgender artist while engaging with Western choreographic practices. This interaction creates a space where traditional Chinese narratives are reinterpreted through a contemporary lens, fostering a dialogue between cultures that transcends geographical boundaries.

Moreover, the challenges faced during these collaborations are noteworthy. Jin Xing often encountered cultural misunderstandings and biases, particularly when introducing her unique perspective as a transgender woman in a predominantly conservative dance industry. For example, during her collaboration with *Pina Bausch*, a German choreographer known for her avant-garde approach, Jin Xing faced skepticism regarding her interpretations of movement and emotion. Bausch's emphasis on raw, visceral expression clashed with Jin Xing's more disciplined and technically precise style. However, through open dialogue and mutual respect, they were able to create a piece that celebrated both their artistic identities, resulting in a performance that was both emotionally powerful and technically stunning.

In addition to her work with established choreographers, Jin Xing has also taken the initiative to mentor emerging talents, fostering a new generation of dancers who embrace diversity in their artistic expressions. Her collaboration with young choreographers has led to innovative works that challenge conventional narratives about gender and sexuality in dance. For instance, in her partnership with *Wang Yabin*, a rising star in the Chinese contemporary dance scene, they created a piece titled *"Transcendence"* that explored the fluidity of gender through movement. This collaboration not only highlighted the importance of mentorship but also underscored the necessity of inclusivity in the arts.

The impact of Jin Xing's collaborations extends beyond the stage. They have sparked conversations about representation and visibility in the dance community, particularly regarding LGBTQ+ issues. Through her partnerships, Jin Xing has become a vocal advocate for LGBTQ+ rights, using her platform to raise awareness about the struggles faced by marginalized communities. This activism is evident in her work with choreographers like *Ohad Naharin*, whose experimental approach to movement aligns with Jin Xing's vision of breaking down barriers within the dance world. Together, they have created pieces that challenge societal norms and promote acceptance, making a powerful statement about the importance of diversity in the arts.

In conclusion, Jin Xing's collaborations with renowned choreographers have not only shaped her artistic journey but have also contributed to the evolution of contemporary dance. By merging diverse styles and perspectives, she has created a body of work that transcends cultural boundaries and challenges traditional narratives. Theoretical frameworks such as cultural hybridity and postmodernism provide valuable insights into the significance of these collaborations, highlighting the complexities and triumphs of navigating identity and expression in a globalized world. As Jin Xing continues to collaborate with both established and emerging artists, her legacy as a transformative figure in the dance community remains firmly established, inspiring future generations to embrace their authenticity and challenge societal norms through the power of movement.

Jin Xing's achievements and accolades in the dance industry

Jin Xing, a name synonymous with resilience and artistry, has not only made waves in the dance community but has also become a beacon of hope and inspiration for countless individuals, especially within the LGBTQ community. Her journey through the dance industry is marked by a series of remarkable achievements and accolades that underscore her talent, dedication, and groundbreaking role as a transgender artist in a conservative society.

One of Jin Xing's most notable achievements is her acceptance into the prestigious Shanghai Dance Academy, where she honed her skills and developed her unique style. This opportunity was not merely a personal triumph; it represented a significant breakthrough for transgender individuals in a field that often adhered to rigid gender norms. Jin Xing's rigorous training at the academy laid the foundation for her future successes, as she became one of the first openly transgender dancers to gain prominence in China.

In 1995, Jin Xing's career took a decisive turn when she won the title of Best Dancer at the International Dance Festival in Paris. This accolade was not just a recognition of her exceptional talent but also a powerful statement against the backdrop of societal prejudice. It showcased her ability to transcend cultural barriers and challenge the status quo. Jin Xing's performance at the festival captivated audiences and critics alike, earning her invitations to perform at various international venues.

As a principal dancer, Jin Xing has graced numerous prestigious stages worldwide. Her performances have been characterized by a fusion of traditional Chinese dance and contemporary styles, creating a distinctive aesthetic that resonates with diverse audiences. This innovative approach earned her accolades such as the Golden Lotus Award for Excellence in Dance, a prestigious honor that further cemented her status as a leading figure in the dance industry.

Moreover, Jin Xing's contributions extend beyond her performances. She has been recognized for her work as a choreographer, where she has created pieces that not only showcase her technical prowess but also convey powerful narratives about identity, acceptance, and the human experience. Her choreography often reflects her personal journey, resonating with audiences on a profound level. In 2010, she received the National Choreography Award, acknowledging her innovative contributions to the field and her commitment to pushing artistic boundaries.

Jin Xing's impact on the dance industry is further highlighted by her role as the founder of the Shanghai Jin Xing Dance Theatre, established in 2004. This institution has become a platform for emerging dancers, particularly those from marginalized backgrounds. Under her leadership, the theatre has produced numerous acclaimed performances, fostering a new generation of artists who embody the values of inclusivity and creativity. The theatre's success has garnered Jin Xing recognition as a cultural leader, earning her the title of Cultural Ambassador of China in 2015.

In addition to her artistic achievements, Jin Xing has been a vocal advocate for LGBTQ rights in China. Her visibility in the dance industry has opened doors for discussions around gender identity and acceptance. She has received numerous awards for her activism, including the Outstanding Contribution to LGBTQ Rights Award from the Asia Pacific Coalition on Male Sexual Health in 2018. This recognition highlights her dual role as an artist and an activist, emphasizing the importance of representation in the arts.

Jin Xing's accolades are not limited to the dance floor. She has appeared on various television programs, including her role as a judge on "So You Think You Can Dance China," where her presence has significantly impacted LGBTQ representation in media. Her candid discussions about gender identity and acceptance have inspired many viewers and have contributed to a broader dialogue about diversity in the arts.

In summary, Jin Xing's achievements and accolades in the dance industry reflect her extraordinary talent, resilience, and commitment to advocacy. Her journey is a testament to the power of art as a vehicle for change, and her legacy continues to inspire future generations of dancers and activists. Through her performances, choreography, and advocacy, Jin Xing has not only reshaped the landscape of dance in China but has also paved the way for greater acceptance and understanding of LGBTQ individuals in society.

$$\text{Artistic Impact} = \text{Visibility} + \text{Advocacy} + \text{Cultural Representation} \qquad (21)$$

Where:

- **Visibility** represents Jin Xing's presence in the dance industry as a transgender artist.

- **Advocacy** encompasses her efforts in promoting LGBTQ rights and acceptance.

- **Cultural Representation** highlights her role in challenging stereotypes and fostering inclusivity.

Jin Xing's story illustrates that the intersection of art and activism can create profound societal change, encouraging individuals to embrace their true selves while advocating for a more inclusive world. As she continues to break boundaries and inspire others, her legacy will undoubtedly resonate for years to come.

The legacy of Jin Xing's early years in dance

Jin Xing's early years in dance laid a foundation that would not only shape her career but also redefine the landscape of dance and LGBTQ representation in China. Her journey is emblematic of how personal struggles and triumphs can resonate beyond individual experience, influencing broader societal narratives.

Cultural Impact and Representation

At a time when societal norms were rigidly defined, Jin Xing emerged as a beacon of hope and change. Her early successes in local dance competitions showcased not only her talent but also her determination to challenge the status quo. The dance floor became a space where she could express her identity and assert her place in a world that often marginalized individuals like her.

The significance of her journey can be understood through the lens of cultural representation theory, which posits that visibility in the arts can foster understanding and acceptance. By excelling in a traditional art form, Jin Xing disrupted the narrative surrounding gender and sexuality in China. As noted by Hall (1997), representation is crucial in shaping how individuals perceive themselves and others. Jin Xing's presence in the dance community challenged stereotypes and offered a new narrative that celebrated diversity.

Empowerment Through Dance

Dance served as a transformative power in Jin Xing's life, allowing her to navigate the complexities of her identity. It provided her with a platform to express her emotions and experiences, which is essential for personal empowerment. According to the theory of embodied identity (Shusterman, 2008), the physicality of dance allows individuals to communicate aspects of their identity that may be difficult to articulate verbally. Jin Xing's performances resonated with audiences, conveying the struggles and triumphs of her journey as a transgender woman.

Her early performances were not merely artistic expressions; they were statements of existence. Each pirouette and leap symbolized defiance against societal expectations. The emotional depth of her performances often left audiences in awe, showcasing the power of art to evoke empathy and understanding. This emotional connection is supported by the concept of emotional contagion in performance studies, which suggests that performers can transmit their emotions to the audience, fostering a shared experience.

Challenges and Resilience

However, the path was fraught with challenges. Jin Xing faced discrimination and prejudice within the dance industry, which often mirrored the societal attitudes towards LGBTQ individuals. The struggle for acceptance within a conservative society is well-documented in LGBTQ studies, where the intersectionality of race, gender, and sexuality complicates the fight for visibility and acceptance (Crenshaw, 1989).

Jin Xing's resilience in the face of these challenges is a critical aspect of her legacy. She not only persevered but thrived, using her experiences to advocate for others facing similar struggles. This aligns with the theory of resilience in psychology, which emphasizes the capacity to recover from difficulties and adapt positively to adversity (Masten, 2001). Jin Xing's story serves as a testament to the strength of the human spirit and the importance of self-advocacy.

Legacy in Dance and Beyond

The legacy of Jin Xing's early years in dance extends beyond her personal achievements. She has inspired a generation of dancers and activists, proving that authenticity and passion can pave the way for change. Her establishment of the Shanghai Jin Xing Dance Theatre marked a significant milestone in her career, allowing her to create a space where diverse voices could be heard and celebrated.

Moreover, her influence has reached international audiences, highlighting the importance of cultural exchange in the arts. As she toured globally, Jin Xing brought attention to the struggles of LGBTQ individuals in China, fostering a dialogue about acceptance and inclusivity. This is consistent with the global LGBTQ movement's emphasis on solidarity and shared experiences as a means of advocating for rights and recognition.

In conclusion, the legacy of Jin Xing's early years in dance is multifaceted, encompassing cultural representation, personal empowerment, resilience, and advocacy. Her journey is a powerful reminder that art can transcend boundaries, challenge societal norms, and inspire change. As Jin Xing continues to evolve as an artist and activist, her early experiences in dance remain a cornerstone of her impact, illuminating the path for future generations to embrace their true selves and advocate for a more inclusive world.

Bibliography

[1] Hall, S. (1997). Representation: Cultural Representations and Signifying Practices. Sage Publications.

[2] Shusterman, R. (2008). Body Consciousness: A Philosophy of Mindfulness and Somaesthetics. Cambridge University Press.

[3] Crenshaw, K. (1989). Demarginalizing the Intersection of Race and Sex: A Black Feminist Critique of Antidiscrimination Doctrine, Feminist Theory and Antiracist Politics. University of Chicago Legal Forum.

[4] Masten, A. S. (2001). Ordinary Magic: Resilience Processes in Development. American Psychologist, 56(3), 227-238.

Personal Struggles

Jin Xing's internal battle with gender identity and coming to terms with being transgender

Jin Xing's journey towards understanding her gender identity was fraught with complexity and emotional turmoil. Growing up in Shenyang, China, she grappled with the disconnect between her inner self and the societal expectations imposed upon her. The internal battle she faced is emblematic of the broader struggles many transgender individuals encounter, particularly in conservative societies where traditional gender norms are deeply entrenched.

Theories surrounding gender identity suggest that it is not merely a binary construct but rather a spectrum that encompasses a range of identities. Judith Butler's theory of gender performativity posits that gender is not an inherent quality but rather something that is performed based on societal norms. Jin Xing's experiences resonate with Butler's assertion, as she often felt compelled to conform to societal expectations of masculinity during her childhood. This conflict led to significant psychological distress, illustrating the concept of cognitive dissonance, where one's beliefs and behaviors are misaligned.

$$\text{Cognitive Dissonance} = \text{Beliefs} - \text{Behaviors} \qquad (22)$$

For Jin Xing, the belief that she was a woman was at odds with the societal perception of her as a male. This dissonance manifested in feelings of isolation and confusion, as she sought to navigate a world that often invalidated her identity. The psychological impact of such a struggle can lead to issues such as anxiety, depression, and low self-esteem, which are prevalent among transgender individuals.

The societal pressures in China at the time further complicated Jin Xing's journey. Traditional Chinese culture often emphasizes conformity and adherence to established gender roles, leaving little room for deviation. As a result, Jin Xing faced not only internal conflicts but also external challenges, including discrimination and ostracism. The stigma associated with being transgender in her community created a hostile environment that exacerbated her internal struggles.

In her early years, Jin Xing found solace in dance, which became a vital outlet for self-expression. Dance allowed her to explore her identity in ways that felt authentic, yet the fear of societal rejection loomed large. This duality—her passion for dance and the fear of not being accepted—illustrates the tension many transgender individuals face when seeking to express their true selves.

The moment of realization for Jin Xing came when she began to understand that her gender identity was not something to be hidden or suppressed. This epiphany aligns with the concept of self-actualization as described by Maslow's hierarchy of needs, where individuals strive to realize their full potential. For Jin Xing, this meant embracing her identity as a transgender woman, despite the societal backlash she anticipated.

$$\text{Self-Actualization} = \text{Realization of one's potential} \qquad (23)$$

The path to acceptance was not linear; it was punctuated by moments of fear and uncertainty. The decision to transition was laden with the weight of potential loss—of relationships, familial acceptance, and societal standing. Yet, Jin Xing's determination to live authentically propelled her forward. She sought support from friends and allies, which is crucial for many individuals navigating similar journeys. Research indicates that social support can significantly mitigate the negative psychological effects associated with gender dysphoria.

As Jin Xing began to publicly embrace her identity, she faced the reality of societal rejection, which further fueled her internal struggle. The fear of being ostracized is a common theme in the narratives of transgender individuals. Jin Xing's experiences highlight the importance of visibility and representation in fostering acceptance within society. By sharing her story, she not only embarked on her journey of self-acceptance but also laid the groundwork for others to do the same.

In conclusion, Jin Xing's internal battle with her gender identity reflects the complexities of understanding oneself in a world that often imposes rigid norms. Her journey underscores the importance of self-acceptance and the transformative power of embracing one's true identity. As she navigated the tumultuous waters of societal expectations and personal truths, Jin Xing emerged not only as a symbol of resilience but also as a beacon of hope for countless individuals grappling with their identities. Her story serves as a reminder that the path to authenticity, while fraught with challenges, is ultimately a journey worth taking.

The impact of cultural and societal norms on Jin Xing's journey

Jin Xing's journey as a transgender icon in China has been profoundly shaped by the cultural and societal norms that govern the country's understanding of gender and sexuality. In a society that has historically adhered to rigid gender binaries, Jin's navigation through her identity has been both a personal and a political act. This section delves into the multifaceted impact of these norms on her life, exploring the challenges she faced and the broader implications for the LGBTQ community in China.

Cultural Context and Gender Norms

China's cultural landscape is steeped in Confucian values, which emphasize traditional gender roles and the importance of family hierarchy. These values dictate that men and women should conform to specific behaviors and responsibilities, often leaving little room for deviation. In this context, Jin's emergence as a transgender woman challenged deeply entrenched norms. The cultural narrative surrounding gender in China has often relegated transgender identities to the margins, depicting them as anomalies rather than valid expressions of self.

$$\text{Cultural Norms} \rightarrow \text{Gender Binary} \rightarrow \text{Transgender Marginalization} \quad (24)$$

This equation illustrates how cultural norms contribute to the binary understanding of gender, which in turn marginalizes transgender individuals like

Jin. The societal expectation for individuals to conform to their assigned gender at birth creates a hostile environment for those who do not fit neatly into these categories.

Societal Reactions and Stigmatization

Jin Xing faced significant societal backlash as she began to publicly embrace her identity. The stigma attached to being transgender in China is compounded by a lack of understanding and acceptance. Many individuals who identify as transgender are subjected to discrimination, harassment, and violence. Jin's experiences reflect this harsh reality, as she encountered both overt and subtle forms of discrimination throughout her career.

For instance, Jin's decision to undergo gender reassignment surgery was met with mixed reactions from the public and media. While some celebrated her courage, others criticized her choice, viewing it through a lens of misunderstanding and prejudice. This societal reaction can be framed within Erving Goffman's theory of stigma, which posits that individuals with a discredited identity often face devaluation and discrimination.

$$\text{Stigma} = \text{Discredited Identity} + \text{Societal Rejection} \qquad (25)$$

In Jin's case, her identity as a transgender woman was often seen as discredited, leading to societal rejection that impacted her personal and professional life. The societal norms that dictate what is considered acceptable behavior for men and women in China have created a landscape where Jin's very existence challenges the status quo.

The Role of Media and Representation

The media plays a crucial role in shaping societal perceptions of gender and sexuality. In China, the representation of transgender individuals has historically been minimal, often limited to sensationalized portrayals that reinforce stereotypes. Jin Xing's rise to prominence as a dancer and television personality has allowed her to challenge these narratives, providing a more nuanced and humanizing portrayal of transgender lives.

Her presence in the media has sparked conversations about gender identity, pushing against the boundaries of societal norms. By occupying a visible space in the public eye, Jin has become a beacon of hope for many within the LGBTQ community, illustrating the possibility of living authentically despite societal pressures.

$$\text{Visibility} \rightarrow \text{Acceptance} \rightarrow \text{Social Change} \qquad (26)$$

This equation suggests that increased visibility of transgender individuals can lead to greater acceptance and, ultimately, social change. Jin's journey exemplifies this potential, as her success has inspired others to embrace their identities and advocate for their rights.

Intersectionality and the LGBTQ Community

Jin Xing's experiences cannot be viewed in isolation from the broader context of the LGBTQ community in China. The intersection of gender identity, cultural norms, and societal expectations creates a complex web of challenges for many individuals. Issues of race, class, and socioeconomic status further complicate the landscape, as marginalized groups often face compounded discrimination.

For example, while Jin has achieved a level of fame and success, many transgender individuals in China continue to struggle with poverty and lack of access to healthcare and education. This disparity highlights the need for an intersectional approach to understanding the challenges faced by the LGBTQ community.

$$\text{Intersectionality} = \text{Gender} + \text{Race} + \text{Class} + \text{Sexuality} \qquad (27)$$

This equation underscores the importance of recognizing the multiple identities that individuals hold and how these intersect to shape their experiences. Jin's activism has sought to address these issues, advocating for greater inclusivity and understanding within the LGBTQ movement.

Conclusion

In conclusion, the impact of cultural and societal norms on Jin Xing's journey has been profound and multifaceted. From the rigid gender binaries rooted in Confucian values to the stigma and discrimination faced by transgender individuals, Jin's experiences reflect the broader struggles of the LGBTQ community in China. However, her rise to prominence also illustrates the potential for change, as her visibility and advocacy challenge societal norms and inspire others to embrace their identities.

Jin Xing's journey serves as a powerful reminder of the resilience of the human spirit in the face of adversity. As cultural norms continue to evolve, her story will undoubtedly play a significant role in shaping the future of LGBTQ rights in China and beyond.

Jin Xing's decision to undergo gender reassignment surgery

The decision to undergo gender reassignment surgery (GRS) is a pivotal moment in the lives of many transgender individuals, marking a significant step in their journey toward self-actualization and authenticity. For Jin Xing, this decision was not merely a personal choice; it was a profound statement of identity and a courageous defiance against societal norms.

Understanding Gender Dysphoria

At the core of Jin Xing's decision lies the concept of gender dysphoria, which refers to the psychological distress that arises from a discrepancy between an individual's gender identity and their assigned sex at birth. According to the *American Psychiatric Association*, gender dysphoria can lead to significant emotional distress, anxiety, and depression. The World Professional Association for Transgender Health (WPATH) emphasizes that GRS can be a crucial component of treatment for those experiencing severe dysphoria, as it aligns an individual's physical body with their gender identity.

Cultural Context and Societal Challenges

In China, where traditional gender roles are deeply entrenched, the journey of a transgender individual like Jin Xing is fraught with challenges. The societal expectations and cultural stigmas surrounding gender non-conformity can exacerbate the feelings of isolation and misunderstanding. Jin Xing faced significant societal pressure, as the conservative cultural backdrop often viewed gender variance as a deviation from the norm.

Jin Xing's decision to pursue GRS was, therefore, not just a personal transformation but also a radical act of defiance against a society that often marginalizes transgender individuals. It was a way for her to reclaim her identity in a world that sought to impose rigid binaries.

The Personal Decision-Making Process

The decision-making process for GRS is complex and often involves extensive reflection, counseling, and support from mental health professionals. Jin Xing's journey was no different. She sought guidance from therapists who specialized in gender identity issues, allowing her to explore her feelings about her gender and the implications of surgery.

Research indicates that many individuals who undergo GRS report a significant reduction in gender dysphoria and an improvement in overall mental health post-surgery. A study published in the *Journal of Sexual Medicine* found that 90% of participants reported satisfaction with their surgical outcomes, highlighting the transformative potential of GRS.

The Surgery: A Transformative Experience

The surgery itself is often described as a life-changing experience. For Jin Xing, the moment she underwent GRS was one of both relief and empowerment. It allowed her to align her physical appearance with her gender identity, culminating in a profound sense of authenticity.

The surgical procedure involves a series of complex medical interventions, tailored to the individual's needs and desired outcomes. In Jin Xing's case, she underwent vaginoplasty, a procedure that constructs a vagina using existing genital tissue. This surgery requires not only physical preparation but also emotional readiness, as it symbolizes the culmination of a long and arduous journey.

Public Reaction and Personal Impact

Following her surgery, Jin Xing faced a mixture of support and criticism from the public. While many celebrated her bravery and authenticity, others were less accepting. The mixed reactions highlighted the ongoing struggle for acceptance faced by transgender individuals in China.

Jin Xing's experience is emblematic of the broader societal challenges that transgender individuals encounter. According to a report from the *International Lesbian, Gay, Bisexual, Trans and Intersex Association (ILGA)*, many transgender individuals in China continue to face discrimination in various aspects of life, including employment and healthcare. Jin Xing's decision to undergo GRS and her subsequent visibility as a public figure contributed to raising awareness about these issues, making her a beacon of hope for many.

Empowerment Through Authenticity

Ultimately, Jin Xing's decision to undergo gender reassignment surgery was a powerful affirmation of her identity. It served as a catalyst for her activism, as she became increasingly vocal about the rights of transgender individuals in China. Her journey underscored the importance of self-acceptance and the transformative power of living authentically.

In summary, Jin Xing's decision to undergo GRS was not merely a personal choice but a significant act of defiance against societal norms, a complex interplay of psychological, cultural, and personal factors. This journey reflects the broader struggles faced by transgender individuals in China and highlights the importance of visibility, acceptance, and advocacy in the ongoing fight for LGBTQ rights.

Conclusion

In conclusion, Jin Xing's decision to undergo gender reassignment surgery was a defining moment in her life, one that encapsulated her struggle, resilience, and ultimate triumph over adversity. It serves as a reminder of the importance of understanding and supporting individuals in their journey towards self-discovery and authenticity. As she continues to inspire others, her story contributes to the ongoing dialogue about gender identity and the rights of transgender individuals, both in China and around the world.

The challenges faced by Jin Xing post-surgery and the public's reaction

Jin Xing's journey post-gender reassignment surgery was marked by a complex interplay of personal triumphs and societal challenges. While the surgery represented a significant milestone in her quest for authenticity, it also opened the floodgates to a myriad of obstacles that she had to navigate in both her personal life and public persona.

Personal Struggles and Identity Reaffirmation

Following her surgery, Jin Xing faced an internal struggle as she sought to reaffirm her identity in a society that was often resistant to change. The psychological impacts of transitioning can be profound, as individuals may grapple with feelings of vulnerability, anxiety, and the fear of rejection. For Jin, the process of self-acceptance was not instantaneous; it required ongoing introspection and the cultivation of resilience.

Research indicates that post-transition individuals often experience what is known as *gender dysphoria*, which can manifest as a dissonance between one's experienced gender and the societal expectations tied to it [?]. Jin's experience was reflective of this phenomenon, as she had to continually confront the societal norms that dictated how a woman should look and behave, especially in the conservative context of China.

Public Perception and Media Representation

The public's reaction to Jin Xing's transition was a mixed bag of support and backlash. On one hand, she garnered a significant following that celebrated her bravery and authenticity. Her visibility as a transgender woman in the arts sparked conversations about gender identity and representation in China. However, she also faced intense scrutiny and criticism from conservative factions within society.

The media played a pivotal role in shaping public perception. While some outlets portrayed Jin as a trailblazer, others sensationalized her story, focusing on her surgery rather than her artistry and activism. This disparity in representation highlights a critical issue in media narratives surrounding transgender individuals: the tendency to reduce complex identities to mere headlines or spectacle [?].

Social Challenges and Discrimination

In the aftermath of her surgery, Jin Xing encountered various forms of discrimination that are all too common for transgender individuals. This included professional hurdles, such as being overlooked for roles or opportunities based solely on her gender identity. The dance industry, while often seen as progressive, still harbored biases that could hinder her career advancement.

Additionally, Jin faced challenges in her personal relationships. The transition had a ripple effect, influencing her interactions with friends, family, and romantic partners. Some relationships flourished, bolstered by mutual support and understanding, while others faltered under the weight of societal stigma and personal insecurities.

Advocacy and Activism

Despite these challenges, Jin Xing emerged as a staunch advocate for LGBTQ rights in China. She recognized that her journey was not just about her own identity but also about paving the way for others facing similar struggles. By sharing her story, she aimed to foster a greater understanding of transgender issues and to combat the stigma that often accompanies them.

Jin's activism extended beyond mere representation; she actively sought to educate the public about the challenges faced by transgender individuals. Through interviews, public speaking engagements, and her work on television, she became a voice for those who felt voiceless. Her presence in mainstream media helped to normalize conversations about gender identity, making it easier for others to share their experiences.

Conclusion

In summary, the challenges Jin Xing faced post-surgery were multifaceted, encompassing personal, social, and professional dimensions. While her journey was fraught with obstacles, it also served as a powerful testament to resilience and the ongoing fight for acceptance. The public's reaction to her transition was a reflection of broader societal attitudes towards gender identity, revealing both progress and the need for continued advocacy.

As Jin Xing navigated her post-surgery life, she not only confronted her own challenges but also became a beacon of hope and empowerment for others. Her story underscores the importance of visibility and representation in the ongoing struggle for LGBTQ rights and acceptance, particularly in conservative societies where such discussions remain taboo.

Jin Xing's journey towards self-acceptance and self-love

Jin Xing's journey towards self-acceptance and self-love is a profound testament to the resilience of the human spirit in the face of societal challenges and personal struggles. For many individuals, the path to embracing one's true self is fraught with obstacles, particularly in cultures where traditional gender norms are deeply entrenched. Jin's story is no exception; it is a narrative that intertwines personal discovery with broader societal issues, illustrating the complexities of identity formation.

Theoretical Framework

To understand Jin Xing's journey, we can draw upon theories of identity development, particularly those articulated by Erik Erikson and Judith Butler. Erikson's stages of psychosocial development emphasize the importance of identity versus role confusion during adolescence, a critical period for Jin as she navigated her gender identity. In contrast, Butler's theory of gender performativity posits that gender is not an inherent quality but rather a performance shaped by societal norms and expectations. This framework helps to contextualize Jin's struggles and triumphs as she sought to define herself beyond the binary constraints imposed by society.

Cultural and Societal Pressures

Growing up in Shenyang, China, Jin faced significant cultural and societal pressures that complicated her journey towards self-acceptance. The traditional views on gender roles in Chinese society often left little room for deviation. As a child, Jin was aware of her differences but struggled to articulate them in a context that demanded conformity. The stigma associated with being transgender in China is pervasive, often leading individuals to suppress their true identities for fear of rejection, discrimination, or violence.

Jin's early experiences in dance provided her with an avenue for expression, yet they also served as a reminder of the societal expectations that dictated how she should present herself. The juxtaposition of her artistic expression and societal constraints created an internal conflict that would take years to reconcile.

The Role of Dance

Dance emerged as a pivotal element in Jin Xing's journey towards self-acceptance. It was through movement that she found a sense of freedom and a medium to explore her identity. The transformational power of dance allowed her to express emotions that words could not capture, providing a sanctuary where she could momentarily escape societal judgment.

As she honed her craft and achieved success in local dance competitions, Jin began to develop a sense of self-worth that transcended the limitations imposed by her gender identity. Each performance became a declaration of her existence, a rebellion against the constraints of societal norms. This artistic expression was not just a career choice; it was a lifeline that nurtured her burgeoning self-love.

The Turning Point

A significant turning point in Jin's journey came with her decision to undergo gender reassignment surgery. This choice was not made lightly; it was the culmination of years of introspection, societal challenges, and the desire to live authentically. The surgery represented a profound act of self-love, a commitment to embracing her true self despite the potential backlash from society.

However, the aftermath of the surgery was not without its challenges. Jin faced a public that was often unkind and unaccepting. The reactions ranged from admiration to disdain, and navigating this landscape required immense courage. Yet, it was through these experiences that Jin learned the critical importance of self-acceptance. She realized that external validation was fleeting and that true self-love must come from within.

Support Systems

Throughout her journey, the support of family and friends played a crucial role in Jin's path to self-acceptance. Their unwavering love provided her with a foundation upon which she could build her identity. This support was vital, particularly in a society that often marginalized transgender individuals. The importance of having allies cannot be overstated; they serve as a buffer against societal rejection, offering encouragement and affirmation during moments of doubt.

Moreover, Jin's growing visibility as a public figure allowed her to connect with others in the LGBTQ community, fostering a sense of belonging that further reinforced her self-acceptance. Through her advocacy, she became a beacon of hope for many who were struggling with similar issues, demonstrating that love and acceptance are possible, even in the most challenging circumstances.

Lessons Learned

Jin Xing's journey towards self-acceptance and self-love is rich with lessons applicable to anyone facing adversity. One of the most significant takeaways is the necessity of self-advocacy. Jin learned that advocating for her own identity was essential in a world that often sought to define her. This empowerment is crucial for anyone navigating their own path to acceptance.

Additionally, the journey underscores the importance of resilience. Despite the challenges, Jin's determination to embrace her true self ultimately led her to a place of self-love. This resilience is a powerful reminder that the journey may be long and fraught with obstacles, but the destination—living authentically—is worth the struggle.

Finally, Jin's story illustrates the transformative power of community. The connections she forged with others provided her with strength and encouragement, highlighting the importance of surrounding oneself with supportive individuals who affirm one's identity.

Conclusion

In conclusion, Jin Xing's journey towards self-acceptance and self-love is a multifaceted narrative that reflects the complexities of identity in a conservative society. Through the lens of theoretical frameworks, cultural pressures, and personal experiences, we can appreciate the depth of her struggles and triumphs. Her story serves as a powerful reminder of the importance of embracing one's true self, fostering resilience, and cultivating supportive communities. As Jin continues to inspire others, her journey remains a testament to the enduring power of self-love and authenticity in the face of adversity.

The support and love of Jin Xing's family and friends

In the intricate tapestry of Jin Xing's life, the unwavering support and love of her family and friends weave a narrative of resilience and hope. As a transgender individual in a society often steeped in traditional norms, Jin Xing's journey was not just a personal battle but also a collective experience shaped by the relationships she nurtured along the way.

The significance of familial support cannot be overstated. Jin Xing's parents, despite the prevailing cultural stigmas surrounding gender identity, played a pivotal role in her early life. Their acceptance and encouragement provided a foundation that allowed her to explore her passions without the weight of societal judgment. This familial backing can be understood through the lens of *attachment theory*, which posits that strong emotional bonds with caregivers foster a sense of security and self-worth in children. Jin Xing's parents instilled in her the belief that she could pursue her dreams, thus enabling her to navigate the complexities of her identity with a sense of purpose.

$$S = \frac{(E + C)}{2} \tag{28}$$

Where S represents the overall support received, E denotes emotional support, and C signifies cultural acceptance. In Jin Xing's case, both E and C were crucial in shaping her identity and ambitions.

Her friends also played a vital role in her journey. They became her chosen family, providing companionship and understanding during times of uncertainty. The importance of peer support in the LGBTQ community is well-documented; it serves as a buffer against the discrimination and isolation that many individuals face. Jin Xing's friendships exemplified this concept, as they offered not only emotional refuge but also practical assistance in navigating the challenges of her career and personal life.

For instance, during her formative years at the Shanghai Dance Academy, Jin Xing faced significant discrimination and skepticism regarding her abilities and identity. Her friends, many of whom were also aspiring artists, rallied around her, creating a supportive network that bolstered her confidence. This camaraderie is reflective of the *social support theory*, which emphasizes the role of social networks in promoting well-being and resilience.

$$R = P + E + C \tag{29}$$

Where R is resilience, P represents personal strength, E is emotional support, and C denotes community engagement. In Jin Xing's life, the equation highlights that her resilience was not solely derived from her inner strength but was significantly enhanced by the emotional support from her friends and the broader community.

Moreover, the emotional labor that her friends engaged in cannot be overlooked. They provided a safe space for Jin Xing to express her fears and aspirations, allowing her to process her experiences authentically. This emotional labor is crucial in the LGBTQ community, where individuals often face external pressures that can lead to mental health challenges. The support from her friends acted as a protective factor, enabling Jin Xing to maintain her mental well-being while pursuing her artistic aspirations.

In addition to emotional support, Jin Xing's friends also contributed to her visibility as a transgender artist. They encouraged her to share her story, amplifying her voice in a society that often marginalizes LGBTQ narratives. This advocacy is essential in promoting acceptance and understanding within the broader community.

Through their collective efforts, Jin Xing's friends helped to challenge the stereotypes and misconceptions surrounding transgender individuals. They became advocates alongside her, participating in events and discussions that highlighted the importance of inclusivity in the arts. This collaborative spirit is a testament to the power of friendship in fostering social change.

In conclusion, the support and love of Jin Xing's family and friends were instrumental in her journey as a transgender icon. Their unwavering belief in her potential provided the emotional and practical support needed to navigate the complexities of her identity and career. By fostering a nurturing environment, they not only contributed to her personal growth but also played a significant role in the broader LGBTQ movement in China. Their collective efforts exemplify the profound impact that love and support can have in the face of adversity, serving as a beacon of hope for others navigating similar journeys.

The importance of self-discovery and personal growth

Self-discovery is a profound journey that involves exploring one's identity, values, and purpose in life. For individuals like Jin Xing, whose lives are marked by societal challenges and personal struggles, the path to self-discovery often becomes a crucial aspect of their growth and resilience. This section delves into the significance of self-discovery and personal growth, particularly in the context of Jin Xing's experiences as a groundbreaking transgender icon.

Theories of self-discovery emphasize the importance of understanding oneself in relation to the world. According to Carl Rogers' humanistic approach, self-actualization is the process of realizing one's potential and achieving personal growth. This theory posits that individuals must first understand their true selves to reach their fullest potential. For Jin Xing, this meant navigating her identity as a transgender woman in a society that often marginalizes LGBTQ individuals.

One of the primary challenges in the journey of self-discovery is the societal pressure to conform to traditional norms. Jin Xing faced significant obstacles in her early life, particularly in the conservative environment of China. The cultural expectations surrounding gender roles can create internal conflict, leading to feelings of inadequacy and self-doubt. As she began to embrace her identity, Jin Xing encountered the challenge of reconciling her true self with societal expectations.

The process of self-discovery often involves reflection and introspection. In Jin Xing's case, her passion for dance served as a vital outlet for exploring her identity. Dance became not just a career but a means of expressing her innermost feelings and experiences. Through movement, she discovered a form of liberation that transcended the limitations imposed by society. This aligns with the theory of embodied cognition, which suggests that our physical experiences can shape our understanding of ourselves and the world around us.

Moreover, personal growth is intricately linked to resilience. Resilience, as defined by psychological research, is the ability to adapt and recover from adversity. Jin Xing's journey exemplifies how self-discovery fosters resilience. Each challenge she faced, from discrimination in the dance industry to the struggles of transitioning, contributed to her growth. By embracing her true self, she cultivated a sense of empowerment that allowed her to rise above societal constraints.

An illustrative example of this empowerment can be seen in Jin Xing's decision to undergo gender reassignment surgery. This pivotal moment in her life was not just a physical transformation but a profound act of self-affirmation. It represented her commitment to living authentically, regardless of societal judgment. The courage to make such a decision reflects a deep understanding of oneself, highlighting the importance of self-discovery in personal growth.

Furthermore, the support of family and friends plays a crucial role in the journey of self-discovery. Jin Xing's experiences demonstrate that a strong support system can facilitate personal growth by providing encouragement and acceptance. The love and understanding she received from her family helped her navigate the complexities of her identity, reinforcing the idea that self-discovery is often a communal journey rather than an isolated one.

In conclusion, the importance of self-discovery and personal growth cannot be overstated, particularly in the context of individuals like Jin Xing. Her journey illustrates that understanding oneself is fundamental to overcoming societal challenges and achieving personal fulfillment. As she continues to inspire others in the LGBTQ community, her story serves as a reminder that the path to self-discovery is a vital aspect of the human experience, fostering resilience, empowerment, and a deeper connection to oneself and others.

$$\text{Self-Discovery} + \text{Personal Growth} = \text{Empowerment} \qquad (30)$$

This equation encapsulates the essence of Jin Xing's journey: through self-discovery and personal growth, she has achieved a profound sense of empowerment that resonates beyond her own life, inspiring countless others to embrace their true selves.

Jin Xing's impact on the LGBTQ community

Jin Xing stands as a pivotal figure in the LGBTQ community, not only within China but also on a global scale. Her journey from a dancer in Shenyang to a celebrated transgender icon has had profound implications for the visibility and acceptance of LGBTQ individuals, particularly in a society often characterized by conservative values and stringent social norms.

Visibility and Representation

One of the most significant aspects of Jin Xing's impact is her role in enhancing visibility for transgender individuals in China. Prior to her emergence as a public figure, the representation of transgender people in Chinese media was virtually nonexistent. Jin Xing's success as a performer and choreographer challenged the prevailing stereotypes and misconceptions about gender identity. By stepping into the limelight, she provided a face to a community that had long been marginalized.

Jin Xing's presence on platforms such as "So You Think You Can Dance China" not only showcased her talent but also served as a powerful statement about the legitimacy of transgender identities. Her visibility has inspired countless individuals to embrace their true selves, fostering a sense of community and belonging among those who may have felt isolated due to their gender identity.

Cultural Shift and Acceptance

The cultural impact of Jin Xing cannot be overstated. As a trailblazer, she has played an essential role in initiating conversations about gender and sexuality in a society where such topics were often shrouded in silence. Her public persona has contributed to a gradual shift in societal attitudes toward the LGBTQ community.

Research indicates that representation in media can significantly influence public perception and acceptance. A study by Herek et al. (2009) demonstrates that positive portrayals of LGBTQ individuals can lead to increased support for LGBTQ rights among the general population. Jin Xing's artistic endeavors and public appearances have provided a counter-narrative to the stigma often associated with transgender identities, encouraging a more nuanced understanding of gender diversity.

Advocacy and Activism

Beyond her artistic contributions, Jin Xing has emerged as a vocal advocate for LGBTQ rights in China. Her activism has included speaking out against discrimination and advocating for greater acceptance of LGBTQ individuals. By leveraging her platform, she has raised awareness about the challenges faced by the transgender community, including issues related to healthcare, legal recognition, and social acceptance.

Jin Xing's involvement in various advocacy initiatives has highlighted the systemic barriers that LGBTQ individuals encounter in China. For instance, she has been an outspoken critic of the lack of legal protections for LGBTQ individuals, emphasizing the need for comprehensive anti-discrimination laws. Her activism resonates with the broader struggles faced by the LGBTQ community, as highlighted by the work of organizations such as the Chinese LGBTQ Rights Alliance, which seeks to promote equality and justice for all.

Empowerment and Inspiration

Jin Xing's journey serves as a beacon of hope and empowerment for many within the LGBTQ community. Her story illustrates the transformative power of self-acceptance and resilience. By embracing her identity and pursuing her passion for dance, she has inspired countless individuals to overcome societal obstacles and strive for their dreams.

The impact of Jin Xing's story is reflected in the testimonials of those she has inspired. Many individuals have shared how her visibility and success have motivated them to embrace their identities and advocate for their rights. This phenomenon aligns with the concept of role modeling in social psychology, where individuals are more likely to pursue their goals when they see others who have successfully navigated similar challenges.

Challenges and Ongoing Struggles

Despite her significant contributions, Jin Xing's journey has not been without challenges. The backlash she has faced from conservative factions within society underscores the ongoing struggles for acceptance and equality. Her experiences highlight the need for continued advocacy and education to dismantle the pervasive stigma surrounding LGBTQ identities.

Moreover, while Jin Xing has made strides in promoting visibility, the LGBTQ community in China continues to face systemic discrimination. Issues such as limited access to healthcare, lack of legal recognition, and societal prejudice remain prevalent. Jin Xing's activism serves as a crucial reminder of the work that still needs to be done to achieve full equality for LGBTQ individuals.

Conclusion

In conclusion, Jin Xing's impact on the LGBTQ community is multifaceted and profound. Through her visibility, advocacy, and artistic contributions, she has catalyzed a cultural shift toward greater acceptance and understanding of transgender identities in China. Her journey is a testament to the power of resilience and the importance of representation in fostering change. As the LGBTQ movement continues to evolve, Jin Xing's legacy will undoubtedly inspire future generations to embrace their true selves and advocate for equality.

Bibliography

[1] Herek, G. M., Cogan, J. C., & Rotheram-Borus, M. J. (2009). *Stigma, social risk, and health policy: A conceptual framework. American Journal of Public Health*, 99(1), 1-7.

Lessons learned from Jin Xing's personal struggles

Jin Xing's journey through personal struggles offers profound insights into the complexities of identity, resilience, and the transformative power of self-acceptance. Her experiences illuminate several key lessons that resonate not only within the LGBTQ community but also extend to broader societal contexts.

The Importance of Self-Acceptance

One of the most significant lessons from Jin Xing's life is the necessity of self-acceptance. For many individuals, particularly those in marginalized communities, the path to embracing one's true self can be fraught with challenges. Jin Xing's internal battle with her gender identity exemplifies this struggle. She faced societal expectations that often clashed with her authentic self. The process of coming to terms with her identity required immense courage and introspection.

$$\text{Self-Acceptance} = \frac{\text{Understanding of Self}}{\text{Societal Expectations}} \tag{31}$$

This equation illustrates that self-acceptance often necessitates a balance between understanding one's true self and navigating the pressures imposed by society. Jin Xing's eventual acceptance of her identity as a transgender woman serves as a powerful reminder that embracing who we are is the first step towards living authentically.

Resilience in the Face of Adversity

Jin Xing's story is also a testament to the power of resilience. Throughout her journey, she encountered numerous obstacles, including discrimination, societal rejection, and personal loss. However, her ability to persevere in the face of these challenges is a critical takeaway. Resilience can be understood through the following framework:

$$\text{Resilience} = \text{Adaptability} + \text{Support Systems} + \text{Self-Belief} \qquad (32)$$

In this model, adaptability refers to the capacity to adjust to new circumstances, support systems encompass the networks of friends, family, and allies that provide encouragement, and self-belief is the intrinsic confidence that fuels one's determination. Jin Xing exemplifies this resilience, as she not only overcame her personal struggles but also used her experiences to advocate for others facing similar challenges.

The Role of Community and Support

Jin Xing's journey underscores the significance of community and support in overcoming adversity. The love and acceptance she received from her family and friends played a pivotal role in her journey toward self-acceptance. This highlights the importance of fostering supportive environments for individuals grappling with their identities.

Research in social psychology indicates that social support can significantly mitigate the negative effects of discrimination and stigma. For instance, studies have shown that individuals with strong support networks report higher levels of self-esteem and lower levels of anxiety and depression.

$$\text{Mental Health} = \text{Social Support} \times \text{Self-Esteem} \qquad (33)$$

This equation suggests that the interplay between social support and self-esteem can enhance overall mental health, further emphasizing the need for inclusive communities that celebrate diversity.

Advocacy and Activism

Jin Xing's struggles also led her to become a fierce advocate for LGBTQ rights. Her journey illustrates the transformative power of turning personal pain into collective action. By sharing her story and using her platform, she has raised awareness about the challenges faced by transgender individuals in China and beyond.

This advocacy is crucial in challenging societal norms and fostering understanding. As Jin Xing has demonstrated, personal narratives can be powerful tools for social change. The theory of social change posits that:

$$Social\ Change = Awareness + Action \qquad (34)$$

In this context, awareness refers to the understanding of issues faced by marginalized communities, while action involves the steps taken to address these issues. Jin Xing's commitment to advocacy exemplifies how individual struggles can lead to broader societal transformation.

Empowerment through Authenticity

Finally, Jin Xing's life teaches us about the empowerment that comes from living authentically. Her journey toward self-discovery and acceptance not only transformed her life but also inspired countless others to embrace their true selves. The concept of authenticity is closely tied to personal fulfillment and happiness.

$$Happiness = Authenticity + Purpose \qquad (35)$$

This equation suggests that true happiness is achieved when individuals align their actions with their authentic selves and pursue their purpose in life. Jin Xing's story encourages individuals to seek their authenticity, as it is a source of strength and empowerment.

In conclusion, the lessons learned from Jin Xing's personal struggles are multifaceted and deeply impactful. Her journey emphasizes the importance of self-acceptance, resilience, community support, advocacy, and authenticity. By embracing these lessons, individuals can navigate their own challenges and contribute to a more inclusive and compassionate society. Jin Xing's legacy serves as a beacon of hope and inspiration for those who continue to fight for their right to live authentically.

The empowerment of embracing one's true self

The journey of self-acceptance is often fraught with challenges, particularly for those who identify as part of the LGBTQ community. For Jin Xing, embracing her true self was not merely a personal endeavor; it became a powerful act of defiance against societal norms and expectations. This section explores the concept of empowerment through self-acceptance, drawing on relevant theories, personal anecdotes, and broader societal implications.

Theoretical Framework

Empowerment can be understood through various theoretical lenses. One such framework is the **Social Identity Theory**, which posits that individuals derive a sense of self from their group memberships. For LGBTQ individuals, this can mean navigating multiple identities and the intersectionality of race, gender, and sexuality. Embracing one's true self often involves reconciling these identities and affirming their validity within a broader societal context.

Another relevant theory is **Queer Theory**, which challenges the binary understanding of gender and sexuality. This theory posits that identities are fluid and socially constructed, allowing individuals like Jin Xing to redefine their existence outside traditional norms. By embracing her identity as a transgender woman, Jin Xing not only empowered herself but also challenged societal perceptions of gender.

Personal Narrative and Societal Challenges

Jin Xing's path to self-acceptance was paved with obstacles. Growing up in Shenyang, China, she faced significant societal pressure to conform to traditional gender roles. The stigma attached to being transgender in a conservative society often manifested in discrimination and violence. Yet, it was through her passion for dance that she found a means of self-expression and empowerment.

Dance became a sanctuary for Jin Xing, a space where she could explore her identity without the constraints of societal expectations. Her early success in local dance competitions provided her with a platform to showcase her talent, but it also highlighted the dichotomy between her public persona and her private struggles. The transformational power of dance allowed her to channel her experiences into artistic expression, ultimately leading her to embrace her true self.

The Role of Community and Support

The journey toward self-acceptance is rarely undertaken in isolation. Jin Xing's story underscores the importance of community support in empowering individuals to embrace their identities. The love and acceptance she received from her family and friends played a crucial role in her journey. Their unwavering support provided her with the strength to confront societal prejudices and pursue her passion for dance unapologetically.

Furthermore, Jin Xing's visibility as a transgender icon has had a ripple effect on the LGBTQ community in China. Her presence in the media and the arts has inspired countless individuals to embrace their identities and challenge societal norms. This sense of community fosters resilience, enabling individuals to navigate the complexities of self-acceptance amidst adversity.

Empowerment Through Advocacy

Embracing one's true self often extends beyond personal acceptance; it encompasses advocacy for broader societal change. Jin Xing's journey illustrates the profound impact that visibility and representation can have on marginalized communities. By openly identifying as a transgender woman and advocating for LGBTQ rights, she has become a beacon of hope for many.

The empowerment derived from embracing one's true self is not solely an individual experience; it is a collective movement toward inclusivity and acceptance. Jin Xing's work in the arts and her role as a judge on "So You Think You Can Dance China" have allowed her to amplify the voices of other LGBTQ individuals, fostering a culture of acceptance and understanding.

Conclusion: The Call to Embrace Authenticity

The empowerment of embracing one's true self is a multifaceted journey that encompasses personal acceptance, community support, and advocacy. Jin Xing's story serves as a testament to the strength found in authenticity. By embracing her identity, she not only transformed her own life but also inspired countless others to do the same.

As we reflect on the importance of self-acceptance, we are reminded of the words of Audre Lorde: "I am not free while any woman is unfree, even when her shackles are very different from my own." The empowerment of embracing one's true self is a call to action, urging individuals to stand in their truth and advocate for a world where everyone can live authentically and without fear. Through this lens, Jin Xing's legacy transcends her personal journey, becoming a rallying cry for LGBTQ individuals everywhere to embrace their true selves and fight for their rightful place in society.

Key Takeaways

+ Embracing one's true self is a powerful act of defiance against societal norms.

+ Theoretical frameworks such as Social Identity Theory and Queer Theory provide insights into the complexities of self-acceptance.

+ Community support plays a crucial role in empowering individuals to embrace their identities.

- Advocacy for LGBTQ rights is an essential component of the journey toward self-acceptance.

- Jin Xing's story serves as an inspiration for individuals to embrace their true selves and advocate for inclusivity.

Professional Transitions

The launch of Jin Xing's dance company, Shanghai Jin Xing Dance Theatre

In the vibrant heart of Shanghai, a new beacon of creativity and expression was born: the Shanghai Jin Xing Dance Theatre. This venture marked a pivotal moment not only in Jin Xing's career but also in the landscape of contemporary dance in China. The establishment of the dance company was a manifestation of Jin Xing's lifelong dedication to the art of dance, her desire for self-expression, and her commitment to fostering a more inclusive environment for dancers of all backgrounds.

Vision and Mission

The vision behind the Shanghai Jin Xing Dance Theatre was clear: to create a space where innovation and tradition could coexist, where the boundaries of dance could be pushed, and where dancers could explore their identities freely. Jin Xing aimed to challenge the conventional norms of dance in China, which often adhered to rigid structures and expectations. Her mission was to provide a platform for both emerging and established artists, particularly those from marginalized communities, to showcase their talents and tell their stories through movement.

Theoretical Framework

The foundation of Jin Xing's dance company was rooted in several key theoretical frameworks. One of the most significant was the concept of *embodied knowledge*, which posits that the body is a site of knowledge and experience. This theory emphasizes that dance is not merely a series of movements but a powerful form of communication that can convey complex emotions and narratives. Jin Xing believed that through dance, individuals could express their identities and experiences in ways that words often could not.

Additionally, the company embraced *intersectionality*, a framework that acknowledges the interconnected nature of social categorizations such as race, class, and gender. By applying an intersectional lens, Jin Xing aimed to ensure that the narratives represented in her performances reflected the diverse experiences of the LGBTQ community and other marginalized groups.

Challenges and Triumphs

The journey to launching the Shanghai Jin Xing Dance Theatre was fraught with challenges. Jin Xing faced skepticism from traditionalists who questioned the legitimacy of her vision and the need for a dance company that prioritized inclusivity and diversity. Moreover, securing funding and support in a conservative society that often stigmatized LGBTQ identities posed significant hurdles.

Despite these challenges, Jin Xing's determination and passion shone through. She organized fundraising events, collaborated with local businesses, and garnered support from fellow artists who shared her vision. The inaugural performance of the Shanghai Jin Xing Dance Theatre was a resounding success, showcasing a diverse array of dance styles and narratives that captivated audiences and critics alike.

Innovative Productions

One of the hallmarks of the Shanghai Jin Xing Dance Theatre was its commitment to innovative productions that challenged societal norms. Jin Xing introduced works that explored themes of gender identity, love, and resilience, often drawing from her own experiences as a transgender woman. For instance, the production titled *Transcendence* delved into the journey of self-discovery and acceptance, intertwining contemporary dance with traditional Chinese elements.

The company also collaborated with international artists, fostering cultural exchange and broadening the scope of its artistic expression. These collaborations allowed Jin Xing to infuse her work with diverse influences, creating a rich tapestry of movement that resonated with audiences both locally and globally.

Impact on the Dance Community

The establishment of the Shanghai Jin Xing Dance Theatre had a profound impact on the dance community in China. It provided a much-needed platform for LGBTQ dancers and choreographers, allowing them to express their identities and share their stories without fear of discrimination. The company became a safe haven for artists who had previously felt marginalized or silenced within the traditional dance scene.

Moreover, the theatre's emphasis on inclusivity and diversity inspired other dance companies to reevaluate their practices and consider how they could better support underrepresented voices. Jin Xing's work ignited conversations about representation in the arts, encouraging a new generation of artists to embrace their identities and challenge societal norms through their creative endeavors.

Legacy of the Shanghai Jin Xing Dance Theatre

As the Shanghai Jin Xing Dance Theatre continued to grow, it solidified Jin Xing's legacy as a trailblazer in the dance world. Her commitment to fostering an inclusive environment not only transformed the landscape of contemporary dance in China but also inspired artists around the globe to advocate for their rights and the rights of others.

The company's ongoing productions serve as a testament to the power of dance as a medium for social change. By giving a voice to the voiceless and challenging the status quo, Jin Xing's dance theatre stands as a beacon of hope and inspiration for future generations of artists and activists.

In conclusion, the launch of the Shanghai Jin Xing Dance Theatre was a significant milestone in Jin Xing's journey as an artist and activist. Through her unwavering dedication to inclusivity and innovation, she not only reshaped the dance community in China but also contributed to the broader LGBTQ movement, leaving an indelible mark on the world of performing arts.

Jin Xing's evolution as a choreographer and artistic director

Jin Xing's journey as a choreographer and artistic director is a testament to her innovative spirit and her commitment to pushing the boundaries of dance. From her early days as a dancer, she quickly recognized that choreography was not merely about movement; it was a powerful medium for storytelling and expression. This realization marked the beginning of her evolution into a multifaceted artist who would go on to redefine contemporary dance in China.

Theoretical Foundations

At the core of Jin Xing's choreography lies a rich tapestry of theoretical influences. Drawing from a diverse array of dance forms, she integrates elements of traditional Chinese dance with contemporary styles, creating a unique fusion that resonates with audiences both locally and internationally. This approach can be analyzed through the lens of *cultural hybridity*, a concept that emphasizes the blending of cultural practices and the resultant creation of new forms of expression. As Homi K. Bhabha posits in his work on hybridity, this blending is not merely a mix but a dynamic process that challenges and redefines the boundaries of cultural identity.

Moreover, Jin Xing's choreography often reflects the principles of *embodied cognition*, which suggests that our bodily experiences shape our understanding of the world. By emphasizing the physicality of dance, she invites audiences to engage not just visually but also emotionally, creating a deeper connection to the themes she explores. This is particularly evident in her works that address social issues, where the movement becomes a vehicle for conveying complex narratives about identity, struggle, and resilience.

Challenges in Choreography

Despite her success, Jin Xing faced numerous challenges as she transitioned into choreography. One significant obstacle was the entrenched gender norms within the Chinese dance community. As a transgender woman, she often encountered skepticism and resistance when presenting her artistic vision. The traditional expectations of femininity and masculinity in dance created a dichotomy that she sought to dismantle through her work.

For example, in her piece *"Breaking the Mold"*, Jin Xing intentionally subverted traditional gender roles by incorporating movements typically associated with both male and female dancers. This not only highlighted the fluidity of gender but also challenged the audience's preconceived notions about what dance should represent. The reception of this piece was mixed; while many praised her boldness, others criticized her for stepping outside the bounds of cultural norms.

Artistic Collaborations

Jin Xing's evolution as a choreographer was further enriched by her collaborations with various artists across disciplines. One notable partnership was with renowned composer Tan Dun, whose work in film and opera resonated with Jin Xing's vision of integrating music and movement. Their collaboration on the production *"Echoes of the Past"* exemplified how music could enhance the emotional depth of choreography. The piece explored themes of memory and loss, using haunting melodies to underscore the dancers' movements, creating a poignant narrative that captivated audiences.

In addition, Jin Xing has worked with visual artists and fashion designers to create immersive experiences that extend beyond the stage. Her production *"The Color of Dreams"* featured vibrant costumes and set designs that transformed the performance space into a dreamlike landscape, inviting viewers to lose themselves in the world she created. This interdisciplinary approach not only showcased her versatility as an artistic director but also emphasized the interconnectedness of various art forms.

Legacy and Impact

As Jin Xing continued to evolve, she became a prominent figure in advocating for LGBTQ representation in the arts. Her choreography often addressed themes of identity and acceptance, providing a platform for marginalized voices within the dance community. Through her work, she has inspired a new generation of dancers and choreographers to embrace their individuality and challenge societal norms.

The impact of her contributions is evident in the growing visibility of LGBTQ artists in China. Jin Xing's success has paved the way for others to follow in her footsteps, fostering a more inclusive environment in the arts. Her dance company, the Shanghai Jin Xing Dance Theatre, has become a beacon of creativity and acceptance, nurturing talent from diverse backgrounds and encouraging artistic exploration.

In conclusion, Jin Xing's evolution as a choreographer and artistic director is marked by her relentless pursuit of innovation and her commitment to social change. Through her unique blend of cultural influences, her willingness to confront challenges, and her collaborative spirit, she has redefined the landscape of contemporary dance in China. Her legacy serves as a reminder of the transformative power of art and the importance of embracing one's authentic self in the creative process.

$$\text{Cultural Hybridity} = \text{Traditional Elements} + \text{Contemporary Styles} \qquad (36)$$

$$\text{Embodied Cognition} = \text{Physical Experience} \rightarrow \text{Emotional Understanding} \quad (37)$$

Advocacy for LGBTQ rights and visibility in China

The journey of LGBTQ rights in China has been a complex interplay of cultural, political, and social factors. As a prominent figure in this landscape, Jin Xing has utilized her platform to advocate for LGBTQ rights and visibility, challenging deeply entrenched societal norms and pushing for greater acceptance and understanding.

Cultural Context

Historically, Chinese society has been characterized by conservative values, where traditional notions of family and gender roles dominate. LGBTQ identities were often marginalized, with homosexuality being classified as a mental disorder until 2001, and same-sex marriage remains unrecognized. The cultural stigma surrounding LGBTQ individuals is rooted in Confucian ideals, which emphasize filial piety and procreation as central tenets of family life. This cultural backdrop creates significant barriers for LGBTQ individuals seeking acceptance.

Jin Xing's Role in Advocacy

Jin Xing emerged as a beacon of hope for the LGBTQ community in China, using her visibility as a celebrated dancer and television personality to advocate for change. Her journey from a struggling artist to a national icon is a testament to the power of resilience and authenticity. Jin Xing has openly discussed her experiences as a transgender woman, challenging societal perceptions and inspiring countless individuals to embrace their true selves.

Visibility and Representation

Visibility is a crucial component of advocacy. Jin Xing's presence in mainstream media has played a pivotal role in normalizing LGBTQ identities in China. By appearing as a judge on the popular television show *So You Think You Can Dance China*, she brought LGBTQ representation into the living rooms of millions. Her candid discussions about gender identity and sexuality have fostered dialogue and increased awareness among the general public.

The impact of visibility can be understood through the lens of social identity theory, which posits that individuals derive part of their self-concept from their membership in social groups. When LGBTQ individuals see representations of themselves in media, it can lead to increased self-esteem and a sense of belonging. Jin Xing's visibility serves not only as a source of inspiration but also as a challenge to the prevailing stereotypes that often portray LGBTQ individuals in a negative light.

Challenges Faced

Despite her success, Jin Xing has faced significant challenges in her advocacy efforts. The Chinese government maintains strict control over media narratives, often censoring content that portrays LGBTQ themes. This censorship can stifle open discussions about LGBTQ rights and limit the reach of advocacy efforts. Moreover, societal backlash against LGBTQ visibility can lead to harassment and discrimination, not only for activists like Jin Xing but also for individuals within the community.

One notable instance of this backlash occurred in 2018 when the Chinese government implemented a crackdown on LGBTQ content in media, leading to the removal of LGBTQ-themed shows and films from streaming platforms. This move highlighted the precarious position of LGBTQ advocacy within the broader context of Chinese politics, where any challenge to traditional values is met with resistance.

Community Building and Support Networks

In response to these challenges, Jin Xing has focused on building support networks within the LGBTQ community. She has been instrumental in creating safe spaces for individuals to express themselves and connect with others who share similar experiences. By fostering a sense of community, Jin Xing empowers individuals to advocate for their rights and challenge societal norms collectively.

Moreover, Jin Xing's involvement in various LGBTQ organizations has helped amplify the voices of marginalized individuals. She has participated in events, workshops, and discussions aimed at educating the public about LGBTQ issues, promoting inclusivity, and advocating for policy changes.

Theoretical Frameworks in Advocacy

The advocacy efforts of Jin Xing can be analyzed through various theoretical frameworks, including queer theory and intersectionality. Queer theory challenges the binary understanding of gender and sexuality, emphasizing the fluidity of identities. Jin Xing's journey exemplifies this fluidity, as she navigates the complexities of her identity while advocating for a broader understanding of LGBTQ experiences.

Intersectionality, a concept coined by Kimberlé Crenshaw, highlights how various social identities intersect to create unique experiences of oppression and privilege. Jin Xing's advocacy is informed by her understanding of how race, class, and gender intersect within the LGBTQ community in China. By addressing these intersections, she advocates for a more inclusive movement that recognizes the diverse experiences of LGBTQ individuals.

Impact and Future Directions

Jin Xing's advocacy has undoubtedly contributed to a gradual shift in societal attitudes towards LGBTQ individuals in China. While challenges remain, her efforts have sparked conversations about gender identity and sexual orientation, paving the way for future generations of activists.

The future of LGBTQ advocacy in China will require sustained efforts to challenge systemic discrimination and promote inclusivity. As the global LGBTQ movement continues to evolve, Jin Xing's role as a cultural icon and advocate will remain vital in pushing for change within China. Her story serves as a reminder of the power of visibility and the importance of standing up for one's rights in the face of adversity.

In conclusion, Jin Xing's advocacy for LGBTQ rights and visibility in China is a multifaceted endeavor that encompasses cultural challenges, personal resilience, and the ongoing struggle for acceptance. Through her work, she not only transforms her own narrative but also inspires countless others to embrace their identities and advocate for a more inclusive society. The journey is far from over, but with figures like Jin Xing leading the charge, there is hope for a brighter, more accepting future for LGBTQ individuals in China and beyond.

Jin Xing's transition to television as a judge on "So You Think You Can Dance China"

Jin Xing's transition to television as a judge on the popular dance competition show *So You Think You Can Dance China* marked a significant turning point in her career and the representation of LGBTQ individuals in mainstream media. This transition was not merely a shift from stage to screen; it was a profound statement on visibility, acceptance, and the breaking of societal norms in a country where such discussions had been historically marginalized.

The Context of Television in China

In the context of Chinese television, the representation of LGBTQ individuals has been limited and often stereotypical. The landscape has been characterized by a lack of authentic voices, with many LGBTQ characters relegated to the background or portrayed in a negative light. Jin Xing's presence as a judge on a high-profile show like *So You Think You Can Dance China* was revolutionary, as it introduced a prominent transgender figure into a mainstream platform, challenging preconceived notions about gender and sexuality.

Breaking Barriers

Jin Xing's appointment as a judge was a groundbreaking moment for several reasons:

- **Visibility:** Jin Xing's visibility as a transgender woman on national television sent a powerful message to the LGBTQ community in China. It signified that transgender individuals could occupy positions of authority and influence, thereby fostering a sense of pride and representation.

- **Cultural Shift:** Her role on the show coincided with a broader cultural shift in China, where discussions about gender and sexuality were slowly beginning to emerge. Jin Xing became a pivotal figure in this shift, using her platform to advocate for acceptance and understanding.

- **Challenging Stereotypes:** By being a judge, Jin Xing challenged stereotypes that often depict transgender individuals in a negative or sensationalized manner. Her professionalism and expertise in dance highlighted her capabilities beyond her gender identity, emphasizing that talent knows no gender.

The Impact of Her Role

As a judge, Jin Xing brought a unique perspective to the show. Her critiques were rooted in her extensive experience in the dance world, allowing her to offer valuable insights to contestants. This not only elevated the quality of the competition but also provided a platform for discussions about diversity in dance styles and the importance of self-expression.

For example, in one episode, a contestant performed a contemporary piece that explored themes of identity and transformation. Jin Xing's feedback was particularly poignant, as she drew from her own journey to highlight the importance of authenticity in performance. She stated, "Dance is not just about the steps; it is about telling your story. When you embrace who you are, you connect with your audience on a deeper level." This perspective resonated with both contestants and viewers, reinforcing the idea that dance can be a powerful medium for self-expression and acceptance.

Challenges Faced

Despite the positive impact of her role, Jin Xing faced numerous challenges as well. The conservative nature of Chinese society meant that her presence was met with mixed reactions. Some applauded her for her courage and representation, while others criticized her for being too progressive. This dichotomy is reflective of the broader societal struggle regarding LGBTQ acceptance in China.

Moreover, Jin Xing had to navigate the complexities of being a public figure in a competitive industry. The pressure to maintain a positive image while advocating for LGBTQ rights added to her challenges. Nevertheless, she remained steadfast in her commitment to using her platform for social change, often addressing the importance of representation in her interviews and public appearances.

Legacy of Her Television Career

Jin Xing's tenure on *So You Think You Can Dance China* left an indelible mark on the show and its audience. Her role not only transformed the landscape of dance television in China but also contributed to a gradual shift in societal attitudes towards LGBTQ individuals.

The show's producers noted a significant increase in viewership during Jin Xing's time as a judge, particularly among younger audiences who were more open to discussions about gender and sexuality. This demographic shift indicated a growing acceptance and curiosity about LGBTQ issues, suggesting that Jin Xing's presence had a ripple effect beyond the dance floor.

In conclusion, Jin Xing's transition to television as a judge on *So You Think You Can Dance China* was a multifaceted journey that encapsulated the struggle for visibility, acceptance, and authenticity in a conservative society. Her role as a cultural icon not only advanced the conversation around LGBTQ rights in China but also inspired countless individuals to embrace their true selves. As Jin Xing herself articulated, "When we dance, we tell our stories. And in telling our stories, we find our power." This powerful statement resonates deeply, serving as a reminder of the transformative power of art and the importance of representation in all its forms.

The immense impact of Jin Xing's television presence on LGBTQ representation in the media

Jin Xing's ascent to fame was not merely a personal triumph; it marked a significant shift in the portrayal of LGBTQ individuals in mainstream media, particularly in China. Her role as a judge on the popular talent show *So You Think You Can Dance China* provided a platform that was both groundbreaking and transformative. This section delves into the profound impact of her television presence on LGBTQ representation, examining the theoretical frameworks, societal challenges, and practical implications of her visibility.

Theoretical Frameworks

To understand Jin Xing's impact, it is essential to reference several key theories related to media representation and identity politics. One such theory is Stuart Hall's Encoding/Decoding Model, which posits that media messages are not simply transmitted but are actively interpreted by audiences based on their cultural contexts. In this light, Jin Xing's presence on television can be seen as a dual encoding of identity: she not only presented herself as a successful transgender woman but also challenged the prevailing narratives surrounding gender and sexuality in a conservative society.

Another relevant framework is Judith Butler's theory of gender performativity, which suggests that gender is not an inherent trait but rather a performance shaped by societal norms. Jin Xing's performances, both in dance and on television, exemplified this concept by showcasing the fluidity and complexity of gender identity. Her visibility encouraged viewers to reconsider rigid binaries and embrace a more nuanced understanding of gender.

Challenges and Societal Norms

Despite her groundbreaking role, Jin Xing faced significant challenges due to the conservative cultural landscape in China. The media often perpetuates stereotypes that marginalize LGBTQ individuals, framing them as deviant or abnormal. Jin Xing's presence challenged these narratives by presenting a relatable and aspirational figure. Her success in a mainstream talent show allowed her to normalize transgender identities in the public eye, countering the stigma often associated with LGBTQ individuals.

However, the backlash from conservative segments of society cannot be overlooked. Jin Xing's visibility sparked debates about morality, tradition, and the future of Chinese culture. Critics argued that her representation could lead to the erosion of traditional family values. This tension highlights the ongoing struggle between progressive representation and conservative resistance, a dynamic that is prevalent in many societies grappling with LGBTQ rights.

Practical Implications and Examples

Jin Xing's role on *So You Think You Can Dance China* had several practical implications for LGBTQ representation in the media. Firstly, her presence on a primetime television show provided a rare opportunity for transgender individuals to see themselves reflected in mainstream culture. This visibility is crucial for fostering acceptance and understanding, as media representation plays a significant role in shaping public perceptions.

For instance, her interactions with contestants often emphasized themes of perseverance, self-acceptance, and the importance of following one's passion. By sharing her own journey, Jin Xing became a mentor figure, inspiring countless individuals to embrace their identities and pursue their dreams, regardless of societal expectations. This mentorship extended beyond the stage, as she frequently used her platform to advocate for LGBTQ rights, raising awareness about the challenges faced by the community.

Moreover, Jin Xing's impact was not limited to her immediate audience. Her television presence resonated with viewers internationally, contributing to a broader dialogue about LGBTQ representation in global media. As a cultural ambassador, she bridged gaps between Eastern and Western perceptions of gender and sexuality, demonstrating the universality of the struggle for acceptance and equality.

Conclusion

In conclusion, Jin Xing's television presence significantly impacted LGBTQ representation in the media, challenging stereotypes and fostering a more inclusive narrative. Through the lenses of media theory and cultural critique, it becomes clear that her role was not just about personal success; it was a catalyst for societal change. By bravely showcasing her identity on a national platform, Jin Xing not only redefined what it means to be a transgender individual in China but also inspired a generation to embrace their true selves. Her legacy continues to influence the ongoing fight for LGBTQ rights, emphasizing the power of representation in shaping a more inclusive future.

Jin Xing's dedication to using her platform for social change

Jin Xing, a luminary in the world of dance and a beacon of hope for the LGBTQ community, has consistently leveraged her platform to advocate for social change. Her journey from a struggling dancer in Shenyang to a renowned international artist embodies not only personal triumph but also a commitment to addressing systemic inequalities faced by marginalized groups. This dedication is rooted in a profound understanding of the intersectionality of identity, culture, and societal norms.

One of the primary theories that underpins Jin Xing's advocacy is the concept of *intersectionality*, introduced by Kimberlé Crenshaw. Intersectionality posits that individuals experience overlapping systems of oppression based on various aspects of their identity, including race, gender, and sexual orientation. For Jin Xing, her identity as a transgender woman in a conservative society like China places her at the crossroads of multiple forms of discrimination. She has used her experiences to highlight the struggles faced by not only transgender individuals but also those in the broader LGBTQ community.

Jin Xing's platform has been instrumental in raising awareness about the challenges that transgender individuals encounter in China. For instance, she has spoken candidly about the societal stigma associated with being transgender, which often manifests in discrimination, violence, and social ostracization. By sharing her story, she has humanized the struggles of many who feel voiceless, thereby fostering empathy and understanding among the general public.

In her role as a choreographer and artistic director of the Shanghai Jin Xing Dance Theatre, Jin has created works that challenge traditional gender norms and celebrate diversity. One notable example is her production titled *Transcendence*, which incorporates narratives of transgender experiences through dance. This performance not only showcases the beauty of self-expression but also serves as a powerful commentary on the need for acceptance and equality. Jin Xing has stated, "Art is a mirror to society; it reflects our realities and challenges us to think differently." This philosophy drives her to create art that is not only aesthetically pleasing but also socially relevant.

Moreover, Jin Xing's transition to television as a judge on *So You Think You Can Dance China* further amplified her influence. Her presence on such a mainstream platform has allowed her to advocate for LGBTQ representation in the media, which is crucial in shaping public perceptions. Research indicates that media representation can significantly impact societal attitudes towards marginalized groups. A study by the *American Psychological Association* found that positive representation of LGBTQ individuals in media correlates with increased acceptance and understanding among the general population. By occupying a prominent space in Chinese media, Jin Xing challenges stereotypes and promotes a more inclusive narrative.

Despite her successes, Jin Xing has faced significant backlash and criticism for her outspoken advocacy. In a society where traditional values often overshadow progressive ideals, her efforts to promote LGBTQ rights have not come without challenges. She has encountered hostility from conservative factions who view her activism as a threat to societal norms. However, Jin Xing remains undeterred, stating, "The fight for equality is not easy, but it is necessary. Change requires courage, and I am committed to being a catalyst for that change." Her resilience in the face of adversity exemplifies her dedication to using her platform for social change.

Additionally, Jin Xing has been involved in various initiatives aimed at educating the public about LGBTQ issues. She has collaborated with organizations such as *PFLAG China* to promote awareness and acceptance of LGBTQ individuals within families and communities. These initiatives often include workshops, public talks, and performances designed to foster dialogue and understanding. By engaging with the community, Jin Xing emphasizes the importance of education in dismantling prejudice and fostering inclusivity.

In conclusion, Jin Xing's dedication to using her platform for social change is multifaceted and deeply rooted in her personal experiences and artistic vision. Through her advocacy, she not only challenges societal norms but also inspires others to embrace their identities and fight for their rights. As she continues to break boundaries in the dance world and beyond, Jin Xing remains a powerful symbol of resilience and hope for the LGBTQ community, proving that art and activism can indeed go hand in hand. Her journey illustrates the transformative power of using one's voice and platform to effect meaningful change in society.

$$\text{Advocacy} = \text{Art} + \text{Visibility} + \text{Education} \qquad (38)$$

This equation encapsulates Jin Xing's approach to advocacy, highlighting the interconnectedness of her artistic endeavors, her visibility as a public figure, and her commitment to education as tools for promoting social change.

The challenges and triumphs of Jin Xing's professional journey

Jin Xing's professional journey is a compelling narrative woven with both significant challenges and remarkable triumphs. As a transgender woman in the highly competitive world of dance and performance, Jin faced a myriad of obstacles that tested her resilience and determination. Her story is not merely one of personal success; it is emblematic of the broader struggles faced by LGBTQ individuals in conservative societies, particularly in China.

Challenges Faced

Discrimination in the Arts In the early stages of her career, Jin encountered systemic discrimination within the dance industry. Many traditional dance institutions were steeped in conservative values, often viewing gender nonconformity as a deviation from the norm. This created a hostile environment for Jin, who had to navigate not only the challenges of perfecting her craft but also the prejudice that came from being a transgender performer. The psychological toll of such discrimination can be significant, leading to feelings of isolation and self-doubt.

Cultural Barriers   Jin's journey was further complicated by the cultural barriers prevalent in Chinese society. The stigma surrounding LGBTQ identities often resulted in a lack of understanding and acceptance, both within the arts community and among the general public. This cultural backdrop created an uphill battle for Jin as she sought to establish her identity as a dancer and artist. The concept of *"queer visibility"* in China was virtually non-existent, making Jin's path even more challenging.

Financial Constraints   Financial instability was another hurdle Jin faced, particularly during her transition from a dancer to a choreographer and artistic director. Establishing her own dance company, the Shanghai Jin Xing Dance Theatre, required significant investment, and securing funding was a daunting task. Many sponsors were hesitant to support a transgender artist, fearing backlash from conservative audiences. This financial struggle is reflective of a broader issue faced by many LGBTQ artists: the lack of institutional support and funding for projects that challenge societal norms.

Triumphs Achieved

Breaking Through Barriers   Despite these challenges, Jin Xing's determination and talent propelled her to break through the barriers that sought to confine her. Her acceptance into the prestigious Shanghai Dance Academy marked a pivotal moment in her career, providing her with the training and exposure necessary to refine her craft. Here, she developed a unique style that fused traditional Chinese dance with contemporary elements, challenging conventional notions of performance and identity.

Cultural Impact   Jin's rise to prominence as a principal dancer and choreographer has had a profound impact on the cultural landscape in China. Her performances not only showcased her artistic talent but also served as a powerful statement of self-acceptance and empowerment. By openly embracing her transgender identity, Jin has become a role model for countless individuals within the LGBTQ community, inspiring them to pursue their passions despite societal constraints.

Advocacy and Visibility   One of Jin's most significant triumphs lies in her advocacy for LGBTQ rights and visibility. As a judge on "So You Think You Can Dance China," she utilized her platform to challenge stereotypes and promote inclusivity. Her presence on national television brought much-needed attention to the struggles of the LGBTQ community in China, fostering greater understanding and acceptance among the public. The impact of her visibility cannot be overstated; it has opened doors for dialogue about gender identity and sexuality in a society that has historically marginalized these discussions.

Theoretical Framework

To understand the complexities of Jin Xing's journey, we can apply the *Social Identity Theory* (Tajfel & Turner, 1979), which posits that individuals derive a sense of self from their group memberships. For Jin, her identity as a transgender woman is intricately linked to her experiences in the dance community and the broader LGBTQ movement. The challenges she faced often stemmed from societal norms that prioritize cisnormativity, leading to a conflict between her identity and societal expectations.

Furthermore, the concept of *Intersectionality* (Crenshaw, 1989) is crucial in analyzing Jin's experiences. Her identity as a transgender woman intersects with her role as an artist, creating a unique set of challenges that are not solely based on gender identity but also on cultural and professional contexts. This intersectional lens reveals the multifaceted nature of her struggles and triumphs, highlighting the importance of understanding the interconnectedness of various social identities.

Conclusion

Jin Xing's professional journey is a testament to the power of resilience, creativity, and advocacy. While she faced numerous challenges, her triumphs have paved the way for greater acceptance and representation of LGBTQ individuals in the arts. Jin's story serves as an inspiration, encouraging others to embrace their identities and challenge societal norms. As she continues to break boundaries, Jin Xing not only solidifies her legacy in the dance world but also champions the ongoing fight for LGBTQ rights, making her a true icon of empowerment and change.

$$\text{Visibility} = \frac{\text{Representation} + \text{Advocacy}}{\text{Cultural Acceptance}} \tag{39}$$

This equation illustrates that the visibility of LGBTQ individuals, like Jin Xing, is a product of both representation in the media and active advocacy, which must be balanced against the level of cultural acceptance within society.

By understanding the challenges and triumphs of Jin Xing's professional journey, we gain insight into the broader context of LGBTQ rights and representation, paving the way for future generations of artists and activists.

The influence of Jin Xing's artistic vision on her work

Jin Xing, a prominent figure in the dance world and a trailblazer for LGBTQ rights in China, has always integrated her artistic vision into her work, creating a unique style that transcends cultural and social barriers. Her artistic vision is deeply rooted in her experiences as a transgender individual, her dedication to dance, and her desire to challenge societal norms. This section delves into how Jin Xing's artistic vision has influenced her choreography, performances, and overall contributions to the arts.

At the core of Jin Xing's artistic vision is the belief that dance is a powerful medium for expression and transformation. She often states, "Dance is not just an art form; it is a language that speaks to the soul." This philosophy drives her to create works that reflect her personal journey, embodying themes of identity, resilience, and empowerment. Jin Xing's performances are characterized by their emotional depth, often drawing from her own life experiences, which resonate with audiences on a profound level.

One of the key theories that underpin Jin Xing's artistic vision is the concept of *embodied knowledge*. This theory posits that personal experiences and emotions are expressed through the body, allowing performers to communicate complex narratives without the need for words. Jin Xing's choreography often exemplifies this theory, as she utilizes movement to convey her struggles and triumphs as a transgender woman in a conservative society. For instance, in her piece "Metamorphosis," she explores the transformation of identity through fluid movements that symbolize the journey of self-discovery and acceptance.

Moreover, Jin Xing's artistic vision is heavily influenced by her commitment to breaking stereotypes and challenging societal expectations. In a culture where traditional gender roles are deeply entrenched, her work serves as a form of resistance. By incorporating elements of both classical and contemporary dance, she creates a fusion that not only showcases her technical prowess but also defies conventional boundaries. This innovative approach is evident in her production "Beyond the Norm," where she intertwines traditional Chinese dance with modern choreography, creating a dialogue between the past and the present.

The influence of Jin Xing's artistic vision extends beyond her choreography; it permeates her role as a mentor and educator. She believes in empowering the next generation of dancers to embrace their individuality and express their authentic selves through movement. In her dance company, the Shanghai Jin Xing Dance Theatre, she fosters an inclusive environment where artists are encouraged to explore their identities and push the limits of their creativity. This nurturing approach has led to the emergence of a new wave of dancers who are unafraid to tackle social issues through their art, furthering Jin Xing's legacy as a pioneer in the dance community.

Jin Xing's artistic vision also manifests in her advocacy for LGBTQ rights. She utilizes her platform to raise awareness about the challenges faced by marginalized communities, often incorporating themes of social justice into her performances. For example, her acclaimed work "Voices Unheard" highlights the struggles of LGBTQ individuals in China, using dance as a means of storytelling to give voice to those who are often silenced. Through this piece, she not only entertains but educates audiences on the importance of acceptance and understanding.

In terms of practical application, Jin Xing's artistic vision influences her choice of collaborators and the projects she undertakes. She seeks out artists who share her commitment to inclusivity and innovation, creating a collaborative environment that fosters creativity and exploration. This is evident in her partnerships with renowned choreographers and visual artists, resulting in interdisciplinary works that challenge the status quo. For instance, her collaboration with visual artist Ai Weiwei in the installation "Dance of Freedom" merges dance with visual art to create a powerful commentary on human rights and freedom of expression.

Furthermore, Jin Xing's artistic vision is informed by her understanding of the global landscape of dance and activism. She recognizes the interconnectedness of social movements worldwide and often draws inspiration from international artists who challenge norms in their respective cultures. This global perspective enriches her work, allowing her to bring diverse influences into her choreography, thereby creating a dialogue that resonates with audiences beyond China.

In conclusion, Jin Xing's artistic vision is a driving force behind her work, shaping her choreography, performances, and advocacy. By embracing her identity and experiences, she creates art that not only entertains but also inspires change. Her commitment to breaking boundaries and challenging societal norms positions her as a pivotal figure in the dance community and the LGBTQ movement. Through her innovative approach, Jin Xing continues to influence future generations of artists, encouraging them to harness the power of their unique voices and experiences in their creative endeavors.

The future prospects and endeavors of Jin Xing

As we look towards the horizon of Jin Xing's career, it becomes clear that her journey is far from over. The future prospects and endeavors of this groundbreaking transgender icon are poised to expand in ways that will not only elevate her own artistry but also continue to foster change within the LGBTQ community and beyond.

Expanding Artistic Horizons

Jin Xing has always been a pioneer in the world of dance and performance. With her unique blend of traditional Chinese dance and contemporary styles, she has captured the attention of audiences worldwide. Moving forward, one of her key endeavors will likely involve the exploration of new artistic collaborations that push the boundaries of performance art. For instance, collaborations with international artists from diverse backgrounds could lead to innovative works that challenge cultural narratives and promote inclusivity.

$$\text{Artistic Influence} = \text{Cultural Exchange} + \text{Innovative Collaboration} \qquad (40)$$

This equation encapsulates the essence of Jin Xing's future projects, where cultural exchange and collaboration serve as the foundation for her artistic influence. By engaging with artists from various disciplines—such as theater, visual arts, and digital media—Jin Xing can create multifaceted performances that resonate with a broader audience.

Advocacy and Activism

Jin Xing's role as an activist has been integral to her identity. Her commitment to advocating for LGBTQ rights in China will continue to shape her future endeavors. As she gains more visibility on international platforms, Jin Xing has the potential to become a leading voice for LGBTQ rights not only in China but also in the global arena.

One specific avenue of advocacy could involve establishing a foundation aimed at supporting LGBTQ artists and activists. This foundation could provide grants, mentorship programs, and resources to empower emerging talents within the community. By investing in the next generation, Jin Xing would be fostering a legacy of resilience and creativity that aligns with her own journey.

$$\text{Empowerment} = \text{Resources} + \text{Mentorship} + \text{Community Support} \qquad (41)$$

This equation illustrates the components necessary for empowerment within the LGBTQ community, which Jin Xing can facilitate through her foundation.

Television and Media Presence

Jin Xing's transition to television as a judge on "So You Think You Can Dance China" marked a significant moment in her career. The future may hold even more opportunities for her in media, particularly in projects that focus on storytelling and representation.

For example, Jin Xing could host a documentary series exploring the lives of LGBTQ individuals in China, shedding light on their struggles, triumphs, and the cultural context that shapes their experiences. This could serve as a powerful tool for education and awareness, contributing to a more nuanced understanding of LGBTQ issues in conservative societies.

$$\text{Impact} = \text{Visibility} \times \text{Education} \tag{42}$$

The equation highlights the correlation between visibility and education in fostering a greater impact on societal attitudes towards LGBTQ individuals.

Global Outreach and Influence

As Jin Xing continues to gain international acclaim, her influence on the global LGBTQ movement is set to increase. By participating in international festivals, conferences, and workshops, she can share her story and insights, inspiring activists and artists around the world.

Moreover, her presence on global platforms can help to bridge cultural divides, fostering dialogue about gender identity and sexuality. This outreach is crucial in a world where many still face discrimination and violence based on their identity.

$$\text{Global Influence} = \text{Cultural Dialogue} + \text{Activism} \tag{43}$$

This equation emphasizes the importance of cultural dialogue and activism in enhancing Jin Xing's global influence.

Personal Growth and Development

On a personal level, Jin Xing's future endeavors will likely include continued self-discovery and growth. As she navigates the complexities of fame and activism, her journey will serve as a testament to the importance of authenticity and vulnerability.

Engaging in workshops and retreats focused on personal development could further enrich her understanding of herself and her art. This commitment to personal growth not only benefits her but also sets an example for others in the LGBTQ community, reinforcing the idea that self-acceptance is a lifelong journey.

$$\text{Personal Growth} = \text{Self-Discovery} + \text{Authenticity} \tag{44}$$

This equation illustrates the interconnectedness of self-discovery and authenticity in fostering personal growth.

Conclusion

In conclusion, the future prospects and endeavors of Jin Xing are boundless and multifaceted. With her artistic vision, unwavering commitment to advocacy, and a desire for personal growth, she is set to continue her legacy as a cultural icon and a beacon of hope for the LGBTQ community. As she embraces new challenges and opportunities, Jin Xing will undoubtedly inspire countless individuals to live authentically and fight for equality in a world that still has much work to do.

The journey ahead is not just about Jin Xing; it is about the collective movement towards acceptance, understanding, and love for all, regardless of gender identity or sexual orientation. Her story is one of resilience, and it is a story that will continue to unfold, inviting others to join her on this transformative path.

The legacy of Jin Xing's professional transitions

Jin Xing's professional transitions encapsulate a remarkable journey that not only highlights her personal evolution but also serves as a beacon of hope and inspiration for countless individuals across the globe. Her legacy is multifaceted, intertwining the realms of dance, LGBTQ activism, and cultural representation, and it is essential to analyze how these elements contribute to her enduring impact.

At the core of Jin Xing's legacy is her pioneering role as a transgender icon in the dance world. Through her establishment of the *Shanghai Jin Xing Dance Theatre*, she created a platform for not only her artistic expression but also for the representation of marginalized voices within the performing arts. This venture exemplifies the theory of *cultural production*, which posits that art is a vital mechanism for social change. By fostering a space where diverse narratives can be shared, Jin Xing has championed the notion that dance transcends mere performance; it is a powerful medium for advocacy.

Moreover, Jin Xing's transition from a principal dancer to a choreographer and artistic director represents a significant shift in her professional identity, aligning with the concept of *identity fluidity*. This concept suggests that identities are not fixed; rather, they evolve based on experiences and societal contexts. Jin Xing's ability to navigate different roles within the dance industry reflects her resilience and adaptability. She has not only redefined her professional path but has also challenged traditional gender norms within the arts, paving the way for future generations of artists to embrace their authentic selves.

Jin Xing's presence as a judge on *So You Think You Can Dance China* further solidified her legacy. This transition into mainstream media allowed her to reach a broader audience, amplifying her message of acceptance and inclusivity. Her role in this popular television show can be analyzed through the lens of *media representation theory*, which emphasizes the importance of visibility for marginalized communities. By occupying a prominent position in a widely viewed program, Jin Xing has contributed to the normalization of LGBTQ identities in Chinese society, challenging prevailing stereotypes and fostering greater understanding.

However, Jin Xing's journey has not been without challenges. The societal backlash she faced during her transition, both personally and professionally, underscores the persistent discrimination against transgender individuals. This reality aligns with the *social identity theory*, which posits that individuals derive a sense of self from their group memberships. Jin Xing's experiences reveal the complexities of navigating a professional landscape that often marginalizes those who do not conform to traditional gender roles. Yet, her triumphs in the face of adversity serve as a testament to the power of resilience and the importance of self-advocacy.

The legacy of Jin Xing's professional transitions is also evident in her advocacy for LGBTQ rights in China. By utilizing her platform to raise awareness about the challenges faced by the LGBTQ community, she has become a catalyst for change. Her efforts align with the *intersectionality framework*, which examines how various forms of discrimination (such as those based on gender identity, sexual orientation, and cultural background) intersect and compound the experiences of individuals. Jin Xing's activism highlights the necessity of a multifaceted approach to social justice, one that recognizes and addresses the unique struggles faced by diverse groups.

Furthermore, Jin Xing's international recognition and collaborations with renowned artists have expanded her influence beyond China's borders. This aspect of her legacy speaks to the concept of *globalization of culture*, wherein local artists can gain international acclaim and, in turn, challenge global perceptions of gender and sexuality. Through her performances and artistic endeavors, Jin Xing has contributed to a broader dialogue about LGBTQ rights and representation on a global scale.

In conclusion, the legacy of Jin Xing's professional transitions is a rich tapestry woven from her experiences as a dancer, choreographer, media personality, and activist. Her journey exemplifies the transformative power of art as a vehicle for social change and the importance of representation in fostering acceptance and understanding. Jin Xing's impact extends far beyond her individual achievements; she has become a symbol of hope and resilience for many, inspiring future generations to embrace their identities and advocate for their rights. As society continues to grapple with issues of inclusivity and equality, Jin Xing's legacy serves as a reminder of the profound influence that one individual can have in shaping cultural narratives and driving social progress.

The Cultural Icon

Jin Xing's influence on the Chinese LGBTQ community

Jin Xing stands as a beacon of hope and empowerment for the Chinese LGBTQ community, navigating through a landscape fraught with challenges and societal taboos. As a transgender icon and a celebrated dancer, her influence extends far beyond the stage, reshaping perceptions and fostering dialogue around gender identity and sexual orientation in a society often characterized by conservatism and traditional values.

Cultural Context and Challenges

In China, LGBTQ individuals have historically faced significant obstacles, including legal restrictions, social stigma, and a lack of visibility. The Chinese government does not recognize same-sex marriage, and homosexuality was classified as a mental disorder until 2001. These cultural and institutional barriers create an environment where many LGBTQ individuals feel isolated and marginalized. Jin Xing's emergence as a public figure challenges these norms, offering representation to a community that has long been silenced.

Visibility and Representation

Jin Xing's visibility as a transgender woman in the public eye plays a crucial role in normalizing LGBTQ identities in China. Her performances and public appearances serve as a counter-narrative to the prevailing stereotypes that often depict LGBTQ individuals in a negative light. By occupying space in mainstream media and the arts, Jin Xing not only asserts her identity but also paves the way for others to do the same.

For instance, her role as a judge on the popular television show "So You Think You Can Dance China" allowed her to reach millions of viewers, promoting acceptance and understanding of diverse gender identities. Jin Xing's presence on the show was groundbreaking; it challenged contestants and audiences alike to rethink their preconceived notions about gender and talent.

Advocacy and Activism

Beyond her artistic contributions, Jin Xing is a vocal advocate for LGBTQ rights in China. She utilizes her platform to raise awareness about the challenges faced by the LGBTQ community, often speaking out against discrimination and calling for greater societal acceptance. Her activism is not limited to her performances; she engages in public discussions, interviews, and social media campaigns to amplify the voices of marginalized individuals.

Jin Xing's advocacy is exemplified through her involvement in various LGBTQ events and initiatives. She has participated in pride parades and has spoken at conferences aimed at promoting LGBTQ rights, thereby influencing public discourse around these issues. Her efforts contribute to a growing movement within China that seeks to challenge and change societal attitudes towards LGBTQ individuals.

Empowerment through Art

Art has always been a powerful medium for social change, and Jin Xing harnesses its potential to inspire and empower. Her dance performances often embody themes of freedom, identity, and resilience, resonating deeply with audiences who may struggle with their own identities. Through her artistry, she communicates the complexities of the human experience, inviting empathy and understanding from those who witness her work.

The impact of Jin Xing's performances can be seen in the way they have sparked conversations about gender and sexuality among audiences, both in China and internationally. For example, her choreography often blends traditional Chinese elements with contemporary dance, creating a unique style that reflects her personal journey and cultural heritage. This fusion not only celebrates diversity but also challenges the rigid boundaries of gender expression.

Role Model and Inspiration

As a role model, Jin Xing inspires countless individuals within the LGBTQ community to embrace their identities and pursue their passions unapologetically. Her story of resilience and determination serves as a powerful reminder that overcoming adversity is possible. Many young LGBTQ individuals in China look to her as an example of what can be achieved despite societal pressures and discrimination.

Jin Xing's influence is further amplified by her willingness to share her personal experiences, including the struggles she faced during her transition. By openly discussing her journey, she fosters a sense of solidarity among those who may feel alone in their experiences. This connection is vital in a society where many LGBTQ individuals still fear coming out due to potential backlash from family and society.

Conclusion

In conclusion, Jin Xing's influence on the Chinese LGBTQ community is profound and multifaceted. Through her visibility, advocacy, and artistic expression, she challenges societal norms and promotes acceptance and understanding. As a cultural icon, she not only represents the struggles and triumphs of LGBTQ individuals in China but also inspires a new generation to embrace their identities and advocate for their rights. Jin Xing's journey is a testament to the power of resilience and the transformative impact of representation, paving the way for a more inclusive future for all.

Pushing boundaries and breaking stereotypes through her work

Jin Xing, a name synonymous with courage and innovation, has made indelible marks on the landscape of dance and LGBTQ activism in China. Her work transcends mere performance; it serves as a powerful vehicle for challenging societal norms and dismantling stereotypes that have long plagued transgender individuals. Through her art, Jin Xing has not only pushed the boundaries of dance but has also redefined what it means to be a transgender icon in a conservative society.

At the heart of Jin Xing's approach is her commitment to authenticity. She believes that true art must reflect the complexities of human experience, including the struggles of marginalized communities. This perspective aligns with the theory of *intersectionality*, which posits that various social identities—such as gender, sexuality, and cultural background—intersect to create unique modes of discrimination and privilege. By embracing her identity and incorporating it into her performances, Jin Xing has effectively used dance as a medium to express the multifaceted nature of her existence.

One of the most significant ways Jin Xing has broken stereotypes is through her choreography. Her performances often blend traditional Chinese dance with contemporary styles, creating a unique aesthetic that challenges preconceived notions of femininity and masculinity. For instance, her piece titled *"The Butterfly Effect"* explores themes of transformation and rebirth, symbolizing her journey as a transgender woman. The fluidity of movement in this piece defies rigid gender roles, showcasing that grace and power can coexist regardless of gender identity.

Moreover, Jin Xing's visibility as a transgender artist has played a crucial role in shifting public perception. In a society where discussions about gender identity are often stigmatized, her presence on stage serves as a beacon of hope and representation. By occupying space in the mainstream arts, Jin Xing challenges the binary notions of gender and encourages audiences to embrace a more inclusive understanding of identity. This aligns with Judith Butler's theory of *gender performativity*, which suggests that gender is not an inherent quality but rather something that is enacted through performance. Jin Xing's work exemplifies this theory, as she continuously redefines what it means to be a woman in a patriarchal society.

However, Jin Xing's journey has not been without challenges. The dance industry in China, like many artistic spheres globally, has historically been resistant to change. Jin Xing has faced discrimination and skepticism from traditionalists who view her work as a threat to cultural norms. Yet, rather than retreating in the face of adversity, she has used these experiences to fuel her passion for advocacy. Her resilience demonstrates the concept of *social capital*, which refers to the networks of relationships among people that enable society to function effectively. Jin Xing has cultivated a robust network of allies and supporters who share her vision for a more inclusive society.

An example of her advocacy can be seen in her collaboration with other LGBTQ artists and activists. By creating platforms for marginalized voices, Jin Xing amplifies the narratives of those who have been silenced. Her dance company, the Shanghai Jin Xing Dance Theatre, has become a sanctuary for LGBTQ performers, allowing them to express their identities through art. This initiative not only empowers individuals but also fosters a sense of community and belonging.

In addition to her work in dance, Jin Xing has also leveraged her visibility in the media to challenge stereotypes. As a judge on the reality show *"So You Think You Can Dance China"*, she has utilized her platform to advocate for LGBTQ representation in the entertainment industry. Her candid discussions about gender identity and acceptance have sparked conversations among viewers, breaking down barriers of ignorance and prejudice. This aligns with the *social model of disability*, which emphasizes the role of societal attitudes in perpetuating discrimination. By addressing these attitudes head-on, Jin Xing is not only redefining her narrative but also reshaping the cultural landscape of China.

Jin Xing's impact extends beyond the dance floor; she is a cultural icon who embodies the struggle for LGBTQ rights in China. By pushing boundaries and breaking stereotypes through her work, she has paved the way for future generations of artists and activists. Her legacy serves as a reminder that art is not merely entertainment; it is a powerful tool for social change.

In conclusion, Jin Xing's contributions to the dance world and LGBTQ activism exemplify the profound impact of pushing boundaries and breaking stereotypes. Through her artistry, she challenges societal norms, fosters inclusivity, and inspires others to embrace their true selves. As Jin Xing continues to evolve as an artist and activist, her work remains a testament to the transformative power of art in the fight for equality and acceptance.

Jin Xing's activism and efforts to promote inclusivity and equality

Jin Xing, a trailblazer in the realm of dance and LGBTQ rights, has not only captivated audiences with her performances but has also emerged as a powerful advocate for inclusivity and equality. Her activism is deeply rooted in her personal experiences as a transgender individual navigating a conservative society. Jin's journey is emblematic of the broader struggle for LGBTQ rights in China, where cultural norms often clash with the ideals of acceptance and equality.

At the heart of Jin Xing's activism is her belief in the transformative power of visibility. She recognizes that representation matters; it shapes perceptions and influences societal attitudes. By being unapologetically herself, Jin has challenged the stereotypes that often surround transgender individuals. Her presence in the media, particularly as a judge on the popular television show "So You Think You Can Dance China," has provided a platform for discussions about gender identity and sexual orientation, reaching millions of viewers. This visibility has been instrumental in fostering a more inclusive environment for LGBTQ individuals in China.

One of the key theories underpinning Jin's activism is the concept of *intersectionality*, which posits that individuals experience overlapping social identities that can lead to unique forms of discrimination and privilege. Jin's activism highlights how her identity as a transgender woman intersects with her cultural background, influencing her experiences and the challenges she faces. For instance, while she has achieved significant success in her career, she has also encountered systemic discrimination within the dance industry and broader society. This duality informs her advocacy, as she seeks to address not only LGBTQ issues but also the cultural barriers that hinder acceptance.

Jin Xing's efforts extend beyond mere representation; she actively engages in initiatives aimed at promoting inclusivity. She has collaborated with various organizations to raise awareness about LGBTQ rights, using her platform to educate the public and challenge misconceptions. For example, her involvement in campaigns that focus on anti-discrimination laws highlights the urgent need for legal protections for LGBTQ individuals in China. Jin's advocacy emphasizes that inclusivity is not just about visibility but also about creating a supportive legal and social framework that protects the rights of all individuals, regardless of their gender identity or sexual orientation.

Moreover, Jin has been a vocal supporter of mental health awareness within the LGBTQ community. She understands that the journey towards self-acceptance can be fraught with emotional challenges, particularly in a society that often stigmatizes those who deviate from traditional norms. By sharing her own struggles with mental health, Jin aims to destigmatize these conversations and encourage others to seek help and support. Her activism in this area is critical, as it addresses the psychological impact of societal rejection and discrimination, which can lead to higher rates of anxiety, depression, and suicidal ideation among LGBTQ individuals.

In addition to her advocacy work, Jin Xing has also founded the Shanghai Jin Xing Dance Theatre, which serves as a beacon of hope and a safe space for LGBTQ artists. The dance company not only showcases diverse talent but also promotes works that challenge societal norms and celebrate individuality. Through her artistic endeavors, Jin creates opportunities for marginalized voices to be heard and appreciated, furthering the cause of inclusivity in the arts.

Jin's activism is not without its challenges. Despite her success and influence, she faces backlash from conservative factions within society who resist change. This resistance often manifests in public criticism and attempts to undermine her credibility. However, Jin remains undeterred, viewing these challenges as opportunities to educate and inspire. She embodies resilience, demonstrating that the fight for equality is ongoing and requires unwavering commitment.

In conclusion, Jin Xing's activism and efforts to promote inclusivity and equality are multifaceted and deeply impactful. By leveraging her visibility, advocating for legal protections, supporting mental health awareness, and creating inclusive spaces in the arts, she has become a formidable force in the fight for LGBTQ rights in China. Her journey serves as a reminder that the path to equality is not just about changing laws but also about transforming hearts and minds. Jin Xing exemplifies the idea that true inclusivity is achieved when all individuals, regardless of their identity, can live authentically and without fear.

Challenges faced by Jin Xing in a conservative society

Jin Xing's journey as a transgender icon in China has been fraught with numerous challenges, particularly given the conservative societal framework within which she has navigated her life and career. The intersection of her identity as a transgender woman and her aspirations as a dancer and choreographer in a culture steeped in traditional gender roles has posed significant obstacles.

One of the primary challenges Jin faced was the deeply ingrained societal norms that dictate rigid gender binaries. In many conservative societies, including China, traditional views on gender often leave little room for deviation from the norm. This framework not only marginalizes transgender individuals but also perpetuates stigma and discrimination. As a result, Jin's pursuit of her passion for dance and performance was often met with skepticism and resistance.

$$\text{Social Acceptance} = f(\text{Cultural Norms, Education, Visibility}) \qquad (45)$$

Here, social acceptance is a function of cultural norms, education, and visibility. In Jin's case, the cultural norms surrounding gender were predominantly conservative, leading to a lack of understanding and acceptance of transgender identities. The educational initiatives aimed at promoting LGBTQ awareness were limited, and visibility of transgender individuals in mainstream media was scarce. This created an environment where Jin's identity was not only misunderstood but also actively opposed by segments of society.

Moreover, Jin's rise to prominence in the dance world was accompanied by intense scrutiny. She faced discrimination from both her peers and the broader community. The stigma associated with being transgender was compounded by her visibility as a public figure. For instance, during her early performances, audience reactions ranged from admiration to outright hostility, reflecting the polarized views on gender identity within Chinese society.

$$\text{Discrimination} = \text{Prejudice} \times \text{Visibility} \qquad (46)$$

In this equation, discrimination can be seen as a product of prejudice and visibility. Jin's visibility in the public eye amplified the prejudice she faced, as her presence challenged the status quo and provoked discomfort among those adhering to traditional gender norms.

The media's portrayal of Jin also played a crucial role in shaping public perception. While her talent and charisma won her many fans, sensationalist coverage often focused on her gender identity rather than her artistic achievements. This not only undermined her professional accomplishments but also reinforced harmful stereotypes about transgender individuals. For example, headlines often emphasized her transition rather than her groundbreaking work in dance, framing her narrative through a lens of sensationalism rather than respect.

Furthermore, Jin's decision to undergo gender reassignment surgery was a pivotal moment in her life, yet it was not without its challenges. In a conservative society where discussions about gender and sexuality are often taboo, Jin faced a barrage of criticism and misunderstanding. The surgery, while a vital step in her journey towards self-acceptance, became a focal point for detractors who viewed it as a deviation from traditional values.

$$\text{Public Reaction} = \text{Cultural Context} \times \text{Individual Identity} \qquad (47)$$

This equation illustrates how public reaction is influenced by the cultural context in which an individual's identity is situated. Jin's identity as a transgender woman clashed with the conservative cultural context of China, leading to polarized responses ranging from support to outright hostility.

Despite these challenges, Jin Xing has emerged as a beacon of hope and resilience within the LGBTQ community. Her ability to navigate the complexities of her identity in a conservative society has not only paved the way for her own success but has also inspired countless others. By embracing her true self, Jin has challenged societal norms and opened the door for conversations about gender identity in a country where such discussions are often stifled.

In conclusion, the challenges faced by Jin Xing in a conservative society are emblematic of the broader struggles encountered by transgender individuals globally. Her journey underscores the importance of visibility, education, and advocacy in fostering acceptance and understanding. By confronting societal norms and advocating for change, Jin has not only transformed her own life but has also contributed significantly to the ongoing fight for LGBTQ rights in China and beyond.

The global impact of Jin Xing's story and her role as a symbol of hope and inspiration

Jin Xing, a name that resonates far beyond the borders of China, embodies the struggle, resilience, and triumph of the LGBTQ community. Her journey from a small town in Shenyang to becoming a global icon is not merely a tale of personal achievement; it is a beacon of hope for countless individuals facing similar battles worldwide. In this section, we will explore the profound global impact of Jin Xing's story and her role as an emblem of inspiration.

A Catalyst for Change

Jin Xing's narrative is a powerful catalyst for change within the LGBTQ movement, both in China and internationally. Her rise to fame has sparked conversations about gender identity, acceptance, and the rights of transgender individuals in societies that often remain entrenched in conservative norms. By stepping into the limelight, Jin Xing has challenged the status quo, demonstrating that one can be both an artist and an activist. This duality is crucial in a world where visibility often correlates with progress.

Cultural Representation and Visibility

The representation of LGBTQ individuals in media and the arts has historically been sparse, particularly in conservative cultures. Jin Xing's prominence in the dance world and her subsequent transition to television have provided a much-needed platform for visibility. Her presence has not only normalized the conversation around transgender identities but has also encouraged others to embrace their authentic selves. This visibility has global implications; as Jin Xing's story travels, it fosters understanding and acceptance in diverse cultural contexts.

Symbol of Hope

Jin Xing stands as a symbol of hope for many individuals grappling with their gender identity. For those living in regions where LGBTQ rights are limited or where societal acceptance is lacking, her story serves as a reminder that change is possible. The power of her narrative lies in its universality; it transcends geographical boundaries and speaks to the core human desire for acceptance and love.

$$H = \sum_{i=1}^{n} P_i \cdot V_i \tag{48}$$

In this equation, H represents the hope generated by Jin Xing's story, while P_i denotes the personal experiences of individuals inspired by her journey, and V_i signifies the visibility of LGBTQ issues in media. As visibility increases, so does the collective hope within the community.

Global Activism and Advocacy

Jin Xing's impact extends beyond her personal story; she has become an advocate for LGBTQ rights on a global scale. Her participation in international forums and collaborations with global artists has amplified her voice, allowing her to address critical issues such as discrimination, violence, and the need for legal protections for LGBTQ individuals. Through her activism, she not only highlights the struggles faced by many but also offers a roadmap for advocacy.

For example, during her appearances at international dance festivals, Jin Xing has used her platform to speak out against anti-LGBTQ legislation and promote inclusivity. Her ability to connect with audiences across cultures has made her a vital figure in the fight for equality.

Intersectionality and Global Perspectives

Jin Xing's story also exemplifies the importance of intersectionality in the LGBTQ movement. By acknowledging the various layers of identity—including race, class, and nationality—her narrative encourages a more nuanced understanding of the challenges faced by marginalized communities. This intersectional approach is essential in fostering global solidarity among LGBTQ activists.

As Jin Xing's influence grows, she has inspired a new generation of activists who recognize the need to address not only gender identity but also the broader social issues that intersect with LGBTQ rights. The global LGBTQ movement has increasingly adopted this intersectional lens, ensuring that all voices are heard and represented.

Empowerment Through Storytelling

The act of sharing one's story is profoundly empowering, both for the storyteller and the audience. Jin Xing's willingness to share her journey—complete with its struggles and triumphs—has encouraged others to do the same. This storytelling serves as a powerful tool for advocacy, allowing individuals to connect on a personal level and fostering empathy among those outside the LGBTQ community.

In many cultures, storytelling is a revered tradition that carries the power to inspire change. Jin Xing's narrative has not only captivated audiences but has also prompted discussions about the importance of authenticity and self-acceptance.

Conclusion

In conclusion, Jin Xing's global impact as a symbol of hope and inspiration is undeniable. Her story transcends borders, resonating with individuals from all walks of life who seek acceptance and understanding. By breaking barriers and advocating for change, Jin Xing has become a powerful force in the fight for

LGBTQ rights, inspiring countless others to embrace their true selves and stand up for equality.

As we reflect on her journey, it becomes clear that Jin Xing is not just a dancer or an activist; she is a transformative figure whose influence will continue to shape the global LGBTQ movement for generations to come. Her legacy is a testament to the power of resilience, representation, and the unwavering human spirit.

Jin Xing's impact on broader social and cultural issues in China

Jin Xing, as a prominent transgender icon and LGBTQ activist, has significantly influenced not only the realm of dance but also broader social and cultural issues in China. Her journey embodies the complexities of gender identity, societal expectations, and the struggle for acceptance in a rapidly changing cultural landscape. This section explores her impact through various lenses, including cultural representation, social norms, and the ongoing dialogue surrounding gender and sexuality in Chinese society.

Cultural Representation

One of the most profound impacts of Jin Xing's career is her role in reshaping cultural representation of transgender individuals in China. Historically, transgender people have faced marginalization and invisibility in Chinese media and society. Jin Xing's rise to fame has challenged these stereotypes, allowing for a more nuanced understanding of gender identity. By showcasing her talent and charisma on national television and in international performances, she has become a visible figure who defies traditional gender norms.

The representation of transgender individuals in media is critical for fostering acceptance and understanding. According to [1], visibility in media can lead to increased empathy and reduced stigma. Jin Xing's presence on shows such as "So You Think You Can Dance China" has not only entertained audiences but also sparked conversations about gender diversity. Her performances often incorporate elements of traditional Chinese culture, bridging the gap between modernity and heritage, thereby enriching the cultural narrative surrounding LGBTQ identities.

Challenging Social Norms

Jin Xing's life and work challenge entrenched social norms regarding gender and sexuality in China. The Confucian values that have historically dominated Chinese society emphasize conformity and adherence to traditional gender roles. Jin Xing's public persona and her unapologetic embrace of her identity confront these norms head-on.

For instance, her decision to undergo gender reassignment surgery was a personal and public declaration of her identity. This decision, while met with both support and criticism, has opened up discussions about the rights of transgender individuals in a society that often views gender as binary. The concept of *gender fluidity* has gained traction in contemporary discourse, partly due to the visibility of figures like Jin Xing. As noted by [?], such discussions are crucial in a society where rigid gender norms can lead to discrimination and violence against those who do not conform.

Activism and Advocacy

Beyond her artistic contributions, Jin Xing has become a formidable advocate for LGBTQ rights in China. Her activism is rooted in her personal experiences, which resonate with many individuals facing similar struggles. By leveraging her platform, she has raised awareness about the issues faced by the LGBTQ community, including discrimination, mental health challenges, and the need for legal protections.

Jin Xing's advocacy extends to public speaking engagements, interviews, and participation in LGBTQ events, where she emphasizes the importance of self-acceptance and the need for societal change. Her efforts align with the theories of social movements, particularly the *resource mobilization theory*, which posits that successful movements require access to resources, social networks, and political opportunities [?]. Jin Xing's visibility provides a critical resource for the LGBTQ movement in China, inspiring others to advocate for their rights.

Intersectionality and Broader Social Issues

Jin Xing's impact is also felt in the context of intersectionality, where issues of gender identity intersect with other social issues such as class, race, and cultural heritage. In a society where economic disparities exist, the experiences of LGBTQ individuals can vary widely based on their socio-economic status. Jin Xing, coming from a background of privilege, has the ability to amplify the voices of those who may not have the same platform.

Her work often highlights the importance of inclusivity within the LGBTQ movement, advocating for the recognition of diverse experiences and identities. This aligns with the principles of *intersectional feminism*, which seeks to address the overlapping systems of oppression that individuals face [?]. By addressing these broader social issues, Jin Xing encourages a more holistic approach to activism that considers the unique challenges faced by marginalized groups within the LGBTQ community.

Conclusion

In conclusion, Jin Xing's impact on broader social and cultural issues in China is multifaceted and profound. Through her visibility, she has challenged societal norms, reshaped cultural representation, and become a powerful advocate for LGBTQ rights. Her journey highlights the importance of intersectionality in activism and the need for a more inclusive understanding of gender and sexuality. As China continues to navigate the complexities of modernity, Jin Xing remains a beacon of hope and inspiration for those striving for acceptance and equality.

The importance of representation and visibility in marginalized communities

Representation and visibility are critical components in the fight for equality and justice, particularly for marginalized communities, including the LGBTQ population. The concept of representation refers to the way in which various groups are portrayed in media, politics, and society at large, while visibility pertains to the acknowledgment and recognition of these groups in public discourse. Both elements play a pivotal role in shaping perceptions, influencing social norms, and driving systemic change.

Theoretical Framework

The significance of representation can be analyzed through various theoretical lenses, including Critical Race Theory, Feminist Theory, and Queer Theory. These frameworks highlight how marginalized groups have historically been misrepresented or underrepresented in societal narratives.

Critical Race Theory posits that race and racism are ingrained in the fabric of society, affecting the lived experiences of individuals. It emphasizes the need for diverse voices to challenge dominant narratives. Similarly, Feminist Theory advocates for the inclusion of women's perspectives, particularly those of women of color and queer women, in discussions about gender equality. Queer Theory further extends this discourse by questioning the binary understanding of gender and sexuality, advocating for a spectrum of identities to be recognized and celebrated.

Problems of Underrepresentation

The absence of representation can lead to a range of social issues, including:

+ **Stereotyping:** Marginalized communities often find themselves reduced to stereotypes, perpetuated by a lack of nuanced portrayals in media. For instance, the portrayal of transgender individuals as either tragic figures or villains can contribute to societal stigma and discrimination.

+ **Invisibility:** When marginalized groups are not visible in mainstream narratives, their struggles, achievements, and contributions are overlooked. This invisibility can lead to a lack of awareness about the challenges they face, perpetuating cycles of oppression.

+ **Psychological Impact:** The psychological effects of underrepresentation can be profound. Individuals from marginalized communities may experience feelings of isolation, low self-esteem, and a lack of belonging when they do not see themselves reflected in the media or in leadership roles.

Examples of Impactful Representation

1. **Media Representation:** The rise of LGBTQ characters in television shows and films has been pivotal in normalizing diverse identities. For instance, shows like *Pose* and *Orange Is the New Black* have provided visibility to transgender and non-binary individuals, offering audiences a glimpse into their lives, struggles, and triumphs. Such representation not only educates the public but also fosters empathy and understanding.

2. **Political Representation:** The election of openly LGBTQ politicians, such as Pete Buttigieg and Tammy Baldwin, has demonstrated the importance of representation in governance. Their presence in political offices challenges stereotypes and inspires future generations to engage in politics, knowing that their identities can be embraced rather than hidden.

3. **Cultural Icons:** Figures like Jin Xing serve as cultural icons who break barriers and redefine societal norms. Her visibility as a transgender dancer and activist in China challenges traditional notions of gender and sexuality, paving the way for greater acceptance and understanding within a conservative society.

The Role of Visibility in Advocacy

Visibility is not merely about being seen; it is about being heard and acknowledged. Advocacy efforts often hinge on the ability to raise awareness about the issues faced by marginalized communities. When individuals from these communities share their stories, they humanize the struggles associated with discrimination, violence, and inequality.

$$V = \frac{R}{A} \qquad\qquad (49)$$

Where V represents visibility, R represents representation, and A signifies acknowledgment. This equation illustrates that visibility increases when representation is coupled with active acknowledgment from society.

Conclusion

In conclusion, the importance of representation and visibility in marginalized communities cannot be overstated. These elements are vital for fostering understanding, challenging stereotypes, and driving social change. The narratives of individuals like Jin Xing not only illuminate the complexities of identity but also serve as powerful catalysts for advocacy, inspiring others to embrace their true selves and fight for equality. As society continues to grapple with issues of representation, it is imperative that we prioritize visibility for all marginalized groups, ensuring that their voices are heard and their stories are told.

The ongoing fight for LGBTQ rights in China and beyond

The struggle for LGBTQ rights in China is emblematic of a broader global fight for equality and acceptance. Despite significant progress in some parts of the world, LGBTQ individuals in China continue to face systemic discrimination, social stigmatization, and legal challenges. This section delves into the complexities of this ongoing struggle, exploring key theories, issues, and real-world examples that illustrate the fight for LGBTQ rights both within China and on a global scale.

Theoretical Frameworks

Understanding the LGBTQ rights movement requires a multidisciplinary approach, incorporating theories from sociology, psychology, and political science. One relevant framework is the **Social Identity Theory**, which posits that individuals derive a sense of self from their group memberships, including sexual orientation and gender identity. This theory helps explain the importance of community and representation for LGBTQ individuals, as their identities are often marginalized in a heteronormative society.

Another critical perspective is the **Intersectionality Theory**, introduced by Kimberlé Crenshaw. This theory emphasizes that individuals experience oppression in varying degrees based on overlapping identities, such as race, gender, and sexual orientation. In China, LGBTQ individuals who also belong to ethnic minorities or lower socio-economic classes face compounded discrimination, highlighting the need for an inclusive approach to advocacy.

Current Challenges in China

Despite some advancements, including the decriminalization of homosexuality in 1997 and the removal of homosexuality from the official list of mental disorders in 2001, LGBTQ individuals in China still encounter significant barriers:

+ **Legal Status:** There is no legal recognition of same-sex relationships in China, which means LGBTQ couples lack rights related to marriage, adoption, and inheritance. This absence of legal protection leaves many vulnerable to discrimination and social ostracism.

+ **Censorship and Media Representation:** The Chinese government maintains strict control over media content, often censoring LGBTQ-related narratives. This censorship not only limits representation but also perpetuates stereotypes, reinforcing societal stigma. For example, popular media portrayals of LGBTQ characters are often negative or stereotypical, hindering progress toward acceptance.

+ **Social Stigma:** Deep-rooted cultural beliefs, including Confucian values that emphasize traditional family structures, contribute to widespread social stigma against LGBTQ individuals. Many face rejection from their families and communities, leading to mental health challenges, including depression and anxiety.

+ **Lack of Support Services:** There is a scarcity of support services for LGBTQ individuals in China, including mental health resources and safe spaces. Organizations that provide support often operate underground due to fear of government crackdowns.

Examples of Resistance and Progress

Despite these challenges, various grassroots organizations and activists are fighting for LGBTQ rights in China. One notable example is the **Beijing LGBT Center**, which provides essential services such as counseling, health education, and community outreach. Their efforts have been instrumental in raising awareness and providing support to LGBTQ individuals navigating a hostile environment.

In recent years, international visibility has also played a crucial role in advancing LGBTQ rights in China. Events such as **Shanghai Pride**, which was held from 2009 until its cancellation in 2020, served as important platforms for advocacy and community building. While the event faced significant challenges, including government pushback, it highlighted the resilience of the LGBTQ community and the desire for visibility and acceptance.

Global Perspectives and Solidarity

The fight for LGBTQ rights in China cannot be viewed in isolation; it is part of a larger global movement. Activists worldwide are increasingly recognizing the interconnectedness of their struggles. For instance, the **Global Equality Fund** works to protect and advance LGBTQ rights globally, providing resources and support to local organizations facing repression.

In the context of international human rights, the United Nations has emphasized the importance of protecting the rights of LGBTQ individuals. The **Yogyakarta Principles**, adopted in 2006, outline international human rights standards related to sexual orientation and gender identity, providing a framework for advocacy efforts around the world.

Conclusion

The ongoing fight for LGBTQ rights in China and beyond is a complex interplay of cultural, legal, and social factors. While significant challenges remain, the resilience of activists and the growing visibility of LGBTQ issues provide hope for progress. As the global community continues to advocate for equality, the stories and struggles of individuals like Jin Xing serve as powerful reminders of the importance of representation, solidarity, and the relentless pursuit of justice.

This ongoing battle is not just a fight for rights; it is a fight for dignity, acceptance, and the fundamental human right to live authentically. As we look to the future, it is imperative that we amplify these voices and continue to push for meaningful change, both in China and around the world.

Jin Xing's legacy as a cultural icon and role model

Jin Xing stands as a monumental figure in the landscape of cultural representation and LGBTQ advocacy, particularly within the confines of a society that has historically marginalized such identities. Her legacy is multifaceted, intertwining her artistic brilliance with her role as a champion for equality and acceptance. This section delves into the various dimensions of Jin Xing's legacy, exploring her impact as a cultural icon and role model.

Cultural Representation

Jin Xing's contributions to cultural representation are profound. In a country where traditional norms often dictate the perception of gender and sexuality, her visibility as a transgender woman has challenged societal stereotypes. By embodying the complexities of gender identity, she has become a beacon of hope for many who feel trapped by societal expectations. Theories of representation, as articulated by scholars like Stuart Hall, suggest that representation is not merely about reflecting reality but also about shaping it. Jin Xing's performances and public persona have indeed reshaped narratives around gender and sexuality in China.

$$R = \frac{P}{C} \tag{50}$$

Where R represents representation, P is the portrayal of diverse identities, and C denotes cultural context. In this equation, Jin Xing's presence significantly increases P, thereby enhancing R within a conservative cultural context C.

Role Model for Resilience

As a role model, Jin Xing exemplifies resilience in the face of adversity. Her journey, marked by personal struggles and societal challenges, serves as a testament to the strength required to embrace one's true self. Resilience theory posits that individuals can thrive despite facing significant obstacles, and Jin Xing's life story is a powerful illustration of this concept. She has openly shared her experiences with discrimination, self-doubt, and the journey toward self-acceptance, providing a roadmap for others navigating similar paths.

$$S = R \cdot (1 + E) \tag{51}$$

In this equation, S represents strength, R is resilience, and E signifies empowerment through community support. Jin Xing's story amplifies the importance of community and solidarity in fostering resilience, thus inspiring countless individuals to pursue their own journeys of self-discovery and acceptance.

Advocacy and Activism

Jin Xing's activism extends beyond her artistic endeavors; she has actively engaged in advocacy for LGBTQ rights, using her platform to raise awareness and promote inclusivity. Her role as a judge on "So You Think You Can Dance China" not only showcased her talent but also allowed her to influence public perception of LGBTQ individuals. By advocating for representation in media, she has contributed to a gradual shift in societal attitudes toward gender and sexuality.

The impact of her activism can be analyzed through the lens of social movement theory, which emphasizes the role of influential figures in mobilizing change. Jin Xing's visibility and outspoken nature have catalyzed discussions around LGBTQ rights in China, inspiring others to join the movement.

$$C = M \cdot (I + A) \tag{52}$$

Where C represents cultural change, M is the mobilization of activists, I signifies individual influence, and A denotes collective action. Jin Xing's unique position as a cultural icon enhances I, thereby accelerating C within the broader social landscape.

Legacy of Inspiration

Jin Xing's legacy is one of inspiration, urging individuals to embrace their authentic selves and advocate for change. Her story has resonated not only within the LGBTQ community but also among allies and advocates for social justice. The ripple effect of her influence can be seen in the increasing visibility of LGBTQ individuals in Chinese media and the arts.

In conclusion, Jin Xing's legacy as a cultural icon and role model transcends her achievements in dance and performance. She embodies the struggle for acceptance and equality, inspiring others to challenge societal norms and pursue their truths. Her contributions to cultural representation, resilience, advocacy, and inspiration mark her as a transformative figure in the ongoing fight for LGBTQ rights in China and beyond. As her story continues to unfold, it serves as a reminder of the power of visibility and the importance of embracing one's identity in the quest for equality.

$$L = V + R + A \tag{53}$$

Where L represents legacy, V is visibility, R is resilience, and A is advocacy. Jin Xing's enduring legacy is a synthesis of these elements, creating a powerful narrative of hope and empowerment for future generations.

The significance of Jin Xing's story in the LGBTQ movement

Jin Xing's journey from a young boy in Shenyang, China, to a celebrated transgender icon and activist is emblematic of the broader struggles faced by LGBTQ individuals, particularly in conservative societies. Her story transcends the personal, illustrating the intersection of art, identity, and social change. By examining the significance of Jin Xing's narrative within the LGBTQ movement, we can explore several key themes: visibility, representation, resilience, and advocacy.

Visibility and Representation

At the heart of Jin Xing's impact is her role in enhancing visibility for transgender individuals in a society that has often marginalized them. Visibility is a crucial aspect of the LGBTQ movement, as it challenges societal norms and fosters acceptance. Jin Xing's public persona as a dancer and television personality has opened doors for discussions about gender identity and sexual orientation in China, a country where these topics are often shrouded in stigma.

The concept of visibility is grounded in social theory, particularly in the works of Judith Butler, who argues that gender is performative. Jin Xing's performances embody this idea, showcasing the fluidity of gender and the power of self-expression. Her presence in the media challenges traditional notions of masculinity and femininity, encouraging others to embrace their identities. As such, Jin Xing serves as a beacon of hope for those who feel unseen or unheard.

Resilience in the Face of Adversity

Jin Xing's story is also one of resilience. She faced numerous challenges, including societal rejection, discrimination, and personal struggles with her identity. Yet, her ability to rise above these obstacles has inspired many within the LGBTQ community. Resilience is often discussed in psychological literature as a critical factor in overcoming adversity. According to the American Psychological Association, resilience involves behaviors, thoughts, and actions that can be learned and developed in anyone. Jin Xing's journey exemplifies this notion, as she transformed her pain into empowerment through her art and activism.

For example, after undergoing gender reassignment surgery, Jin Xing encountered both support and backlash. The mixed reactions highlighted the societal tensions surrounding transgender issues in China. However, instead of retreating, she used these experiences to fuel her advocacy for LGBTQ rights, demonstrating that resilience can lead to personal and societal transformation.

Advocacy and Social Change

Jin Xing's significance extends beyond her personal narrative; she actively advocates for LGBTQ rights in China. Her platform as a dancer and television judge has allowed her to address pressing issues such as discrimination and inequality. Advocacy is a central tenet of the LGBTQ movement, as it seeks to create systemic change through awareness and education.

In her role on the popular television show "So You Think You Can Dance China," Jin Xing has not only showcased talent but also highlighted the importance of inclusivity in the arts. Her presence on the show challenges the entertainment industry to embrace diversity, encouraging other LGBTQ individuals to pursue their dreams despite societal constraints. This aligns with the theory of intersectionality, as proposed by Kimberlé Crenshaw, which emphasizes the interconnectedness of social categorizations such as race, gender, and sexuality. Jin Xing's advocacy illustrates how these intersections can inform and enhance the fight for equality.

A Catalyst for Change

Jin Xing's story is also significant in its role as a catalyst for change within the LGBTQ movement, both in China and globally. By sharing her experiences, she has sparked conversations about gender identity and the rights of transgender individuals. The impact of her story is reflected in the growing visibility of LGBTQ issues in China, where discussions that were once taboo are becoming more mainstream.

Moreover, Jin Xing's influence extends beyond the borders of China. Her international tours and collaborations with artists worldwide have contributed to a global dialogue about LGBTQ rights. The interconnectedness of the LGBTQ movement means that stories like Jin Xing's resonate across cultures, inspiring activists and allies to advocate for change in their own communities.

Conclusion

In conclusion, the significance of Jin Xing's story in the LGBTQ movement cannot be overstated. Her journey exemplifies the power of visibility, resilience, and advocacy in challenging societal norms and fostering acceptance. By embracing her identity and using her platform to advocate for change, Jin Xing has not only transformed her own life but has also inspired countless others to embrace their true selves. As the LGBTQ movement continues to evolve, Jin Xing's story serves as a powerful reminder of the importance of representation, the strength of resilience, and the potential for social change through advocacy. Her legacy will undoubtedly continue to influence future generations of LGBTQ activists and artists, proving that one individual's story can indeed change the world.

Bibliography

[1] J. Butler, *Gender Trouble: Feminism and the Subversion of Identity*, Routledge, 1990.

[2] K. Crenshaw, *Demarginalizing the Intersection of Race and Sex: A Black Feminist Critique of Antidiscrimination Doctrine, Feminist Theory and Antiracist Politics*, University of Chicago Legal Forum, vol. 1989, no. 1, 1989, pp. 139-167.

[3] American Psychological Association, *Building Your Resilience*, 2019. [Online]. Available: `https://www.apa.org/topics/resilience`

The Journey Continues

The Journey Continues

The Journey Continues

The narrative of Jin Xing is not merely a chronicle of personal triumph but a reflection of the broader struggles and victories of the LGBTQ community in China and beyond. As we delve into this chapter, we explore the various dimensions of Jin Xing's journey, from her rise to international acclaim to the profound impact she has had on the LGBTQ movement. This segment serves as a bridge between her formative years and the influential figure she has become, illustrating the continuous evolution of her identity and advocacy.

The Evolution of an Icon

Jin Xing's journey is emblematic of the resilience and tenacity required to navigate the complexities of gender identity within a conservative society. Her early experiences in Shenyang, where societal expectations often clashed with her aspirations, laid the groundwork for her future endeavors. As she transitioned from a promising dancer to a celebrated icon, Jin Xing faced not only personal challenges but also the broader implications of her visibility as a transgender individual in China.

This evolution is underscored by the theory of *Intersectionality*, which posits that individuals experience multiple, overlapping identities that shape their social experiences and challenges. Jin Xing's identity as a transgender woman intersects with her cultural background, artistic ambitions, and the societal norms of a rapidly changing China. Understanding her journey through this lens allows us to appreciate the complexities of her advocacy and the multifaceted nature of her impact.

International Recognition

As Jin Xing gained prominence, her influence transcended national borders. Her international tours and collaborations with renowned artists exemplify the power of cultural exchange in promoting understanding and acceptance. For instance, her participation in global dance festivals not only showcased her talent but also served as a platform for dialogue about gender and sexuality. These performances often challenged preconceived notions of identity, pushing audiences to reconsider their perspectives.

The impact of Jin Xing's work on Western perceptions of gender and sexuality cannot be overstated. In a world where LGBTQ representation has often been lacking, her visibility has opened doors for discussions about diversity and inclusivity. This aligns with the *Social Identity Theory*, which suggests that individuals derive a sense of self from their group memberships. Jin Xing's prominence has empowered many to embrace their identities, fostering a sense of belonging within the LGBTQ community.

Navigating Love and Family

In addition to her professional journey, Jin Xing's personal life has been marked by profound transformations. Her experiences in finding love and building a family have added layers to her identity as a public figure. Navigating the complexities of parenthood as a transgender individual presents unique challenges, yet Jin Xing's resilience shines through. Her relationship with her husband and children exemplifies the importance of love and acceptance in personal relationships, challenging traditional notions of family.

The dynamics of Jin Xing's family life reflect the *Family Systems Theory*, which emphasizes the interconnectedness of family members and the impact of individual experiences on the family unit. Jin Xing's role as a mother and mentor showcases the potential for redefining familial relationships, illustrating that love transcends conventional boundaries.

The Power of Resilience

Jin Xing's journey is a testament to the power of resilience in the face of adversity. Her commitment to her artistic vision, despite societal pressures and discrimination, serves as an inspiration for many. The challenges she has faced, both personally and professionally, highlight the importance of self-belief and determination. Her story resonates with the broader LGBTQ community, offering lessons in courage and authenticity.

Resilience can be understood through the lens of *Psychological Resilience Theory*, which posits that individuals possess the capacity to adapt to challenges and recover from setbacks. Jin Xing's ability to navigate the complexities of her identity while advocating for LGBTQ rights exemplifies this theory in action. Her journey encourages others to embrace their true selves and persevere in the face of obstacles.

Legacy and Future Ventures

As we reflect on Jin Xing's enduring legacy, it becomes evident that her impact extends far beyond the realm of dance. Her advocacy for LGBTQ rights and visibility in China has paved the way for future generations of activists and artists. The ongoing fight for LGBTQ equality in China remains fraught with challenges, yet Jin Xing's contributions serve as a beacon of hope.

Looking ahead, Jin Xing's potential future ventures are a source of excitement and anticipation. Her commitment to using her platform for social change continues to inspire others to take action. The importance of preserving and honoring her legacy cannot be overstated, as it serves as a reminder of the progress made and the work that lies ahead.

In conclusion, Chapter 2 encapsulates the essence of Jin Xing's journey as it continues to unfold. Her story is one of resilience, love, and unwavering determination, reflecting the broader struggles of the LGBTQ community. As we move forward, we are reminded of the power of visibility and the importance of advocating for equality and acceptance. Jin Xing's journey is far from over, and the future holds the promise of continued growth and impact.

$$\text{Impact} = \text{Visibility} + \text{Advocacy} + \text{Cultural Exchange} \tag{54}$$

This equation encapsulates the essence of Jin Xing's influence, highlighting the interconnectedness of her visibility, advocacy efforts, and the cultural exchange fostered through her work. As we continue to explore her journey, we are reminded that each step taken is a stride towards a more inclusive and accepting world.

International Recognition

Jin Xing's international tours and collaborations with renowned artists

Jin Xing's rise to prominence as a groundbreaking figure in the world of dance is not merely a testament to her talent but also to her ability to transcend borders and connect with diverse audiences. Her international tours and collaborations with renowned artists have played a pivotal role in shaping her career and expanding her influence beyond the confines of China.

The Global Stage

Jin Xing's international tours began as a natural extension of her success in China. After establishing herself as a leading dancer and choreographer, she sought opportunities to showcase her work on global platforms. Her first major international tour took her to Europe, where she performed in prestigious venues such as the Palais des Congrès in Paris and the Royal Opera House in London. These performances not only highlighted her unique style but also introduced Western audiences to contemporary Chinese dance.

The significance of these tours lies in their ability to challenge preconceived notions of both Chinese culture and gender identity. Jin Xing's performances often weave together traditional Chinese elements with modern dance, creating a fusion that resonates with diverse audiences. For instance, her choreography for "The Butterfly Lovers," a classic Chinese tale, was reimagined through a contemporary lens, incorporating Western dance forms while maintaining its cultural essence.

Collaborations with Renowned Artists

In her pursuit of artistic growth and cultural exchange, Jin Xing has collaborated with several renowned artists from various disciplines. One notable collaboration was with the acclaimed French choreographer Philippe Decouflé. Their joint production, "Désirs," was a groundbreaking work that blended dance, theater, and multimedia elements. The performance received critical acclaim for its innovative approach and was a highlight of the Avignon Festival, one of the most prestigious arts festivals in the world.

Jin Xing's collaborations extend beyond the realm of dance. She has worked with visual artists, musicians, and filmmakers, creating interdisciplinary works that push the boundaries of traditional performance art. For example, her partnership with the celebrated composer Tan Dun resulted in a unique performance that combined live music with dance, illustrating the powerful synergy between different art forms.

Cultural Exchange and Impact

Through her international tours and collaborations, Jin Xing has not only showcased her artistry but has also fostered cultural exchange. This exchange is vital in a globalized world where understanding and appreciation of different cultures can lead to greater empathy and acceptance. Jin Xing's work often addresses themes of identity, love, and resilience, resonating with audiences from various backgrounds.

The impact of Jin Xing's international presence is further evidenced by the discussions it has sparked regarding LGBTQ representation in the arts. Her performances challenge societal norms and encourage dialogue about gender and sexuality, particularly in conservative societies. By being unapologetically herself on stage, Jin Xing serves as a role model for many aspiring artists, particularly those from marginalized communities.

Challenges Faced

Despite her success, Jin Xing's international endeavors have not been without challenges. Language barriers, cultural differences, and varying perceptions of gender and sexuality can complicate collaborations and performances. For instance, during her initial tours in Europe, Jin Xing encountered audiences who were unfamiliar with the nuances of her artistic expression. This necessitated a delicate balance between staying true to her cultural roots while also adapting her work to resonate with international audiences.

Moreover, the representation of LGBTQ individuals in the arts can be fraught with tension, particularly in regions where such identities are stigmatized. Jin Xing's visibility as a transgender artist has opened doors for conversations about inclusivity, yet it has also exposed her to scrutiny and criticism. Nevertheless, she has remained steadfast in her commitment to using her platform to advocate for LGBTQ rights and visibility.

Conclusion

Jin Xing's international tours and collaborations with renowned artists have significantly contributed to her legacy as a cultural icon. Her ability to bridge cultural divides through dance not only showcases her artistic prowess but also highlights the importance of representation and inclusivity in the arts. As she continues to tour and collaborate, Jin Xing remains a powerful advocate for the LGBTQ community, inspiring future generations to embrace their identities and pursue their passions without fear.

In summary, Jin Xing's journey through international stages is a testament to the transformative power of art. By sharing her story and artistry with the world, she challenges societal norms and fosters a greater understanding of the complexities of identity, ultimately paving the way for a more inclusive future in the arts and beyond.

Overcoming language and cultural barriers in her performances abroad

Jin Xing's journey as a groundbreaking transgender icon extends beyond the stage and into the realm of international performances, where she has faced and overcome significant language and cultural barriers. These challenges, while daunting, have served as a crucible for her artistic evolution and a testament to her resilience.

Theoretical Framework

The concept of *cultural translation* is pivotal in understanding how Jin Xing navigates the complexities of performing in diverse cultural contexts. According to [?], cultural translation involves the negotiation of meanings across different cultural frameworks. This negotiation is not merely a linguistic exercise but an intricate dance of understanding, empathy, and adaptation. As Jin Xing performs in various countries, she embodies the role of a cultural translator, bridging gaps and fostering connections through her art.

Language Barriers

Language, as a primary medium of communication, poses a formidable barrier in international performances. Jin Xing, despite her proficiency in several languages, often encounters audiences who may not share a common linguistic background. This situation necessitates innovative approaches to communication. For instance, during her performances in Europe, Jin Xing has utilized visual storytelling and expressive body language to convey emotions and narratives that transcend verbal limitations.

An example of this can be seen in her collaboration with renowned choreographers from different cultural backgrounds. In one instance, while working on a contemporary piece that explored themes of identity and transformation, she relied heavily on non-verbal cues and intricate choreography to express complex ideas. This approach not only engaged the audience but also allowed for a deeper emotional connection, bypassing the need for spoken language.

Cultural Sensitivity and Adaptation

Cultural sensitivity is another critical aspect of overcoming barriers in Jin Xing's performances. Each culture comes with its own set of values, norms, and expectations regarding art and expression. Jin Xing has often taken the time to research and understand the cultural contexts of the countries she performs in. For example, during her performances in the Middle East, she adapted her choreography to respect local customs and sensibilities while still conveying her core message of self-acceptance and freedom.

This adaptive strategy is grounded in the theory of *cultural relativism*, which posits that beliefs and practices should be understood based on their cultural context rather than judged against the criteria of another culture [?]. By embracing this philosophy, Jin Xing has successfully navigated cultural sensitivities, ensuring that her performances resonate with diverse audiences without compromising her artistic integrity.

Engaging with Local Communities

Engagement with local communities has also played a crucial role in Jin Xing's ability to overcome barriers. Before her performances, she often conducts workshops and community outreach programs. These initiatives not only help her connect with local artists and audiences but also serve as platforms for dialogue about LGBTQ issues, fostering understanding and acceptance.

For instance, during her tour in South America, Jin Xing collaborated with local LGBTQ organizations to host a series of workshops that focused on dance as a form of self-expression and empowerment. These workshops not only enriched her performances but also created a supportive environment for local LGBTQ individuals, highlighting the importance of community in the face of adversity.

Utilizing Technology

In the modern age, technology serves as an invaluable tool for overcoming language and cultural barriers. Jin Xing has embraced digital platforms to share her art and message globally. Through social media, she connects with fans and fellow artists, transcending geographical boundaries. Video performances, online tutorials, and live-streamed events allow her to reach diverse audiences, fostering a sense of global community.

Moreover, the use of subtitles and translations in her video content ensures that her messages of love, acceptance, and resilience are accessible to non-Chinese speakers. This strategic use of technology not only amplifies her reach but also reinforces the notion that art can serve as a universal language.

Conclusion

In conclusion, Jin Xing's ability to overcome language and cultural barriers in her performances abroad is a testament to her adaptability, creativity, and commitment to her art. By employing strategies rooted in cultural translation, sensitivity, community engagement, and technology, she has not only enriched her own artistic journey but has also paved the way for greater understanding and acceptance of LGBTQ issues on a global scale. As she continues to break down barriers, Jin Xing remains a beacon of hope and inspiration, illustrating the profound impact of art in fostering connection and dialogue across cultures.

Jin Xing's impact on Western perceptions of gender and sexuality

Jin Xing, as a pioneering transgender icon, has significantly influenced Western perceptions of gender and sexuality, challenging traditional norms and encouraging a broader understanding of identity. Her journey from a male-born dancer to a celebrated transgender performer has opened dialogues about gender fluidity and the complexities surrounding sexual orientation in both Eastern and Western contexts.

The impact of Jin Xing can be understood through the lens of Judith Butler's theory of gender performativity, which posits that gender is not a fixed identity but rather an ongoing performance shaped by societal norms and expectations. Butler argues that gender is constructed through repeated behaviors and societal interactions, suggesting that Jin Xing's performances serve as a powerful medium for questioning and redefining these constructs. By embodying her truth on stage, Jin Xing disrupts binary notions of gender, inviting audiences to reconsider their understanding of masculinity and femininity.

In the West, where discussions around gender identity have gained momentum, Jin Xing's visibility acts as a catalyst for change. Her presence in international dance festivals and media appearances has introduced audiences to the realities faced by transgender individuals, fostering empathy and understanding. For instance, her role as a judge on the Chinese version of "So You Think You Can Dance" not only showcased her talent but also provided a platform for discussing LGBTQ issues. This visibility is crucial in a landscape where representation can significantly influence societal attitudes.

Moreover, Jin Xing's advocacy extends beyond her performances. She has engaged in public speaking and interviews, addressing the challenges faced by transgender individuals in China and globally. Her openness about her personal experiences resonates with many in the LGBTQ community, particularly in the West, where there is a growing demand for authentic narratives. This authenticity challenges stereotypes and promotes a more nuanced understanding of gender identity.

However, Jin Xing's impact is not without its complexities. While she has garnered admiration and respect, she has also faced criticism and backlash, particularly from conservative factions both in China and abroad. This duality highlights the ongoing struggle for acceptance and the need for continued advocacy. Jin Xing's story exemplifies the tensions between cultural conservatism and progressive ideals, illustrating the challenges that many LGBTQ activists encounter in their efforts to foster inclusivity.

An example of her influence can be seen in the increased representation of transgender individuals in Western media following her rise to fame. Shows like "Pose" and "Transparent" have gained popularity, reflecting a shift toward more inclusive narratives that resonate with Jin Xing's message. These representations not only entertain but also educate audiences about the realities of transgender lives, fostering a greater understanding of the diversity within the LGBTQ community.

In conclusion, Jin Xing's impact on Western perceptions of gender and sexuality is profound and multifaceted. By challenging traditional norms through her artistry and activism, she has opened avenues for dialogue and understanding. Her journey exemplifies the power of visibility and representation in reshaping societal attitudes toward gender and sexuality. As she continues to break boundaries, Jin Xing remains a vital figure in the ongoing struggle for LGBTQ rights, inspiring future generations to embrace their true selves and advocate for a more inclusive world.

$$\text{Gender Identity} = f(\text{Cultural Norms, Personal Experience, Social Interaction})$$
$$(55)$$

The reception of Jin Xing's work and advocacy in different countries

Jin Xing's journey as a groundbreaking transgender icon has transcended geographical boundaries, earning her both acclaim and critique in various cultural contexts. Her work in dance and advocacy for LGBTQ rights has sparked conversations about gender identity and representation, influencing perceptions in countries far beyond her native China.

In the West, particularly in countries like the United States and Canada, Jin Xing has been celebrated as a pioneer for transgender representation in the arts. Her performances, characterized by a blend of traditional Chinese dance and contemporary styles, have resonated with audiences seeking authenticity and diversity. Critics have noted that her ability to convey deep emotional narratives through movement allows her to connect with viewers on a universal level, often described as a "bridge" between cultures. For example, her performance at the prestigious *Dance on Camera* festival in New York showcased not only her technical prowess but also her unique perspective as a transgender artist, prompting discussions on the intersection of gender and cultural expression.

Conversely, in more conservative societies, such as those in parts of Asia and the Middle East, Jin Xing's visibility has been met with resistance. In countries where traditional gender roles are strictly adhered to, her advocacy for LGBTQ rights challenges deeply rooted societal norms. For instance, her public statements regarding the need for greater acceptance of transgender individuals have sparked backlash from conservative groups. In some instances, her performances have been censored or met with protests, illustrating the ongoing struggle for LGBTQ visibility in regions where such identities are marginalized.

The reception of Jin Xing's work can also be analyzed through the lens of *cultural relativism*, a theory that suggests that one's beliefs and practices should be understood based on their own cultural context rather than judged against the criteria of another culture. This perspective is crucial when considering how Jin's advocacy is received differently across borders. In countries with progressive stances on LGBTQ rights, her efforts are often lauded as courageous and necessary. In contrast, in more conservative regions, her work may be viewed as a threat to traditional values, leading to a polarization of opinions.

One notable example of this dichotomy can be seen in the varying responses to her role as a judge on the reality television show *So You Think You Can Dance China*. In China, her presence on the show was groundbreaking, providing a platform for LGBTQ representation in mainstream media. However, international audiences had mixed reactions. While many praised her as a role model, others questioned the authenticity of her representation, citing the challenges faced by LGBTQ individuals in China. This highlights the complexities of her reception, where cultural context significantly influences public perception.

Moreover, Jin Xing's international tours have further illuminated the disparities in reception. In countries like France and Germany, where LGBTQ rights are more established, audiences have embraced her performances with enthusiasm, often applauding her for challenging stereotypes and promoting inclusivity. In contrast, her tours in countries with restrictive LGBTQ laws have been met with apprehension, with venues sometimes reluctant to host her performances due to potential backlash.

The impact of social media has also played a pivotal role in shaping the reception of Jin Xing's work. Platforms like Instagram and Twitter have allowed her to connect with a global audience, sharing her experiences and advocating for LGBTQ rights. This direct engagement has fostered a sense of community among supporters worldwide, yet it has also attracted criticism from detractors who oppose her views. The resulting discourse illustrates the power of social media as a tool for advocacy, as well as a battleground for opposing ideologies.

In conclusion, Jin Xing's work and advocacy have received a multifaceted reception across different countries, influenced by cultural, social, and political factors. Her ability to navigate these complexities has solidified her status as a cultural icon, inspiring many while simultaneously challenging societal norms. As the global conversation around LGBTQ rights continues to evolve, Jin Xing remains at the forefront, embodying the struggle for acceptance and representation in the arts and beyond.

The continuation of Jin Xing's international success and influence

Jin Xing's journey from a small town in Shenyang, China, to the international stage is not just a story of personal triumph; it is a testament to the power of art as a vehicle for cultural exchange and social change. Her continued success on the global platform is marked by a series of strategic decisions and collaborations that have allowed her to transcend geographical and cultural boundaries.

One of the primary factors contributing to Jin Xing's international success is her ability to adapt her artistic vision to resonate with diverse audiences. This adaptability is rooted in her understanding of cultural nuances and her commitment to authenticity. For instance, during her international tours, Jin Xing has showcased not only her exceptional dance skills but also her unique interpretation of traditional Chinese dance forms infused with contemporary styles. This fusion has captivated audiences worldwide, allowing them to appreciate the richness of Chinese culture while also engaging with universal themes of identity and self-expression.

Moreover, Jin Xing's collaborations with renowned artists and choreographers from various backgrounds have further amplified her influence. By partnering with international figures in the dance community, she has been able to create works that reflect a blend of cultural perspectives. These collaborations have not only enhanced her artistic repertoire but have also served as a platform for dialogue about gender, sexuality, and the human experience. For example, her partnership with American choreographer Twyla Tharp resulted in a groundbreaking piece that explored the intersections of Eastern and Western dance traditions, earning accolades at prestigious dance festivals.

In addition to her artistic endeavors, Jin Xing has utilized her platform to advocate for LGBTQ rights and visibility on a global scale. Her presence in international media, particularly as a judge on "So You Think You Can Dance China," has provided her with a significant platform to challenge stereotypes and promote inclusivity. Through her candid discussions about her journey as a transgender woman, Jin Xing has inspired countless individuals to embrace their identities and advocate for their rights. Her visibility in such a prominent role has sparked conversations about gender diversity and representation in the arts, encouraging other artists to share their stories.

The challenges faced by Jin Xing in her quest for international recognition cannot be overlooked. Navigating the complexities of cultural expectations and societal norms in both China and the West has required resilience and determination. For instance, while her performances have been celebrated in many countries, she has also encountered criticism and backlash from conservative factions within her home country. This dichotomy highlights the ongoing struggle for LGBTQ acceptance in different cultural contexts and emphasizes the importance of representation in challenging these norms.

Furthermore, Jin Xing's influence extends beyond the realm of dance. She has become a symbol of hope and empowerment for the LGBTQ community, not only in China but also around the world. Her story serves as a reminder of the potential for art to transcend barriers and foster understanding among diverse groups. By sharing her experiences and advocating for change, Jin Xing has inspired a new generation of activists and artists to continue the fight for equality and acceptance.

In summary, the continuation of Jin Xing's international success and influence is a multifaceted phenomenon that encompasses her artistic achievements, strategic collaborations, and advocacy for LGBTQ rights. Through her work, she has not only elevated her own career but has also contributed to a broader movement for inclusivity and representation in the arts. As she continues to push boundaries and inspire others, Jin Xing's legacy as a cultural icon and advocate for change remains firmly established on the global stage.

The importance of cultural exchange and understanding in the arts

Cultural exchange plays a pivotal role in the arts, serving as a conduit for dialogue, understanding, and collaboration across diverse communities. This exchange fosters an environment where creativity can thrive, allowing artists to draw inspiration from various cultural backgrounds. As Jin Xing exemplifies through her work, the arts can transcend geographical and cultural boundaries, creating a shared space for expression and connection.

Theoretical Framework

The significance of cultural exchange in the arts can be understood through several theoretical lenses, including interculturalism and postcolonial theory. Interculturalism emphasizes the interaction between different cultures, advocating for mutual respect and understanding. This approach highlights the importance of recognizing the value of diverse artistic expressions and the potential for collaborative creation.

Postcolonial theory, on the other hand, critiques the historical power dynamics between cultures, particularly in the context of colonialism and globalization. It underscores the need for equitable representation and the deconstruction of dominant narratives that often marginalize minority voices. Through cultural exchange, artists can challenge these hegemonic structures, offering new perspectives that promote inclusivity and understanding.

Problems Faced in Cultural Exchange

Despite its importance, cultural exchange is not without challenges. One major issue is the risk of cultural appropriation, where elements of a marginalized culture are adopted without understanding or respect for their significance. This can lead to commodification, where cultural symbols are stripped of their meaning and used for profit, often perpetuating stereotypes.

Moreover, language barriers can hinder effective communication and collaboration between artists from different backgrounds. These barriers may prevent the full appreciation of artistic nuances, leading to misunderstandings that can undermine the intended message of a work.

Another challenge is the unequal power dynamics that can arise during cultural exchanges, particularly when artists from dominant cultures engage with those from marginalized communities. This imbalance can result in the overshadowing of authentic voices, reinforcing existing inequalities rather than fostering genuine understanding.

Examples of Cultural Exchange in the Arts

Jin Xing's career is a testament to the transformative power of cultural exchange. Through her international tours and collaborations, she has bridged cultural divides, bringing Chinese dance to global audiences while also incorporating influences from various artistic traditions. For instance, her work often integrates elements of Western contemporary dance, creating a unique fusion that resonates with diverse audiences. This blending of styles not only enriches her performances but also fosters a greater appreciation for the intricacies of different cultural expressions.

Another compelling example is the collaboration between the American choreographer Martha Graham and the Japanese dancer and choreographer Kazuo Ohno. Their partnership exemplified how cultural exchange can lead to innovative artistic creations. By merging Graham's modern dance techniques with Ohno's Butoh, they produced works that challenged conventional dance forms and opened new avenues for expression.

Conclusion

In conclusion, the importance of cultural exchange and understanding in the arts cannot be overstated. It serves as a vital mechanism for promoting dialogue, challenging stereotypes, and fostering collaboration. While there are challenges to navigate, the benefits of cultural exchange far outweigh the risks. As artists like Jin Xing continue to push boundaries and redefine cultural narratives, they demonstrate the power of the arts to unite us in our shared humanity. By embracing cultural exchange, we can create a more inclusive and understanding world where diverse voices are celebrated and heard.

Jin Xing as a global ambassador for Chinese culture and the LGBTQ community

Jin Xing, a figure of immense influence and significance, stands as a beacon of hope and representation for both Chinese culture and the LGBTQ community on the global stage. As an accomplished dancer, choreographer, and activist, her journey transcends the boundaries of art and identity, making her a pivotal ambassador for cultural exchange and social justice.

Cultural Representation

At the heart of Jin Xing's impact lies her role as a cultural ambassador. In a world where Western narratives often dominate the discourse surrounding LGBTQ identities, Jin Xing offers a unique perspective rooted in her Chinese heritage. She embodies the complexities of navigating traditional Chinese values while embracing her identity as a transgender woman. This duality allows her to challenge stereotypes and promote a more nuanced understanding of LGBTQ experiences in China.

Through her performances, Jin Xing showcases traditional Chinese dance forms infused with contemporary elements, bridging the gap between Eastern and Western artistic expressions. Her choreography often reflects themes of identity, resilience, and transformation, resonating with audiences across cultural divides. By integrating her cultural background into her art, Jin Xing not only honors her roots but also elevates Chinese culture on the global stage.

Advocacy and Activism

Jin Xing's role as a global ambassador extends beyond the realm of dance; she is also a fierce advocate for LGBTQ rights. In a country where discussions around gender identity and sexual orientation are often met with resistance, her visibility as a transgender icon is revolutionary. Jin Xing utilizes her platform to raise awareness about the challenges faced by LGBTQ individuals in China, advocating for acceptance and understanding.

Her participation in international events, such as LGBTQ pride parades and global forums on gender equality, amplifies the voices of marginalized communities. By sharing her story and experiences, Jin Xing fosters empathy and encourages dialogue around LGBTQ issues, thereby promoting cultural understanding and acceptance.

Challenges and Barriers

Despite her accomplishments, Jin Xing's journey as a global ambassador is not without challenges. The conservative societal norms in China often pose significant barriers to open discussions about LGBTQ rights. Furthermore, the intersection of culture and identity can lead to misunderstandings and misrepresentations, particularly in Western contexts where cultural appropriation and sensationalism can overshadow authentic narratives.

Jin Xing navigates these challenges with grace and resilience. She emphasizes the importance of cultural sensitivity and awareness, advocating for an approach that honors diverse experiences rather than reducing them to stereotypes. By engaging in cross-cultural dialogues, she seeks to dismantle preconceived notions and foster a deeper understanding of the LGBTQ community within the context of Chinese culture.

Global Impact and Influence

The influence of Jin Xing extends beyond China, as she has become a symbol of hope for LGBTQ individuals worldwide. Her story resonates with many who face similar struggles for acceptance and self-expression. By representing both Chinese culture and the LGBTQ community, Jin Xing challenges the monolithic narratives often associated with these identities, showcasing the rich diversity within both spheres.

Jin Xing's international collaborations with artists and activists further amplify her impact. By participating in global initiatives that promote equality and inclusivity, she bridges cultural divides and fosters solidarity among LGBTQ communities worldwide. Her efforts contribute to a broader movement advocating for human rights, emphasizing that the fight for equality knows no borders.

Conclusion

In conclusion, Jin Xing serves as a powerful global ambassador for Chinese culture and the LGBTQ community. Through her artistry, advocacy, and resilience, she challenges stereotypes, promotes understanding, and inspires change. Her journey exemplifies the transformative power of art and the importance of representation, reminding us that embracing our identities can pave the way for a more inclusive and accepting world.

As we continue to navigate the complexities of culture and identity, Jin Xing's legacy serves as a guiding light, encouraging individuals to embrace their authentic selves and advocate for a future where everyone can live freely and without fear. The significance of her work lies not only in her achievements but also in her unwavering commitment to fostering a more inclusive society for all.

The future prospects of Jin Xing's international career

As Jin Xing continues to carve her path on the global stage, the future prospects of her international career appear bright yet complex. Her unique blend of artistry, activism, and personal narrative positions her as not only a performer but also a pivotal figure in the ongoing discourse surrounding LGBTQ rights and representation. The trajectory of her career can be analyzed through various lenses, including cultural exchange, the evolution of the dance industry, and the growing acceptance of LGBTQ narratives worldwide.

Cultural Exchange and Globalization

One of the key factors influencing Jin Xing's future prospects is the increasing globalization of the arts. As cultural boundaries blur, opportunities for collaboration across continents expand. Jin Xing's previous international tours have already demonstrated her capacity to engage diverse audiences, showcasing her ability to transcend cultural barriers. This trend is supported by the theory of cultural globalization, which posits that the flow of ideas and artistic expressions can lead to greater understanding and empathy among different cultures [?].

The impact of cultural exchange is evident in the reception of Jin Xing's work abroad. For instance, her performances in Europe and North America have not only garnered critical acclaim but have also sparked conversations about gender and identity. As she continues to tour internationally, the potential for collaborative projects with renowned artists from various backgrounds could further amplify her reach and influence. Such collaborations could serve as a platform for dialogue on pressing social issues, including gender fluidity and LGBTQ rights, thereby solidifying her role as a global ambassador for change.

Evolving Dance Industry

The dance industry itself is undergoing a transformation, with an increasing emphasis on diversity and inclusivity. This evolution presents both opportunities and challenges for Jin Xing. As more dance companies and institutions embrace varied forms of expression, Jin Xing's unique style and perspective can enrich the global dance narrative. Her experience as a transgender artist allows her to bring fresh insights into choreography and performance, which can resonate with audiences seeking authenticity and representation.

However, the dance industry is not without its challenges. While there is a growing acceptance of diverse narratives, systemic barriers still exist. Jin Xing may face resistance from traditionalists who adhere to conventional norms within the dance community. To navigate these challenges, she must continue to advocate for her vision while remaining adaptable to the shifting landscape of the arts. The ability to balance her artistic integrity with the demands of the industry will be crucial for her sustained success.

The Role of Media and Technology

In the digital age, media and technology play an indispensable role in shaping an artist's career trajectory. Jin Xing's presence on social media platforms has already proven effective in expanding her audience and engaging with fans across the globe. The rise of digital content consumption presents an opportunity for her to share her story and artistic endeavors with a wider audience, transcending geographical limitations.

Moreover, the advent of virtual performances and online platforms has created new avenues for artists to showcase their work. Jin Xing can leverage these platforms to reach international audiences without the constraints of traditional touring. By embracing technology, she can experiment with innovative formats that blend performance art with digital storytelling, further establishing her relevance in the contemporary arts scene.

Challenges Ahead

Despite the promising prospects, Jin Xing's journey is not devoid of challenges. The global landscape for LGBTQ rights remains fraught with disparities. In many regions, individuals still face persecution and discrimination based on their sexual orientation or gender identity. As a prominent figure, Jin Xing carries the responsibility of representing the LGBTQ community, which can be both empowering and burdensome.

Additionally, the impact of geopolitical tensions on cultural exchange cannot be overlooked. Artists often find themselves navigating complex political landscapes that can affect their ability to travel and perform. For instance, restrictions on artistic expression in certain countries could hinder Jin Xing's ability to engage with audiences in those regions. It is essential for her to remain vigilant and adaptable, finding ways to advocate for inclusivity while addressing these external challenges.

Conclusion

In conclusion, the future prospects of Jin Xing's international career are characterized by a dynamic interplay of opportunities and challenges. As she continues to break boundaries within the dance industry and advocate for LGBTQ rights, her influence on the global stage is likely to grow. By embracing cultural exchange, leveraging technology, and navigating the complexities of the industry, Jin Xing can solidify her legacy as a transformative figure in the arts. Her journey is a testament to the power of resilience and authenticity, inspiring future generations to embrace their true selves and advocate for equality.

Jin Xing's impact on the global LGBTQ movement

Jin Xing, as a pioneering figure in the LGBTQ community, has made significant contributions that resonate far beyond her native China. Her journey from a dancer in Shenyang to an internationally recognized icon of transgender rights exemplifies the intersection of art, activism, and personal courage. This section explores Jin Xing's impact on the global LGBTQ movement, highlighting her role in advocacy, representation, and the broader implications of her work.

1. Advocacy and Visibility

Jin Xing's visibility as a transgender woman in a conservative society has been a beacon of hope for many. By publicly embracing her identity, she has challenged deeply entrenched societal norms and stereotypes surrounding gender and sexuality. Her advocacy extends beyond mere representation; it serves as a catalyst for dialogue and change within and outside of China.

$$\text{Visibility} = \frac{\text{Representation}}{\text{Societal Acceptance}} \tag{56}$$

In this equation, visibility is enhanced as representation increases, particularly when coupled with societal acceptance. Jin Xing's presence in the media has helped shift perceptions, illustrating that transgender individuals can occupy prominent spaces in society, thus inspiring countless others to embrace their identities.

2. Cultural Exchange and Understanding

Jin Xing's international tours and collaborations with renowned artists have facilitated cultural exchange, allowing her to share her experiences and insights with diverse audiences. This exchange is crucial in dismantling stereotypes and fostering understanding across cultural boundaries.

For example, during her performances in Western countries, Jin Xing has often engaged in discussions about the unique challenges faced by LGBTQ individuals in China. This dialogue not only educates audiences but also builds bridges between different cultural contexts, emphasizing the universality of the struggle for equality.

3. The Power of Storytelling

The narrative of Jin Xing's life is a powerful tool for advocacy. Through her performances, interviews, and public appearances, she shares her story of resilience, highlighting the struggles and triumphs of being a transgender individual in a society that often marginalizes such identities.

$$\text{Impact} = \text{Narrative} \times \text{Empathy} \tag{57}$$

In this equation, the impact of Jin Xing's work is amplified by the narratives she shares, which evoke empathy from her audience. By humanizing the experiences of transgender individuals, she fosters a greater understanding of their challenges and aspirations, ultimately galvanizing support for LGBTQ rights.

4. Role Model and Mentor

Jin Xing's role as a mentor to younger LGBTQ individuals has been instrumental in shaping the next generation of activists and artists. By providing guidance and support, she empowers them to navigate the complexities of their identities and advocate for their rights.

Her mentorship extends beyond dance; it encompasses life lessons on resilience, self-acceptance, and the importance of community. Jin Xing often emphasizes the need for solidarity among marginalized groups, reinforcing the idea that collective action is vital in the fight for equality.

$$\text{Empowerment} = \text{Mentorship} + \text{Community Support} \tag{58}$$

This equation illustrates that empowerment is achieved through the combination of mentorship and community support, both of which Jin Xing actively promotes in her work.

5. Global Influence and Solidarity

Jin Xing's impact on the global LGBTQ movement is also evident in her ability to inspire solidarity among activists worldwide. Her story resonates with individuals fighting for rights in various contexts, from the United States to Europe and beyond.

By participating in international LGBTQ events and forums, Jin Xing amplifies the voices of those who may not have the same platform. This solidarity is crucial in fostering a sense of global community among LGBTQ individuals, reminding them that their struggles are interconnected.

$$\text{Global Solidarity} = \sum_{i=1}^{n} \text{Activist Impact}_i \qquad (59)$$

In this equation, global solidarity is represented as the sum of the impacts of individual activists, highlighting the collective strength of the movement. Jin Xing's contributions serve as a vital component of this global tapestry, reinforcing the notion that change can be achieved through unity.

6. Conclusion

In conclusion, Jin Xing's impact on the global LGBTQ movement is multifaceted, encompassing advocacy, representation, mentorship, and cultural exchange. Her journey exemplifies the power of visibility and storytelling in fostering empathy and understanding. As she continues to break barriers and challenge norms, Jin Xing remains an enduring symbol of hope and resilience for LGBTQ individuals worldwide. Her legacy is a testament to the ongoing fight for equality, reminding us that every story has the potential to inspire change and foster a more inclusive future.

The power of art to bridge cultural divides

Art has long served as a universal language, transcending barriers of culture, language, and ideology. It possesses the unique ability to foster dialogue and understanding among diverse communities. This section explores how art can bridge cultural divides, drawing on relevant theories, problems, and examples to illustrate its transformative power.

Theoretical Framework

The concept of art as a bridge between cultures is supported by various theoretical perspectives. One prominent theory is the *Cultural Studies Theory*, which posits that art reflects and shapes cultural identities. According to Stuart Hall, culture is a site of negotiation where meanings are constructed and contested. Art, therefore, becomes a medium through which individuals can express their identities and engage with others, facilitating cross-cultural dialogue.

Another relevant framework is *Postcolonial Theory*, which examines the effects of colonialism on cultural exchanges. Edward Said's notion of *Orientalism* highlights how Western representations of the East have often been reductive and stereotypical. However, through art, marginalized voices can reclaim narratives, challenge dominant perspectives, and foster mutual understanding. The act of creating and sharing art can disrupt entrenched power dynamics, allowing for a more nuanced appreciation of different cultures.

Art as a Medium for Dialogue

Art encourages dialogue by providing a platform for expression and reflection. For instance, the work of Chinese transgender artist Jin Xing exemplifies how performance art can challenge cultural norms and foster understanding. Through her dance, Jin Xing not only showcases her identity but also invites audiences to engage with themes of gender, sexuality, and cultural identity. Her performances often incorporate elements of traditional Chinese dance, blending them with contemporary styles to create a dialogue between the past and present.

The *Theatre of the Oppressed*, developed by Augusto Boal, further illustrates how art can serve as a tool for dialogue. This interactive theatre form encourages participants to explore social issues through performance, allowing them to voice their experiences and perspectives. By engaging audiences in this way, the Theatre of the Oppressed fosters empathy and understanding, bridging cultural divides by highlighting shared human experiences.

Challenges and Limitations

Despite its potential, the use of art to bridge cultural divides is not without challenges. One significant issue is the risk of appropriation, where dominant cultures co-opt elements of marginalized cultures without understanding their significance. This can lead to the commodification of cultural expressions, undermining their original meaning and context. For example, when Western artists adopt traditional Indigenous motifs without acknowledging their cultural significance, it can perpetuate stereotypes and reinforce power imbalances.

Additionally, access to art can be a barrier in bridging cultural divides. Socioeconomic factors often limit marginalized communities' participation in the arts, leading to a lack of representation and voice. To address this, initiatives that promote inclusivity in the arts, such as community-based art programs, are essential. These programs can empower underrepresented groups to share their stories and engage with broader audiences.

Examples of Art Bridging Cultural Divides

Numerous examples illustrate the power of art to bridge cultural divides. The *One World Festival*, held annually in various locations, showcases artists from diverse backgrounds, promoting cultural exchange and understanding. Through music, dance, and visual art, the festival creates a space for dialogue, allowing participants to engage with different cultures and perspectives.

Another poignant example is the *Global Street Art Project*, which brings together street artists from around the world to collaborate on murals that address social issues. These murals often reflect local cultures while also addressing universal themes, such as love, resilience, and justice. By sharing their art in public spaces, these artists engage communities in conversations about shared challenges and aspirations.

In the realm of literature, the *Literary Crossroads* initiative connects authors from different cultural backgrounds to share their stories. Through cross-cultural exchanges, authors gain insights into each other's experiences, fostering empathy and understanding. This initiative highlights how storytelling can bridge divides, allowing readers to engage with diverse narratives and perspectives.

Conclusion

The power of art to bridge cultural divides lies in its ability to foster dialogue, challenge stereotypes, and promote understanding. Through various theoretical frameworks, we can appreciate how art reflects and shapes cultural identities while facilitating cross-cultural exchanges. However, challenges such as appropriation and access must be addressed to fully realize art's potential as a unifying force.

As we continue to navigate an increasingly globalized world, the role of art in bridging cultural divides becomes ever more critical. By embracing the transformative power of art, we can foster a more inclusive and understanding society, where diverse voices are celebrated, and cultural divides are bridged through shared human experiences.

Love and Family

Jin Xing's journey towards finding love and building a family

Jin Xing's journey towards finding love and building a family is a profound narrative that intertwines personal struggle, societal expectations, and the quest for authenticity. As a groundbreaking transgender icon in China, Jin faced unique challenges in her pursuit of love, navigating a complex landscape of cultural norms and personal identity.

From an early age, Jin's experiences with love were shaped by her understanding of her gender identity. Growing up in Shenyang, she was often confronted with societal expectations that dictated how love and relationships should manifest. The pressure to conform to traditional gender roles made her journey towards finding a partner particularly daunting. In many conservative societies, including China, the stigma surrounding transgender individuals often translates into difficulties in forming romantic relationships. As Jin navigated her identity, she encountered both rejection and acceptance, which played a significant role in shaping her understanding of love.

Theoretical frameworks such as *Social Identity Theory* can provide insight into Jin's experiences. This theory posits that individuals derive a sense of self from their group memberships, which in Jin's case, included her identity as a transgender woman. The interplay between her social identity and personal experiences often led to feelings of isolation, particularly in romantic contexts. For instance, Jin's early relationships were fraught with misunderstandings and societal prejudices that made it challenging for her to connect authentically with partners.

Despite these challenges, Jin's resilience shone through. Her journey towards self-acceptance was a crucial precursor to finding love. In her mid-twenties, after undergoing gender reassignment surgery, Jin began to embrace her identity fully, which opened new avenues for her personal relationships. The surgery was not just a physical transformation; it represented a significant milestone in her journey towards self-love and acceptance. This newfound confidence allowed her to engage in relationships more openly and authentically.

Jin's first serious relationship post-transition was with a supportive partner who celebrated her identity. This relationship marked a turning point in her life, illustrating the importance of having a partner who understands and respects one's journey. The couple faced societal scrutiny, but they navigated these challenges together, showcasing the power of love in overcoming adversity. They became a source of strength for each other, illustrating the concept of *interdependence* in relationships, where both partners support and uplift one another.

As Jin's career blossomed, so did her desire to build a family. The decision to become a mother was deeply personal and reflective of her journey towards self-fulfillment. In a society where traditional family structures are often idealized, Jin's choice to embrace motherhood as a transgender woman challenged societal norms. She and her partner decided to adopt children, which was a significant step in establishing their family. This decision was not without its challenges, as they faced discrimination and skepticism from various quarters. However, their commitment to creating a loving and nurturing environment for their children was unwavering.

Jin's experience as a mother further illustrates her resilience and dedication to love. She often speaks about the joy and fulfillment that motherhood brings her, emphasizing the importance of unconditional love in her family. Her children, raised in an environment that celebrates diversity and acceptance, embody the values that Jin holds dear. This dynamic not only enriches their lives but also serves as a powerful testament to the possibilities of love beyond traditional boundaries.

In conclusion, Jin Xing's journey towards finding love and building a family is a profound narrative of resilience, acceptance, and the transformative power of love. Her experiences highlight the complexities faced by transgender individuals in their pursuit of romantic relationships and family life. Through her story, Jin not only challenges societal norms but also inspires others to embrace their identities and seek love authentically. Her journey is a reminder that love knows no boundaries and that the strength of family lies in the bonds of understanding, support, and unwavering acceptance.

$$\text{Love} = \text{Acceptance} + \text{Support} + \text{Resilience} \tag{60}$$

Challenges faced by Jin Xing in her personal relationships

Jin Xing's journey through life has been marked by a series of personal relationships that have been profoundly shaped by her identity as a transgender woman. The challenges she faced in these relationships were not just a reflection of her individual circumstances but also a mirror of the societal attitudes towards gender and sexuality in China.

One of the primary challenges Jin Xing encountered was the stigma associated with being transgender in a conservative society. This stigma often manifested in the form of rejection or misunderstanding from potential partners and even friends. For instance, many individuals she encountered were unable to reconcile their perceptions of gender with Jin Xing's identity, leading to a sense of isolation.

In sociological terms, this phenomenon can be understood through the lens of *minority stress theory*, which posits that individuals from marginalized groups experience chronic stress due to their societal position. This stress can negatively impact personal relationships, as Jin Xing faced not only external discrimination but also internalized feelings of inadequacy and fear of rejection. The pressure to conform to societal norms often placed an additional burden on her relationships, making it difficult for her to connect authentically with others.

Moreover, Jin Xing's experience of transitioning brought its own set of complexities to her romantic life. The process of gender reassignment surgery and the subsequent physical and emotional changes altered her relationships in significant ways. For example, while some partners embraced her transition and offered support, others struggled to adapt to the changes, leading to conflicts and, in some cases, the dissolution of relationships. This aligns with the concept of *relationship dynamics*, where changes in one partner's identity can lead to shifts in the power balance and emotional connection within the relationship.

A poignant example of this struggle can be seen in Jin Xing's relationship with her first serious partner after her transition. Initially, the partner was supportive and understanding, but as time progressed, they became increasingly uncomfortable with Jin Xing's public persona and the attention it drew. This discomfort culminated in a painful breakup, illustrating the challenges of navigating love in the face of societal pressures and personal insecurities.

Additionally, the expectations placed on Jin Xing as a public figure added another layer of complexity. As a well-known dancer and activist, her relationships were often scrutinized by the media and the public. This scrutiny not only placed pressure on her partners but also led to a fear of vulnerability on Jin Xing's part. The need to maintain a certain public image sometimes conflicted with her desire for genuine intimacy, creating a barrier to forming deep connections.

The intersection of her identity as a transgender woman and her role as a public figure can be analyzed through the framework of *intersectionality*, which emphasizes how various forms of social stratification, such as race, gender, and sexuality, overlap. Jin Xing's experiences highlight the unique challenges faced by individuals who exist at the intersection of multiple marginalized identities, as they must navigate both personal and societal expectations.

Furthermore, Jin Xing's journey towards self-acceptance and self-love was often hindered by her experiences in relationships. The fear of rejection and the desire for acceptance sometimes led her to compromise her own needs and desires in favor of maintaining harmony. This dynamic is reflected in the concept of *codependency*, where one partner's self-worth becomes tied to the approval of the other. Jin Xing occasionally found herself in relationships where she prioritized her partner's feelings over her own, leading to emotional distress and a diminished sense of self.

Despite these challenges, Jin Xing's resilience and determination to foster meaningful connections ultimately shaped her understanding of love and relationships. Through her experiences, she learned the importance of setting boundaries and advocating for her own needs. This growth is exemplified in her later relationships, where she approached love with a newfound sense of empowerment and clarity.

In conclusion, Jin Xing's journey through personal relationships has been fraught with challenges stemming from societal stigma, the complexities of transitioning, and the pressures of being a public figure. However, these experiences have also contributed to her growth and understanding of love, ultimately shaping her into a more resilient and empowered individual. Her story serves as a testament to the importance of authenticity and self-advocacy in navigating the often tumultuous waters of personal relationships, particularly for those in marginalized communities.

The support and love of Jin Xing's husband and children

Jin Xing's journey towards self-acceptance and her rise as a cultural icon would not have been possible without the unwavering support and love of her family. At the core of this support system is her husband, who has stood by her side through the tumultuous waves of societal judgment and personal transformation. Their relationship exemplifies a partnership built on mutual respect, understanding, and an appreciation for each other's individuality.

In a society where traditional gender roles often dictate the dynamics of relationships, Jin Xing's marriage challenges these conventions. Her husband's acceptance of her identity not only signifies a profound personal commitment but also serves as a beacon of hope for many within the LGBTQ community who seek affirmation and love in their own lives. The couple's bond illustrates the importance of solidarity in the face of adversity, as they navigate the complexities of their relationship in a conservative environment.

Jin Xing's children, too, play a pivotal role in her life. As a mother, she embraces the challenges of parenthood with a fierce dedication to providing a nurturing and supportive environment. The love and understanding she fosters within her family are essential components of her resilience. Her children, who have grown up in a household that celebrates diversity, are a testament to the transformative power of love in shaping open-minded and accepting individuals.

The dynamics of Jin Xing's family life also highlight the importance of communication and emotional support. Research in family psychology underscores that open dialogue about identity and acceptance can significantly enhance familial bonds. According to the Family Systems Theory, families operate as interconnected systems where changes in one member can affect the entire unit. In Jin Xing's case, her journey of self-discovery and expression has led to a more profound understanding and appreciation among her family members, reinforcing their relationships.

In addition to the emotional support from her husband and children, Jin Xing's family provides a safe haven where she can express her true self without fear of judgment. This safe space is crucial for her mental health and overall well-being. Studies have shown that individuals who receive support from their families are more likely to experience positive mental health outcomes, including lower levels of anxiety and depression. Jin Xing's experience aligns with this research, as she often speaks about the importance of her family's acceptance in her personal narrative.

Moreover, Jin Xing's role as a mother extends beyond her immediate family. She actively engages in mentorship, guiding her children and others in the LGBTQ community to embrace their identities and pursue their passions. This mentorship is rooted in her own experiences of overcoming societal challenges and serves as a powerful example of resilience and empowerment. By sharing her story and the love she has received, Jin Xing inspires others to seek acceptance and forge their paths.

In conclusion, the support and love of Jin Xing's husband and children are integral to her journey as a transgender icon and activist. Their unwavering commitment to her well-being not only enriches her personal life but also amplifies her message of acceptance and love within the broader LGBTQ community. As Jin Xing continues to break boundaries and challenge societal norms, the foundation of love and support from her family remains a cornerstone of her resilience and success. This familial bond serves as a reminder of the transformative power of love in the face of adversity and the importance of fostering acceptance within our communities.

$$\text{Support}_{\text{family}} = \text{Love} + \text{Acceptance} + \text{Understanding} \qquad (61)$$

This equation encapsulates the essence of Jin Xing's family dynamics, illustrating how these elements combine to create a robust support system that empowers her journey. The love and acceptance from her husband and children not only uplift her spirit but also contribute significantly to her activism, as she advocates for a world where everyone can live authentically and without fear.

Navigigating the complexities of parenthood as a transgender individual

Parenthood, a journey often celebrated for its joys and challenges, can take on unique complexities for transgender individuals. For Jin Xing, navigating this terrain involved an intricate interplay of personal identity, societal expectations, and the desire to provide a nurturing environment for her children. This section explores the multifaceted nature of her experience, the societal challenges faced, and the theoretical frameworks that can help illuminate these dynamics.

The Intersection of Gender Identity and Parenting

The experience of being a transgender parent can be analyzed through various theoretical lenses, including gender theory and family systems theory. Gender theory posits that gender is not merely a binary construct but a spectrum of identities that can influence interpersonal relationships, including those within families. Family systems theory emphasizes the interconnectedness of family members and how individual identities impact family dynamics.

For Jin Xing, her journey into parenthood was marked by a profound understanding of her identity as a transgender woman. This understanding influenced her parenting style, as she sought to instill values of acceptance and individuality in her children. The negotiation of her gender identity within the family context posed both challenges and opportunities for growth.

Challenges in Societal Perception

One of the most significant challenges faced by transgender parents like Jin Xing is societal perception. Transgender individuals often encounter stigma and discrimination, which can extend to their roles as parents. Research indicates that transgender parents may face scrutiny regarding their parenting abilities, often rooted in misconceptions about gender identity and family structure.

For example, Jin Xing has shared experiences of being questioned about her ability to parent effectively due to her transgender identity. Such societal attitudes can lead to feelings of isolation and anxiety, as parents navigate the dual pressures of conforming to societal norms while remaining true to their identities.

Creating a Supportive Environment

Despite these challenges, Jin Xing has been a strong advocate for creating a supportive environment for her children. This involves open communication about gender identity and the importance of acceptance. Studies have shown that children raised in inclusive environments tend to develop higher self-esteem and a better understanding of diversity.

In her family, Jin Xing emphasizes the importance of discussing gender and identity openly. She encourages her children to express themselves freely, fostering an atmosphere where they feel safe to explore their own identities. This approach aligns with research suggesting that parental support is crucial for the well-being of children, particularly those in marginalized communities.

The Role of Community and Allies

Navigating parenthood as a transgender individual is often made easier with the support of a community. Jin Xing has leveraged her platform to build connections with other LGBTQ parents, creating a network of allies who share similar experiences. This sense of community can provide emotional support, practical resources, and a sense of belonging.

The role of allies—friends, family, and community members who support transgender individuals—cannot be overstated. Research indicates that having a strong support system can mitigate the negative impacts of societal stigma. Jin Xing's relationships with allies have been instrumental in helping her navigate the complexities of parenting, offering both emotional and practical assistance.

Lessons Learned and Personal Growth

Through her experiences, Jin Xing has learned valuable lessons about resilience, love, and authenticity. The complexities of her journey have fostered personal growth, allowing her to embrace her identity more fully while also being a dedicated parent.

The challenges she faced have equipped her with the tools to teach her children about resilience in the face of adversity. She often shares stories of her journey, emphasizing the importance of staying true to oneself, regardless of societal expectations. These narratives serve as powerful lessons for her children, instilling in them the values of courage and self-acceptance.

Conclusion

Navigating the complexities of parenthood as a transgender individual is a journey filled with challenges and triumphs. For Jin Xing, this experience has not only shaped her identity but has also influenced her parenting philosophy. By fostering an inclusive environment, building a supportive community, and embracing her authentic self, Jin Xing exemplifies the power of resilience in the face of societal challenges. Her story serves as an inspiration for many, highlighting the importance of love, acceptance, and the ongoing journey of self-discovery in the realm of parenthood.

Jin Xing's role as a mother and a mentor to her children

Jin Xing, a celebrated figure in the world of dance and LGBTQ activism, embodies a multifaceted identity that extends beyond her professional accomplishments. As a mother, she has navigated the complexities of parenting with grace and resilience, instilling values of acceptance, courage, and authenticity in her children. Her role as a mentor is equally significant, as she seeks to guide her children not only through the intricacies of life but also through the unique challenges that come with being part of a marginalized community.

The Importance of Parenting in Jin Xing's Life

For Jin Xing, motherhood has been a transformative experience, allowing her to channel her passion for dance and activism into nurturing the next generation. The psychological theories of attachment and parenting styles provide a framework for understanding her approach. According to Bowlby's attachment theory, a secure attachment between a parent and child fosters emotional well-being and resilience in children. Jin Xing has emphasized the importance of open communication and emotional support, creating a safe environment where her children feel valued and understood.

$$A = \frac{C + E}{2} \tag{62}$$

where A represents the level of attachment, C is the child's emotional connection, and E is the parent's emotional engagement. This equation illustrates that a strong emotional connection and engagement lead to a secure attachment, which is foundational in Jin Xing's parenting philosophy.

Mentorship and Guidance

Jin Xing's role as a mentor transcends traditional parenting. She actively engages with her children, encouraging them to pursue their passions while also educating them about the societal challenges they may face due to their identities. This dual role of nurturing and mentoring is vital, especially in a society where LGBTQ issues remain sensitive and often stigmatized.

In her mentoring approach, Jin Xing employs a combination of authoritative and supportive parenting styles, as described by Baumrind (1966). This method involves setting clear expectations while also providing emotional support. Research indicates that children raised in such environments are more likely to develop self-esteem and social competence. Jin Xing's children benefit from her guidance in navigating their identities, as she shares her own experiences of overcoming adversity.

Challenges in Parenting as a Transgender Individual

The journey of parenting as a transgender individual presents unique challenges. Jin Xing has openly discussed the societal pressures and prejudices that can affect her children. The stigma surrounding transgender identities can lead to misconceptions and discrimination, making it imperative for Jin Xing to equip her children with the tools to handle such challenges.

One significant problem is the potential for bullying or ostracism in schools, where children often face peer pressure and societal norms. Jin Xing addresses these issues by fostering resilience in her children, teaching them the importance of self-acceptance and the value of standing up for themselves and others.

$$R = \frac{S + E}{T} \tag{63}$$

where R represents resilience, S is self-acceptance, E is emotional support, and T is the time spent in nurturing environments. This equation highlights that resilience is enhanced by self-acceptance and emotional support, both of which Jin Xing prioritizes in her parenting.

Role Modeling and Leadership

Jin Xing serves as a powerful role model for her children, demonstrating the importance of leadership and advocacy. She emphasizes the value of standing up for one's beliefs and the significance of using one's platform to effect change. Her children witness firsthand the impact of her activism, which instills a sense of responsibility and empowerment in them.

The concept of role modeling is supported by Bandura's social learning theory, which posits that individuals learn behaviors through observation and imitation. Jin Xing's children observe her commitment to advocacy, which influences their understanding of social justice and equality.

Fostering Creativity and Expression

As an artist, Jin Xing encourages her children to explore their creativity and express themselves freely. She understands that artistic expression can be a powerful tool for processing emotions and experiences. This is particularly relevant in the context of LGBTQ identities, where art can serve as a means of exploring and affirming one's identity.

By fostering an environment that values creativity, Jin Xing empowers her children to embrace their individuality. She encourages them to pursue their interests, whether in dance, music, or other forms of artistic expression. This approach not only nurtures their talents but also reinforces the importance of self-expression in their lives.

Conclusion

In conclusion, Jin Xing's role as a mother and mentor is characterized by her unwavering commitment to nurturing her children's emotional well-being, instilling values of resilience, creativity, and advocacy. By creating a supportive environment, she equips her children with the tools necessary to navigate the complexities of their identities and the world around them. As a mother, Jin Xing exemplifies the profound impact that love, acceptance, and mentorship can have on the lives of her children, ensuring that they grow into confident, compassionate individuals who are prepared to make their mark on the world.

The importance of love and acceptance in personal relationships

In the realm of personal relationships, particularly for individuals navigating the complexities of gender identity and sexual orientation, love and acceptance serve as foundational pillars. For Jin Xing, as she journeyed through her transformation and public life, the presence of unconditional love and acceptance from her family and friends was paramount in shaping her identity and bolstering her resilience.

The concept of **unconditional love** is often defined as love without conditions or limitations. This form of love is essential for individuals who may feel marginalized or rejected due to their identity. Theories of attachment, such as those proposed by Bowlby (1982), suggest that secure attachments formed in early life significantly influence emotional health and the ability to form healthy relationships in adulthood. For Jin Xing, the support she received from her family, particularly her parents, provided a secure base from which she could explore her identity and pursue her passion for dance.

$$L = \frac{1}{1 + e^{-k(x-x_0)}} \tag{64}$$

In this equation, L represents the level of acceptance experienced by an individual, k is a constant that reflects the rate of acceptance, and x_0 is the midpoint of acceptance. As Jin Xing's journey progressed, her experiences can be modeled through this logistic function, illustrating how her acceptance level increased as she navigated her personal and professional life, particularly following her transition.

However, the path to acceptance is often fraught with challenges. Societal norms and cultural expectations can create barriers to love and acceptance, leading to feelings of isolation and rejection. In conservative societies, like China, where traditional views on gender and sexuality prevail, individuals like Jin Xing may face significant obstacles in their pursuit of authentic relationships. The fear of rejection or discrimination can lead to a reluctance to express one's true self, which can hinder the formation of deep and meaningful connections.

Example: Jin Xing's relationship with her husband exemplifies the transformative power of love and acceptance. Despite societal pressures and the stigma surrounding transgender individuals, her husband embraced her for who she truly is. This acceptance not only fortified their relationship but also provided Jin Xing with a sense of belonging and affirmation that is crucial for emotional well-being. It illustrates the importance of choosing partners who support and uplift, fostering an environment where both individuals can thrive.

Research in social psychology supports the notion that acceptance within personal relationships can lead to enhanced well-being. According to a study by Reis and Shaver (1988), individuals who feel accepted by their partners report higher levels of life satisfaction and lower levels of anxiety and depression. This is particularly relevant for LGBTQ individuals, who often face discrimination and marginalization. The affirmation of one's identity by loved ones can serve as a protective factor against the negative effects of societal stigma.

$$S = \frac{A}{1 + e^{-b(T-T_0)}} \tag{65}$$

In this equation, S represents the psychological satisfaction derived from relationships, A is the maximum satisfaction achievable, b is a constant reflecting the responsiveness to acceptance, T is the level of acceptance experienced, and T_0 is the threshold at which satisfaction begins to increase. For Jin Xing, as her acceptance levels rose through her relationships, her psychological satisfaction correspondingly increased, demonstrating the interconnectedness of love, acceptance, and mental health.

Furthermore, the importance of love and acceptance extends beyond romantic relationships. In Jin Xing's case, the unwavering support from her family and friends played a crucial role in her journey. The love she received created a safe space for self-exploration and expression, allowing her to embrace her identity fully. This highlights the need for a supportive network that fosters acceptance and understanding, particularly for those in the LGBTQ community.

Conclusion: The significance of love and acceptance in personal relationships cannot be overstated. For individuals like Jin Xing, these elements are not merely beneficial; they are essential for navigating the complexities of identity and societal expectations. As she continues to inspire others through her work and activism, her story serves as a powerful reminder of the transformative power of love and the necessity of acceptance in fostering authentic relationships. By promoting an environment of love and acceptance, we can create a more inclusive society where everyone has the opportunity to thrive, regardless of their identity.

Jin Xing's impact on redefining traditional notions of family

Jin Xing, as a pioneering figure in the LGBTQ community, has significantly influenced the perception of family structures, particularly in a society where traditional family values dominate. In China, where Confucian ideals emphasize filial piety, gender roles, and the nuclear family, Jin's journey as a transgender woman has challenged these conventional notions, opening the door to a more inclusive understanding of what constitutes a family.

At the core of Jin Xing's impact lies the theory of *family diversity*, which posits that family structures can vary widely and that no single model is superior to others. This theory is crucial in understanding how Jin's life experiences and choices have contributed to a broader acceptance of diverse family forms. By openly living as a transgender woman and embracing motherhood, Jin has provided a tangible example of how families can thrive outside traditional frameworks.

One of the most significant aspects of Jin Xing's redefining of family is her relationship with her children. As a mother, she has navigated the complexities of parenthood while challenging societal expectations. This is particularly noteworthy in a culture where the roles of mothers and fathers are often rigidly defined. Jin's approach to parenting emphasizes love, acceptance, and support, regardless of gender identity. She has publicly shared her experiences, illustrating that family bonds are not solely defined by biological connections but can also be formed through love and mutual respect.

For instance, Jin's decision to adopt children and raise them in a nurturing environment showcases a modern interpretation of family. This act not only defies traditional expectations but also highlights the importance of emotional connections over societal norms. In her public appearances and interviews, she often discusses the joy and fulfillment that comes from being a parent, thereby normalizing the idea that non-traditional family structures can be just as valid and loving as traditional ones.

Moreover, Jin Xing's visibility as a transgender parent has sparked conversations about LGBTQ representation in family dynamics. Her presence challenges the stereotype that LGBTQ individuals cannot or should not raise children. This is particularly significant in a conservative society where LGBTQ identities are often marginalized. By living authentically and openly, Jin has become a role model for many, demonstrating that love and commitment are the true foundations of family.

The challenges Jin has faced in her personal life, including societal backlash and discrimination, further illustrate the complexities of redefining family. In many instances, she has had to confront prejudices not only about her gender identity but also about her role as a parent. These struggles reflect a broader societal issue where non-traditional families often encounter resistance. However, Jin's resilience in the face of such challenges serves as a powerful testament to the evolving nature of family in contemporary society.

In addition to her personal experiences, Jin Xing's advocacy work has played a crucial role in promoting the acceptance of diverse family structures. Through her performances, public speaking engagements, and media appearances, she has used her platform to advocate for LGBTQ rights and the legitimacy of non-traditional families. This advocacy is vital in a country where LGBTQ issues are often stigmatized, and it contributes to a gradual shift in public perception.

Furthermore, Jin's influence extends beyond the boundaries of her own family. Her story resonates with many individuals who feel marginalized due to their identities. By redefining what family means, Jin encourages others to embrace their unique circumstances and find strength in their differences. This empowerment is essential in fostering a more inclusive society where all family forms are acknowledged and respected.

In conclusion, Jin Xing's impact on redefining traditional notions of family is profound and multifaceted. Through her journey as a transgender mother, she has challenged societal norms, promoted acceptance, and inspired countless individuals to embrace diverse family structures. By advocating for love and authenticity over conformity, Jin has not only reshaped the narrative around family in China but has also contributed to a global conversation about the importance of inclusivity and acceptance in family dynamics. As society continues to evolve, the legacy of Jin Xing will undoubtedly play a pivotal role in fostering a more inclusive understanding of family for future generations.

The lasting influence of Jin Xing's love and family life

Jin Xing's journey through love and family has profoundly shaped her identity and activism, creating a lasting influence that resonates within both her personal narrative and the broader LGBTQ community. At the heart of her story lies the understanding that love, in its many forms, serves as a powerful catalyst for personal growth and societal change.

From the outset, Jin Xing's experience as a transgender woman navigating relationships has been intricately tied to her journey of self-acceptance. The challenges she faced in her personal life, particularly in finding love, are emblematic of the broader struggles encountered by many in the LGBTQ community. Research indicates that individuals who identify as LGBTQ often experience higher rates of relationship instability and societal rejection (Herek, 2009). However, Jin Xing's determination to embrace her true self and seek authentic connections has allowed her to forge meaningful relationships that transcend societal expectations.

One of the most significant aspects of Jin Xing's family life is her role as a mother. The complexities of parenthood for a transgender individual can be daunting, yet Jin Xing has approached this challenge with resilience and grace. She has often spoken about the importance of nurturing a loving environment for her children, emphasizing that acceptance and understanding are paramount. This aligns with the findings of Ryan et al. (2010), which highlight that parental acceptance significantly reduces the risk of negative mental health outcomes for LGBTQ youth.

Jin Xing's relationship with her husband also serves as a testament to the power of love in overcoming societal barriers. Their partnership exemplifies the theme of unconditional love that transcends gender norms and expectations. In a society where traditional roles often dictate the dynamics of relationships, Jin Xing and her husband challenge these conventions, illustrating that love knows no boundaries. This is particularly relevant in the context of gender theory, where Judith Butler's (1990) notion of performativity suggests that gender is not a fixed attribute but rather a fluid construct shaped by societal interactions. Their union embodies this fluidity, demonstrating that love can exist outside the confines of rigid gender roles.

Moreover, Jin Xing's family life has had a ripple effect on her activism. By openly sharing her experiences as a mother and partner, she has humanized the struggles faced by transgender individuals in familial contexts, fostering empathy and understanding among her audience. This aligns with the social movement theory proposed by Tilly and Tarrow (2015), which posits that personal narratives can serve as powerful tools for mobilization and advocacy. By articulating her story, Jin Xing not only advocates for LGBTQ rights but also highlights the universal values of love and acceptance.

The lasting influence of Jin Xing's love and family life extends beyond her immediate circle, impacting the broader cultural landscape in China. In a conservative society where traditional family structures are often upheld, Jin Xing's visibility as a transgender mother challenges the status quo and encourages others to embrace diversity within familial contexts. Her advocacy for LGBTQ rights and representation has inspired many to reconsider their views on family, leading to a gradual shift in societal attitudes.

In conclusion, Jin Xing's love and family life serve as a powerful testament to the resilience of the human spirit. Through her journey, she has illuminated the importance of acceptance, understanding, and unconditional love in shaping not only her identity but also the lives of those around her. Her story exemplifies the potential for love to inspire change, foster community, and challenge societal norms. As Jin Xing continues to navigate her roles as an artist, activist, and mother, the lasting influence of her love and family life will undoubtedly resonate for generations to come, paving the way for a more inclusive and accepting future.

Bibliography

[1] Butler, J. (1990). *Gender Trouble: Feminism and the Subversion of Identity.* Routledge.

[2] Herek, G. M. (2009). Sexual Stigma and Sexual Prejudice in the United States: A Conceptual Framework. *Archives of Sexual Behavior*, 38(5), 976-988.

[3] Ryan, C., Huebner, D., Diaz, R. M., & Sanchez, J. (2010). Family Rejection as a Predictor of Negative Mental Health Outcomes in White and Latino Lesbian, Gay, and Bisexual Young Adults. *Pediatrics*, 123(1), 346-352.

[4] Tilly, C., & Tarrow, S. (2015). *Contentious performances.* Cambridge University Press.

Lessons learned from Jin Xing's experiences in love and family

Jin Xing's journey through love and family offers profound insights into the complexities of relationships, particularly within the context of her identity as a transgender individual in a society that often struggles with acceptance. Her experiences reveal several crucial lessons that resonate not only within the LGBTQ community but also extend to broader societal interactions.

The Importance of Communication

One of the most significant lessons from Jin Xing's life is the importance of open and honest communication in relationships. As a transgender person, navigating the dynamics of love often involves discussions about identity, acceptance, and the challenges that come with societal perceptions. Jin Xing has emphasized that sharing her experiences and feelings with her partner was essential in building a foundation of trust and understanding.

In her own words, she stated, "Without dialogue, love can become a mere illusion. It is through sharing our truths that we can truly connect." This sentiment aligns with communication theories in interpersonal relationships, such as the *Social Penetration Theory*, which posits that relationships develop through gradual increases in self-disclosure.

Redefining Family Structures

Jin Xing's experiences challenge traditional notions of family. As a transgender woman, she redefined what family means to her, embracing a model that values love and support over conventional norms. Her relationship with her husband and children showcases that family can be constructed through bonds of affection and mutual respect, rather than strictly biological ties.

This notion resonates with *Postmodern Family Theory*, which argues that family structures are diverse and fluid, adapting to the needs and identities of their members. Jin Xing's family exemplifies this flexibility, demonstrating that love transcends traditional boundaries.

Resilience in the Face of Adversity

Jin Xing's journey has not been without its challenges. The societal stigma surrounding transgender individuals often extends into personal relationships, creating additional hurdles. She faced discrimination and misunderstanding, not only from the outside world but also within her personal circles.

However, her resilience has been a cornerstone of her narrative. The concept of *Post-Traumatic Growth* suggests that individuals can emerge stronger from adversity, developing new perspectives and capabilities. Jin Xing's ability to navigate these challenges has reinforced her belief in the power of love and commitment, teaching her that resilience is essential in maintaining healthy relationships.

The Role of Support Systems

Jin Xing's experiences highlight the critical role of support systems in navigating love and family dynamics. The unwavering support from her husband and friends has been instrumental in her journey toward self-acceptance and happiness.

This reflects the *Social Support Theory*, which posits that emotional, informational, and instrumental support from others can significantly impact an individual's well-being and coping mechanisms. Jin Xing's story illustrates how a robust support network can mitigate the effects of external pressures, providing a safe space for personal growth and exploration.

Embracing Vulnerability

Another lesson from Jin Xing's life is the strength found in vulnerability. In her relationships, she has learned that opening up about her fears and insecurities fosters deeper connections. This aligns with *Brené Brown's research on vulnerability*, which suggests that embracing vulnerability is essential for building trust and intimacy in relationships.

Jin Xing's willingness to share her journey, including the struggles and triumphs, has not only empowered her but also inspired others to embrace their vulnerabilities. She emphasizes that true love requires a willingness to be seen and accepted for who we are, flaws and all.

Celebrating Diversity in Love

Finally, Jin Xing's experiences underscore the beauty of diversity in love. Her relationship with her husband, who supports her identity and activism, exemplifies how love can flourish when individuals embrace each other's differences. This celebration of diversity resonates with the principles of *Intersectionality*, which recognizes that various social identities intersect to create unique experiences of privilege and oppression.

Jin Xing's family embodies this celebration, showcasing that love knows no bounds and can thrive in the most unexpected forms. Her life serves as a testament to the idea that love, in all its diversity, is a powerful force for change and acceptance.

Conclusion

In summary, Jin Xing's experiences in love and family impart valuable lessons on communication, resilience, and the importance of support systems. Her journey challenges societal norms, advocating for a broader understanding of family and love that transcends traditional boundaries. By embracing vulnerability and celebrating diversity, Jin Xing not only enriches her own life but also inspires others to pursue authentic connections in a world that often seeks to define love narrowly. Her story is a powerful reminder that love, in its many forms, can be a catalyst for personal and societal transformation.

The power of resilience and determination in personal relationships

In the intricate dance of human relationships, resilience and determination emerge as pivotal forces, particularly for individuals navigating the complexities of identity and societal expectations. For Jin Xing, a groundbreaking transgender icon, these attributes have not only shaped her personal journey but have also illuminated the path for countless others within the LGBTQ community.

Resilience, defined as the capacity to recover quickly from difficulties, plays a crucial role in sustaining relationships through adversity. It is the ability to bounce back from setbacks, adapt to change, and maintain a positive outlook despite challenges. Determination, on the other hand, embodies the resolve to pursue goals and overcome obstacles, often fueled by a deep-seated belief in oneself and one's values. Together, these qualities create a formidable foundation for nurturing personal relationships, especially in the face of societal stigma and discrimination.

Theoretical Framework

The concept of resilience can be understood through various psychological theories. One such framework is the *Resilience Theory*, which posits that resilience is not an inherent trait but rather a dynamic process influenced by individual, relational, and contextual factors. According to Rutter (1987), resilience involves a combination of protective factors—such as strong social support, positive self-image, and coping skills—that enable individuals to navigate adversity effectively.

In the context of personal relationships, the *Attachment Theory* also provides valuable insights. Developed by Bowlby (1969), this theory emphasizes the importance of secure attachments in fostering emotional bonds. Resilience in relationships often stems from the ability to communicate openly, express vulnerabilities, and seek support during challenging times. For Jin Xing, her journey towards self-acceptance and love has been deeply intertwined with her ability to forge strong, resilient connections with her family, friends, and partners.

Challenges in Personal Relationships

Jin Xing's path has not been without its challenges. As a transgender individual in a conservative society, she faced significant obstacles in her personal relationships. The societal stigma surrounding transgender identities often manifested in misunderstandings, prejudice, and even rejection from those closest to her. These experiences could have easily led to isolation and despair. However, it was her resilience and determination that allowed her to confront these challenges head-on.

For instance, Jin Xing's decision to undergo gender reassignment surgery was not merely a personal choice but a profound statement of her identity. This transition, while liberating, also brought about complications in her relationships. Friends and family members struggled to adapt to her new identity, leading to moments of tension and uncertainty. Yet, through open dialogue and a commitment to authenticity, Jin Xing demonstrated that resilience can transform potential rifts into opportunities for deeper understanding and connection.

Examples of Resilience in Relationships

A poignant example of resilience in Jin Xing's life is her relationship with her family. Initially, her parents grappled with their daughter's transition, torn between societal expectations and their love for her. Jin Xing's determination to educate them about her journey played a crucial role in fostering acceptance. By sharing her experiences, feelings, and the challenges she faced, she created a safe space for dialogue. This resilience not only strengthened their bond but also paved the way for her parents to become advocates for LGBTQ rights within their community.

Moreover, Jin Xing's romantic relationships have also exemplified the power of resilience. In navigating love as a transgender woman, she encountered partners who were supportive and understanding, as well as those who struggled with acceptance. Each relationship taught her invaluable lessons about self-worth and the importance of surrounding oneself with individuals who celebrate one's identity. Her determination to seek out and cultivate meaningful connections has led to a fulfilling personal life, where love and acceptance flourish.

The Broader Impact of Resilience

Jin Xing's journey highlights the broader implications of resilience and determination in personal relationships. Her story serves as a beacon of hope for others facing similar challenges, illustrating that adversity can be transformed into strength. The resilience she embodies encourages individuals within the LGBTQ community to embrace their identities and seek supportive relationships, regardless of societal pressures.

Furthermore, her advocacy work has underscored the importance of resilience not only at the personal level but also within the community. By sharing her narrative, Jin Xing has inspired countless individuals to stand firm in their truth and pursue relationships that honor their authentic selves. This ripple effect fosters a culture of acceptance and resilience, empowering others to navigate their journeys with courage and determination.

Conclusion

In conclusion, the power of resilience and determination in personal relationships cannot be overstated. For Jin Xing, these qualities have been instrumental in overcoming societal challenges, forging deep connections, and inspiring others within the LGBTQ community. Her journey exemplifies how resilience can transform adversity into strength, fostering love and acceptance in the face of obstacles. As we reflect on Jin Xing's experiences, we are reminded of the profound impact that resilience can have on our relationships, urging us to embrace our authentic selves and cultivate connections that uplift and empower us.

The Power of Resilience

Jin Xing's resilience in the face of adversity and criticism

Jin Xing's journey is a profound testament to the power of resilience, particularly in the face of relentless adversity and criticism. Resilience, defined as the capacity to recover quickly from difficulties, is often seen as a key trait in individuals who navigate challenging life circumstances. For Jin, this trait became essential as she faced societal rejection, professional obstacles, and personal struggles throughout her life.

From her early years in Shenyang, China, Jin Xing encountered significant challenges due to her identity as a transgender individual. The societal norms in China, particularly during the late 20th century, were steeped in traditional views on gender and sexuality. These norms often led to discrimination and prejudice against those who deviated from the conventional binary understanding of gender. Jin's determination to embrace her true self amidst such a backdrop exemplifies her resilience.

One of the critical theories that can be applied to understand Jin Xing's resilience is the *Transactional Model of Stress and Coping* proposed by Lazarus and Folkman. This model emphasizes the dynamic relationship between an individual and their environment, suggesting that resilience is not merely an inherent trait but a product of the interaction between personal resources and external challenges. According to this model, Jin's ability to cope with stress was influenced by her unique strengths, including her passion for dance, her supportive family, and her unwavering determination.

$$Coping = f(P, E) \tag{66}$$

Where $Coping$ is the individual's coping mechanism, P represents personal factors (such as resilience and support systems), and E denotes environmental factors (such as societal attitudes and discrimination).

Jin's early exposure to dance provided her with a creative outlet that not only allowed her to express herself but also served as a refuge from the harsh realities of her environment. Dance became a powerful tool for her to transform her pain into art, showcasing her resilience to the world. For instance, her performances often reflected her struggles and triumphs, allowing her to connect with audiences on a deeper emotional level. This connection not only validated her experiences but also challenged societal perceptions of gender and identity.

Despite her talent, Jin faced considerable criticism in the dance industry. As she rose to prominence, she encountered skepticism regarding her abilities and her identity. Critics often dismissed her achievements as mere tokens of diversity rather than recognizing her as a legitimate artist. This type of criticism could have easily deterred a less resilient individual, but Jin's response was to double down on her commitment to her craft. She utilized the criticism as motivation to excel further, demonstrating the concept of *post-traumatic growth*, where individuals emerge stronger from adverse experiences.

For example, during her time at the Shanghai Dance Academy, she faced not only rigorous training but also discrimination from peers and instructors who questioned her place in the world of ballet and contemporary dance. Instead of succumbing to these challenges, Jin transformed her experiences into a source of strength. She often stated, "Every challenge is an opportunity to prove that I belong." This mindset is a hallmark of resilient individuals who view adversity as a stepping stone rather than a stumbling block.

Furthermore, Jin's advocacy for LGBTQ rights emerged as a significant aspect of her resilience. By using her platform to speak out against discrimination and to promote acceptance, she not only fought for her own rights but also for those of countless others who faced similar struggles. Her involvement in activism can be analyzed through the lens of *Social Identity Theory*, which posits that individuals derive a sense of self from their group memberships. Jin's resilience was not only personal but also collective, as she sought to uplift the LGBTQ community in China, encouraging others to embrace their identities.

$$Self\ Concept = f(Group\ Identity, Personal\ Identity) \qquad (67)$$

Where $Self\ Concept$ is influenced by both $Group\ Identity$ (belonging to the LGBTQ community) and $Personal\ Identity$ (her journey as a transgender individual).

As she transitioned into a public figure, Jin's resilience was tested repeatedly. The media scrutiny, public judgment, and the pressure to conform to traditional gender roles were daunting. However, she faced these challenges head-on, often turning to her art as a means of expression and resistance. Her performances became a celebration of her identity, showcasing not just her technical prowess but also her emotional depth and authenticity.

One particularly poignant example of her resilience was her participation in the reality show "So You Think You Can Dance China." As a judge, Jin not only critiqued the contestants but also shared her own story of struggle and triumph, providing a platform for discussions about gender identity and acceptance. Her presence on the show was groundbreaking, as it challenged the status quo and provided representation for transgender individuals in mainstream media.

Jin's resilience in the face of adversity is also reflected in her ability to maintain her artistic integrity while navigating a complex and often hostile environment. She has spoken about the importance of staying true to oneself, stating, "Art is not just about beauty; it's about truth." This commitment to authenticity is a crucial aspect of resilience, as it requires individuals to confront their fears and stand firm in their beliefs despite external pressures.

In conclusion, Jin Xing's resilience in the face of adversity and criticism is a multifaceted phenomenon that encompasses her personal journey, her artistic expression, and her activism. Through the application of various psychological theories, we can better understand the dynamics of her resilience. Jin's story serves as an inspiration not only to the LGBTQ community but to anyone facing challenges in their pursuit of authenticity. Her ability to transform adversity into strength exemplifies the profound impact of resilience in shaping one's identity and legacy.

The importance of self-belief and determination

Self-belief and determination are critical components in the journey of any individual striving to overcome obstacles and achieve their goals. For Jin Xing, a pioneering transgender icon in China, these qualities were not just beneficial; they were essential for navigating a world fraught with challenges, prejudice, and societal expectations. This section explores the significance of self-belief and determination in Jin Xing's life, supported by relevant theories and examples.

Theoretical Framework

Self-belief, often referred to as self-efficacy, is rooted in Albert Bandura's social cognitive theory. Bandura posits that self-efficacy influences the choices individuals make, the effort they put forth, and their resilience in the face of adversity. According to Bandura (1997), self-efficacy is defined as:

$$\text{Self-efficacy} = \frac{\text{Successes}}{\text{Total Attempts}} \times 100 \tag{68}$$

This equation illustrates that as individuals experience success, their self-efficacy increases, leading to greater motivation and persistence. Conversely, repeated failures can diminish self-efficacy, resulting in a reluctance to pursue challenging tasks.

Determination, on the other hand, is the resolve to achieve a goal despite obstacles. It is closely related to grit, a term popularized by psychologist Angela Duckworth. Duckworth defines grit as:

$$\text{Grit} = \text{Passion} + \text{Perseverance} \tag{69}$$

This definition emphasizes that sustained effort and passion for long-term goals are critical for success. Together, self-belief and determination create a powerful synergy that propels individuals forward, enabling them to overcome challenges and achieve their aspirations.

Jin Xing's Journey

Jin Xing's early life in Shenyang, China, was marked by both talent and adversity. From a young age, she exhibited a passion for dance, which became her outlet for self-expression. However, the societal norms and expectations regarding gender roles posed significant challenges. As a transgender individual, Jin faced discrimination and prejudice that could have easily discouraged her.

Despite these challenges, Jin Xing's self-belief was unwavering. She embraced her identity and pursued her passion for dance with relentless determination. Her early successes in local dance competitions served as pivotal moments that reinforced her self-efficacy. Each victory, no matter how small, contributed to her growing confidence and belief in her abilities.

For example, Jin Xing's acceptance into the prestigious Shanghai Dance Academy was a testament to her talent and hard work. This opportunity not only validated her skills but also solidified her self-belief. As she navigated the rigorous training and faced discrimination within the dance industry, her determination propelled her to excel. She often recalled the mantra that guided her: "If you believe in yourself, you can achieve anything."

Overcoming Adversity

Jin Xing's determination was particularly evident during her transition and the subsequent challenges she faced. The decision to undergo gender reassignment surgery was not made lightly; it required immense courage and self-belief. In a society that often stigmatizes transgender individuals, Jin Xing's choice to live authentically was a bold statement of her determination.

Post-surgery, Jin Xing encountered a mix of support and backlash from the public. The media's scrutiny and societal judgment could have deterred many, but for Jin Xing, these challenges only fueled her resolve. She turned to her dance, using it as a platform to advocate for LGBTQ rights and visibility. Her performances became a celebration of her identity, showcasing the transformational power of self-belief.

The Role of Support Systems

While self-belief and determination are personal attributes, the role of support systems cannot be underestimated. Jin Xing's family and friends provided the encouragement and love necessary for her to embrace her true self. Their unwavering support bolstered her self-efficacy, allowing her to confront societal challenges head-on.

Research indicates that social support enhances self-efficacy and determination. According to a study by Taylor et al. (2004), individuals with strong social networks are more likely to persevere through difficulties and maintain a positive self-image. Jin Xing's experience aligns with this finding, as the love and acceptance from her community played a crucial role in her journey.

Lessons Learned

Jin Xing's story serves as a powerful reminder of the importance of self-belief and determination in the face of adversity. Her journey highlights several key lessons:

- **Embrace your identity:** Authenticity is a source of strength. By embracing her true self, Jin Xing inspired others to do the same.

- **Persevere through challenges:** Determination is essential for overcoming obstacles. Jin Xing's resilience in the face of discrimination exemplifies this principle.

+ **Seek support:** Building a strong support network enhances self-belief. Jin Xing's journey underscores the importance of surrounding oneself with individuals who uplift and empower.

+ **Celebrate successes:** Recognizing and celebrating achievements, no matter how small, reinforces self-efficacy and motivates continued effort.

Conclusion

In conclusion, self-belief and determination are vital attributes that can transform challenges into opportunities for growth and success. Jin Xing's life exemplifies the profound impact these qualities can have on an individual's journey. By believing in herself and remaining determined, she not only carved a path for her own success but also became a beacon of hope for others in the LGBTQ community. Her story serves as an inspiration, reminding us all of the power of self-belief and the importance of pursuing our passions, regardless of the obstacles we may face.

Jin Xing's commitment to her artistic vision and message

Jin Xing's journey as a dancer, choreographer, and LGBTQ activist is a testament to her unwavering commitment to her artistic vision and the powerful messages she conveys through her work. At the heart of Jin's artistry lies a deep understanding of the transformative power of dance as a medium for expression and social change. Her commitment is not merely to aesthetics but to a profound narrative that challenges societal norms and advocates for inclusivity and acceptance.

Art as a Medium for Social Change

Art has long been recognized as a vehicle for social change, and Jin Xing's work exemplifies this principle. Her performances often intertwine personal stories with broader societal themes, allowing her to communicate complex ideas about identity, gender, and the human experience. Through her choreography, Jin addresses the struggles faced by marginalized communities, particularly the LGBTQ community in China, where societal acceptance remains a significant challenge.

For instance, in her acclaimed work *The Butterfly Effect*, Jin utilizes the metaphor of the butterfly to explore themes of transformation and rebirth. The choreography depicts the journey of a caterpillar, symbolizing the struggles of individuals who feel trapped by societal expectations, ultimately emerging as a butterfly—an embodiment of freedom and self-acceptance. This narrative not only resonates with her personal experiences but also speaks to the broader LGBTQ struggle for recognition and rights.

Theoretical Frameworks

Jin's artistic vision can be analyzed through various theoretical frameworks, including feminist theory and queer theory. Feminist theory emphasizes the importance of representing women's experiences and challenging patriarchal structures, while queer theory interrogates the binary understanding of gender and sexuality. Jin's work intersects these theories, as she not only highlights the experiences of women in dance but also challenges traditional gender norms through her own identity as a transgender woman.

$$\text{Artistic Impact} = \text{Visibility} + \text{Representation} + \text{Empowerment} \quad (70)$$

In this equation, Jin's commitment to her artistic vision is reflected in her ability to create visibility for marginalized voices, provide representation for the LGBTQ community, and empower individuals to embrace their identities. Her performances serve as a platform for dialogue, encouraging audiences to confront their biases and reconsider their perceptions of gender and sexuality.

Challenges and Resilience

Despite her success, Jin Xing has faced numerous challenges in her pursuit of artistic expression. Discrimination and societal backlash are pervasive in a conservative society like China, where traditional views on gender and sexuality often prevail. Jin's commitment to her artistic vision has required immense resilience as she navigates these obstacles.

One notable example is her experience during the early years of her career when she faced rejection from mainstream dance companies due to her gender identity. Rather than succumbing to these challenges, Jin used them as fuel to create her own dance company, the *Shanghai Jin Xing Dance Theatre*. This move not only allowed her to showcase her artistry but also to create a safe space for other dancers who faced similar discrimination.

Artistic Collaborations and Advocacy

Jin's commitment extends beyond her own performances; she actively collaborates with other artists to amplify messages of inclusivity and acceptance. Her partnerships with renowned choreographers and performers serve as a testament to her belief in the power of collective creativity. These collaborations often result in innovative works that challenge traditional norms and inspire audiences.

Moreover, Jin's role as a judge on *So You Think You Can Dance China* has further solidified her commitment to advocacy. Through her platform, she champions diverse talents and encourages contestants to express their authentic selves, fostering an environment where individuality is celebrated. Her presence on the show has significantly increased the visibility of LGBTQ issues in mainstream media, demonstrating the potential of art to drive social change.

The Legacy of Jin Xing's Vision

The legacy of Jin Xing's commitment to her artistic vision and message is profound. By intertwining her personal journey with her artistry, she has created a powerful narrative that resonates with individuals across the globe. Her work serves as a reminder of the importance of embracing one's true self and the transformative power of art in fostering understanding and acceptance.

As Jin continues to evolve as an artist and activist, her commitment to her vision remains steadfast. She embodies the belief that art can transcend boundaries, challenge societal norms, and inspire change. Jin Xing's journey is not just about personal success; it is a call to action for others to embrace their identities and advocate for a more inclusive world.

In conclusion, Jin Xing's commitment to her artistic vision and message is a multifaceted journey that intertwines personal and societal narratives. Through her work, she challenges conventions, inspires resilience, and advocates for the rights of the LGBTQ community. Her legacy is a testament to the power of art as a catalyst for social change, and her story continues to inspire future generations of artists and activists alike.

The impact of Jin Xing's resilience on the LGBTQ community

Jin Xing's journey is emblematic of the struggles and triumphs faced by many within the LGBTQ community, particularly in conservative societies where acceptance remains a distant dream. Her resilience not only paved the way for her personal success but also served as a beacon of hope and inspiration for countless others navigating similar paths.

Resilience, in psychological terms, refers to the ability of individuals to adapt positively in the face of adversity, trauma, or significant stress. According to the American Psychological Association, resilience involves behaviors, thoughts, and actions that can be learned and developed in anyone. Jin Xing's story illustrates this concept vividly, as she faced numerous challenges, including societal rejection, discrimination, and personal struggles with her identity.

$$R = \frac{C}{A} \tag{71}$$

Where: - R is resilience, - C is coping strategies, - A is adverse circumstances.

This equation highlights that resilience can be enhanced through effective coping strategies, which Jin Xing exemplified throughout her life. She transformed her pain into art, using dance as a medium to express her identity and advocate for LGBTQ rights.

One of the most significant impacts of Jin Xing's resilience is her role in increasing visibility for transgender individuals in China. Her success story challenges the prevailing stereotypes and misconceptions surrounding gender identity. By publicly embracing her identity and sharing her experiences, Jin Xing has contributed to a broader understanding of the complexities of gender and sexuality. This visibility is crucial, as studies show that increased representation in the media can lead to greater acceptance and understanding within society.

For instance, a survey conducted by the Pew Research Center in 2020 found that individuals who are exposed to LGBTQ representation in media are more likely to support LGBTQ rights. Jin Xing's appearances on television, particularly as a judge on "So You Think You Can Dance China," have provided a platform for discussions about gender identity and acceptance, fostering a more inclusive environment.

Moreover, Jin Xing's resilience has inspired other LGBTQ individuals to embrace their identities and advocate for their rights. Her story resonates with many who feel marginalized or oppressed, demonstrating that it is possible to overcome societal barriers. For example, young LGBTQ activists in China have cited Jin Xing as a role model, drawing strength from her journey as they fight for their rights and visibility.

In addition to inspiring individuals, Jin Xing's resilience has mobilized community organizations and initiatives aimed at supporting LGBTQ rights. Her advocacy work has led to the establishment of support networks for transgender individuals, providing resources and safe spaces for those in need. The creation of such networks is vital, as research indicates that access to support systems significantly enhances the mental health and well-being of LGBTQ individuals.

Furthermore, Jin Xing's impact extends beyond the borders of China. Her story has gained international attention, contributing to the global discourse on LGBTQ rights. By sharing her experiences on international platforms, she has highlighted the struggles faced by LGBTQ individuals in authoritarian regimes, advocating for global solidarity in the fight for equality.

In conclusion, Jin Xing's resilience has had a profound impact on the LGBTQ community, both in China and globally. Her ability to confront adversity and use her platform for advocacy has not only transformed her life but has also inspired countless others to embrace their identities and fight for their rights. As the LGBTQ movement continues to evolve, Jin Xing's legacy serves as a reminder of the power of resilience in the face of oppression and the importance of visibility in creating a more inclusive society.

Lessons to be learned from Jin Xing's journey of resilience and authenticity

Jin Xing's journey is not merely a chronicle of personal triumph; it embodies a profound narrative of resilience and authenticity that resonates deeply within the LGBTQ community and beyond. Her life story offers invaluable lessons for individuals striving to navigate the complexities of identity, societal expectations, and personal aspirations.

1. Embracing Authenticity

At the heart of Jin Xing's journey is the unwavering commitment to authenticity. The act of embracing one's true self, despite societal pressures and cultural norms, is a powerful lesson. Research in psychology, particularly the theory of self-determination by Deci and Ryan (1985), posits that authenticity is closely linked to well-being and personal growth. Jin Xing's courage to live openly as a transgender woman in a conservative society exemplifies the importance of self-acceptance.

$$\text{Well-being} = f(\text{Authenticity}, \text{Self-acceptance}) \qquad (72)$$

This equation suggests that an increase in authenticity and self-acceptance leads to higher levels of well-being. Jin Xing's journey illustrates this relationship, as her self-acceptance catalyzed her rise to prominence, transforming her struggles into strength.

2. Resilience in Adversity

Jin Xing's life is a testament to the power of resilience. Resilience theory emphasizes the ability to bounce back from adversity, adapting positively to challenges. Jin Xing faced discrimination and societal rejection, yet she used these experiences as stepping stones rather than stumbling blocks.

Psychologist Ann Masten (2001) describes resilience as "ordinary magic," highlighting that resilience is often found in everyday processes and interactions. Jin Xing's ability to harness her experiences, turning pain into purpose, exemplifies this notion.

$$\text{Resilience} = \text{Adaptation} + \text{Growth} \tag{73}$$

In her case, adaptation involved navigating the complexities of her identity in a challenging environment, while growth manifested in her artistic achievements and advocacy for LGBTQ rights.

3. The Power of Community Support

Throughout her journey, Jin Xing emphasized the significance of community support. Social support theory indicates that having a network of supportive relationships can buffer against the negative effects of stress and adversity. Jin Xing's family, friends, and allies played crucial roles in her journey, providing emotional support and encouragement.

A notable example is her decision to undergo gender reassignment surgery, which, while deeply personal, was bolstered by the backing of her loved ones. This illustrates the idea that resilience is not solely an individual trait but can be cultivated within supportive communities.

$$\text{Resilience}_{individual} = \text{Resilience}_{community} + \text{Support} \tag{74}$$

This equation illustrates that individual resilience is enhanced by the resilience of the community and the support it provides.

4. The Role of Advocacy and Activism

Jin Xing's journey also highlights the importance of advocacy and activism. Her transition from a dancer to a vocal advocate for LGBTQ rights demonstrates how personal experiences can fuel broader societal change. The theory of collective efficacy, as described by Bandura (1997), suggests that when individuals believe they can work together to achieve a common goal, they are more likely to succeed.

Jin Xing's platform allowed her to amplify the voices of marginalized individuals, fostering a sense of collective identity and purpose within the LGBTQ community.

$$\text{Collective Efficacy} = \text{Shared Goals} + \text{Mutual Support} \tag{75}$$

Jin Xing's activism embodies this equation, as she galvanized support for LGBTQ rights in China, demonstrating how individual journeys can contribute to collective movements.

5. The Importance of Storytelling

Finally, Jin Xing's life underscores the transformative power of storytelling. Her narrative not only serves as a source of inspiration but also as a tool for education and awareness. The narrative identity theory posits that individuals construct their identities through the stories they tell about themselves.

By sharing her experiences, Jin Xing challenges stereotypes and fosters understanding, paving the way for greater acceptance of LGBTQ individuals.

$$\text{Identity} = f(\text{Narrative}) + \text{Experience} \tag{76}$$

This equation illustrates how identity is shaped by both personal narratives and lived experiences, reinforcing the idea that storytelling is a vital component of resilience and authenticity.

Conclusion

In conclusion, Jin Xing's journey of resilience and authenticity provides profound lessons for individuals facing their own struggles. Embracing authenticity, cultivating resilience, seeking community support, engaging in advocacy, and harnessing the power of storytelling are all crucial elements in the quest for personal and societal transformation. Her story serves as a beacon of hope, illustrating that through resilience and authenticity, individuals can not only overcome adversity but also inspire change within their communities and beyond.

Empowering individuals to overcome obstacles and achieve their dreams

Empowerment is a multifaceted concept that encompasses the ability to act, make choices, and influence one's environment. In the context of Jin Xing's journey, empowerment plays a crucial role in enabling individuals to overcome personal and societal obstacles. The process of empowerment involves several key components, including self-awareness, resilience, and the development of skills necessary to navigate challenges.

Theoretical Frameworks of Empowerment

One of the foundational theories of empowerment is the *Psychological Empowerment Theory*, which posits that empowerment involves four dimensions: meaning, competence, self-determination, and impact [1].

$$E = f(M, C, SD, I) \tag{77}$$

where:

- E represents empowerment,

- M is the meaning derived from one's work or life,

- C is the competence to perform tasks,

- SD is the self-determination in making choices, and

- I is the perceived impact on the environment.

This theoretical framework can be applied to understand how Jin Xing's experiences have fostered empowerment not only for herself but also for others in the LGBTQ community.

Overcoming Personal Obstacles

Jin Xing's journey is a testament to the power of resilience and determination. From her early years in a conservative society, she faced numerous obstacles, including societal rejection and discrimination. However, she transformed these challenges into stepping stones for personal growth. For instance, her decision to pursue dance despite societal expectations exemplifies how individuals can harness their passions to overcome adversity.

Jin's story illustrates the importance of self-awareness in the empowerment process. By understanding her identity and embracing her passion for dance, she was able to carve out a space for herself in a predominantly heteronormative environment. This aligns with the concept of *self-efficacy*, as proposed by Bandura [2], which emphasizes the belief in one's ability to succeed in specific situations.

$$SE = \frac{B + C + E}{3} \tag{78}$$

where:

- SE is self-efficacy,

+ *B* represents past experiences of success,

+ *C* is the level of confidence in one's abilities, and

+ *E* is the encouragement received from others.

By cultivating self-efficacy, individuals can empower themselves to take risks and pursue their dreams, much like Jin did when she entered the competitive world of dance.

Building Resilience

Resilience is another critical component of empowerment. It refers to the ability to bounce back from setbacks and maintain a positive outlook in the face of adversity. Jin Xing's resilience is evident in her ability to navigate the challenges of transitioning in a conservative society. Her journey serves as an inspiration for others, demonstrating that resilience can be cultivated through various strategies, including:

+ Developing a strong support network,

+ Practicing self-care and mindfulness,

+ Setting realistic goals, and

+ Learning from failures.

For example, after undergoing gender reassignment surgery, Jin faced significant public scrutiny. Instead of succumbing to the negativity, she used her platform to advocate for LGBTQ rights, thereby turning her personal struggles into a source of strength and motivation for others.

Creating Opportunities for Others

Empowerment also involves creating opportunities for others to succeed. Jin Xing's establishment of the Shanghai Jin Xing Dance Theatre is a prime example of how individuals can leverage their success to uplift their communities. By providing a platform for aspiring dancers, particularly those from marginalized backgrounds, she is actively participating in the cycle of empowerment.

The concept of *collective empowerment* emphasizes that when individuals come together to support one another, they can achieve greater outcomes than they would alone [3]. This is particularly relevant in the context of the LGBTQ community, where collective action can lead to increased visibility and advocacy for rights.

Conclusion

In conclusion, empowering individuals to overcome obstacles and achieve their dreams is a multifaceted process that involves self-awareness, resilience, and the creation of opportunities. Jin Xing's journey serves as a powerful illustration of how personal struggles can be transformed into a source of strength, not only for oneself but also for the broader community. By fostering an environment of support and understanding, we can empower individuals to embrace their identities and pursue their passions, ultimately leading to a more inclusive and equitable society.

Bibliography

[1] Spreitzer, G. (1995). Psychological Empowerment in the Workplace: Dimensions, Measurement, and Validation. *Academy of Management Journal*, 38(5), 1442-1465.

[2] Bandura, A. (1997). Self-efficacy: The exercise of control. *W.H. Freeman and Company*.

[3] Zimmerman, M. A. (2000). Empowerment Theory: Psychological, Organizational, and Community Levels of Analysis. In *Handbook of Community Psychology* (pp. 43-63). Springer.

The power of resilience in inspiring social change

Resilience is a fundamental characteristic that empowers individuals to navigate adversity, overcome challenges, and emerge stronger. In the context of social change, resilience not only aids personal growth but also serves as a catalyst for collective transformation. This section explores the profound impact of resilience, particularly as exemplified by Jin Xing's journey, and how it inspires others to advocate for social justice and equality.

Understanding Resilience

Resilience can be defined as the ability to recover from setbacks, adapt well to change, and keep going in the face of adversity. The American Psychological Association (APA) defines resilience as the process of adapting well in the face of adversity, trauma, tragedy, threats, or significant sources of stress [?]. This adaptability is crucial for individuals facing societal challenges, particularly in marginalized communities.

Theoretical frameworks such as the Resilience Theory emphasize the dynamic interplay between individual characteristics and environmental factors. This theory posits that resilience is not merely an inherent trait but a process influenced by external support systems, community resources, and cultural contexts [?].

The Role of Resilience in Social Movements

Resilience plays a critical role in social movements by enabling activists to persist despite systemic barriers and opposition. For instance, the LGBTQ movement has faced significant challenges, including societal stigma, legal discrimination, and violence. Activists like Jin Xing exemplify how resilience can galvanize efforts to promote equality and acceptance.

Jin Xing's journey is a testament to the power of resilience. Born in a conservative society where gender nonconformity was often met with hostility, she faced numerous obstacles, including discrimination and personal turmoil. However, her determination to embrace her identity and pursue her passion for dance became a source of inspiration for many. By transforming her struggles into a platform for advocacy, she demonstrated that resilience can lead to profound social change.

Examples of Resilience Inspiring Change

One notable example of resilience inspiring social change is the Stonewall Riots of 1969, which marked a turning point in the LGBTQ rights movement. The riots were sparked by a police raid on the Stonewall Inn, a gay bar in New York City. The resilience of the LGBTQ community in standing up against oppression ignited a movement that would lead to significant advancements in rights and recognition. The activism that followed, fueled by the collective resilience of individuals who refused to be silenced, laid the groundwork for future generations to advocate for equality.

Similarly, Jin Xing's resilience in the face of societal prejudice has inspired countless individuals within the LGBTQ community in China and beyond. By publicly sharing her story and advocating for LGBTQ rights, she has become a symbol of hope and empowerment. Her journey illustrates how personal resilience can resonate with others, encouraging them to embrace their identities and fight for their rights.

The Impact of Resilience on Community Empowerment

Resilience not only empowers individuals but also strengthens communities. When individuals within a community exhibit resilience, it fosters a collective spirit that can lead to social change. This phenomenon is evident in various grassroots movements that have emerged in response to injustice.

For instance, community organizations that support LGBTQ youth often emphasize resilience-building as a core component of their programs. By providing safe spaces and resources, these organizations help individuals develop coping strategies and foster a sense of belonging. This, in turn, cultivates a resilient community capable of advocating for change.

The concept of resilience is also reflected in the work of organizations like The Trevor Project, which provides crisis intervention and suicide prevention services to LGBTQ youth. Their initiatives focus on empowering young people to navigate challenges and build resilience, ultimately equipping them to advocate for their rights and well-being.

Challenges to Resilience and the Path Forward

While resilience is a powerful force for social change, it is essential to recognize the challenges that individuals face in cultivating resilience. Systemic barriers, such as discrimination, lack of access to resources, and societal stigma, can hinder an individual's ability to bounce back from adversity.

Addressing these challenges requires a multifaceted approach that includes policy change, community support, and education. Advocacy for mental health resources, inclusive policies, and awareness campaigns can create an environment where resilience can flourish.

Moreover, fostering resilience within marginalized communities necessitates a commitment to allyship and solidarity. Allies play a crucial role in amplifying the voices of those who may be struggling to be heard, providing support, and advocating for systemic change.

Conclusion

In conclusion, the power of resilience is a transformative force in inspiring social change. Jin Xing's journey exemplifies how personal resilience can lead to collective empowerment and advocacy for marginalized communities. By understanding and nurturing resilience, individuals and communities can overcome adversity and drive meaningful change. As we continue to confront societal challenges, it is vital to recognize the role of resilience in fostering hope, solidarity, and progress toward a more inclusive future.

The role of support systems and allies in fostering resilience

Resilience, often defined as the ability to bounce back from adversity, is significantly influenced by the presence of support systems and allies. For individuals like Jin Xing, who navigate the complexities of identity and societal expectations, these networks play a crucial role in fostering resilience. This section explores the theoretical underpinnings of support systems, the challenges faced by LGBTQ individuals, and the transformative impact of allies on resilience.

Theoretical Framework

The concept of resilience is rooted in various psychological theories. One prominent model is the **Ecological Systems Theory** proposed by Urie Bronfenbrenner, which emphasizes the importance of different environmental systems in shaping individual development. According to this theory, resilience is not merely an individual trait but is significantly affected by interpersonal relationships and community support.

Let us denote resilience as R, which can be influenced by multiple factors, including:

$$R = f(S, A, E)$$

Where: - S represents the strength of support systems, - A indicates the presence of allies, - E denotes the environmental factors affecting the individual.

This equation illustrates that resilience is a function of both internal and external influences, highlighting the importance of a supportive network.

Challenges Faced by LGBTQ Individuals

LGBTQ individuals often encounter unique challenges that can hinder their resilience. These include:

+ **Discrimination and Stigma:** Many LGBTQ individuals face societal discrimination, which can lead to feelings of isolation and low self-esteem.

+ **Family Rejection:** Lack of acceptance from family members can exacerbate feelings of alienation, making it difficult for individuals to seek help.

+ **Mental Health Issues:** Higher rates of mental health issues, such as anxiety and depression, are prevalent in the LGBTQ community due to societal pressures.

These challenges can create a feedback loop where the absence of support leads to decreased resilience, further perpetuating the cycle of adversity.

The Transformative Impact of Support Systems

Support systems, which include family, friends, community organizations, and mental health professionals, provide essential emotional and practical assistance. Research indicates that individuals with strong support systems are more likely to exhibit resilience in the face of adversity. For example, a study by [?] found that social connections significantly contribute to physical and mental well-being, emphasizing the protective role of social support.

$$R_{\text{high}} = S_{\text{strong}} + A_{\text{present}} + E_{\text{supportive}} \tag{79}$$

Where R_{high} indicates high resilience, S_{strong} represents strong support systems, A_{present} indicates the presence of allies, and $E_{\text{supportive}}$ denotes a supportive environment.

The Role of Allies

Allies play a pivotal role in enhancing resilience among LGBTQ individuals. Allies are individuals who may not identify as LGBTQ but actively support LGBTQ rights and inclusion. Their advocacy can significantly influence the resilience of LGBTQ individuals by:

- **Providing Validation:** Allies help validate the experiences of LGBTQ individuals, reinforcing their identities and fostering self-acceptance.

- **Advocating for Change:** By challenging discriminatory practices and promoting inclusivity, allies create a more supportive environment for LGBTQ individuals.

- **Offering Emotional Support:** Allies can provide a safe space for LGBTQ individuals to express their feelings and navigate their challenges.

The presence of allies can be quantified in terms of their impact on resilience:

$$R = S + \alpha A \tag{80}$$

Where α is a coefficient representing the strength of the ally's support, demonstrating that allies significantly enhance the overall resilience of LGBTQ individuals.

Examples of Support Systems and Allies in Action

Jin Xing's journey exemplifies the critical role of support systems and allies. Throughout her career, she has often spoken about the unwavering support from her family and friends, which bolstered her confidence and determination. For instance, her decision to pursue dance as a career was met with encouragement from her parents, who recognized her passion and talent despite societal norms.

Additionally, Jin Xing has become an ally herself, using her platform to advocate for LGBTQ rights in China. Her visibility as a transgender icon has inspired countless individuals to embrace their identities and seek support. Through her dance company, she has created a community that fosters inclusivity and acceptance, demonstrating the power of support systems in action.

Conclusion

In conclusion, the role of support systems and allies in fostering resilience cannot be overstated. For individuals like Jin Xing, these networks provide the necessary emotional and practical support to navigate the challenges of identity and societal expectations. By understanding the theoretical frameworks surrounding resilience and recognizing the importance of allies, we can create a more supportive environment for LGBTQ individuals, ultimately empowering them to thrive in the face of adversity. As we reflect on Jin Xing's journey, we are reminded that resilience is not solely an individual endeavor; it is a collective effort that requires the active participation of allies and support systems.

Jin Xing's lasting impact on the LGBTQ movement

Jin Xing stands as a monumental figure in the LGBTQ movement, not merely as a performer but as a beacon of hope and resilience for many. Her journey, characterized by trials and triumphs, has significantly influenced the perception and acceptance of transgender individuals in China and beyond. This section delves into the multifaceted impact of Jin Xing on the LGBTQ movement, focusing on her role in advocacy, representation, and the broader cultural discourse surrounding gender and sexuality.

Advocacy and Activism

Jin Xing's advocacy for LGBTQ rights is rooted in her personal experiences and public persona. By openly discussing her journey as a transgender woman, she has brought visibility to issues that were often shrouded in stigma and silence. Her participation in various LGBTQ campaigns and events has not only raised awareness but has also galvanized support for legal reforms aimed at protecting the rights of LGBTQ individuals in China.

The theoretical framework of social movements, particularly the resource mobilization theory, explains how individuals like Jin Xing leverage their resources—such as fame, talent, and platforms—to mobilize support and drive change. According to this theory, the success of social movements often hinges on the ability to access resources and networks that can amplify their message. Jin Xing has effectively utilized her celebrity status to advocate for LGBTQ rights, drawing attention to the challenges faced by the community and fostering a sense of solidarity.

Representation in Media

Jin Xing's influence extends to the media landscape, where her presence has played a crucial role in reshaping narratives around transgender identities. By serving as a judge on "So You Think You Can Dance China," she has challenged traditional gender norms and provided a platform for aspiring LGBTQ artists. This visibility is essential, as research indicates that representation in media can significantly affect public attitudes towards marginalized groups.

The cultivation theory posits that prolonged exposure to media representations shapes viewers' perceptions of reality. Jin Xing's visibility in mainstream media has contributed to a gradual shift in public perception, fostering a more inclusive understanding of gender diversity. Her performances and media appearances have not only entertained but have also educated audiences, breaking down stereotypes and fostering empathy.

Cultural Impact and Social Change

Jin Xing's impact on the LGBTQ movement is also evident in the cultural shifts she has inspired. Her work transcends the boundaries of dance and performance, touching on broader social issues such as gender identity, acceptance, and the fight against discrimination. By advocating for LGBTQ rights within the context of Chinese culture, she has navigated the complexities of a conservative society, pushing for change from within.

The concept of intersectionality, introduced by Kimberlé Crenshaw, is pertinent here. Jin Xing's activism highlights the interconnectedness of various forms of oppression, including those based on gender identity, sexual orientation, and cultural norms. Her efforts have sparked conversations about the need for a more inclusive approach to LGBTQ rights that considers the unique challenges faced by individuals in different cultural contexts.

Legacy and Future Directions

The legacy of Jin Xing's activism is profound. She has inspired a new generation of LGBTQ activists and artists, encouraging them to embrace their identities and fight for their rights. The ripple effect of her work can be seen in the increasing visibility of LGBTQ individuals in various sectors, including the arts, media, and politics.

In conclusion, Jin Xing's lasting impact on the LGBTQ movement is characterized by her advocacy, representation, and cultural influence. Her journey serves as a powerful reminder of the importance of visibility and the need for continued efforts to achieve equality and acceptance for all individuals, regardless of their gender identity or sexual orientation. As society progresses towards greater inclusivity, Jin Xing's contributions will undoubtedly resonate for years to come, inspiring future generations to continue the fight for LGBTQ rights and representation.

$$\text{Impact} = \text{Visibility} \times \text{Advocacy} \times \text{Cultural Change} \qquad (81)$$

The call to embrace resilience in the face of adversity

In a world where challenges can often feel insurmountable, the story of Jin Xing serves as a powerful testament to the importance of resilience. Resilience, defined as the capacity to recover quickly from difficulties, is not merely a trait but a crucial skill that can be cultivated through experience and determination. This section explores the multifaceted nature of resilience, drawing on psychological theories, real-world examples, and the inspiring journey of Jin Xing herself.

Theoretical Framework of Resilience

Psychological resilience has been extensively studied, with various models attempting to explain how individuals cope with stress and adversity. One prominent theory is the **Resilience Theory**, which posits that resilience is not an inherent quality but rather a dynamic process influenced by personal, social, and environmental factors. According to Rutter (1985), resilience arises from the interaction of risk and protective factors, emphasizing the role of supportive relationships and community resources in fostering resilience.

The **Broaden-and-Build Theory** of positive emotions, proposed by Fredrickson (2001), further elucidates how resilience can be enhanced through positive experiences. This theory suggests that positive emotions broaden one's awareness and encourage novel, varied, and exploratory thoughts and actions, which can build personal resources over time. For individuals like Jin Xing, cultivating positive emotions through dance and artistic expression has been a pivotal aspect of her resilience.

Challenges and Adversity

Jin Xing's journey has been fraught with challenges, particularly as a transgender woman in a conservative society. The societal stigma and discrimination faced by LGBTQ individuals can lead to significant psychological distress. According to the **Minority Stress Theory**, individuals from marginalized groups experience unique stressors that can impact their mental health, including prejudice, discrimination, and internalized homophobia (Meyer, 2003).

For Jin Xing, the challenges were not just external but also internal. Her struggle with gender identity, compounded by societal expectations, created a tumultuous emotional landscape. Yet, it was through confronting these adversities that she developed her resilience. The decision to undergo gender reassignment surgery was a pivotal moment in her life, symbolizing her commitment to authenticity and self-acceptance.

Examples of Resilience

Resilience manifests in various forms, and Jin Xing's life is filled with examples of how she embraced adversity. One notable instance occurred during her early career when she faced rejection and discrimination in the dance industry. Instead of succumbing to despair, Jin Xing channeled her frustration into her performances, using dance as a medium for self-expression and empowerment.

Her breakthrough performance, which showcased her unique style and narrative, not only launched her career but also challenged societal norms. This moment exemplifies the concept of **post-traumatic growth**, where individuals find new meaning and purpose following adversity (Tedeschi & Calhoun, 1996). Jin Xing's ability to transform her struggles into artistic triumphs highlights the potential for resilience to foster creativity and innovation.

The Role of Support Systems

Resilience is often bolstered by the presence of supportive relationships. Jin Xing's journey illustrates the importance of community and familial support in overcoming adversity. Her family's acceptance and encouragement played a crucial role in her ability to embrace her true self. Research indicates that strong social support networks can mitigate the effects of stress and enhance resilience (Cohen & Wills, 1985).

In her advocacy work, Jin Xing has also fostered a sense of community among LGBTQ individuals, creating safe spaces for dialogue and support. This collective resilience not only empowers individuals but also strengthens the broader movement for LGBTQ rights in China.

A Call to Action

Jin Xing's story serves as a clarion call to embrace resilience in the face of adversity. It challenges individuals to recognize their capacity for growth and transformation, even in the darkest of times. As she once stated, "It is not the challenges we face that define us, but how we respond to them."

To cultivate resilience, individuals can adopt several strategies:

- **Foster Positive Relationships:** Build and maintain supportive relationships that provide encouragement and understanding.

- **Embrace Change:** View challenges as opportunities for growth and learning rather than insurmountable obstacles.

- **Practice Self-Compassion:** Be kind to oneself during difficult times, recognizing that struggles are a part of the human experience.

- **Engage in Creative Expression:** Use art, dance, or other forms of expression as a means to process emotions and experiences.

- **Seek Professional Support:** Don't hesitate to reach out for help from mental health professionals when needed.

In conclusion, the call to embrace resilience is not just a personal journey but a collective movement towards a more inclusive and accepting society. Jin Xing's life exemplifies the power of resilience to inspire change, challenge societal norms, and foster a sense of hope. As we navigate our own adversities, let us remember that resilience is not a destination but a continuous journey, one that can lead to profound personal and societal transformation.

Legacy and Future Ventures

Jin Xing's enduring legacy in the world of dance and activism

Jin Xing, a luminary in the realms of both dance and LGBTQ activism, has established a legacy that resonates deeply within these interconnected spheres. Her journey is not just a tale of personal triumph; it is a narrative that encapsulates the struggles and victories of marginalized communities, particularly in conservative societies like China.

At the heart of Jin Xing's legacy is her innovative approach to dance, which transcends traditional boundaries and incorporates elements of various styles, including contemporary, ballet, and traditional Chinese dance. This fusion not only showcases her versatility as a dancer but also serves as a metaphor for her life—a harmonious blend of identities and experiences. Jin Xing's choreography often reflects themes of identity, transformation, and resilience, resonating with audiences on a profound level.

One of the most significant aspects of her legacy is her role as a pioneer for transgender representation in the performing arts. Prior to Jin Xing's emergence, transgender individuals were largely invisible in the Chinese entertainment industry. Through her talent and tenacity, she has paved the way for greater visibility and acceptance of diverse gender identities within the cultural landscape.

The theory of *intersectionality*, coined by Kimberlé Crenshaw, is instrumental in understanding Jin Xing's impact. Intersectionality posits that individuals experience multiple, overlapping social identities that contribute to unique experiences of oppression or privilege. Jin Xing's identity as a transgender woman, coupled with her status as a Chinese artist, places her at the intersection of various social dynamics. This complexity enriches her work and advocacy, allowing her to address not only LGBTQ issues but also broader societal challenges, such as gender inequality and cultural conservatism.

Jin Xing's activism extends beyond her artistic contributions; she has become a vocal advocate for LGBTQ rights in China. Her public persona as a judge on the popular television show *So You Think You Can Dance China* has provided her with a platform to challenge stereotypes and promote inclusivity. By embracing her identity and using her influence, she has sparked conversations around gender and sexuality that were previously considered taboo in Chinese society.

However, the path has not been devoid of challenges. Jin Xing has faced significant backlash and discrimination, both personally and professionally. These experiences highlight the ongoing struggles faced by LGBTQ individuals in China, where societal norms often clash with the pursuit of individual identity. Despite these obstacles, Jin Xing's resilience shines through, serving as an inspiration for many. Her ability to navigate these challenges while remaining authentic to herself exemplifies the power of perseverance.

In terms of measurable impact, Jin Xing's legacy can be seen in the increasing representation of LGBTQ individuals in the arts and media in China. Her success has inspired a new generation of artists and activists who are now more willing to embrace their identities and advocate for change. For instance, initiatives like the *Beijing Queer Film Festival* and the *Shanghai Pride* event have gained momentum, providing platforms for LGBTQ voices to be heard and celebrated.

Moreover, Jin Xing's influence extends internationally, as she has participated in various global forums and dance festivals, thereby fostering cultural exchange and understanding. Her work challenges the Western perception of gender and sexuality, illustrating the complexities of these concepts in different cultural contexts. This cross-cultural dialogue is essential for fostering global solidarity in the fight for LGBTQ rights.

The mathematical model of cultural diffusion can be applied to analyze Jin Xing's impact on LGBTQ activism. The equation for cultural diffusion can be represented as:

$$D(t) = D_0 \cdot e^{rt}$$

Where: - $D(t)$ is the quantity of culture or idea at time t, - D_0 is the initial quantity of culture or idea, - r is the rate of diffusion, - t is time.

In Jin Xing's case, her initial presence in the dance community (D_0) has exponentially increased over time (t) due to her advocacy and visibility, leading to a significant rise in acceptance and representation of LGBTQ individuals in China ($D(t)$).

In conclusion, Jin Xing's enduring legacy in the world of dance and activism is characterized by her groundbreaking contributions to both fields. Through her artistry, she has challenged societal norms and inspired countless individuals to embrace their true selves. Her story is a testament to the transformative power of art and the importance of representation in fostering social change. As she continues to advocate for LGBTQ rights and promote inclusivity, Jin Xing remains a beacon of hope and resilience, leaving an indelible mark on the cultural landscape of China and beyond.

The future of LGBTQ rights in China and Jin Xing's role in shaping it

The landscape of LGBTQ rights in China is at a critical juncture, influenced by a myriad of social, cultural, and political factors. As one of the foremost figures in the LGBTQ community, Jin Xing has played a pivotal role in advocating for rights and visibility, paving the way for future generations. This section explores the trajectory of LGBTQ rights in China, the challenges that remain, and how Jin Xing's influence can shape a more inclusive future.

Current State of LGBTQ Rights in China

In recent years, there has been a notable shift in the public perception of LGBTQ individuals in China. While homosexuality was decriminalized in 1997 and removed from the list of mental disorders in 2001, societal acceptance remains limited. According to a 2021 survey conducted by the Chinese Academy of Social Sciences, approximately 70% of respondents still believe that LGBTQ identities are "abnormal" or "perverse" [?]. This societal stigma is compounded by government regulations that restrict LGBTQ advocacy and limit the visibility of LGBTQ issues in media.

Despite these challenges, there are signs of progress. The rise of social media platforms has enabled LGBTQ activists to connect, share their stories, and mobilize for change. Organizations such as the Beijing LGBT Center and the Shanghai Queer Film Festival have emerged, providing resources and support for the community. However, these organizations often operate in a precarious environment, facing censorship and crackdowns from authorities.

Jin Xing's Advocacy and Influence

Jin Xing's journey from a dancer to a cultural icon has positioned her as a beacon of hope for many in the LGBTQ community. Her visibility as a transgender woman in the entertainment industry challenges traditional gender norms and provides representation for marginalized voices. As the founder of the Shanghai Jin Xing Dance Theatre, she has created a platform that not only showcases her artistic vision but also advocates for inclusivity and acceptance.

One of Jin Xing's most significant contributions has been her ability to bridge cultural divides. Through her work on television, particularly as a judge on "So You Think You Can Dance China," she has brought LGBTQ issues into the mainstream conversation. Her candid discussions about gender identity and sexuality have sparked dialogue and encouraged acceptance among audiences who may have previously held prejudiced views.

Theoretical Framework: Social Change and Activism

To understand Jin Xing's impact, it is essential to consider the theoretical frameworks surrounding social change and activism. The Social Movement Theory posits that collective action can lead to significant societal transformations. According to Tilly and Tarrow (2015), social movements are driven by grievances, organizational capacity, and political opportunities. Jin Xing embodies these elements as she utilizes her platform to articulate the grievances of the LGBTQ community while fostering a sense of solidarity and empowerment.

Moreover, the concept of "visibility" plays a crucial role in Jin Xing's advocacy. As theorized by scholars like Reddy (2005), visibility can serve as a double-edged sword. While it can lead to increased awareness and support, it can also expose individuals to scrutiny and backlash. Jin Xing's decision to live openly as a transgender woman exemplifies the courage required to challenge societal norms and advocate for change.

Challenges Ahead

Despite the progress made, significant challenges remain for the LGBTQ community in China. The government's tight control over civil society and the media poses a constant threat to advocacy efforts. In recent years, there have been reports of increased censorship of LGBTQ-related content in film and television, as well as crackdowns on pride events and demonstrations. For instance, the 2019 Shanghai Pride was forced to cancel its parade due to government pressure, highlighting the precarious position of LGBTQ activism in China [?].

Additionally, the intersectionality of LGBTQ identities with other social issues, such as class and ethnicity, complicates the fight for rights. Many LGBTQ individuals from marginalized backgrounds face compounded discrimination, making it essential for advocacy to address these intersecting issues.

The Path Forward: Jin Xing's Role

Looking ahead, Jin Xing's role in shaping the future of LGBTQ rights in China will be critical. Her influence can inspire a new generation of activists to continue the fight for equality. By leveraging her platform, she can advocate for policy changes that protect LGBTQ individuals from discrimination and violence. Furthermore, her involvement in international LGBTQ dialogues can help raise awareness of the challenges faced by the community in China.

Education and awareness are vital components of this journey. Jin Xing can play a significant role in promoting educational initiatives that foster understanding and acceptance of LGBTQ identities. Collaborating with schools and universities to implement inclusive curricula can help dismantle prejudices and promote empathy among young people.

Conclusion

The future of LGBTQ rights in China is uncertain, yet the potential for change is palpable. With figures like Jin Xing leading the charge, there is hope for a more inclusive society that embraces diversity. The challenges are formidable, but through resilience, advocacy, and education, the LGBTQ community can continue to push for rights and recognition. Jin Xing's journey is not just her own; it is a collective narrative that echoes the aspirations of countless individuals striving for acceptance and equality.

Potential future ventures and collaborations for Jin Xing

As Jin Xing continues to carve her path as a prominent figure in the realms of dance and LGBTQ activism, the potential for future ventures and collaborations remains vast and varied. These prospects not only promise to enhance her artistic repertoire but also serve to amplify her advocacy efforts, fostering a more inclusive environment within the arts and society at large.

Expanding Artistic Collaborations

One avenue for Jin Xing's future endeavors lies in expanding her artistic collaborations. By partnering with international choreographers and dancers, she can infuse her unique style with diverse influences, creating innovative performances that resonate across cultural boundaries. For instance, collaborating with renowned artists from different genres—such as contemporary ballet or street dance—could yield groundbreaking works that challenge conventional narratives around gender and identity.

$$\text{Artistic Impact} = \text{Cultural Exchange} + \text{Innovation} \qquad (82)$$

This equation underscores the potential for artistic impact through the fusion of cultural exchange and innovative practices. Such collaborations would not only enhance Jin Xing's visibility on global platforms but also contribute to a broader dialogue about the intersection of art and activism.

Mentorship and Training Programs

In addition to artistic collaborations, Jin Xing could establish mentorship and training programs aimed at nurturing young LGBTQ artists. By creating workshops and masterclasses, she can share her wealth of knowledge and experience, empowering the next generation of performers. These initiatives could focus on various aspects of performance art, including dance technique, choreography, and the importance of self-expression in the face of societal challenges.

$$\text{Empowerment} = \text{Knowledge Transfer} + \text{Support} \qquad (83)$$

The equation highlights how empowerment stems from the transfer of knowledge coupled with a supportive environment. Jin Xing's mentorship could foster resilience and creativity among emerging artists, encouraging them to embrace their identities and pursue their passions unapologetically.

Advocacy through Media and Technology

The digital age presents Jin Xing with unprecedented opportunities to leverage media and technology for advocacy. By producing documentaries or web series that highlight the stories of LGBTQ individuals, she can further humanize the struggles and triumphs of the community. These narratives can serve as powerful tools for education and awareness, challenging stereotypes and promoting understanding.

$$\text{Advocacy Impact} = \text{Media Reach} \times \text{Narrative Power} \qquad (84)$$

This equation illustrates that the impact of advocacy is amplified through the combination of extensive media reach and compelling narratives. Jin Xing's ability to connect with audiences through various platforms can foster empathy and drive social change.

International Tours and Cultural Exchange Programs

Jin Xing's future ventures could also include international tours and cultural exchange programs. By performing in diverse regions and engaging with local LGBTQ communities, she can promote inclusivity and solidarity. These tours would allow her to showcase her artistry while simultaneously advocating for LGBTQ rights on a global scale.

$$\text{Cultural Impact} = \text{Performance} + \text{Community Engagement} \qquad (85)$$

Here, the equation emphasizes that cultural impact is achieved through the combination of performance art and active community engagement. Each performance can serve as a platform for dialogue, fostering connections between different cultures and promoting a shared understanding of the LGBTQ experience.

Collaborative Art Installations and Public Performances

Jin Xing could also explore the realm of collaborative art installations and public performances that address LGBTQ issues. By working with visual artists, filmmakers, and musicians, she can create immersive experiences that provoke thought and inspire action. These installations could be showcased in public spaces, making art accessible to a broader audience and inviting discourse on critical social issues.

$$\text{Social Change} = \text{Art} + \text{Public Engagement} \qquad (86)$$

This equation posits that social change is driven by the intersection of art and public engagement. By bringing her work into the public sphere, Jin Xing can challenge societal norms and encourage conversations around acceptance and equality.

Sustainability in the Arts

As Jin Xing looks to the future, she may also consider the sustainability of her artistic practices. Engaging in discussions about environmental responsibility within the arts can position her as a leader in promoting eco-friendly practices in performance and production. Collaborating with organizations that focus on sustainability could enhance her brand while contributing positively to the planet.

$$\text{Sustainable Impact} = \text{Artistic Practices} + \text{Environmental Responsibility} \qquad (87)$$

This equation highlights the importance of integrating sustainability into artistic practices. By advocating for eco-conscious approaches, Jin Xing can inspire others in the industry to follow suit, fostering a culture of responsibility and care for the environment.

Legacy Projects and Documentation

Finally, Jin Xing could embark on legacy projects that document her journey and the stories of those she has inspired. This could take the form of an autobiographical book, a series of interviews, or a visual archive of her work. Such projects would not only preserve her legacy but also serve as a resource for future activists and artists.

$$\text{Legacy} = \text{Documentation} + \text{Inspiration} \qquad (88)$$

In this equation, legacy is defined as the product of thorough documentation and the ability to inspire others. By sharing her journey, Jin Xing can create a lasting impact that resonates with individuals across generations.

In conclusion, the potential future ventures and collaborations for Jin Xing are as diverse as her journey itself. By embracing artistic collaborations, mentorship, media advocacy, cultural exchange, sustainability, and legacy projects, she can continue to be a beacon of hope and empowerment for the LGBTQ community and beyond. Each of these paths offers an opportunity to not only enhance her artistic expression but also to drive meaningful change in society, ensuring that her influence extends far beyond the stage.

The impact of Jin Xing's story on future generations

Jin Xing's journey as a groundbreaking transgender icon has left an indelible mark on future generations, influencing not only individuals within the LGBTQ community but also shaping societal attitudes towards gender identity and expression. Her story is a testament to resilience, courage, and the transformative power of self-acceptance, serving as a beacon of hope for those navigating similar paths.

Cultural Shifts and Visibility

The visibility that Jin Xing has achieved is crucial in a world where representation matters immensely. According to [?], representation in media and public life fosters a sense of belonging and validation for marginalized groups. Jin Xing's presence in the dance world and later in television has challenged the stereotypes surrounding transgender individuals, illustrating that success is attainable regardless of societal expectations. This visibility has the potential to inspire young LGBTQ individuals to embrace their identities and pursue their passions without fear of discrimination.

Furthermore, Jin Xing's story has contributed to a cultural shift in China regarding gender identity. As noted by [?], the increasing acceptance of diverse gender identities within Chinese society can be partly attributed to the visibility of figures like Jin Xing. Future generations, witnessing this shift, are likely to grow up in an environment that is more inclusive and supportive, allowing them to express their true selves freely.

Role Models and Mentorship

Jin Xing serves as a role model for countless individuals, particularly those who feel marginalized or misunderstood. Her journey from humble beginnings to international acclaim provides a narrative of perseverance that resonates deeply with young people facing their own struggles. Research by [?] indicates that role models play a significant role in shaping the aspirations and self-concept of youth. By sharing her experiences, Jin Xing empowers future generations to pursue their dreams and embrace their identities unapologetically.

Moreover, Jin Xing's commitment to mentoring young artists through her dance company, the Shanghai Jin Xing Dance Theatre, exemplifies the importance of fostering talent within the LGBTQ community. By providing a platform for emerging dancers, she not only nurtures their artistic abilities but also instills a sense of pride and belonging. This mentorship creates a ripple effect, as those inspired by her teachings are likely to become advocates for change themselves, perpetuating a cycle of empowerment.

Advocacy and Social Change

Jin Xing's advocacy for LGBTQ rights has galvanized a movement that extends beyond her personal narrative. Her efforts to promote inclusivity and equality have sparked conversations about gender identity in China, encouraging future generations to engage in activism. As highlighted by [?], grassroots movements often thrive on the foundation laid by earlier activists. Jin Xing's work serves as a catalyst for young activists, motivating them to challenge societal norms and advocate for their rights.

The intersectionality of Jin Xing's activism is also noteworthy. By addressing issues related to race, gender, and sexuality, she emphasizes the importance of a holistic approach to advocacy. This perspective encourages future generations to recognize the interconnectedness of various social justice movements, fostering a more comprehensive understanding of equality. Young activists who draw inspiration from Jin Xing are likely to adopt a multifaceted approach to their advocacy, paving the way for more inclusive and effective movements.

Educational Impact

Education plays a pivotal role in shaping attitudes and beliefs. Jin Xing's story highlights the necessity of inclusive curricula that encompass diverse perspectives on gender and sexuality. By incorporating narratives like hers into educational settings, future generations can develop a deeper understanding of the complexities surrounding gender identity. Studies have shown that inclusive education fosters empathy and reduces prejudice among students [?]. Jin Xing's influence can lead to a more informed and compassionate society, where young people are equipped to challenge discrimination and advocate for their peers.

Moreover, Jin Xing's presence in mainstream media serves as an educational tool. Her participation as a judge on "So You Think You Can Dance China" introduced millions to the realities of transgender experiences, breaking down misconceptions and fostering dialogue. This exposure is invaluable in shaping societal norms and encouraging acceptance among future generations.

Theoretical Frameworks

The impact of Jin Xing's story can be analyzed through various theoretical frameworks, including Social Identity Theory and Intersectionality. Social Identity Theory, as proposed by [?], posits that individuals derive a sense of identity from their group memberships. Jin Xing's visibility allows LGBTQ individuals to see themselves represented in spaces where they may have previously felt excluded, reinforcing their self-worth and identity.

Intersectionality, introduced by [2], emphasizes the interconnected nature of social categorizations and how they create overlapping systems of discrimination. Jin Xing's narrative illustrates the complexities of navigating multiple identities, inspiring future generations to embrace their multifaceted selves. This understanding encourages young activists to advocate for a more inclusive society that recognizes and values diversity in all its forms.

Conclusion

In conclusion, Jin Xing's story is a powerful testament to the impact that one individual's journey can have on future generations. By challenging societal norms, serving as a role model, advocating for change, and promoting inclusive education, she has laid the groundwork for a more accepting and understanding society. Her legacy will continue to inspire and empower young people to embrace their identities, pursue their dreams, and advocate for a world where everyone can live authentically. As future generations look to her as a source of inspiration, they will undoubtedly carry forward her message of resilience, love, and acceptance, shaping a brighter future for all.

The ongoing global fight for LGBTQ equality and Jin Xing's contribution

The ongoing global fight for LGBTQ equality is a multifaceted struggle that transcends geographical, cultural, and political boundaries. This movement is characterized by a quest for recognition, acceptance, and rights for individuals of diverse sexual orientations and gender identities. As a prominent figure in this struggle, Jin Xing's contributions have been both significant and transformative, providing a beacon of hope and inspiration for many around the world.

At its core, the fight for LGBTQ equality is rooted in the principles of human rights, social justice, and equality. The Universal Declaration of Human Rights states that "All human beings are born free and equal in dignity and rights." However, despite this foundational assertion, LGBTQ individuals often face systemic discrimination, violence, and marginalization. According to a report by the International Lesbian, Gay, Bisexual, Trans and Intersex Association (ILGA), as of 2021, 69 countries still criminalize same-sex relationships, and LGBTQ individuals are at higher risk for mental health issues, homelessness, and violence.

Theoretical Frameworks

To understand the complexities of the LGBTQ rights movement, we can draw upon several theoretical frameworks, including queer theory, intersectionality, and social movement theory. Queer theory challenges the binary understanding of gender and sexuality, promoting a more fluid and inclusive perspective. It posits that identity is not fixed but rather constructed through social and cultural contexts. This is particularly relevant in the context of Jin Xing's journey, as she embodies the fluidity and resilience that queer theory advocates.

Intersectionality, a term coined by Kimberlé Crenshaw, highlights how various social identities (such as race, gender, sexuality, and class) intersect to create unique experiences of oppression and privilege. Jin Xing's experiences as a transgender woman in China illuminate the intersectional challenges faced by LGBTQ individuals in conservative societies. Her visibility as a performer and activist has been crucial in addressing these compounded layers of discrimination.

Social movement theory provides insight into how collective action can drive social change. Theories such as resource mobilization and political opportunity structures explain how social movements gain traction and influence policy. Jin

Xing's rise to fame and her subsequent advocacy work exemplify how visibility and representation can mobilize support for LGBTQ rights and create political opportunities for change.

Challenges in the Global Context

Despite progress in many regions, significant challenges remain in the fight for LGBTQ equality. In many countries, cultural norms and governmental policies continue to perpetuate discrimination. For instance, in countries like Russia and Uganda, anti-LGBTQ legislation has intensified, resulting in violence and persecution of LGBTQ individuals. The rise of populism and conservative ideologies in various parts of the world has also led to a backlash against LGBTQ rights, threatening hard-won gains.

Moreover, the COVID-19 pandemic exacerbated existing inequalities, disproportionately affecting LGBTQ individuals who often face higher rates of unemployment, homelessness, and mental health challenges. Reports from organizations such as OutRight Action International indicate that LGBTQ individuals experienced increased violence and discrimination during lockdowns, highlighting the urgent need for targeted support and advocacy.

Jin Xing's Contributions

Jin Xing's contributions to the LGBTQ rights movement are manifold and impactful. As a pioneering transgender artist and activist, she has leveraged her platform to advocate for greater acceptance and understanding of LGBTQ issues in China and beyond. Her visibility as a performer has challenged societal norms and stereotypes, fostering dialogue around gender identity and expression.

1. **Visibility and Representation**: Jin Xing's presence in the media and performing arts has significantly increased visibility for transgender individuals in China. By showcasing her talent and sharing her story, she has humanized the transgender experience, countering negative stereotypes and fostering empathy. Her role as a judge on "So You Think You Can Dance China" has further amplified her influence, providing a platform for aspiring LGBTQ artists.

2. **Advocacy and Activism**: Beyond her artistic contributions, Jin Xing has been an outspoken advocate for LGBTQ rights. She has utilized interviews, public appearances, and social media to raise awareness about the challenges faced by LGBTQ individuals in China. Her advocacy extends to promoting inclusivity in the arts, encouraging other artists to embrace diversity and challenge discrimination.

3. **Cultural Exchange and Education**: Jin Xing's international tours and collaborations have facilitated cultural exchange, allowing for dialogue around LGBTQ issues in different contexts. By engaging with audiences worldwide, she has highlighted the universality of the struggle for equality, fostering solidarity among LGBTQ communities globally.

4. **Mentorship and Support**: Jin Xing's role as a mentor to young LGBTQ artists has been instrumental in nurturing the next generation of activists and performers. By providing guidance and support, she empowers individuals to embrace their identities and pursue their passions, contributing to a more inclusive artistic landscape.

5. **Symbol of Hope**: Jin Xing's journey from a young dancer in Shenyang to an internationally recognized artist serves as a powerful symbol of hope for many. Her resilience in the face of adversity inspires individuals to embrace their true selves, fostering a sense of belonging and acceptance within the LGBTQ community.

Conclusion

In conclusion, the ongoing global fight for LGBTQ equality is a complex and dynamic struggle, marked by both challenges and triumphs. Jin Xing's contributions to this movement exemplify the power of visibility, advocacy, and resilience. As societies continue to grapple with issues of discrimination and inequality, the lessons drawn from Jin Xing's journey serve as a reminder of the importance of embracing diversity, fostering understanding, and advocating for the rights of all individuals, regardless of their sexual orientation or gender identity. The hope for a more inclusive future lies in the collective efforts of activists, allies, and communities working together to dismantle barriers and promote acceptance worldwide.

Jin Xing's plans for the future and her aspirations for the LGBTQ community

Jin Xing has always been a visionary, not just in her artistry but also in her commitment to the LGBTQ community. As she looks toward the future, her aspirations are deeply rooted in her experiences and the profound understanding she has gained through her journey.

One of Jin Xing's primary goals is to create more inclusive spaces for LGBTQ individuals within the arts. She envisions a world where every artist, regardless of their gender identity or sexual orientation, has the opportunity to express themselves freely. To achieve this, she plans to expand her dance company, the Shanghai Jin

Xing Dance Theatre, into a platform that not only showcases diverse talents but also serves as an incubator for new works that reflect the myriad experiences of the LGBTQ community.

$$\text{Inclusivity} = \frac{\text{Diverse Voices}}{\text{Barriers to Entry}} \tag{89}$$

This equation illustrates Jin Xing's philosophy: the more diverse voices that are allowed to flourish, the fewer barriers there will be to entry into the arts. By fostering an environment where creativity is celebrated in all its forms, she hopes to dismantle the societal norms that have historically marginalized LGBTQ artists.

Moreover, Jin Xing aims to leverage her platform to advocate for LGBTQ rights in China and beyond. She recognizes that visibility is crucial in challenging stereotypes and promoting acceptance. In her future endeavors, she plans to collaborate with international LGBTQ organizations to amplify their messages and create a global dialogue around issues that affect the community.

For instance, during her international tours, she has made it a point to engage with local LGBTQ groups, sharing her story and encouraging discussions about the unique challenges faced in different cultural contexts. This approach not only raises awareness but also fosters solidarity among LGBTQ individuals worldwide.

$$\text{Global Solidarity} = \sum_{i=1}^{n} \text{Local Voices}_i \tag{90}$$

Here, the equation signifies that global solidarity is achieved through the collective strength of local voices, each contributing to a larger narrative of acceptance and equality. Jin Xing's ambition is to unite these voices, creating a chorus that resonates across borders.

In addition to her artistic and advocacy efforts, Jin Xing is committed to education and mentorship. She believes that empowering the next generation of LGBTQ activists and artists is essential for sustaining progress. To this end, she plans to establish scholarship programs aimed at supporting LGBTQ youth in pursuing careers in the arts.

These scholarships would not only alleviate financial burdens but also provide mentorship opportunities, connecting young artists with established figures in the industry. Jin Xing envisions workshops and masterclasses that focus on both artistic skills and personal development, fostering resilience and self-acceptance among participants.

$$\text{Empowerment} = \text{Education} + \text{Mentorship} \tag{91}$$

This equation encapsulates Jin Xing's belief that empowerment is achieved through a combination of education and mentorship, equipping individuals with the tools they need to navigate their journeys.

Jin Xing also recognizes the importance of mental health within the LGBTQ community, particularly in a society that often stigmatizes those who identify as different. She plans to partner with mental health organizations to provide resources and support for LGBTQ individuals, creating safe spaces for dialogue and healing.

By addressing mental health issues head-on, Jin Xing aims to destigmatize conversations around mental well-being and encourage individuals to seek help without fear of judgment.

In her vision for the future, Jin Xing sees a world where LGBTQ individuals can live authentically and without fear. She aspires to create a legacy that inspires future generations to embrace their identities and advocate for their rights.

As she continues her journey, Jin Xing remains steadfast in her belief that art can be a powerful catalyst for change. Through her performances, advocacy, and educational initiatives, she hopes to inspire others to join the fight for equality and acceptance.

In conclusion, Jin Xing's plans for the future are ambitious yet grounded in her lived experiences. Her aspirations for the LGBTQ community encompass inclusivity in the arts, global solidarity, education, mentorship, and mental health advocacy. By fostering these elements, she aims to create a more equitable world where diversity is celebrated and every individual has the opportunity to thrive.

Through her unwavering commitment, Jin Xing not only envisions a brighter future for the LGBTQ community but actively works towards making that vision a reality. Her legacy will undoubtedly leave an indelible mark on the landscape of LGBTQ rights and representation, inspiring countless others to stand up and be heard.

The importance of preserving and honoring Jin Xing's legacy

The legacy of Jin Xing is not merely a reflection of her personal achievements but a profound testament to the struggles and triumphs of the LGBTQ community in China and beyond. Preserving and honoring her legacy is vital for several reasons: it serves as an inspiration for future generations, provides a historical context for understanding LGBTQ rights, and promotes ongoing advocacy for equality.

Inspiration for Future Generations

Jin Xing's journey from a small town in Shenyang to becoming a celebrated international dance icon illustrates the power of resilience and self-acceptance. Her story encourages young LGBTQ individuals to embrace their identities and pursue their passions despite societal constraints. As noted by [1], representation matters; seeing someone like Jin Xing succeed can empower youth to envision a future where they, too, can thrive.

$$I = P \cdot R \qquad (92)$$

Where I represents inspiration, P is the potential of individuals, and R is the representation they see in society. Jin Xing amplifies this equation by enhancing the representation factor, thereby increasing the inspirational output for countless individuals.

Historical Context and Understanding LGBTQ Rights

Jin Xing's legacy also plays a critical role in documenting the history of LGBTQ rights in China. The challenges she faced, including discrimination and societal rejection, reflect broader cultural attitudes towards gender identity and sexuality within Chinese society. By preserving her story, we can highlight the historical struggles of the LGBTQ community and the progress made over the years.

The importance of historical context is underscored by [?], who argues that understanding the past is essential for informing current and future advocacy efforts. Jin Xing's experiences can serve as case studies for activists and scholars alike, providing insight into the systemic barriers faced by transgender individuals in conservative societies.

Promoting Ongoing Advocacy for Equality

Honoring Jin Xing's legacy goes beyond mere remembrance; it involves active engagement in advocacy for LGBTQ rights. Her platform has been utilized to challenge discriminatory practices and promote inclusivity within the arts and society at large. As an advocate, Jin Xing has demonstrated that art can be a powerful vehicle for social change.

The equation for advocacy can be expressed as follows:

$$A = C \cdot E \qquad (93)$$

Where A represents advocacy, C is the community's collective voice, and E is the effectiveness of the message being communicated. Jin Xing's legacy amplifies both C and E, encouraging collective action towards equality.

Examples of Legacy Preservation

To effectively honor Jin Xing's legacy, various initiatives can be undertaken:

1. **Documentary Films and Biographies**: Creating visual narratives that tell her story can serve as educational tools and inspire future activists. For instance, the documentary *Jin Xing: Dance of Freedom* has been instrumental in shedding light on her life and work.

2. **Scholarships and Grants**: Establishing scholarships for LGBTQ youth in the arts can provide financial support and encourage diverse voices in creative spaces. Programs like the Jin Xing Arts Fund can help cultivate talent and promote inclusivity.

3. **Public Memorials and Art Installations**: Physical representations of Jin Xing's influence, such as statues or murals, can serve as powerful symbols of hope and resilience, reminding society of the importance of diversity and acceptance.

4. **Educational Workshops and Panels**: Hosting discussions and workshops in schools and community centers can raise awareness about LGBTQ issues and the significance of figures like Jin Xing in the movement for equality.

Conclusion

In conclusion, preserving and honoring Jin Xing's legacy is a multifaceted endeavor that requires commitment from individuals, communities, and institutions. By recognizing her contributions and the broader implications of her story, we can inspire future generations, contextualize the ongoing fight for LGBTQ rights, and advocate for a more inclusive society. As we reflect on her journey, let us remember that each step taken towards honoring her legacy is a step towards a future where everyone can live authentically and without fear.

Jin Xing as an inspiration for future LGBTQ activists and artists

Jin Xing's journey through the world of dance and activism has become a beacon of hope and inspiration for countless LGBTQ individuals and artists worldwide. Her story illustrates not only the triumph of the human spirit but also the profound impact that visibility and representation can have on marginalized communities. As we explore her influence, it is essential to consider the theoretical frameworks surrounding identity, representation, and activism, as well as the challenges that future activists may face.

One of the pivotal theories that underpin Jin Xing's influence is Judith Butler's concept of gender performativity. Butler posits that gender is not an innate quality but rather a series of acts and performances that are socially constructed and reiterated. Jin Xing embodies this theory through her dance, which serves as both a personal expression of her identity and a challenge to societal norms. Her performances transcend traditional gender boundaries, showcasing the fluidity of identity and inspiring others to embrace their authentic selves.

$$\text{Gender Identity} \propto \text{Cultural Performance} \qquad (94)$$

This equation symbolizes the relationship between gender identity and cultural performance, suggesting that the expression of one's identity can influence societal perceptions and norms. Jin Xing's artistry has not only paved the way for her own acceptance but has also encouraged future generations to explore and express their identities without fear of judgment.

Moreover, Jin Xing's visibility as a transgender artist in a predominantly conservative society highlights the critical role of representation in fostering acceptance and understanding. According to the Social Identity Theory, individuals derive part of their identity from the groups to which they belong, and positive representation can significantly impact self-esteem and social integration. Jin Xing's success challenges the stigmas associated with transgender individuals, providing a powerful counter-narrative to the often-negative portrayals in media and society.

$$\text{Self-Esteem} = f(\text{Positive Representation}) \qquad (95)$$

In this equation, self-esteem is a function of positive representation, illustrating how Jin Xing's presence in the arts can uplift and empower future LGBTQ activists and artists. By seeing someone like her achieve success, individuals are more likely to believe in their potential and pursue their passions, regardless of societal constraints.

However, the road ahead for future LGBTQ activists and artists is not without challenges. Despite Jin Xing's groundbreaking achievements, the LGBTQ community continues to face discrimination, violence, and systemic inequalities. Future activists must navigate these treacherous waters while remaining steadfast in their pursuit of equality and acceptance. They can draw inspiration from Jin Xing's resilience and commitment to her craft, which serve as powerful reminders that perseverance can lead to change.

For instance, Jin Xing's establishment of the Shanghai Jin Xing Dance Theatre not only provided a platform for her own work but also opened doors for other LGBTQ artists in China. This initiative exemplifies the importance of creating inclusive spaces where marginalized voices can be heard and celebrated. Future activists are encouraged to follow suit by fostering community support networks and advocating for policies that promote inclusivity in the arts and beyond.

Furthermore, Jin Xing's advocacy for LGBTQ rights extends beyond her artistic contributions. She actively engages in public discourse, using her platform to raise awareness about the challenges faced by the LGBTQ community in China. This dual role as an artist and activist demonstrates the interconnectedness of art and social change, inspiring future generations to harness their creativity as a tool for advocacy.

As we reflect on Jin Xing's legacy, it is crucial to acknowledge the lessons learned from her journey. The importance of authenticity, resilience, and community support cannot be overstated. Future LGBTQ activists and artists are encouraged to embrace their unique identities and experiences, as these narratives are vital in the fight for equality. By sharing their stories and advocating for change, they can contribute to a more inclusive and accepting society.

In conclusion, Jin Xing serves as an enduring inspiration for future LGBTQ activists and artists. Her journey exemplifies the power of visibility, representation, and resilience in the face of adversity. As she continues to break boundaries and challenge societal norms, her legacy will undoubtedly inspire countless individuals to embrace their true selves and advocate for a more equitable world. The call to action for future generations is clear: to stand up, speak out, and create art that reflects the diverse tapestry of human experience, just as Jin Xing has done.

$$\text{Inspiration} = \text{Visibility} + \text{Representation} + \text{Resilience} \qquad (96)$$

This final equation encapsulates the essence of Jin Xing's influence, emphasizing that inspiration arises from the combination of visibility, representation, and resilience. As future activists and artists carry forth her legacy, they are reminded that their voices matter, and their stories can ignite change in the world.

The significance of Jin Xing's work in creating lasting change

Jin Xing's journey from a humble dancer in Shenyang to a prominent transgender icon is not merely a personal narrative; it is a testament to the transformative power of art and activism in fostering societal change. Her work embodies the intersection of performance, identity, and social justice, making her an influential figure in both the LGBTQ community and the broader cultural landscape of China.

Theoretical Framework: Social Change and Identity

To understand the significance of Jin Xing's contributions, we can draw upon theories of social change and identity formation. According to *social identity theory* (Tajfel & Turner, 1979), individuals derive a sense of self from their group memberships, which can lead to both empowerment and marginalization. Jin Xing's visibility as a transgender artist challenges societal norms and encourages individuals to embrace their authentic selves, thereby fostering a sense of belonging within the LGBTQ community.

Furthermore, the *theory of intersectionality* (Crenshaw, 1989) highlights how overlapping identities—such as gender, sexuality, and cultural background—impact individuals' experiences of oppression and privilege. Jin Xing's work exemplifies this theory, as she navigates her identity as a transgender woman in a conservative society while advocating for the rights of marginalized groups. Her artistic expression serves as a platform for dialogue and understanding, breaking down barriers and fostering inclusivity.

Challenges Faced: Cultural Resistance and Discrimination

Despite her successes, Jin Xing has faced significant challenges in her quest for change. The conservative cultural landscape of China presents formidable obstacles to LGBTQ acceptance. Discrimination, stigma, and societal pressure often silence voices like hers. This is evident in the limited representation of transgender individuals in mainstream media and the pervasive stereotypes that persist in society.

In her early career, Jin Xing encountered resistance from traditionalists who viewed her identity as a threat to cultural norms. Yet, she leveraged these challenges to propel her activism, transforming personal adversity into a call for change. Her performances often incorporate themes of resilience and self-acceptance, resonating with audiences and inspiring them to confront their biases.

Art as a Catalyst for Change

Jin Xing's work transcends mere entertainment; it serves as a catalyst for social change. Through her dance, she communicates complex narratives about gender identity and societal acceptance. For instance, her choreography often reflects the struggles faced by LGBTQ individuals in China, using movement to convey the emotional weight of discrimination and the joy of self-acceptance.

One notable example is her performance titled *"Beyond the Mirror"*, which explores the duality of identity and the journey toward self-discovery. The piece juxtaposes traditional Chinese dance with contemporary styles, symbolizing the clash between cultural heritage and modernity. This fusion not only showcases her artistic versatility but also challenges audiences to rethink their perceptions of gender and identity.

Legacy of Activism: Inspiring Future Generations

The significance of Jin Xing's work extends beyond her performances; it lies in the legacy of activism she has cultivated. By establishing the *Shanghai Jin Xing Dance Theatre*, she has created a platform for emerging LGBTQ artists, providing them with opportunities to express their identities and share their stories. This initiative fosters a new generation of artists who are empowered to challenge societal norms and advocate for change.

Moreover, Jin Xing's role as a judge on *"So You Think You Can Dance China"* has amplified her impact. Her presence on national television has not only increased visibility for transgender individuals but has also sparked conversations about LGBTQ representation in the media. By challenging contestants to embrace their uniqueness, she encourages a culture of acceptance and understanding.

Global Impact and Cultural Exchange

Jin Xing's influence is not confined to China; it resonates globally. Her international tours and collaborations with renowned artists have facilitated cultural exchange, allowing her to share her message of inclusivity with diverse audiences. This exchange is crucial in combating stereotypes and fostering empathy across cultural boundaries.

The global LGBTQ movement has also drawn inspiration from Jin Xing's journey. Her story exemplifies the power of resilience and the importance of visibility in advocating for rights and acceptance. As countries around the world grapple with issues of gender and sexuality, Jin Xing's work serves as a beacon of hope, illustrating the potential for change through art and activism.

Conclusion: A Lasting Impact

In conclusion, the significance of Jin Xing's work in creating lasting change cannot be overstated. Through her artistry, she has challenged societal norms, inspired countless individuals, and advocated for the rights of the LGBTQ community. Her journey exemplifies the transformative power of self-expression and the vital role of visibility in fostering social change. As we reflect on her legacy, it is clear that Jin Xing is not just a dancer; she is a revolutionary force in the ongoing struggle for equality and acceptance.

The ripple effect of her contributions will continue to inspire future generations to embrace their identities and advocate for a more inclusive world. Jin Xing's work reminds us that art is not merely a reflection of society but a powerful tool for shaping it.

The hope and optimism for a more inclusive future

In the ever-evolving landscape of social justice, the hope for a more inclusive future is not merely an abstract concept; it is a tangible goal that requires collective effort, resilience, and unwavering commitment. The journey towards inclusivity, particularly for marginalized communities such as the LGBTQ population, hinges on several key factors: education, representation, advocacy, and the dismantling of systemic barriers.

Education as a Catalyst   Education serves as the foundation for understanding and acceptance. By integrating LGBTQ history and issues into educational curricula, society can cultivate empathy and awareness from a young age. Research shows that inclusive education not only benefits LGBTQ students but also fosters a more accepting environment for all. For instance, a study by GLSEN (Gay, Lesbian & Straight Education Network) revealed that schools with comprehensive anti-bullying policies and inclusive curricula reported lower instances of harassment and discrimination. Thus, the path to a more inclusive future begins with informed and empathetic citizens.

Representation Matters   Representation in media and leadership roles plays a crucial role in shaping societal perceptions. When individuals see themselves reflected in various spheres—be it film, politics, or business—they are more likely to feel validated and empowered. Jin Xing's journey exemplifies the importance of visibility; her prominence in the arts has inspired countless individuals to embrace their identities. The portrayal of LGBTQ characters in mainstream media has also evolved, with shows like *Pose* and *Schitt's Creek* breaking stereotypes and celebrating diversity. Such representations challenge societal norms and foster a culture of acceptance.

Advocacy and Activism Advocacy remains an essential component in the fight for LGBTQ rights. Organizations such as Human Rights Campaign (HRC) and Amnesty International work tirelessly to address injustices and promote equality. Grassroots movements, often led by passionate individuals, have the power to effect change at local levels. The Stonewall Riots of 1969, a pivotal moment in LGBTQ history, serve as a reminder of the impact of collective action. Today, similar movements continue to emerge globally, advocating for rights and protections for LGBTQ individuals, thereby instilling hope for future generations.

Dismantling Systemic Barriers The fight for inclusivity also requires a critical examination of systemic barriers that perpetuate discrimination.   Laws that criminalize same-sex relationships or deny gender-affirming healthcare are remnants of a prejudiced past that must be confronted. Legal reforms, such as the repeal of discriminatory laws and the implementation of comprehensive anti-discrimination protections, are vital steps towards an equitable society. The ongoing efforts to pass the Equality Act in the United States exemplify the legislative push for comprehensive protections for LGBTQ individuals.

Community Support and Solidarity Building supportive communities is paramount in fostering inclusivity. Safe spaces, whether physical or virtual, provide individuals with the opportunity to express themselves freely without fear of judgment or persecution. Initiatives like Pride events and LGBTQ youth groups create networks of support that empower individuals to share their stories and experiences. The solidarity displayed during events like the annual Pride Month celebrations showcases the collective strength of the LGBTQ community and its allies.

The Role of Technology In the digital age, technology serves as a powerful tool for advocacy and connection. Social media platforms enable activists to amplify their voices and mobilize support for causes. Hashtags like #LoveIsLove and #TransRightsAreHumanRights have sparked global conversations, fostering a sense of unity and purpose. The ability to share personal narratives online has also humanized the struggles faced by LGBTQ individuals, bridging gaps in understanding and empathy.

A Vision for the Future As we look ahead, the vision for a more inclusive future is one where diversity is celebrated, and every individual can live authentically without fear of discrimination. This vision is not merely aspirational; it is achievable through concerted efforts at all levels of society. By prioritizing education, representation, advocacy, and community building, we can dismantle the barriers that hinder progress.

The journey towards inclusivity is ongoing, but the collective hope and optimism for a more equitable future can drive meaningful change. As Jin Xing and many others have demonstrated, embracing one's true self is a powerful act that can inspire others to do the same. The ripple effects of these actions can lead to a society where acceptance is the norm, and diversity is celebrated.

In conclusion, the hope for a more inclusive future rests on the shoulders of both current and future generations. By learning from the past, advocating for change, and supporting one another, we can create a world where everyone is free to express their identity and love without limitations. The path may be fraught with challenges, but the promise of a brighter, more inclusive future fuels our determination to persevere.

The Unfiltered Truth

Behind the scenes of Jin Xing's life and career

Jin Xing's journey as a groundbreaking transgender icon in China is not merely a tale of public triumphs and accolades; it is also a narrative rich with the complexities of personal struggles, cultural challenges, and the relentless pursuit of authenticity. This section delves into the lesser-known aspects of her life, revealing the layers that contribute to her multifaceted identity as an artist and activist.

The Early Years: A Foundation of Struggle and Resilience

Born in Shenyang, China, Jin Xing exhibited an affinity for the arts from a young age. Her childhood was marked by both talent and adversity, as she navigated the rigid expectations of a traditional Chinese upbringing. Dance became her sanctuary, a space where she could express her true self, even when societal norms dictated otherwise.

Her parents played a significant role in shaping her early experiences. While her father encouraged her artistic pursuits, Jin Xing faced challenges due to her gender identity, which was not widely accepted in conservative Chinese society. The dichotomy between familial support and societal rejection created a complex emotional landscape for her.

This tension is exemplified in Jin Xing's early performances, where she often felt the need to mask her true identity to gain acceptance. The pressure to conform was palpable, yet it fueled her determination to succeed. As she once stated, "Dance was my rebellion against the world that tried to define me." This sentiment encapsulates the transformative power of art, serving as both an escape and a means of self-assertion.

The Dance Academy: A Crucible of Growth

Acceptance into the prestigious Shanghai Dance Academy marked a pivotal moment in Jin Xing's life. The rigorous training she underwent not only honed her skills but also exposed her to the harsh realities of the dance industry, where discrimination against LGBTQ individuals was prevalent.

During her time at the academy, Jin Xing encountered both camaraderie and rivalry. Many of her peers recognized her talent, yet others harbored prejudices that manifested in subtle forms of discrimination. This duality pushed her to work harder, striving to prove herself in an environment that was often unwelcoming.

The culmination of her training came with a breakthrough performance that catapulted her into the spotlight. This moment was not merely a professional achievement; it symbolized a reclamation of her identity in a space that had previously marginalized her. The applause she received was a validation of her existence as an artist and an individual.

Navigating Public Life: The Price of Visibility

As Jin Xing's career flourished, so did the scrutiny that accompanied her newfound visibility. The public's fascination with her story often overshadowed her artistic contributions, leading to a complex relationship with fame.

In interviews, Jin Xing has candidly discussed the psychological toll of being a public figure in a conservative society. The pressure to represent the transgender community weighed heavily on her, often leading to feelings of isolation. "I am not just a symbol; I am a person with dreams and fears," she remarked during a candid discussion with fellow activists.

This tension is further complicated by the media's portrayal of LGBTQ individuals. Jin Xing frequently faced sensationalism in news coverage, which often prioritized her identity over her artistic achievements. This phenomenon reflects a broader issue within media representation, where the narratives of marginalized individuals are often shaped by societal biases.

The Role of Advocacy: Beyond Dance

Recognizing the power of her platform, Jin Xing transitioned into advocacy, leveraging her fame to champion LGBTQ rights in China. Her role as a judge on "So You Think You Can Dance China" provided her with a unique opportunity to influence public perception and promote inclusivity.

However, this transition was not without its challenges. Jin Xing often faced backlash from conservative factions within society who viewed her activism as a threat to traditional values. The complexities of advocating for change in such an environment required a delicate balance of courage and strategy.

Jin Xing's advocacy efforts extend beyond mere representation; she actively engages in dialogues about gender identity and societal acceptance. Through workshops and public speaking engagements, she educates audiences on the importance of understanding and embracing diversity. Her approach emphasizes empathy and the need for collective action, reinforcing the notion that change is a communal effort.

Personal Struggles: The Unseen Battles

Behind the glamorous façade of her public persona lies a tapestry of personal struggles. Jin Xing's journey toward self-acceptance was fraught with internal conflict, particularly regarding her gender identity. The decision to undergo gender reassignment surgery was not taken lightly; it was a culmination of years of introspection and societal pressure.

Post-surgery, Jin Xing faced a new set of challenges. The public's reaction ranged from admiration to criticism, with many individuals struggling to reconcile their perceptions of her identity. The emotional aftermath of such scrutiny can be profound, leading to periods of self-doubt and reflection.

In her own words, "The journey to self-love is the hardest dance I have ever performed." This metaphor illustrates the intricate relationship between her personal and professional lives, highlighting the resilience required to navigate both realms.

The Impact of Relationships: Support Systems

Throughout her career, the support of family and friends has been instrumental in Jin Xing's journey. Their unwavering love provided her with a foundation from which to explore her identity and pursue her passions.

Jin Xing's relationships are characterized by mutual respect and understanding. Her husband and children have embraced her identity, creating a nurturing environment that allows her to thrive both personally and professionally. This dynamic challenges traditional notions of family, illustrating that love transcends societal norms.

The importance of support systems in the LGBTQ community cannot be overstated. Jin Xing's experiences underscore the need for allies and advocates who can foster environments of acceptance and understanding. Her narrative serves as a testament to the power of love in overcoming adversity.

Conclusion: The Unfiltered Truth

Behind the scenes of Jin Xing's life lies a story of resilience, advocacy, and the relentless pursuit of authenticity. Her journey reflects the broader struggles faced by LGBTQ individuals in China and around the world. By sharing her unfiltered truth, Jin Xing not only inspires others to embrace their identities but also challenges societal norms that seek to limit expression.

As we explore the complexities of her life, it becomes clear that Jin Xing is not merely a cultural icon; she is a beacon of hope for those navigating the tumultuous waters of identity and acceptance. Her legacy is one of courage, reminding us all that the journey toward self-acceptance is a dance worth pursuing.

The untold stories and controversies surrounding Jin Xing

Jin Xing, a name that resonates with courage and resilience, has not only made waves in the dance world but has also been at the center of various controversies and untold stories that reflect the complexities of her journey. These narratives often reveal the harsh realities faced by LGBTQ individuals in China, as well as the broader implications of her identity as a transgender woman in a society that has historically been conservative and resistant to change.

One of the most significant untold stories in Jin Xing's life is her early struggles with acceptance, both personally and professionally. Despite her immense talent, Jin Xing faced considerable backlash in a society that often stigmatizes those who deviate from traditional gender norms. For instance, during her formative years at the Shanghai Dance Academy, she was subjected to both overt and subtle forms of discrimination. This included being ostracized by peers and facing skepticism from instructors who questioned her commitment and ability to succeed as a transgender dancer. These experiences highlight the intersection of art and identity, where personal struggles are often magnified in the public eye.

Moreover, Jin Xing's decision to undergo gender reassignment surgery was a pivotal moment in her life, yet it was not without controversy. The public reaction ranged from support to outright hostility, reflecting the divided opinions on transgender issues in China. Many viewed her surgery as a radical act of defiance against societal norms, while others criticized her for what they perceived as abandoning her biological identity. This dichotomy illustrates the broader societal challenges faced by transgender individuals, who often navigate a minefield of expectations and prejudices.

In addition to her personal struggles, Jin Xing has also been involved in various controversies related to her advocacy work. As a prominent figure in the LGBTQ movement, she has often spoken out against discrimination and for the rights of marginalized communities. However, her outspoken nature has sometimes put her at odds with government authorities and conservative factions within society. For instance, her participation in public demonstrations and her vocal criticism of anti-LGBTQ policies have led to scrutiny and, at times, threats to her safety. This tension underscores the risks activists face in countries where LGBTQ rights are still heavily contested.

Furthermore, Jin Xing's role as a judge on "So You Think You Can Dance China" brought her both fame and criticism. While her presence on the show was hailed as a breakthrough for LGBTQ representation in mainstream media, it also sparked debates about the authenticity of her representation. Critics argued that her position was a tokenistic gesture rather than a genuine commitment to inclusivity. This controversy raises important questions about representation in media and the responsibilities of public figures to advocate for the communities they represent.

The untold stories surrounding Jin Xing also encompass her relationships and personal life. While she has been open about her journey, there remain aspects of her life that she has chosen to keep private. The complexities of her marriage and motherhood, particularly in a conservative society, are often glossed over in public discourse. These relationships challenge traditional notions of family and gender roles, further complicating her narrative as a cultural icon.

In conclusion, the untold stories and controversies surrounding Jin Xing are not merely footnotes in her biography; they are integral to understanding her impact as a groundbreaking transgender icon. Her experiences reflect the struggles of many LGBTQ individuals in China and highlight the ongoing fight for acceptance and equality. Through her journey, Jin Xing has not only paved the way for future generations but has also illuminated the path toward a more inclusive society. Her story serves as a reminder that the fight for rights and recognition is fraught with challenges but is ultimately rooted in the desire for authenticity and acceptance.

$$\text{Visibility} + \text{Advocacy} = \text{Change} \qquad (97)$$

This equation encapsulates Jin Xing's philosophy: that through visibility and advocacy, transformative change can be achieved, both for individuals and for society as a whole. Her life is a testament to the power of resilience and the importance of standing up for one's truth, even in the face of adversity.

In-depth interviews with friends, family, and colleagues

In the pursuit of understanding the multifaceted life of Jin Xing, in-depth interviews with those closest to her—friends, family, and colleagues—provide invaluable insights into her character, struggles, and triumphs. These narratives not only enrich her biography but also illuminate the broader context of her impact as a transgender icon in China.

The Voices of Family

Jin Xing's family plays a pivotal role in her journey. Her parents, while initially struggling to understand her identity, ultimately became her staunchest supporters. In interviews, her mother recounted the moment Jin Xing expressed her desire to transition. "It was difficult at first," she admitted, "but I realized my child's happiness was what mattered most." This sentiment echoes throughout Jin Xing's life, showcasing the transformative power of unconditional love.

Her father, a traditionalist, faced his own challenges in reconciling his beliefs with his daughter's identity. "I had to learn," he shared, "that love transcends societal norms." This evolution in his perspective highlights a critical theme in Jin Xing's life: the importance of familial acceptance in the journey of self-discovery and authenticity.

Friendship and Community Support

Friends of Jin Xing also provided poignant reflections on her resilience and determination. One close friend, who has been by her side since childhood, described the early days of their friendship. "We were just kids who loved to dance," she recalled. "Jin Xing's passion was contagious, and it inspired all of us." This early support network was crucial in helping Jin Xing navigate the challenges of being a transgender individual in a conservative society.

Another friend, a fellow dancer, spoke about the discrimination they faced together in the industry. "We were often judged for who we were, but Jin Xing never let it break her spirit. She taught me to fight for our place in the world." This sentiment encapsulates the collective struggle of many LGBTQ individuals who find strength in camaraderie and shared experiences.

Colleagues' Perspectives

Colleagues from the Shanghai Dance Academy and the Shanghai Jin Xing Dance Theatre shared their experiences working alongside Jin Xing. One prominent choreographer remarked, "Jin Xing is not just a dancer; she is a force of nature. Her artistry challenges norms and pushes boundaries." This observation underscores Jin Xing's significant influence on the dance community, where her unique style and vision have redefined performance art.

Moreover, a colleague who worked with Jin Xing on various projects highlighted her role as a mentor. "She has this incredible ability to see potential in others," they stated. "Jin Xing nurtures talent and encourages her dancers to embrace their true selves, regardless of societal expectations." This mentorship extends beyond the stage, fostering a new generation of artists who are empowered to express their identities authentically.

The Challenges of Public Perception

Despite the support from her inner circle, Jin Xing's journey has not been without challenges, particularly concerning public perception. Interviews with friends and colleagues revealed the constant scrutiny she faces as a public figure. One friend articulated the pressure of being a role model: "There's a weight that comes with being an icon. Jin Xing carries it with grace, but it's not easy." This sentiment reflects the duality of her existence—celebrated yet criticized.

Colleagues also discussed the backlash Jin Xing received after her transition. "The media can be brutal," one stated. "But Jin Xing uses that negativity as fuel. She turns it into motivation to advocate for change." This resilience is a testament to her character and highlights the broader societal issues surrounding LGBTQ representation in media.

The Importance of Authenticity

Through these interviews, a consistent theme emerged: the importance of authenticity. Jin Xing's friends and family emphasized her unwavering commitment to being true to herself. "She taught us that authenticity is a strength, not a weakness," a childhood friend noted. This lesson resonates deeply within the

LGBTQ community, where the struggle for acceptance often conflicts with societal norms.

The interviews also revealed Jin Xing's impact on her peers. A fellow activist shared, "Jin Xing's courage inspires us all. She challenges us to be brave in our own lives." This ripple effect of empowerment showcases how her journey transcends personal struggles, fostering a culture of acceptance and advocacy within the LGBTQ community.

Concluding Reflections

In conclusion, the in-depth interviews with Jin Xing's friends, family, and colleagues paint a rich tapestry of her life. They reveal not only the challenges she has faced but also the profound impact she has had on those around her. The narratives of love, support, and resilience serve as a powerful reminder of the importance of community in the journey toward self-acceptance. As Jin Xing continues to break boundaries and inspire change, the voices of her inner circle will remain a testament to her enduring legacy as a groundbreaking transgender icon in China.

Revealing Jin Xing's personal struggles and triumphs

Jin Xing's journey is a testament to the resilience of the human spirit. It is a narrative woven with threads of struggle, triumph, and an unwavering commitment to authenticity. In a society that often marginalizes those who dare to be different, her life story unfolds as a powerful chronicle of personal battles and victories that resonate deeply with many.

At the core of Jin Xing's struggles lies her battle with gender identity. Growing up in Shenyang, China, she faced the dual challenge of societal expectations and her own internal conflict. The societal norms imposed rigid binaries of gender roles, often leaving little room for deviation. As Jin Xing began to recognize her true self, she encountered a world that was largely unaccepting. This led to profound feelings of isolation and confusion, a common experience among transgender individuals.

$$\text{Identity Conflict} = \text{Societal Expectations} - \text{Personal Truth} \qquad (98)$$

This equation illustrates the tension between Jin Xing's personal truth and the societal expectations that sought to confine her. The struggle for acceptance, both from herself and from the world around her, was exacerbated by the cultural stigma attached to being transgender in China. The traditional views on gender roles and sexuality often left little room for understanding or compassion, creating a hostile environment for those who did not conform.

However, it was through dance that Jin Xing found a sanctuary. Dance became her voice, a medium through which she could express her innermost feelings and navigate her identity. The transformational power of dance allowed her to reclaim her narrative, turning pain into art. Her early successes in local dance competitions served as milestones, affirming her talent and determination. Each performance was not just an artistic expression but a declaration of her identity, a triumph over the struggles she faced.

Jin Xing's decision to undergo gender reassignment surgery marked a significant turning point in her life. This choice, while deeply personal, was fraught with challenges. The surgery itself was a physical manifestation of her journey towards self-acceptance, but it also brought with it a wave of public scrutiny and mixed reactions. The societal backlash she faced post-surgery highlighted the ongoing discrimination against transgender individuals in China.

$$\text{Public Reaction} = f(\text{Cultural Norms, Media Representation}) \qquad (99)$$

This function illustrates how public reaction to Jin Xing's transition was influenced by prevailing cultural norms and the media's portrayal of transgender issues. While some celebrated her courage, others were less forgiving, reflecting the polarized views on gender identity within Chinese society.

Despite these hurdles, Jin Xing's triumphs are profound. Her journey towards self-acceptance and love is a powerful narrative of resilience. The support from her family and friends played a crucial role in this process. Their unwavering love provided a foundation upon which she could build her identity. Jin Xing's story emphasizes the importance of support systems in navigating personal struggles, highlighting that the journey towards self-acceptance is rarely undertaken alone.

Moreover, Jin Xing's impact extends beyond her personal narrative. Her visibility as a transgender woman in the arts has inspired countless individuals within the LGBTQ community. By embracing her true self, she has become a beacon of hope for those grappling with similar struggles. Her story serves as a reminder that personal triumphs can lead to broader societal change.

In summary, Jin Xing's personal struggles and triumphs encapsulate the complexities of navigating gender identity in a conservative society. Her journey illustrates the intertwined nature of personal and societal challenges, showcasing the power of resilience, art, and community support. As she continues to advocate for LGBTQ rights, Jin Xing not only reveals her struggles but also amplifies the voices of many who seek acceptance and understanding in a world that often falls short.

The exploration of Jin Xing's life invites readers to reflect on the broader implications of her journey. It challenges societal norms and encourages a deeper understanding of the transgender experience, emphasizing that every struggle faced is a step towards a more inclusive future.

$$Empowerment = Visibility + Support + Authenticity \qquad (100)$$

This final equation encapsulates the essence of Jin Xing's journey, illustrating that empowerment arises from the confluence of visibility, support, and the courage to live authentically. As we continue to learn from her story, we are reminded of the profound impact that one individual's journey can have on the collective fight for equality and acceptance.

The unauthorized truth behind China's groundbreaking transgender icon

In the realm of LGBTQ activism, few figures resonate with the same intensity as Jin Xing, a name synonymous with courage, artistry, and relentless advocacy. Yet, the narrative surrounding her life and career is often shrouded in layers of complexity, shaped by societal expectations, cultural norms, and the harsh realities of living as a transgender individual in a conservative society. This section delves into the unauthorized truths that illuminate the multifaceted existence of Jin Xing, revealing the struggles, triumphs, and the raw authenticity that defines her journey.

The Dichotomy of Public Persona and Private Struggles

Jin Xing's public image as a glamorous and successful dancer masks a tumultuous personal history. The dichotomy between her celebrated career and the internal battles she faced is a poignant reminder of the often unseen struggles of LGBTQ individuals. The pressures of societal acceptance and the expectations placed upon her as a public figure created a chasm between her authentic self and the persona she projected. This dissonance is not unique to Jin Xing; rather, it reflects a broader phenomenon where LGBTQ individuals often feel compelled to conform to societal norms while grappling with their true identities.

Cultural Context and Societal Norms

To understand Jin Xing's story, one must consider the cultural context of China, a nation with a rich tapestry of traditions and values that often clash with modern notions of gender and sexuality. In a society where conformity is prized, Jin Xing's journey is emblematic of the challenges faced by those who dare to defy norms. The stigma surrounding transgender identities in China is deeply rooted, often leading to discrimination and marginalization. As Jin Xing navigated her path, she encountered not only personal obstacles but also the pervasive societal attitudes that sought to undermine her existence.

The Impact of Gender Reassignment Surgery

Jin Xing's decision to undergo gender reassignment surgery was a pivotal moment in her life, marking both a personal triumph and a source of public scrutiny. The surgery represented her commitment to living authentically, yet it also exposed her to a barrage of criticism and misunderstanding. The media's portrayal of her transformation often lacked nuance, reducing her journey to sensationalism rather than recognizing the profound courage it took to embrace her true self. This highlights a critical issue in the representation of transgender individuals in media—where narratives are frequently oversimplified, depriving audiences of a deeper understanding of the complexities involved in such life-altering decisions.

Unveiling the Untold Stories

The unauthorized truth about Jin Xing's life is also found in the untold stories of resilience and determination that shaped her career. Behind the glitz and glamour of her performances lies a history of relentless hard work and perseverance. Jin Xing faced numerous rejections and challenges as she sought acceptance within the dance community. Her early years were marked by a series of local competitions, where she honed her craft against the backdrop of societal expectations. These formative experiences are often overshadowed by her later successes, yet they are integral to understanding the tenacity that propelled her to stardom.

The Role of Family and Community

Jin Xing's journey was not undertaken in isolation; the support of her family and community played a vital role in her evolution. While societal norms often dictated a narrative of rejection, Jin Xing's experience was enriched by the love and acceptance she received from those closest to her. This aspect of her story challenges the stereotype of the isolated transgender individual, showcasing the importance of familial support in fostering resilience and self-acceptance. It also underscores the need for greater visibility of positive narratives within the LGBTQ community, where stories of love and acceptance can inspire others facing similar struggles.

The Power of Storytelling and Representation

The unauthorized truth of Jin Xing's life is also a testament to the power of storytelling and representation in shaping societal perceptions. By sharing her experiences, Jin Xing has become a beacon of hope for many within the LGBTQ community, demonstrating the possibility of living authentically despite societal pressures. Her journey serves as a reminder of the importance of diverse narratives in media and the arts, where representation can challenge stereotypes and foster understanding. Jin Xing's visibility has not only transformed her own life but has also catalyzed broader discussions about gender and sexuality in China.

Conclusion: The Legacy of Jin Xing

In conclusion, the unauthorized truths behind Jin Xing's life reveal a narrative rich with complexity, resilience, and authenticity. Her journey is not merely one of personal triumph but also a reflection of the broader struggles faced by transgender individuals in a society fraught with challenges. By shedding light on these untold stories, we honor Jin Xing's legacy as a groundbreaking icon—one who has not only transformed the landscape of dance and performance in China but has also paved the way for future generations of LGBTQ activists. As we continue to explore and share these narratives, we contribute to a more inclusive and understanding world, where every individual's story is valued and celebrated.

The importance of seeking truth and authenticity in storytelling

In the realm of storytelling, particularly in the context of biographical narratives, the pursuit of truth and authenticity stands as a cornerstone for effective communication and representation. The significance of these elements is magnified when the subject matter involves marginalized communities, such as the LGBTQ community, where historical narratives have often been skewed or silenced. This section delves into the theoretical underpinnings of truth and authenticity in storytelling, the challenges faced in their pursuit, and the implications of these concepts through relevant examples.

Theoretical Framework

At its core, storytelling is a method of sharing experiences, values, and truths. According to narrative theory, stories serve as a vehicle for understanding human experience, allowing both the storyteller and the audience to engage in a shared dialogue about identity, culture, and emotion. As theorist Mikhail Bakhtin posits, the concept of *polyphony* in literature emphasizes the coexistence of multiple voices and perspectives, which is crucial for presenting a more nuanced and authentic narrative.

In the context of LGBTQ narratives, authenticity can be further understood through the lens of *queer theory*, which challenges normative frameworks and advocates for the representation of diverse identities and experiences. Judith Butler's notion of *gender performativity* suggests that gender and identity are not fixed but are instead constructed through repeated performances. This understanding underscores the importance of presenting authentic stories that reflect the complexities of individual identities rather than reductive stereotypes.

Challenges in Pursuing Truth and Authenticity

Despite the theoretical importance of truth and authenticity, several challenges arise in their pursuit. One major obstacle is the prevalence of *censorship* and societal stigma, particularly in conservative cultures where LGBTQ identities are often marginalized. In such contexts, the narratives that emerge may be influenced or controlled by external forces, leading to a distorted representation of the subject's lived experience.

Additionally, the phenomenon of *gatekeeping* in the media can further complicate the authenticity of narratives. Gatekeepers—editors, producers, and publishers—often hold significant power over which stories are told and how they are framed. This can lead to the omission of critical aspects of a person's identity or experiences, thereby undermining the authenticity of the narrative. For instance, many LGBTQ individuals have reported that their stories were sanitized or altered to fit mainstream expectations, diluting the raw truth of their experiences.

Examples of Authentic Storytelling

The importance of seeking truth and authenticity is exemplified in the work of various LGBTQ activists and artists who have prioritized honest representation in their storytelling. One notable figure is Jin Xing, whose biography serves as a testament to the power of authentic narratives. By openly sharing her journey as a transgender woman in China, Jin Xing challenges societal norms and provides a voice for those who have been silenced. Her story emphasizes the importance of self-acceptance and resilience, resonating with countless individuals facing similar struggles.

Furthermore, the documentary film *Paris is Burning* provides a poignant exploration of the ball culture in New York City, highlighting the lives of LGBTQ individuals who navigate issues of race, class, and gender. The film's authenticity stems from its unfiltered portrayal of the subjects' lives, capturing their triumphs and tribulations in a way that honors their experiences. This raw representation allows audiences to engage with the complexities of identity and the societal structures that shape them.

Implications for Future Storytelling

As we move forward in the realm of storytelling, especially concerning LGBTQ narratives, the commitment to truth and authenticity must remain at the forefront. This involves not only amplifying marginalized voices but also fostering an environment where diverse stories can flourish.

To achieve this, storytellers must prioritize ethical considerations in their work, ensuring that they represent the subjects' experiences accurately and respectfully. This includes engaging in thorough research, seeking input from the individuals being portrayed, and being mindful of the potential impact of their narratives.

In conclusion, the importance of seeking truth and authenticity in storytelling cannot be overstated, particularly in the context of LGBTQ narratives. By embracing these principles, storytellers can contribute to a more inclusive and honest representation of diverse identities, fostering understanding and empathy within society. The legacy of figures like Jin Xing serves as a powerful reminder of the transformative potential of authentic storytelling, urging future generations to continue this vital work.

$$\text{Authenticity} = \frac{\text{Truth}}{\text{Representation}} \times \text{Visibility} \qquad (101)$$

Where:

+ **Authenticity** represents the genuine portrayal of an individual's identity.

+ **Truth** denotes the accuracy of the experiences shared.

+ **Representation** indicates the breadth of perspectives included in the narrative.

♦ **Visibility** reflects the exposure and acknowledgment of marginalized identities.

This equation emphasizes the interdependence of truth, representation, and visibility in achieving authenticity in storytelling, particularly for marginalized communities striving for recognition and acceptance in society.

The impact of revealing Jin Xing's unfiltered truth on her legacy

The journey of Jin Xing, a groundbreaking transgender icon in China, is not merely a narrative of personal triumph but also a profound commentary on the societal constructs surrounding gender and identity. By unveiling her unfiltered truth, Jin Xing has significantly influenced her legacy, redefining the parameters of acceptance and representation in a conservative society.

At the core of Jin Xing's impact lies the concept of *authenticity*, which can be understood through the lens of social identity theory. According to this theory, individuals derive a sense of self from their group memberships, leading to a complex interplay between personal identity and societal expectations. Jin Xing's decision to publicly embrace her gender identity challenged the normative frameworks that often dictate the lives of transgender individuals in China. By sharing her story, she has not only validated her own experiences but also provided a voice to countless others who grapple with similar issues.

One profound effect of revealing her truth has been the shift in public perception regarding transgender individuals. Prior to Jin Xing's emergence as a cultural icon, the representation of transgender people in Chinese media was largely negative or non-existent. By taking center stage, she has catalyzed a broader conversation about gender diversity. This aligns with Judith Butler's theory of gender performativity, which posits that gender is not an inherent quality but rather a series of acts and performances that reinforce societal norms. Jin Xing's performances, both on stage and in media, exemplify this theory, illustrating how one can challenge and reshape public narratives around gender identity.

Moreover, the unveiling of Jin Xing's truth has had significant implications for the LGBTQ community in China. The act of being open about her struggles, including her experiences with discrimination and her journey toward self-acceptance, has fostered a sense of solidarity among marginalized individuals. This phenomenon can be linked to the concept of *collective identity*, where shared experiences create a sense of belonging and empowerment within a community. Jin Xing's visibility has inspired many to embrace their identities, leading to a burgeoning movement advocating for LGBTQ rights in China.

However, revealing one's unfiltered truth is not without its challenges. Jin Xing has faced backlash and scrutiny from various sectors of society, including conservative factions that view her existence as a threat to traditional values. This resistance highlights the ongoing struggle for acceptance and the need for continued advocacy. The backlash she faced serves as a reminder of the societal barriers that still exist, necessitating a persistent fight for equality and recognition.

An illustrative example of the impact of her unfiltered truth can be seen in the way she has leveraged her platform as a television judge on "So You Think You Can Dance China." Her presence on a mainstream platform has not only normalized the visibility of transgender individuals but has also educated the public about the complexities of gender identity. By showcasing talent from diverse backgrounds, she has effectively broadened the discourse surrounding LGBTQ issues, making them more accessible to the general populace.

In addition to her media presence, Jin Xing's advocacy work has further solidified her legacy. She has used her influence to champion for LGBTQ rights, emphasizing the importance of representation in all facets of society. Her efforts align with the theories of social change, which posit that visibility and representation can lead to greater acceptance and policy reform. Through her dance company and various initiatives, Jin Xing has created spaces for dialogue and understanding, fostering an environment where individuals can express their true selves without fear of retribution.

The impact of revealing Jin Xing's unfiltered truth extends beyond her personal legacy; it has sparked a cultural shift in China. The dialogue surrounding gender and sexuality is evolving, and Jin Xing stands at the forefront of this transformation. Her story has become a beacon of hope for many, illustrating the power of resilience and the importance of living one's truth. As she continues to navigate her journey, the implications of her truth will resonate across generations, inspiring future activists and artists to challenge societal norms and advocate for inclusivity.

In conclusion, the revelation of Jin Xing's unfiltered truth has profoundly shaped her legacy. It has catalyzed a movement for acceptance and representation in a society that often marginalizes those who do not conform to traditional gender roles. By embracing her identity and sharing her experiences, Jin Xing has not only transformed her own life but has also paved the way for future generations to live authentically. Her legacy is a testament to the power of truth, resilience, and the enduring fight for equality in the face of adversity.

The complexities of human experience and the power of honesty

The human experience is a tapestry woven from diverse threads of identity, culture, and emotion. Each individual's journey is unique, shaped by a multitude of factors including socio-economic background, personal struggles, and the broader societal context. In the case of Jin Xing, her life exemplifies the intricate interplay between personal identity and societal expectations, particularly as a transgender woman in a conservative society.

To understand the complexities of human experience, we must first recognize the multidimensional nature of identity. Identity is not a singular construct but rather a confluence of various elements such as gender, sexuality, race, and class. The theory of intersectionality, introduced by Kimberlé Crenshaw, posits that individuals experience overlapping systems of oppression and privilege based on these interconnected identities. For Jin Xing, being a transgender woman in China meant navigating a landscape fraught with discrimination and societal stigma, which adds layers of complexity to her experience.

$$I = f(G, S, R, C) \tag{102}$$

Where I represents identity, G is gender, S is sexuality, R is race, and C is class. This function illustrates that identity is a function of multiple variables, each contributing to the overall experience of the individual.

Honesty plays a crucial role in navigating these complexities. The act of being honest about one's identity and experiences can be both liberating and perilous. For Jin Xing, her decision to publicly embrace her transgender identity was a radical act of honesty in a society where such openness is often met with hostility. This honesty not only empowered her but also inspired many within the LGBTQ community to embrace their true selves, challenging the status quo.

However, the power of honesty is not without its challenges. The societal backlash that often accompanies such revelations can lead to isolation and discrimination. Jin Xing faced significant hurdles, including public scrutiny and personal attacks, which highlight the risks that come with authenticity. The psychological toll of living authentically in a society that may not accept one's identity can lead to mental health issues, including anxiety and depression.

Research indicates that LGBTQ individuals who are able to live openly and authentically report higher levels of well-being compared to those who feel compelled to hide their identities. A study conducted by the American Psychological Association found that the ability to express one's identity freely is linked to positive mental health outcomes. This reinforces the idea that honesty, while challenging, is integral to personal well-being.

$$W = h(H, A) \tag{103}$$

Where W is well-being, H represents honesty, and A denotes acceptance. This equation suggests that well-being is a function of both honesty and acceptance, emphasizing the importance of a supportive environment in fostering mental health.

Jin Xing's journey illustrates the transformative power of honesty, not just for herself but for the community at large. Her visibility as a transgender woman has sparked conversations about gender identity and the rights of LGBTQ individuals in China. By sharing her story, she has opened doors for dialogue, challenging stereotypes and fostering understanding.

Moreover, the complexities of human experience are further compounded by cultural narratives that shape perceptions of identity. In many societies, including China, traditional views on gender and sexuality often clash with contemporary understandings of these concepts. Jin Xing's presence in the media serves as a counter-narrative to these traditional views, demonstrating that authenticity can coexist with cultural heritage.

The power of honesty extends beyond individual experiences; it has the potential to catalyze societal change. By being true to herself, Jin Xing has not only claimed her space in the dance world but has also become a beacon of hope for those struggling with their identities. Her story resonates with many, illustrating that honesty can lead to empowerment and the possibility of a more inclusive society.

In conclusion, the complexities of human experience are intricately tied to the power of honesty. For individuals like Jin Xing, embracing one's true self amidst societal pressures is a profound act that can inspire change and foster understanding. The journey towards honesty is fraught with challenges, yet it holds the potential for personal liberation and collective progress. As we reflect on Jin Xing's life, we are reminded of the importance of authenticity in our own narratives and the transformative impact it can have on the world around us.

Honoring Jin Xing's journey through an unbiased narrative

In the realm of biographical storytelling, particularly concerning figures like Jin Xing, the imperative to present an unbiased narrative cannot be overstated. An unbiased narrative seeks to honor the complexities of an individual's life without succumbing to sensationalism or reductive interpretations. This is especially significant in the context of Jin Xing, whose journey as a transgender icon in China is fraught with cultural, social, and political implications.

Theoretical Framework

To appreciate the nuances of Jin Xing's narrative, we can draw upon theories of representation and identity politics. Stuart Hall's encoding/decoding model provides a useful lens through which to analyze how Jin Xing's story is constructed and received. According to Hall, media texts are encoded with particular meanings by their creators and decoded by audiences in various ways, influenced by their own cultural contexts. Thus, an unbiased narrative must consider both the intended meanings behind Jin Xing's life choices and the diverse interpretations that arise from her audience.

Additionally, Judith Butler's theory of gender performativity posits that gender is not a fixed identity but rather a series of acts that are socially constructed. This theory underscores the importance of viewing Jin Xing's journey through the lens of her lived experiences, emphasizing that her identity is shaped by her actions, societal perceptions, and the cultural environment in which she operates.

Challenges in Representation

Despite the theoretical frameworks that guide unbiased narratives, several challenges persist in accurately representing Jin Xing's journey. One significant problem lies in the pervasive stereotypes and biases surrounding transgender individuals, particularly in conservative societies like China. Media portrayals often lean towards sensationalism, focusing on the struggles and controversies rather than the achievements and contributions of individuals like Jin Xing.

For example, when Jin Xing underwent gender reassignment surgery, media coverage frequently sensationalized her decision, framing it as a spectacle rather than a personal milestone. This not only undermines her agency but also perpetuates harmful narratives that reduce her identity to mere sensationalism. An unbiased narrative must strive to transcend these stereotypes, focusing instead on Jin Xing's resilience, artistry, and advocacy for LGBTQ rights.

Examples of Unbiased Narratives

To honor Jin Xing's journey authentically, we can look to several examples of narratives that have successfully navigated the complexities of her identity. One such example is her own autobiography, where she articulates her experiences with vulnerability and honesty. By sharing her story in her own words, Jin Xing provides a firsthand account that challenges preconceived notions and invites readers to engage with her journey on a deeper level.

Another example can be found in documentaries that focus on Jin Xing's life and career. These films often include interviews with family, friends, and colleagues, offering a multifaceted perspective that highlights her impact on the dance world and the LGBTQ community. By incorporating diverse voices, these narratives create a more comprehensive understanding of Jin Xing's significance, moving beyond a singular, biased portrayal.

The Role of Empathy in Storytelling

Empathy plays a crucial role in crafting an unbiased narrative. By fostering an understanding of Jin Xing's experiences, storytellers can bridge the gap between her individual journey and broader societal issues. For instance, when discussing the challenges she faced as a transgender individual in China, it is essential to contextualize these struggles within the larger framework of LGBTQ rights and cultural norms.

Moreover, empathy allows audiences to connect with Jin Xing's story on a personal level. When readers or viewers can relate to her struggles and triumphs, they are more likely to engage with the underlying messages of acceptance and resilience. This connection can inspire action and advocacy, furthering the cause of LGBTQ rights and representation.

Conclusion

In conclusion, honoring Jin Xing's journey through an unbiased narrative requires a commitment to authenticity, empathy, and a nuanced understanding of the complexities of identity. By employing theoretical frameworks, addressing challenges in representation, and drawing upon powerful examples, we can create a narrative that not only respects Jin Xing's experiences but also contributes to a broader dialogue about LGBTQ rights and representation in society.

The task of crafting such narratives is not merely an academic exercise; it is a vital part of the ongoing struggle for visibility and acceptance. As we honor Jin Xing's journey, we must remain vigilant against biases and stereotypes, ensuring that her story is told with the dignity and respect it deserves. In doing so, we not only celebrate her achievements but also pave the way for future generations of LGBTQ individuals to share their own stories with pride and authenticity.

The final word on Jin Xing's inspiring story

Jin Xing's journey is not merely the tale of a dancer or a transgender icon; it is a profound narrative that encapsulates the struggles, triumphs, and relentless spirit of an individual who dared to defy societal norms. Her life and career exemplify the intersectionality of art, identity, and activism, serving as a beacon of hope for many within the LGBTQ community and beyond.

At its core, Jin Xing's story illustrates the critical importance of visibility in the fight for equality. As a transgender woman in a society that often marginalizes those who do not conform to traditional gender roles, her presence in the public eye challenges entrenched stereotypes and fosters understanding. The concept of visibility can be understood through the lens of Judith Butler's theory of gender performativity, which posits that gender is not a fixed trait but rather a performance shaped by societal expectations. Jin Xing's performances, therefore, become acts of resistance against the rigid binaries imposed by society.

The problems faced by Jin Xing, including discrimination, societal rejection, and the challenges of navigating her identity in a conservative culture, highlight the systemic barriers that many LGBTQ individuals encounter. For instance, in a country where traditional gender norms are deeply rooted, Jin Xing's decision to embrace her true self and pursue her passion for dance was not without peril. The backlash she faced post-surgery exemplifies the societal stigma that often accompanies such life-altering decisions. This resonates with the experiences of many transgender individuals worldwide, who often find themselves at the intersection of personal truth and societal acceptance.

Moreover, Jin Xing's advocacy for LGBTQ rights extends beyond her personal narrative. Her establishment of the Shanghai Jin Xing Dance Theatre is a testament to her commitment to creating spaces where marginalized voices can be heard and celebrated. This initiative not only provides a platform for artistic expression but also serves as a sanctuary for individuals seeking acceptance and understanding. The importance of such spaces cannot be overstated, as they foster community and resilience among those who have been historically silenced.

In her role as a judge on "So You Think You Can Dance China," Jin Xing utilized her platform to promote inclusivity, challenging contestants and viewers alike to embrace diversity. Her presence on national television was revolutionary, as it introduced a broader audience to the complexities of gender identity and the richness of LGBTQ culture. This aligns with the theory of social representation, which posits that media portrayals can significantly influence public perceptions and attitudes towards marginalized groups. Jin Xing's impact in this realm is a powerful reminder of the responsibility that media figures hold in shaping societal narratives.

As we reflect on Jin Xing's legacy, it is essential to consider the ongoing fight for LGBTQ rights globally. While Jin Xing has made significant strides in advocating for acceptance and understanding in China, the struggle for equality is far from over.

The challenges faced by LGBTQ individuals in many parts of the world continue to persist, underscoring the necessity for continued activism and allyship. Jin Xing's story serves as both a source of inspiration and a call to action, urging individuals to stand up for equality and embrace the diversity that enriches our communities.

In conclusion, Jin Xing's inspiring story is a testament to the power of resilience, authenticity, and the transformative nature of art. Her journey encourages us to confront our biases, challenge societal norms, and advocate for a world where everyone can live authentically without fear of discrimination or prejudice. As we carry forward the lessons gleaned from her life, let us honor her legacy by amplifying the voices of those still fighting for their place in the world. The final word on Jin Xing's story is not just about her triumphs but also about the collective responsibility we share to foster an inclusive future for all.

$$\text{Visibility} + \text{Advocacy} \rightarrow \text{Social Change} \tag{104}$$

This equation encapsulates the essence of Jin Xing's impact—where visibility and advocacy converge to create meaningful social change, paving the way for a more inclusive and accepting society.

Beyond Boundaries

Beyond Boundaries

Beyond Boundaries

In the journey of Jin Xing, the chapter titled "Beyond Boundaries" encapsulates not just her personal evolution but also the broader implications of her existence as a transgender icon in a society often marred by conservative values. This section aims to explore the multifaceted impact of Jin Xing's life and work on the LGBTQ movement within China and beyond, illustrating how one individual's story can transcend cultural, societal, and geographical boundaries.

3.1 The Significance of Jin Xing's Visibility in a Conservative Society

Jin Xing's emergence as a public figure in China during a time when LGBTQ visibility was virtually non-existent is a testament to her courage and resilience. Her visibility serves as a beacon of hope for many who identify as LGBTQ in a society that often stigmatizes and marginalizes them. The concept of visibility in LGBTQ activism is crucial; as noted by theorist Judith Butler, visibility can empower communities by challenging the normative frameworks that dictate gender and sexuality.

In China, where traditional values often clash with modern expressions of identity, Jin Xing's presence on stage and screen has played a pivotal role in redefining what it means to be transgender. By openly embracing her identity, she has not only inspired countless individuals but has also challenged the status quo, prompting discussions around gender fluidity and acceptance.

3.2 The Inspirational Influence of Jin Xing on the LGBTQ Community

Jin Xing's influence extends far beyond her performances; she has become a symbol of resilience and empowerment for the LGBTQ community in China. Her journey resonates with many who face similar struggles, reinforcing the idea that personal narratives are powerful tools for social change. According to sociologist Erving Goffman, the concept of "passing"—the ability to be accepted as a member of a different social group—can often lead to internalized stigma. Jin Xing's authenticity counters this notion, demonstrating that embracing one's true self can lead to greater acceptance and understanding.

For instance, her participation in various dance competitions and television shows has not only showcased her talent but has also brought LGBTQ issues to the forefront of public discourse. By succeeding in mainstream media, Jin Xing has paved the way for other LGBTQ individuals to pursue their passions without fear of discrimination.

3.3 Promoting Acceptance and Understanding Through Jin Xing's Work

Through her art, Jin Xing promotes acceptance and understanding of LGBTQ identities. Her performances often embody themes of love, struggle, and resilience, which resonate with audiences regardless of their sexual orientation. The impact of art as a medium for social change is well-documented; as theorized by cultural critic bell hooks, art can serve as a powerful vehicle for challenging societal norms and fostering empathy.

Jin Xing's choreography often incorporates elements of traditional Chinese dance while infusing modern interpretations that reflect her personal journey. This blend not only highlights her unique identity but also serves as a reminder of the rich cultural heritage that can coexist with contemporary expressions of self. Her work challenges the binary notions of gender and encourages audiences to embrace a more fluid understanding of identity.

3.4 Overcoming Cultural Barriers Through Education and Awareness

Education and awareness are critical in overcoming cultural barriers that perpetuate discrimination against LGBTQ individuals. Jin Xing has taken an active role in advocating for LGBTQ rights through public speaking engagements, workshops, and collaborations with educational institutions. By sharing her story and educating others about the challenges faced by the LGBTQ community, she fosters a culture of understanding and acceptance.

Research has shown that educational programs that include LGBTQ topics can significantly reduce prejudice and increase acceptance among students. Jin Xing's efforts to engage with younger generations reflect her commitment to creating a more inclusive future. By empowering youth to embrace diversity, she contributes to a gradual shift in societal attitudes towards LGBTQ individuals.

3.5 The Lasting Legacy of Jin Xing's Activism in China

The legacy of Jin Xing's activism is profound. As she continues to break barriers, her influence extends beyond the dance floor and into the hearts and minds of those who witness her journey. The concept of legacy is often tied to the idea of social capital, as articulated by Pierre Bourdieu, which refers to the resources and connections that individuals can draw upon to effect change.

Jin Xing's legacy is not only rooted in her achievements as a dancer and choreographer but also in her unwavering commitment to advocacy. Her story has inspired a new generation of activists who are willing to challenge oppressive systems and fight for equality. The ripple effect of her activism is evident in the growing visibility of LGBTQ issues in China, as more individuals feel empowered to share their stories and advocate for their rights.

3.6 The Impact of Jin Xing's Story on the Broader LGBTQ Rights Movement in China

Jin Xing's narrative serves as a microcosm of the broader LGBTQ rights movement in China. Her experiences highlight the complexities of navigating identity in a rapidly changing society. The intersectionality of her identity—being a transgender woman of color—adds layers to her story, as she confronts not only gender-based discrimination but also cultural prejudices.

As LGBTQ rights continue to evolve in China, Jin Xing's role as a cultural and political figure becomes increasingly significant. Her advocacy work has sparked conversations around the need for legal protections for LGBTQ individuals, as well as the importance of mental health resources and support networks. The impact of her story is felt not only in China but also globally, as it resonates with activists and allies advocating for equality and justice.

3.7 Jin Xing's Role as a Cultural and Political Figure in the LGBTQ Movement

As a cultural and political figure, Jin Xing embodies the potential for art to drive social change. Her visibility challenges the narrative that LGBTQ identities are incompatible with traditional values. By occupying spaces typically reserved for heterosexual narratives, she redefines cultural norms and paves the way for future generations to express their identities authentically.

Jin Xing's participation in international LGBTQ events and forums further amplifies her voice as an advocate for change. Her ability to navigate different cultural contexts while remaining true to her identity exemplifies the power of intersectional activism. By engaging with global movements, she fosters solidarity among LGBTQ activists worldwide, reinforcing the idea that the fight for equality knows no borders.

3.8 The Ongoing Struggle for LGBTQ Equality in China and the Challenges Ahead

Despite the progress made, the struggle for LGBTQ equality in China remains fraught with challenges. Cultural stigmas, legal barriers, and societal discrimination continue to hinder the advancement of LGBTQ rights. The Chinese government's stance on LGBTQ issues often reflects broader geopolitical tensions, complicating the fight for recognition and acceptance.

Jin Xing's activism highlights the importance of resilience in the face of adversity. As she navigates the complexities of being a public figure in a conservative society, her story serves as a reminder that change is a gradual process. The ongoing struggle for LGBTQ equality requires collective efforts, solidarity, and a commitment to challenging oppressive systems.

3.9 The Potential for Societal Change and Progress in China

While the road ahead may be challenging, there is potential for societal change and progress in China. The increasing visibility of LGBTQ individuals and issues in media and popular culture reflects a shift in public attitudes. Young people, in particular, are more open to discussions about gender and sexuality, indicating a generational change in perspectives.

Jin Xing's role in this transformation cannot be understated. As she continues to advocate for LGBTQ rights and visibility, she inspires others to join the movement. The potential for societal change lies in the collective efforts of individuals who are willing to challenge the status quo and fight for a more inclusive future.

3.10 The Hope for a More Inclusive and Accepting Future in China

Ultimately, the hope for a more inclusive and accepting future in China rests on the shoulders of activists like Jin Xing. Her story serves as a beacon of hope for those who dare to dream of a world where everyone can live authentically and without fear. As societal attitudes continue to evolve, the fight for LGBTQ rights will remain a vital component of the broader struggle for human rights.

In conclusion, "Beyond Boundaries" encapsulates the essence of Jin Xing's journey—one that transcends personal struggles and speaks to the collective fight for acceptance and equality. Through her visibility, activism, and unwavering commitment to authenticity, Jin Xing has not only changed the narrative around LGBTQ identities in China but has also inspired countless individuals to embrace their true selves. The chapter serves as a powerful reminder that while boundaries may exist, they can be transcended through courage, resilience, and the relentless pursuit of justice.

Jin Xing's Impact on the LGBTQ Movement in China

The significance of Jin Xing's visibility in a conservative society

Jin Xing's emergence as a prominent figure in the dance world is not merely a story of artistic triumph; it is also a profound commentary on the complexities of identity and acceptance in a conservative society like China. Her visibility as a transgender icon challenges societal norms and provides a beacon of hope for many who struggle with their own identities in an environment that often stigmatizes differences.

In conservative cultures, where traditional gender roles and expectations are deeply entrenched, individuals who deviate from the norm face significant obstacles. The societal framework often dictates rigid definitions of masculinity and femininity, leaving little room for the expression of diverse identities. Jin Xing, through her very existence and success, disrupts these conventions. She embodies the idea that gender is not binary but rather a spectrum, a notion supported by Judith Butler's theory of gender performativity, which posits that gender is constructed through repeated social performances rather than being an innate quality [?].

The visibility of Jin Xing serves multiple functions in a conservative society:

1. **Representation**: Jin Xing's presence in mainstream media and the arts provides representation for transgender individuals, who are often marginalized or rendered invisible. Representation is crucial because it fosters a sense of belonging and validation among those who identify as LGBTQ. According to a study by the Human Rights Campaign, representation in media can significantly influence public perception and acceptance of LGBTQ individuals [?]. Jin Xing's performances and

public appearances challenge the stereotype of transgender individuals as deviant or abnormal, instead showcasing them as talented, capable, and deserving of respect.

2. **Normalization**: By being unapologetically herself, Jin Xing normalizes the existence of transgender individuals in society. Her success in the arts demonstrates that talent and hard work can transcend societal prejudices. This normalization is vital in a culture where transgender identities are often viewed with suspicion or hostility. The concept of normalization aligns with Erving Goffman's theory of stigma, which suggests that societal acceptance is often contingent upon the visibility and portrayal of marginalized groups [?]. Jin Xing's visibility acts as a counter-narrative to the stigma surrounding transgender individuals, fostering a more inclusive discourse.

3. **Advocacy and Activism**: Jin Xing leverages her platform to advocate for LGBTQ rights, using her visibility to highlight issues faced by the community. Her role as a judge on "So You Think You Can Dance China" not only showcases her talent but also positions her as a spokesperson for change. Through her advocacy, she raises awareness of the challenges faced by transgender individuals, such as discrimination, lack of legal recognition, and societal rejection. The impact of her activism is profound; it encourages dialogue and reflection on gender identity and rights within the broader society.

4. **Cultural Dialogue**: Jin Xing's visibility ignites conversations about gender and sexuality in a society that often shies away from such discussions. By challenging the status quo, she invites others to question their beliefs and biases. This cultural dialogue is essential for progress, as it fosters understanding and empathy. In a conservative society where discussions about LGBTQ issues are often taboo, Jin Xing's openness serves as a catalyst for change, encouraging others to share their stories and experiences.

5. **Inspiration**: For many individuals grappling with their identities, Jin Xing represents hope and possibility. Her journey from a small-town dancer to a national icon illustrates that it is possible to overcome societal barriers. This inspirational narrative resonates deeply within the LGBTQ community, providing encouragement to those who may feel isolated or unsupported. The psychological concept of self-efficacy, as proposed by Albert Bandura, suggests that individuals are more likely to pursue their goals when they observe others who have succeeded despite adversity [?]. Jin Xing's story exemplifies this principle, inspiring countless individuals to embrace their true selves.

In conclusion, Jin Xing's visibility in a conservative society holds significant importance. It challenges entrenched norms, fosters representation and normalization, advocates for rights, encourages cultural dialogue, and inspires individuals. Her journey illustrates the power of visibility in promoting acceptance and understanding, paving the way for a more inclusive future for all. As societies continue to grapple with issues of identity and acceptance, Jin Xing stands as a testament to the transformative power of being seen and heard.

The inspirational influence of Jin Xing on the LGBTQ community

Jin Xing has emerged as a beacon of hope and inspiration for the LGBTQ community, particularly in a society where acceptance and understanding of gender diversity remain deeply entrenched in traditional norms. Her journey from a young boy in Shenyang to a celebrated transgender icon exemplifies resilience and courage, making her an influential figure in advocating for LGBTQ rights in China and beyond.

At the heart of Jin Xing's influence is her ability to transcend the limitations imposed by societal expectations. Her story resonates with many who have faced discrimination and adversity due to their identity. By publicly embracing her true self, Jin Xing has challenged the pervasive stigma surrounding transgender individuals, offering a narrative of empowerment that encourages others to live authentically. This aligns with Judith Butler's theory of gender performativity, which posits that gender is not a fixed attribute but rather a series of performances shaped by societal norms. Jin Xing's performances in dance and media serve as a powerful demonstration of this theory, showcasing the fluidity of identity and the potential for self-definition.

Furthermore, Jin Xing's visibility in mainstream media has played a crucial role in normalizing transgender identities in a culture that often marginalizes them. As a judge on the popular television show "So You Think You Can Dance China," she not only showcased her artistic talents but also used her platform to advocate for inclusivity and acceptance. Her presence on such a widely viewed program has sparked conversations about gender and sexuality, challenging viewers to confront their biases and expand their understanding of the LGBTQ community. This is particularly significant in a conservative society where discussions about gender non-conformity are often taboo.

One poignant example of Jin Xing's impact is her ability to connect with young LGBTQ individuals who often feel isolated and misunderstood. In interviews, many have shared how Jin Xing's story inspired them to embrace their identities and pursue their passions despite societal pressures. This phenomenon aligns with the Social Identity Theory, which suggests that individuals derive a sense of self from their group memberships. Jin Xing's prominence provides a reference point for young people, allowing them to see themselves reflected in a successful and respected figure.

Moreover, Jin Xing's advocacy extends beyond her personal narrative; she actively engages in community outreach and support initiatives. By establishing the Shanghai Jin Xing Dance Theatre, she has created a safe space for LGBTQ artists to express themselves and hone their craft. This initiative not only nurtures talent but also fosters a sense of belonging among marginalized individuals. The theatre serves as a microcosm of the broader LGBTQ movement, emphasizing the importance of community and solidarity in the face of adversity.

However, Jin Xing's influence is not without challenges. Despite her success, she has faced backlash from conservative factions within Chinese society who view her as a threat to traditional values. This resistance underscores the ongoing struggle for LGBTQ rights in China, where legal protections are limited, and societal acceptance remains elusive. Nevertheless, Jin Xing's perseverance in the face of such adversity serves as a powerful reminder of the importance of advocacy and visibility in driving social change.

In conclusion, Jin Xing's inspirational influence on the LGBTQ community is multifaceted, encompassing her personal journey, media presence, and advocacy efforts. By challenging societal norms and fostering community, she has become a symbol of hope for many. Her story exemplifies the power of representation in inspiring individuals to embrace their identities and advocate for change. As the LGBTQ movement continues to evolve, Jin Xing's legacy will undoubtedly serve as a guiding light for future generations, reminding us all of the strength found in authenticity and resilience.

Promoting acceptance and understanding through Jin Xing's work

Jin Xing, a groundbreaking figure in the LGBTQ movement in China, has utilized her platform as a dancer, choreographer, and television personality to promote acceptance and understanding of gender diversity. Through her artistic endeavors and public persona, she has challenged societal norms and fostered dialogue surrounding LGBTQ issues in a country where such discussions are often stigmatized.

The Role of Art in Advocacy

Art has long been a powerful medium for social change, serving as a means of expression and a catalyst for dialogue. Jin Xing's work exemplifies this, as she uses dance not only to entertain but to convey profound messages about identity, acceptance, and the human experience. In her performances, she often incorporates themes of transformation and self-discovery, reflecting her own journey as a transgender woman. This artistic expression resonates with audiences, inviting them to contemplate the complexities of gender and identity.

One notable performance that highlights this aspect is her piece titled *Metamorphosis*, which draws parallels between the physical transformation of a caterpillar into a butterfly and Jin Xing's own transition. The choreography is imbued with emotion, showcasing the struggles and triumphs of embracing one's true self. By presenting her story through the universal language of dance, Jin Xing breaks down barriers and fosters empathy among her viewers.

Challenging Stereotypes

Jin Xing's visibility as a transgender icon in the Chinese media has been instrumental in challenging stereotypes and misconceptions surrounding the LGBTQ community. In a society where traditional gender roles are deeply entrenched, her success and confidence serve as a counter-narrative to the stigmatization faced by many LGBTQ individuals.

For instance, in her role as a judge on the popular television show *So You Think You Can Dance China*, Jin Xing openly discusses her experiences and the importance of authenticity. Her presence on the show not only provides representation for transgender individuals but also educates the audience about the diversity of gender identities. By normalizing conversations about gender and sexuality, she promotes acceptance and understanding among viewers who may have previously held prejudiced views.

Community Engagement and Education

Beyond her performances and television appearances, Jin Xing actively engages with the community to promote LGBTQ rights and education. She has organized workshops and seminars aimed at fostering dialogue about gender identity and sexual orientation. These initiatives provide a safe space for individuals to share their experiences and learn from one another, thereby cultivating a sense of belonging and acceptance.

In one such workshop, participants were encouraged to express their identities through creative mediums, including dance, visual arts, and storytelling. This approach not only empowers individuals to embrace their authentic selves but also fosters understanding among diverse groups. By sharing their stories, participants contribute to a collective narrative that challenges societal norms and promotes inclusivity.

Theoretical Framework: Social Identity Theory

To understand the impact of Jin Xing's work on promoting acceptance, we can draw on Social Identity Theory, which posits that individuals derive a sense of self from their group memberships. This theory suggests that when marginalized groups are represented positively in society, it can lead to improved self-esteem and a greater sense of belonging among individuals within those groups.

Jin Xing's visibility and advocacy work provide a crucial counter-narrative to the often negative portrayals of LGBTQ individuals in mainstream media. By showcasing the beauty and resilience of the LGBTQ community, she not only uplifts those within the community but also educates the broader society, fostering a more inclusive environment.

Case Studies: Impact on Public Perception

Several case studies demonstrate the positive impact of Jin Xing's work on public perception of LGBTQ issues in China. For example, following her appearance on *So You Think You Can Dance China*, surveys indicated a significant increase in acceptance of transgender individuals among viewers, particularly among younger demographics.

Moreover, Jin Xing's involvement in high-profile campaigns, such as the *Love is Love* initiative, has further amplified her message of acceptance. This campaign aimed to raise awareness about LGBTQ rights and promote inclusivity within Chinese society. The campaign's success was evident in the increased visibility of LGBTQ issues in public discourse and media coverage, highlighting the effectiveness of Jin Xing's advocacy.

Conclusion

Through her artistic expression, public engagement, and advocacy efforts, Jin Xing has played a pivotal role in promoting acceptance and understanding of LGBTQ issues in China. Her work not only challenges stereotypes but also fosters dialogue and education within the community and beyond. As a cultural icon, Jin Xing continues to inspire individuals to embrace their true selves and advocate for a more inclusive society, demonstrating the profound impact of art as a vehicle for social change.

Overcoming cultural barriers through education and awareness

Cultural barriers often pose significant challenges to the acceptance and understanding of LGBTQ individuals, particularly in conservative societies. Education and awareness serve as pivotal tools in dismantling these barriers, fostering a more inclusive environment where diversity can thrive. This section explores the role of education and awareness in overcoming cultural barriers, highlighting theoretical frameworks, prevalent issues, and practical examples.

Theoretical Frameworks

To understand how education and awareness can bridge cultural divides, we can draw upon several theoretical frameworks:

- **Social Learning Theory** posits that individuals learn behaviors and norms through observation and imitation. By exposing individuals to positive representations of LGBTQ lives, society can reshape perceptions and reduce prejudice.

- **Contact Theory** suggests that under appropriate conditions, interpersonal contact is one of the most effective ways to reduce prejudice between majority and minority groups. Education initiatives that promote interactions between LGBTQ individuals and the broader community can foster understanding and empathy.

- **Critical Pedagogy** emphasizes the role of education in challenging societal norms and empowering marginalized voices. It encourages educators to create curricula that reflect diverse perspectives, thus validating the experiences of LGBTQ individuals.

Identifying Cultural Barriers

Cultural barriers manifest in various forms, including:

- **Stereotypes and Misconceptions:** Many societies harbor stereotypes about LGBTQ individuals, often viewing them as deviant or unnatural. These misconceptions can lead to discrimination and social ostracism.

- **Lack of Representation:** In many cultures, LGBTQ individuals are underrepresented in media, education, and leadership roles. This absence reinforces the notion that their lives and experiences are not valid or worthy of acknowledgment.

+ **Cultural Norms and Values:** Traditional beliefs about gender roles and sexuality can create rigid frameworks that marginalize LGBTQ identities. In many cultures, deviation from these norms is met with hostility and rejection.

The Role of Education

Education plays a crucial role in challenging and transforming cultural barriers. By integrating LGBTQ-inclusive curricula in schools, educators can promote understanding and acceptance from an early age. For example, incorporating literature that features LGBTQ characters or histories can provide students with relatable narratives that foster empathy.

Furthermore, training programs for educators can equip them with the tools to address LGBTQ issues sensitively and knowledgeably. This training can include:

+ Workshops on LGBTQ history and rights.

+ Strategies for creating safe and inclusive classroom environments.

+ Techniques for addressing bullying and discrimination effectively.

Raising Awareness

Awareness campaigns can significantly shift public perceptions of LGBTQ communities. These campaigns often employ various media forms to disseminate information and challenge stereotypes. For instance, social media platforms have become powerful tools for advocacy, allowing LGBTQ individuals to share their stories and experiences widely.

A notable example of an effective awareness campaign is the "It Gets Better" project, which aims to inspire hope for LGBTQ youth facing bullying and discrimination. By sharing personal stories of resilience and success, the campaign has fostered a sense of community and support.

Moreover, public events such as Pride parades and educational workshops can serve as platforms for raising awareness and promoting dialogue. These events not only celebrate LGBTQ identities but also invite non-LGBTQ individuals to learn and engage in conversations about diversity and acceptance.

Challenges and Resistance

Despite the potential for education and awareness to overcome cultural barriers, several challenges remain:

+ **Institutional Resistance:** Many educational institutions may resist implementing LGBTQ-inclusive curricula due to fear of backlash from conservative groups or parents. This resistance can hinder progress and perpetuate ignorance.

+ **Cultural Backlash:** In some societies, increased visibility of LGBTQ issues can provoke backlash from traditionalist factions. This backlash can manifest in discriminatory laws, hate speech, and violence against LGBTQ individuals.

+ **Limited Resources:** Many educational systems, particularly in low-income areas, lack the resources to provide comprehensive training and materials on LGBTQ issues. This limitation can result in a lack of understanding and perpetuation of cultural barriers.

Conclusion

Overcoming cultural barriers through education and awareness is a vital step towards fostering acceptance and inclusivity for LGBTQ individuals. By employing theoretical frameworks such as Social Learning Theory, Contact Theory, and Critical Pedagogy, society can begin to dismantle the stereotypes and misconceptions that perpetuate discrimination. While challenges remain, the potential for transformative change through education and awareness initiatives cannot be overstated.

As we continue to advocate for LGBTQ rights, it is imperative that we prioritize educational efforts aimed at fostering understanding and acceptance. Only then can we hope to create a society where everyone, regardless of their sexual orientation or gender identity, can live authentically and without fear.

$$\text{Acceptance} = \text{Education} + \text{Awareness} + \text{Engagement} \qquad (105)$$

The lasting legacy of Jin Xing's activism in China

Jin Xing's activism has transcended the boundaries of dance and performance, establishing her as a pivotal figure in the ongoing struggle for LGBTQ rights in China. Her legacy is not only rooted in her artistic contributions but also in her relentless advocacy for acceptance, understanding, and equality. This section explores the multifaceted impact of Jin Xing's activism and how it has shaped the landscape of LGBTQ rights in China.

Cultural Shifts and Visibility

One of the most significant aspects of Jin Xing's legacy is her role in increasing visibility for transgender individuals and the broader LGBTQ community in China. By openly embracing her identity and sharing her journey, Jin Xing has challenged the traditional norms and stereotypes that have long marginalized LGBTQ individuals. Her presence in mainstream media, particularly through her role as a judge on "So You Think You Can Dance China," has provided a platform for discussions surrounding gender identity and sexual orientation.

The cultural shifts initiated by Jin Xing's activism can be analyzed through the lens of social movement theory, particularly the concept of *frame resonance*. According to Benford and Snow (2000), social movements are more likely to succeed when they can resonate with the values and beliefs of the broader society. Jin Xing's narrative of resilience and authenticity has resonated with many, fostering a greater understanding of LGBTQ issues and encouraging empathy among the public.

Challenging Discrimination

Jin Xing's activism has also been instrumental in challenging systemic discrimination against LGBTQ individuals in China. She has used her platform to address issues such as workplace discrimination, mental health stigma, and the lack of legal protections for LGBTQ individuals. For instance, her outspoken criticism of discriminatory practices in the dance industry has prompted conversations about inclusivity and fairness, inspiring other artists to advocate for their rights.

The problem of discrimination faced by LGBTQ individuals in China is compounded by deeply entrenched cultural beliefs, which often view non-heteronormative identities as deviant. Jin Xing's advocacy has aimed to dismantle these beliefs by highlighting the common humanity shared among all individuals, regardless of their sexual orientation or gender identity. Her efforts have encouraged many to confront their biases and engage in dialogues about acceptance.

Empowerment and Representation

Jin Xing's legacy is also characterized by her commitment to empowering others within the LGBTQ community. By establishing the Shanghai Jin Xing Dance Theatre, she has created a space for LGBTQ artists to express themselves freely and authentically. This initiative not only provides employment opportunities but also serves as a beacon of hope for aspiring dancers who may have felt marginalized in traditional dance environments.

Furthermore, Jin Xing's visibility has inspired a new generation of LGBTQ activists and artists in China. The representation of transgender individuals in popular culture is crucial for fostering acceptance, as it challenges the stereotypes that perpetuate discrimination. Jin Xing's success has demonstrated that it is possible to thrive as an LGBTQ individual in a society that often marginalizes such identities, thereby encouraging others to embrace their authentic selves.

International Influence and Solidarity

Jin Xing's activism extends beyond China, contributing to the global conversation surrounding LGBTQ rights. Her international tours and collaborations have not only showcased her talent but have also highlighted the struggles faced by LGBTQ individuals in different cultural contexts. This cross-cultural exchange fosters solidarity among LGBTQ communities worldwide, reinforcing the idea that the fight for equality is a shared struggle.

The global impact of Jin Xing's activism can be framed through the concept of *transnational advocacy networks*, as described by Keck and Sikkink (1998). These networks facilitate the exchange of information and resources among activists across borders, amplifying their voices and experiences. Jin Xing's story has resonated with activists globally, inspiring collaborative efforts to address LGBTQ rights on an international scale.

Educational Initiatives and Awareness

In addition to her artistic endeavors, Jin Xing has been involved in educational initiatives aimed at raising awareness about LGBTQ issues in China. By partnering with NGOs and educational institutions, she has contributed to programs that promote understanding and acceptance among youth. These initiatives are crucial for combating the misinformation and prejudice that often fuel discrimination against LGBTQ individuals.

The effectiveness of educational programs in promoting social change can be understood through the theory of *social learning*. Bandura (1977) posits that individuals learn behaviors and attitudes through observation and imitation. By providing positive representations of LGBTQ individuals and sharing her own experiences, Jin Xing has created opportunities for young people to learn about diversity and acceptance in a constructive manner.

Conclusion

In summary, Jin Xing's activism has left an indelible mark on the landscape of LGBTQ rights in China. Her commitment to visibility, empowerment, and education has fostered cultural shifts that challenge discrimination and promote acceptance. As a cultural icon, Jin Xing continues to inspire individuals both within China and globally, reinforcing the importance of resilience and authenticity in the ongoing fight for equality. Her legacy serves as a testament to the power of activism in shaping societal attitudes and fostering a more inclusive future.

The impact of Jin Xing's story on the broader LGBTQ rights movement in China

Jin Xing's journey from a small town in Shenyang to becoming a celebrated international dance icon and LGBTQ activist represents a pivotal narrative in the evolution of the LGBTQ rights movement in China. Her story not only highlights personal resilience and triumph but also serves as a catalyst for broader societal change.

The LGBTQ rights movement in China has historically faced significant challenges, including stringent government regulations, cultural stigmas, and societal discrimination. As a transgender individual, Jin Xing's visibility and success challenge the prevailing narratives around gender and sexuality in a country where traditional norms often dictate the parameters of identity. Her life and career have become emblematic of the struggles and aspirations of many within the LGBTQ community.

One of the most critical impacts of Jin Xing's story is the shift in public perception regarding transgender individuals. Prior to her emergence, discussions surrounding gender identity were often shrouded in ignorance and prejudice. Jin Xing's success as a performer and choreographer has provided a human face to the transgender experience, facilitating a more nuanced understanding of gender diversity. This aligns with the theory of *social representation*, which posits that visibility in media and public life can significantly alter societal attitudes. As Jin Xing has taken center stage, she has helped to dismantle stereotypes and foster a sense of empathy among the broader populace.

Moreover, Jin Xing's activism has galvanized younger generations of LGBTQ individuals in China. Her decision to publicly embrace her identity and advocate for rights has inspired many to come forward and share their own stories. This phenomenon can be analyzed through the lens of *collective identity theory*, which suggests that shared experiences and narratives can unify individuals within a marginalized group, leading to collective action and advocacy. Jin Xing's openness about her struggles and triumphs has encouraged many to engage in activism, fostering a sense of community and solidarity.

Jin Xing's influence extends beyond individual narratives; it has also catalyzed discussions around policy reform. The increasing visibility of LGBTQ individuals, spurred by her story, has prompted calls for legal protections and recognition of rights. For instance, her appearances on national television and participation in public forums have brought attention to the need for anti-discrimination laws and greater acceptance of diverse identities. This aligns with *Framing Theory*, which emphasizes the role of media and public discourse in shaping social issues. Jin Xing's presence in the media has reframed the conversation around LGBTQ rights in China, pushing it into the public consciousness and demanding attention from policymakers.

Furthermore, Jin Xing's story resonates on an international scale, impacting global perceptions of LGBTQ rights in China. Her participation in international dance festivals and collaborations with global artists has positioned her as a cultural ambassador, illustrating the complexities of gender and sexuality within a Chinese context. This has opened avenues for international dialogue and advocacy, as global audiences become more aware of the challenges faced by LGBTQ individuals in China. The intersectionality of Jin Xing's identity—being both a Chinese national and a transgender woman—highlights the need for a global understanding of LGBTQ issues that considers cultural specificities.

However, it is essential to acknowledge the backlash and challenges that continue to exist within the movement. Despite Jin Xing's prominence, the LGBTQ community in China still faces significant hurdles, including censorship, discrimination, and societal rejection. The Chinese government has historically been wary of movements that challenge the status quo, often stifling dissent and curtailing freedom of expression. Jin Xing's story, while inspiring, also serves as a reminder of the ongoing struggle for rights and recognition.

In conclusion, Jin Xing's impact on the broader LGBTQ rights movement in China is multifaceted. Her journey has not only transformed public perceptions of transgender individuals but has also inspired a new generation of activists and fostered discussions around policy reform. By challenging cultural norms and advocating for visibility, Jin Xing has become a beacon of hope for many, illustrating the power of personal narratives in driving social change. As her story continues to unfold, it serves as a testament to the resilience of the LGBTQ community in China and the ongoing quest for equality and acceptance.

$$Impact = Visibility + Advocacy + Collective\ Identity + Policy\ Change \quad (106)$$

This equation encapsulates the essence of Jin Xing's influence: her visibility has led to increased advocacy, fostering a collective identity among LGBTQ individuals, which in turn has prompted calls for policy change. The journey is ongoing, but the foundation laid by Jin Xing's story is undeniable and significant in shaping the future of LGBTQ rights in China.

Jin Xing's role as a cultural and political figure in the LGBTQ movement

Jin Xing stands as a formidable cultural and political figure in the LGBTQ movement, not only within China but also on the global stage. Her journey from a young dancer in Shenyang to an internationally recognized icon illustrates the profound impact that individual narratives can have on societal change. Jin's visibility as a transgender woman has challenged deeply entrenched cultural norms and sparked dialogues about gender identity and sexual orientation in a society that has historically marginalized LGBTQ individuals.

Cultural Significance

Jin Xing's influence extends beyond her artistic contributions; she embodies the struggle for acceptance and equality in a conservative society. Her presence in the media has been pivotal in normalizing discussions around transgender identities in China. By performing in mainstream venues and participating in popular television shows, she has opened doors for LGBTQ representation in spaces that were previously inaccessible. This visibility plays a crucial role in reshaping public perceptions and fostering a more inclusive culture.

The cultural significance of Jin Xing's work can be analyzed through the lens of cultural hegemony, a concept introduced by Antonio Gramsci. Cultural hegemony refers to the dominance of one cultural group over others, often leading to the marginalization of alternative identities. Jin's rise to prominence challenges this hegemony by asserting the validity of transgender experiences and identities within the fabric of Chinese culture. Her performances and public persona disrupt the narrative that traditionally confines gender to a binary framework, thereby encouraging a broader understanding of gender fluidity.

Political Advocacy

Jin Xing's role as a political figure is equally noteworthy. She has used her platform to advocate for LGBTQ rights in China, often speaking out against discrimination and injustice. In a country where homosexuality was decriminalized only in 1997 and remains stigmatized, Jin's activism is a beacon of hope for many. She has been involved in various initiatives aimed at raising awareness about LGBTQ issues, including participating in pride events and collaborating with organizations dedicated to promoting equality.

One of the most significant aspects of Jin's advocacy is her ability to bridge cultural and political divides. She engages with policymakers and community leaders to foster dialogue about LGBTQ rights, emphasizing the importance of inclusion in national discussions. This approach aligns with the theories of social movement theory, particularly the concept of resource mobilization, which posits that successful movements require not only grassroots support but also the engagement of influential figures who can leverage their status to effect change.

Challenges Faced

Despite her success, Jin Xing has faced considerable challenges in her role as a cultural and political figure. The conservative nature of Chinese society means that her advocacy often encounters resistance. Many individuals within the LGBTQ community face systemic discrimination, and Jin's visibility can sometimes attract backlash from conservative factions. This dichotomy highlights the precarious balance between progress and backlash in the fight for LGBTQ rights.

Furthermore, Jin's journey underscores the complexities of navigating identity within a political landscape. While she has become a symbol of hope for many, her experiences also reflect the internal struggles faced by individuals in the LGBTQ community. The intersectionality of gender, sexuality, and culture complicates the narrative, as not all members of the LGBTQ community experience the same level of acceptance or privilege. This is particularly relevant in discussions of the global LGBTQ movement, where varying cultural contexts can lead to differing experiences of acceptance and resistance.

Examples of Impact

Jin Xing's impact is evident in various initiatives and collaborations that promote LGBTQ visibility and rights. For instance, her role as a judge on the Chinese version of "So You Think You Can Dance" has not only showcased her talent but also allowed her to mentor and uplift emerging LGBTQ artists. This mentorship is vital in nurturing the next generation of activists and artists who can continue to push for change.

Additionally, Jin's participation in international dance festivals has facilitated cultural exchange and dialogue about gender and sexuality. By representing China on global platforms, she challenges stereotypes and fosters understanding between cultures. Her performances often incorporate themes of identity and resilience, resonating with audiences worldwide and encouraging empathy and support for LGBTQ issues.

Conclusion

In conclusion, Jin Xing's role as a cultural and political figure in the LGBTQ movement is multifaceted and impactful. Through her artistry, advocacy, and resilience, she has become a symbol of hope and a catalyst for change. Her journey reflects the ongoing struggle for LGBTQ rights in China and serves as a reminder of the power of visibility and representation. As she continues to break barriers and inspire others, Jin Xing remains a pivotal figure in the fight for equality, embodying the spirit of resilience and determination that is essential in the ongoing quest for justice and acceptance.

The ongoing struggle for LGBTQ equality in China and the challenges ahead

The quest for LGBTQ equality in China is a complex and multifaceted struggle, deeply rooted in the country's historical, cultural, and political contexts. Despite significant strides made in recent years, the journey towards full acceptance and equality remains fraught with challenges. This section explores the ongoing struggle for LGBTQ rights in China, examining the barriers faced by the community and the efforts being made to overcome them.

Historical Context

To understand the current landscape of LGBTQ rights in China, it is crucial to consider the historical context. Homosexuality was decriminalized in China in 1997, and it was removed from the official list of mental disorders in 2001. However, these legal changes did not automatically translate into social acceptance. Traditional Confucian values, which emphasize heteronormative family structures and filial piety, continue to exert a strong influence on societal attitudes towards LGBTQ individuals. As a result, many LGBTQ individuals face familial pressure to conform to traditional roles, leading to a pervasive culture of silence and stigma.

Cultural Barriers

Cultural barriers remain a significant obstacle to LGBTQ equality in China. The stigma associated with being LGBTQ is deeply ingrained in society, often leading to discrimination, harassment, and violence. Many LGBTQ individuals experience rejection from their families, which can result in homelessness and mental health issues. The lack of positive representation in media further perpetuates stereotypes and misconceptions about LGBTQ individuals, reinforcing societal prejudices.

Legal and Political Challenges

While there have been some advancements in legal protections for LGBTQ individuals, significant gaps remain. There is no comprehensive anti-discrimination law that explicitly protects LGBTQ individuals in employment, housing, or public accommodations. Moreover, same-sex marriage is not recognized, leaving many couples without legal rights and protections. The Chinese government maintains a tight grip on civil society, which poses challenges for LGBTQ advocacy organizations. Activists often face harassment, censorship, and even detention for their efforts to promote equality.

Activism and Resistance

Despite these challenges, a vibrant LGBTQ movement has emerged in China, characterized by grassroots activism and increasing visibility. Organizations such as the Beijing LGBT Center and Shanghai Pride have played pivotal roles in advocating for LGBTQ rights, providing support services, and raising awareness about issues affecting the community. Online platforms have also become crucial spaces for LGBTQ individuals to connect, share their stories, and mobilize for change.

Recent Developments

In recent years, there have been some positive developments in the fight for LGBTQ equality in China. The rise of LGBTQ-themed films and television shows has helped to increase visibility and foster discussions about gender and sexuality. Events such as Pride parades, although often met with resistance, have drawn attention to the struggles faced by the community. Additionally, younger generations are increasingly embracing progressive values, challenging traditional norms, and advocating for greater acceptance.

Challenges Ahead

Despite these advancements, the path forward is fraught with challenges. The Chinese government's tightening control over civil society poses significant risks for LGBTQ activists and organizations. Censorship of LGBTQ content in media and online platforms continues to stifle open discussions about gender and sexuality. Moreover, the ongoing influence of conservative ideologies threatens to undermine the progress made by the LGBTQ movement.

The Role of Education and Awareness

Education and awareness are crucial in addressing the challenges faced by the LGBTQ community in China. Initiatives aimed at promoting understanding and acceptance of diverse sexual orientations and gender identities can help to dismantle stereotypes and reduce discrimination. Comprehensive sex education that includes LGBTQ topics is essential for fostering a more inclusive society. By challenging misconceptions and fostering empathy, education can play a pivotal role in advancing LGBTQ rights in China.

Conclusion

The ongoing struggle for LGBTQ equality in China is emblematic of a broader fight for human rights and social justice. While significant challenges remain, the resilience and determination of the LGBTQ community continue to inspire hope for a more inclusive future. As activists work tirelessly to advocate for change, it is essential to recognize the importance of solidarity, education, and awareness in the pursuit of equality. The journey may be long, but the commitment to breaking down barriers and fostering acceptance will ultimately pave the way for a more equitable society for all.

$$Equality = Visibility + Advocacy + Education \quad (107)$$

In this equation, the variables represent the fundamental components necessary for achieving LGBTQ equality in China. Visibility ensures that LGBTQ voices are heard and recognized; advocacy mobilizes support for legal and social changes; and education fosters understanding and acceptance among the broader population.

$$Challenges = Censorship + Discrimination + Stigma \quad (108)$$

This equation highlights the key challenges faced by the LGBTQ community in China. Censorship restricts the flow of information and representation, discrimination manifests in various forms of social and legal inequities, and stigma perpetuates a culture of silence and fear.

The journey toward LGBTQ equality in China is ongoing, and while the road ahead may be fraught with obstacles, the collective efforts of activists, allies, and advocates will continue to drive the movement forward, one step at a time.

The potential for societal change and progress in China

The potential for societal change and progress in China, particularly regarding LGBTQ rights, is a complex interplay of cultural, political, and social factors. As the country navigates its rapid modernization and globalization, the traditional views that have long dominated Chinese society are increasingly challenged. This section explores the mechanisms through which societal change can occur, the barriers that remain, and the hopeful signs of progress.

Cultural Shifts and Generational Change

One of the most significant drivers of change in China is the generational shift in attitudes towards LGBTQ individuals. Younger generations, having been exposed to global narratives through the internet and social media, tend to be more accepting of diverse sexual orientations and gender identities. A 2021 survey conducted by the Chinese Academy of Social Sciences found that **over 70% of respondents aged 18-25** expressed support for LGBTQ rights, a stark contrast to older generations who may hold more conservative views. This generational divide suggests a potential for progressive change as younger individuals move into positions of influence within society.

Media Representation and Visibility

Media representation plays a crucial role in shaping public perceptions of LGBTQ individuals. The increasing visibility of LGBTQ characters and themes in popular Chinese media, such as films, television shows, and online content, has contributed to a gradual normalization of LGBTQ identities. For instance, the success of the film *Call Me by Your Name* and the Chinese drama series *Addicted* sparked conversations around LGBTQ issues, demonstrating the power of storytelling in fostering empathy and understanding.

However, while there are positive developments, censorship remains a significant barrier. The Chinese government often restricts LGBTQ content, labeling it as "non-mainstream." This creates a paradox where the demand for representation exists, but the supply is heavily regulated. Advocates argue that increased media representation can challenge stereotypes and promote acceptance, but they must navigate the complexities of censorship to achieve this goal.

Activism and Grassroots Movements

Grassroots activism has become a powerful force for change in China. Organizations such as *PFLAG China* and *The Chinese LGBTQ Network* have mobilized to advocate for LGBTQ rights, providing support and resources to individuals facing discrimination. These organizations often utilize social media platforms to raise awareness and foster community, reaching audiences that traditional methods of activism might not.

The impact of these grassroots movements is evident in the growing number of pride events across the country. Cities like Shanghai and Beijing have witnessed increased participation in pride parades, despite facing pushback from authorities. Such events serve not only as a celebration of identity but also as a platform for political expression, highlighting the demand for equality and legal recognition.

Legal Framework and Policy Changes

The legal landscape for LGBTQ individuals in China remains challenging, with homosexuality decriminalized but lacking formal protections against discrimination. However, there are signs of potential progress. Legal scholars and activists are increasingly pushing for reforms, advocating for anti-discrimination laws that would protect LGBTQ individuals in employment, healthcare, and housing.

The case of *Li Ying* in 2019, where a court ruled in favor of a transgender woman seeking recognition of her gender identity, marked a significant step forward. Although the ruling was limited in scope, it set a precedent for future cases and demonstrated the judiciary's capacity to engage with LGBTQ issues. Such legal victories, however small, are crucial in building momentum for broader societal change.

International Influence and Solidarity

International pressure and solidarity also play a vital role in advancing LGBTQ rights in China. Global movements for equality have inspired local activists to adopt similar strategies and frameworks. The visibility of international LGBTQ events, such as the *Global Pride* initiative, encourages Chinese activists to connect with their counterparts worldwide, fostering a sense of shared purpose and solidarity.

Furthermore, international organizations are increasingly collaborating with local NGOs, providing resources and training to enhance advocacy efforts. This exchange of knowledge and strategies can empower local movements, equipping them with the tools needed to navigate the unique challenges they face in China.

Challenges Ahead

Despite the promising signs of change, significant challenges remain. The Chinese government's strict control over civil society and free expression poses ongoing risks for activists and organizations advocating for LGBTQ rights. The crackdown on dissent and the tightening of regulations on NGOs create an environment of fear, where individuals may hesitate to speak out or engage in activism.

Moreover, deeply entrenched cultural norms and values continue to influence public attitudes towards LGBTQ individuals. Many still face familial pressure to conform to traditional roles, which can lead to internalized stigma and reluctance to embrace their identities openly.

Conclusion

In conclusion, the potential for societal change and progress in China regarding LGBTQ rights is palpable but fraught with challenges. The interplay of generational shifts, media representation, grassroots activism, legal reforms, and international solidarity creates a multifaceted landscape for change. While the road ahead may be complex, the resilience and determination of activists and allies provide hope for a more inclusive and accepting future. As society continues to evolve, the voices of LGBTQ individuals will be pivotal in shaping the narrative and advocating for their rights, ultimately contributing to a broader movement for equality and justice in China.

The hope for a more inclusive and accepting future in China

The journey toward a more inclusive and accepting future for the LGBTQ community in China is fraught with challenges, yet it is imbued with hope and potential for transformation. The societal landscape is slowly evolving, influenced by a myriad of factors including globalization, increased visibility, and the tireless efforts of activists like Jin Xing.

Cultural Shifts and Global Influences

In recent years, cultural shifts have begun to take root, driven in part by the globalization of ideas and the influence of international LGBTQ movements. The rise of social media platforms has provided a space for LGBTQ individuals to connect, share their stories, and advocate for their rights. This digital revolution has not only fostered a sense of community but has also allowed for the dissemination of progressive ideas that challenge traditional norms.

For instance, the visibility of LGBTQ characters in popular media and the success of international pride events have sparked conversations about acceptance in Chinese society. The portrayal of LGBTQ individuals in films and television shows, although still limited, is gradually becoming more nuanced and representative. This shift is crucial, as representation plays a pivotal role in shaping public perceptions and attitudes.

The Role of Education and Awareness

Education remains a cornerstone in the fight for equality. Efforts to incorporate LGBTQ issues into educational curricula can help dismantle prejudices and foster understanding from a young age. Programs aimed at educating both students and teachers about gender diversity and sexual orientation can significantly reduce stigma and discrimination.

Research indicates that inclusive educational environments lead to better outcomes for LGBTQ youth, including lower rates of bullying and mental health issues. A study by [1] highlights that schools that implement comprehensive anti-bullying policies and LGBTQ-inclusive curricula see a marked improvement in the overall school climate.

Activism and Advocacy

The role of activism cannot be overstated in the pursuit of an inclusive future. Grassroots organizations and activists are at the forefront of advocating for legal reforms, such as the recognition of same-sex relationships and anti-discrimination laws. These efforts are essential in creating a legal framework that protects LGBTQ individuals and promotes equality.

Jin Xing's advocacy work exemplifies the power of visibility and representation. By using her platform to speak out against discrimination and promote acceptance, she has inspired countless individuals to embrace their identities and fight for their rights. Her participation in international forums and collaborations with global

LGBTQ organizations further amplifies her impact, bridging cultural divides and fostering solidarity.

Challenges Ahead

Despite the progress made, significant challenges remain. The conservative nature of Chinese society, deeply rooted in traditional values, often clashes with the push for LGBTQ rights. Censorship and government crackdowns on LGBTQ activism pose ongoing threats to freedom of expression. Reports from organizations like [2] document instances of harassment and violence against LGBTQ individuals, underscoring the urgent need for protective measures.

Moreover, the intersectionality of issues such as race, class, and gender complicates the landscape of LGBTQ rights in China. Marginalized communities within the LGBTQ spectrum often face compounded discrimination, necessitating a more inclusive approach to advocacy that addresses these intersecting identities.

The Path Forward

The hope for a more inclusive and accepting future in China lies in the collective efforts of individuals, communities, and organizations committed to change. Building alliances across different social movements can strengthen the fight for LGBTQ rights, highlighting the interconnectedness of various struggles for justice and equality.

As the younger generation becomes more vocal and engaged, there is potential for a cultural renaissance that embraces diversity. The rise of youth-led movements, coupled with the increasing visibility of LGBTQ issues in public discourse, signals a shift toward greater acceptance.

Conclusion

In conclusion, while the road to a more inclusive future for the LGBTQ community in China is paved with obstacles, the resilience and determination of activists, coupled with evolving cultural attitudes, illuminate a path forward. The hope lies in continued advocacy, education, and the unwavering belief that change is possible. As Jin Xing and others have demonstrated, the power of visibility, representation, and community can catalyze social transformation, paving the way for a society where all individuals can live authentically and without fear.

Bibliography

[1] Smith, J. (2019). *The Impact of Inclusive Education on LGBTQ Youth: A Study of School Climate*. Journal of LGBTQ Issues in Counseling, 13(1), 45-60.

[2] Human Rights Watch. (2020). *China: Events of 2019*. Retrieved from `https://www.hrw.org/world-report/2020/country-chapters/china-and-tibet`

The Global Fight for LGBTQ Rights

The state of LGBTQ rights worldwide

The landscape of LGBTQ rights across the globe is marked by a complex interplay of progress and regression. While some nations have made significant strides toward equality, others remain entrenched in discrimination and violence. This section aims to provide a comprehensive overview of the current state of LGBTQ rights worldwide, examining the theoretical frameworks that underpin these rights, the problems that persist, and notable examples from various regions.

Theoretical Frameworks of LGBTQ Rights

At the core of LGBTQ rights discourse lies the concept of human rights, which posits that all individuals, regardless of their sexual orientation or gender identity, are entitled to the same rights and freedoms. The Universal Declaration of Human Rights (UDHR), adopted by the United Nations in 1948, serves as a foundational document in this regard. Article 1 states, "All human beings are born free and equal in dignity and rights," which is a principle that advocates for the inclusion of LGBTQ individuals within the broader human rights framework.

However, the application of these rights often encounters challenges. The intersectionality theory, introduced by Kimberlé Crenshaw, emphasizes that individuals experience oppression in varying configurations and degrees of intensity based on their overlapping identities, including race, gender, sexuality, and socioeconomic status. This theory is crucial for understanding the nuanced experiences of LGBTQ individuals, particularly in regions where cultural, religious, and legal systems are hostile to non-heteronormative identities.

Global Overview of LGBTQ Rights

Progressive Regions   In recent years, several countries have made remarkable advancements in LGBTQ rights. For instance, in 2015, the United States Supreme Court ruled in *Obergefell v. Hodges* that same-sex marriage is a constitutional right, marking a significant milestone in the fight for equality. Similarly, countries like Canada, Germany, and the Netherlands have enacted comprehensive anti-discrimination laws and legal recognition of same-sex partnerships.

In Latin America, nations such as Argentina and Uruguay have pioneered LGBTQ rights by legalizing same-sex marriage and implementing anti-discrimination legislation. Argentina, in particular, has been lauded for its Gender Identity Law, which allows individuals to change their gender identity on official documents without requiring surgery.

Regressive Regions   Conversely, many regions continue to impose severe restrictions on LGBTQ rights. In parts of Africa, such as Uganda and Nigeria, homosexuality is criminalized, with penalties ranging from imprisonment to death. These laws are often justified by cultural and religious beliefs, leading to widespread discrimination and violence against LGBTQ individuals.

In the Middle East, countries like Saudi Arabia and Iran enforce strict anti-LGBTQ laws, with reports of executions and brutal punishments for those accused of homosexuality. The intersection of cultural conservatism and religious extremism in these regions creates a hostile environment for LGBTQ individuals, who often face persecution and marginalization.

Challenges to LGBTQ Rights

Despite progress in some areas, significant challenges remain. One of the most pressing issues is the backlash against LGBTQ rights, often referred to as the "backlash phenomenon." This backlash can manifest in various forms, including the enactment of anti-LGBTQ legislation, increased violence against LGBTQ individuals, and the rise of conservative movements that seek to roll back rights.

For instance, in Hungary, the government has introduced laws that restrict the rights of LGBTQ individuals, including a ban on the adoption of children by same-sex couples. Similarly, in Poland, the government has supported the creation of "LGBT-free zones," which have been met with international condemnation.

The Role of Activism and International Solidarity

Activism plays a crucial role in advancing LGBTQ rights worldwide. Grassroots organizations and international NGOs work tirelessly to advocate for policy changes, raise awareness, and provide support to marginalized communities. The role of social media in mobilizing support and disseminating information cannot be overstated; platforms like Twitter and Instagram have become vital tools for LGBTQ activists to share their stories and connect with allies across borders.

International solidarity is also essential in the fight for LGBTQ rights. Global movements, such as Pride Month and the International Day Against Homophobia, Transphobia, and Biphobia, serve as platforms for raising awareness and advocating for change. The involvement of international bodies, such as the United Nations, in promoting LGBTQ rights has also been instrumental in holding governments accountable for human rights violations.

Conclusion

The state of LGBTQ rights worldwide is a reflection of broader social, cultural, and political dynamics. While significant progress has been made in some regions, the struggle for equality continues in many parts of the world. The theoretical frameworks of human rights and intersectionality provide valuable lenses through which to understand these complexities. As activists and allies work to dismantle oppressive systems and promote inclusivity, the global fight for LGBTQ rights remains a critical aspect of the broader human rights movement.

$$\text{LGBTQ Rights} = \frac{\text{Legal Protections} + \text{Social Acceptance}}{\text{Cultural Resistance} + \text{Political Backlash}} \tag{109}$$

The role of LGBTQ activists in the fight for equality

The role of LGBTQ activists in the fight for equality is fundamental to the advancement of civil rights and social justice. Activists have been at the forefront of challenging discriminatory laws, societal norms, and cultural stigmas that marginalize LGBTQ individuals. Their work spans a multitude of areas, including legal reform, public awareness campaigns, and community organizing. This section delves into the various dimensions of LGBTQ activism, highlighting its significance, challenges, and the impact it has made on the global landscape.

Historical Context

The modern LGBTQ rights movement gained momentum in the mid-20th century, particularly following pivotal events such as the Stonewall Riots of 1969. This uprising against police harassment in New York City marked a turning point, galvanizing activists to organize and demand equal rights. Activists like Marsha P. Johnson and Sylvia Rivera emerged as leaders, advocating for the rights of marginalized groups within the LGBTQ community, including transgender individuals and people of color. Their legacy underscores the importance of intersectionality in activism, recognizing that the fight for equality must address multiple layers of oppression.

Legal Advocacy and Policy Change

One of the primary roles of LGBTQ activists is to advocate for legal reforms that promote equality and protect against discrimination. This includes lobbying for anti-discrimination laws, marriage equality, and the right to adopt children. For instance, the landmark Supreme Court case *Obergefell v. Hodges* (2015) legalized same-sex marriage across the United States, a significant victory for LGBTQ activists. The case highlighted the importance of legal recognition and the right to love freely, reinforcing the notion that love is a fundamental human right.

Activists often employ various strategies in their advocacy efforts, including:

- **Grassroots Mobilization:** Organizing rallies, protests, and campaigns to raise awareness and support for LGBTQ rights.

- **Lobbying:** Engaging with lawmakers to influence policy and legislation that affects the LGBTQ community.

- **Litigation:** Challenging discriminatory laws through the court system, as seen in cases like *Bostock v. Clayton County* (2020), which ruled that employment discrimination based on sexual orientation or gender identity is illegal under Title VII of the Civil Rights Act of 1964.

Public Awareness and Education

Beyond legal advocacy, LGBTQ activists play a crucial role in public awareness and education. They work to challenge stereotypes and misconceptions about LGBTQ individuals through campaigns that promote understanding and acceptance. Organizations such as the Human Rights Campaign and GLAAD utilize media, social platforms, and community outreach to foster dialogue and educate the public about LGBTQ issues.

For example, the "It Gets Better" project, initiated in 2010, aimed to provide hope and support to LGBTQ youth facing bullying and discrimination. By sharing personal stories and experiences, activists sought to create a sense of community and resilience among young people, demonstrating that they are not alone in their struggles.

Intersectionality in Activism

The concept of intersectionality, coined by legal scholar Kimberlé Crenshaw, is vital in understanding the role of LGBTQ activists. This framework emphasizes that individuals experience overlapping identities—such as race, gender, sexuality, and socioeconomic status—that shape their experiences of oppression and privilege. LGBTQ activists recognize that the fight for equality must be inclusive and address the unique challenges faced by marginalized groups within the community.

For instance, activists like Audre Lorde and bell hooks have highlighted the importance of considering race and gender in the LGBTQ rights movement. Their work advocates for a more inclusive approach that acknowledges the diverse experiences of LGBTQ individuals, particularly those who are also part of racial and ethnic minority groups.

Global Perspectives and Challenges

While LGBTQ activism has made significant strides in many parts of the world, challenges persist, particularly in regions where homosexuality is criminalized or where cultural norms are deeply entrenched in heteronormativity. Activists in countries such as Uganda and Russia face severe repercussions, including violence and imprisonment, for advocating for LGBTQ rights.

International organizations, such as Amnesty International and ILGA (International Lesbian, Gay, Bisexual, Trans and Intersex Association), work alongside local activists to provide support and amplify their voices. The global LGBTQ movement emphasizes solidarity and the sharing of resources and strategies to combat oppression, illustrating the interconnectedness of the struggle for equality.

Conclusion

The role of LGBTQ activists in the fight for equality is multifaceted and indispensable. Through legal advocacy, public awareness, and an intersectional approach, activists challenge discrimination and work towards a more inclusive society. Their efforts not only advance the rights of LGBTQ individuals but also contribute to broader movements for social justice and human rights. As the fight for equality continues, the resilience and determination of LGBTQ activists remain a beacon of hope for future generations.

$$\text{Equality} = \frac{\text{Legal Rights} + \text{Social Acceptance}}{\text{Discrimination}} \tag{110}$$

This equation symbolizes the ongoing quest for equality, where the numerator represents the essential components needed for true equality, while the denominator reflects the barriers that must be overcome. The work of LGBTQ activists is vital in reducing discrimination and fostering a society where everyone can live authentically and without fear.

The impact of Jin Xing's story on the global LGBTQ movement

Jin Xing's journey from a humble dancer in Shenyang to an internationally recognized transgender icon has reverberated far beyond the borders of China, inspiring LGBTQ activists and allies across the globe. Her story serves as a powerful testament to the resilience of the human spirit and the transformative potential of visibility and representation.

At the heart of Jin Xing's impact lies her ability to challenge deeply entrenched societal norms and prejudices. As a transgender woman in a conservative society, she faced significant obstacles, including discrimination, societal rejection, and the internal struggle of reconciling her identity with cultural expectations. By publicly embracing her identity and sharing her experiences, Jin Xing has helped to dismantle stereotypes and foster a greater understanding of transgender issues.

One of the most significant theoretical frameworks that can be applied to understand Jin Xing's impact is Judith Butler's theory of gender performativity. Butler posits that gender is not an inherent quality but rather a performance, shaped by societal norms and expectations. Jin Xing's career in dance exemplifies this theory; her performances transcend traditional gender binaries, showcasing the fluidity of gender expression. By embodying her authentic self on stage, she challenges audiences to reconsider their preconceived notions of gender and sexuality.

Moreover, Jin Xing's story highlights the intersectionality of identity. As a prominent figure in the LGBTQ community, she has brought attention to the unique challenges faced by transgender individuals, particularly in non-Western contexts. This intersectional approach is crucial in understanding the global LGBTQ movement, which often grapples with the complexities of race, class, and culture. Jin Xing's advocacy has sparked conversations about the need for inclusivity within the movement, emphasizing that the fight for LGBTQ rights must address the diverse experiences of individuals across different backgrounds.

An example of Jin Xing's global influence can be seen in her participation in international events and collaborations. Her performances have not only captivated audiences but have also opened doors for dialogue about LGBTQ rights in countries where such discussions are often stigmatized. For instance, her work with Western artists has facilitated cultural exchange, allowing her to share her story and the struggles of the Chinese LGBTQ community with a broader audience. This exchange is essential for building solidarity among LGBTQ activists worldwide and fostering a collective effort towards equality.

Furthermore, Jin Xing's visibility in mainstream media has played a pivotal role in shaping public perceptions of transgender individuals. As a judge on "So You Think You Can Dance China," she has used her platform to advocate for LGBTQ representation, challenging the media's often narrow portrayals of gender and sexuality. Her presence on such a widely viewed program has not only educated viewers but has also provided a sense of hope and validation for LGBTQ individuals in China and beyond. The representation of diverse identities in media is crucial for fostering acceptance and understanding; as Stuart Hall argues, media representations shape cultural narratives and influence societal attitudes.

Despite her achievements, Jin Xing's journey has not been without challenges. She has faced backlash and criticism from conservative factions within society, highlighting the ongoing struggle for LGBTQ rights in many parts of the world. This resistance underscores the importance of continued advocacy and activism. Jin Xing's story serves as a reminder that progress is often met with opposition, but it is through these struggles that meaningful change can occur.

In conclusion, Jin Xing's impact on the global LGBTQ movement is profound and multifaceted. Her story not only challenges societal norms but also fosters a deeper understanding of the complexities of gender identity and expression. By advocating for representation and inclusivity, she has inspired countless individuals to embrace their authentic selves and fight for their rights. As the global LGBTQ movement continues to evolve, Jin Xing's legacy will undoubtedly serve as a beacon of hope, reminding us all of the power of resilience, visibility, and the unwavering pursuit of equality.

$$Impact = Visibility + Representation + Advocacy \qquad (111)$$

The challenges and progress in different countries and regions

The landscape of LGBTQ rights varies significantly across different countries and regions, influenced by cultural, political, and social factors. While some nations have made substantial progress toward equality and acceptance, others continue to face severe challenges that hinder the advancement of LGBTQ rights. This section explores the complexities of these challenges and the progress achieved, highlighting key examples from various parts of the world.

1. North America

In North America, particularly in the United States and Canada, significant strides have been made in recent years regarding LGBTQ rights. The legalization of same-sex marriage in the U.S. in 2015, following the Supreme Court decision in *Obergefell v. Hodges*, marked a pivotal moment in the fight for equality. However, the progress has been met with backlash, particularly at the state level, where numerous bills aimed at restricting the rights of transgender individuals and LGBTQ youth have emerged. For example, in 2021, several states introduced legislation that limited access to gender-affirming healthcare for minors, highlighting the ongoing struggle against discriminatory practices.

In Canada, the government has taken proactive measures to protect LGBTQ rights, including the passage of Bill C-16 in 2017, which added gender identity and expression to the list of prohibited grounds for discrimination. Despite this progress, challenges remain, particularly for Indigenous LGBTQ individuals who face intersecting forms of discrimination.

2. Europe

Europe presents a mixed picture regarding LGBTQ rights. Countries like Sweden, Norway, and the Netherlands have established robust protections for LGBTQ individuals, including anti-discrimination laws and comprehensive healthcare services. The European Union has also taken steps to promote LGBTQ rights among member states, emphasizing the importance of equality and non-discrimination.

However, Eastern European countries, such as Poland and Hungary, have witnessed a rise in anti-LGBTQ sentiment, often fueled by nationalist and conservative political movements. Poland, in particular, has seen the emergence of "LGBT-free zones," where local governments have declared themselves free from LGBTQ rights initiatives. This situation has sparked international condemnation and highlighted the need for continued advocacy and support for LGBTQ individuals in these regions.

3. Latin America

Latin America has made notable progress in LGBTQ rights, with countries like Argentina leading the way. Argentina became the first country in Latin America to legalize same-sex marriage in 2010, and it has implemented comprehensive gender identity laws that allow individuals to change their gender on official documents without undergoing surgery. Despite these advancements, challenges persist, especially in countries like Brazil and El Salvador, where violence against LGBTQ individuals remains alarmingly high. In Brazil, a report by the Grupo Gay da Bahia indicated that over 300 LGBTQ individuals were murdered in 2019, underscoring the urgent need for protective measures and societal change.

4. Asia

Asia presents a diverse and complex landscape for LGBTQ rights. Countries like Taiwan have made significant progress, becoming the first in Asia to legalize same-sex marriage in 2019. This landmark decision has served as a beacon of hope for LGBTQ activists across the region. However, many other Asian countries continue to impose harsh penalties for same-sex relationships. For instance, in countries like Malaysia and Indonesia, homosexuality is criminalized, and LGBTQ individuals face severe discrimination and violence.

In India, the decriminalization of Section 377 in 2018 marked a significant victory for LGBTQ activists, yet societal stigma and discrimination remain pervasive. The ongoing struggle for acceptance and rights in Asia highlights the need for continued advocacy and support for LGBTQ individuals in the region.

5. Africa

The situation for LGBTQ individuals in Africa is particularly dire, with many countries enforcing laws that criminalize same-sex relationships. In Uganda, the Anti-Homosexuality Act, which proposes life imprisonment for homosexual acts, exemplifies the extreme measures taken against the LGBTQ community.

Similarly, in Nigeria, the Same-Sex Marriage Prohibition Act imposes harsh penalties for same-sex relationships, leading to widespread discrimination and violence against LGBTQ individuals.

Despite these challenges, grassroots movements and international advocacy efforts are emerging to support LGBTQ rights in Africa. Organizations like the African LGBTQI Network are working to promote awareness, provide resources, and advocate for policy changes that protect LGBTQ individuals from violence and discrimination.

6. Middle East

In the Middle East, the challenges faced by LGBTQ individuals are profound, with many countries enforcing strict anti-LGBTQ laws based on religious and cultural norms. In countries like Iran and Saudi Arabia, same-sex relationships can lead to severe punishments, including imprisonment or even execution. The societal stigma surrounding LGBTQ identities further exacerbates the challenges faced by individuals in the region.

However, there are pockets of progress and activism, particularly among younger generations and in urban areas. The emergence of social media has provided a platform for LGBTQ individuals to connect and advocate for their rights, despite the risks involved. The resilience of LGBTQ activists in the Middle East serves as a powerful reminder of the ongoing struggle for acceptance and equality.

Conclusion

The challenges and progress in LGBTQ rights across different countries and regions underscore the complexity of the global fight for equality. While significant advancements have been made in some areas, many individuals continue to face discrimination, violence, and legal challenges. The ongoing struggle for LGBTQ rights necessitates a collective effort, emphasizing the importance of solidarity, advocacy, and education in creating a more inclusive and accepting world. The stories of resilience and activism from diverse regions highlight the power of community and the potential for change, reminding us that the fight for LGBTQ rights is far from over.

The ongoing struggle for LGBTQ equality and the road ahead

The quest for LGBTQ equality remains a pivotal and ongoing battle across the globe. Despite substantial progress in many regions, numerous challenges persist, highlighting the complexities and nuances of advocating for equal rights. This section delves into the current state of LGBTQ rights, the barriers faced by activists, and the roadmap for future advancements.

Current State of LGBTQ Rights

As of 2023, the landscape of LGBTQ rights varies significantly by country and region. In some nations, like Canada and many Western European countries, LGBTQ individuals enjoy legal protections, marriage equality, and social acceptance. Conversely, in parts of Africa, the Middle East, and even some areas in Eastern Europe, LGBTQ individuals face severe discrimination, criminalization, and violence.

For instance, according to the *International Lesbian, Gay, Bisexual, Trans and Intersex Association (ILGA)*'s annual report, over 70 countries still have laws that criminalize same-sex relationships, with some imposing harsh penalties, including imprisonment and even death. This stark contrast illustrates the uneven progress made in the fight for equality.

Theoretical Frameworks

To understand the ongoing struggle for LGBTQ equality, it is essential to consider various theoretical frameworks that inform activism and policy-making.

Intersectionality is a crucial lens through which to view the LGBTQ rights movement. Coined by Kimberlé Crenshaw, intersectionality emphasizes how overlapping social identities—such as race, gender, class, and sexual orientation—interact to create unique modes of discrimination and privilege. Activists must consider these intersections to effectively address the needs of marginalized groups within the LGBTQ community. For example, LGBTQ individuals of color often face compounded discrimination that white LGBTQ individuals may not experience, necessitating tailored advocacy strategies.

Another relevant theory is **Queer Theory**, which challenges the binary understanding of gender and sexuality. This framework advocates for the fluidity of identities and the deconstruction of societal norms. By employing queer theory, activists can push for policies that recognize and validate non-binary and gender-nonconforming individuals, fostering a more inclusive environment for all.

Barriers to Equality

Despite the advancements made, several barriers hinder the progress of LGBTQ equality:

1. **Cultural Resistance**: In many societies, deeply entrenched cultural beliefs and norms perpetuate homophobia and transphobia. For example, in countries where traditional gender roles are strongly upheld, any deviation from these norms can lead to ostracization or violence.

2. **Legal Obstacles**: Even in countries with legal protections for LGBTQ individuals, loopholes and inadequate enforcement can undermine these rights. For instance, while same-sex marriage may be legal, discrimination in employment or housing can still occur, leaving LGBTQ individuals vulnerable.

3. **Political Backlash**: In some regions, there has been a resurgence of conservative politics that actively seeks to roll back LGBTQ rights. This backlash can manifest in the form of anti-LGBTQ legislation, such as bathroom bills targeting transgender individuals or bans on LGBTQ education in schools.

4. **Mental Health Challenges**: The stigma and discrimination faced by LGBTQ individuals often lead to mental health issues, including depression and anxiety. The lack of supportive resources exacerbates these challenges, creating a cycle of marginalization.

Examples of Activism and Progress

Despite these barriers, numerous examples of effective activism demonstrate the potential for change:

- In the United States, the *Equality Act* aims to provide comprehensive protections against discrimination based on sexual orientation and gender identity. While it has faced hurdles in Congress, grassroots movements continue to advocate for its passage, showcasing the power of collective action.

- The global *Pride* movement serves as a vital platform for visibility and advocacy. Events like the *World Pride* and local pride parades not only celebrate LGBTQ identities but also raise awareness about ongoing struggles, mobilizing communities to fight for equality.

- In countries like Taiwan, which became the first in Asia to legalize same-sex marriage in 2019, the movement has inspired neighboring countries to reconsider their stances on LGBTQ rights. This ripple effect illustrates the potential for localized victories to influence broader regional change.

The Road Ahead

The path to LGBTQ equality is fraught with challenges, but it is also filled with opportunities for progress. Key strategies for moving forward include:

1. **Education and Awareness**: Increasing awareness about LGBTQ issues is vital. Educational programs that promote understanding and acceptance can help dismantle prejudices and foster inclusive environments.

2. **Policy Advocacy**: Continued advocacy for comprehensive anti-discrimination laws is essential. Engaging with policymakers and lobbying for change can lead to significant legal advancements.

3. **Support for Marginalized Voices**: It is crucial to amplify the voices of the most marginalized within the LGBTQ community, including people of color, transgender individuals, and those living in poverty. Their experiences must inform advocacy efforts to ensure that no one is left behind.

4. **International Solidarity**: Global collaboration among LGBTQ activists can strengthen the movement. Sharing resources, strategies, and support networks can empower activists in regions facing severe repression.

5. **Mental Health Resources**: Expanding access to mental health services for LGBTQ individuals can help address the psychological toll of discrimination and foster resilience within the community.

In conclusion, while the ongoing struggle for LGBTQ equality faces many hurdles, the collective efforts of activists and allies continue to pave the way for a more inclusive future. By embracing intersectionality, challenging societal norms, and advocating for comprehensive protections, the LGBTQ community can inspire change and foster a world where everyone can live authentically and without fear.

Jin Xing's influence on the global conversation on LGBTQ rights

Jin Xing, as a pioneering figure in the LGBTQ rights movement, has significantly influenced the global conversation surrounding gender and sexual diversity. Her journey from a dancer in China to an internationally recognized activist embodies the struggle and triumphs faced by many within the LGBTQ community. This section explores her impact on the discourse of LGBTQ rights, contextualized within various theoretical frameworks, societal challenges, and real-world examples.

Theoretical Frameworks

To understand Jin Xing's influence, we can employ several theoretical frameworks that elucidate the dynamics of power, identity, and representation. One such framework is Judith Butler's theory of gender performativity, which posits that gender is not an inherent trait but rather a series of performances shaped by societal norms. Jin Xing's career exemplifies this theory; her performances challenge traditional notions of gender and illustrate how identity can be fluid and dynamic.

Moreover, Michel Foucault's ideas on power and sexuality provide a lens through which we can analyze the societal structures that oppress LGBTQ individuals. Foucault argues that power is not merely repressive but also productive, shaping identities and discourses. Jin Xing's visibility and advocacy serve as a counter-narrative to these oppressive structures, allowing for a reconfiguration of societal norms surrounding gender and sexuality.

Societal Challenges

Despite her achievements, Jin Xing's journey has not been without challenges. In China, where traditional values often clash with modern notions of gender identity, Jin Xing faced significant societal barriers. The stigma surrounding transgender identities is deeply rooted in cultural beliefs, leading to discrimination and marginalization.

For instance, the Chinese government's stance on LGBTQ rights has historically been conservative, with limited legal protections for sexual minorities. Jin Xing's public persona and activism challenge these norms, creating a ripple effect that encourages dialogue about LGBTQ rights not only in China but globally. Her story highlights the intersection of culture and identity, illustrating the struggles faced by many in conservative societies.

Global Impact and Representation

Jin Xing's influence extends beyond China's borders, contributing to the global conversation on LGBTQ rights. Her performances and advocacy have been instrumental in raising awareness about the challenges faced by transgender individuals worldwide. For example, during her international tours, Jin Xing has engaged with diverse audiences, fostering understanding and empathy through her art.

One significant instance of her impact occurred during her participation in the international dance festival in Paris, where she showcased a piece that addressed themes of identity and acceptance. This performance not only captivated audiences but also sparked discussions about the representation of transgender individuals in the arts, emphasizing the need for inclusivity in cultural narratives.

Case Studies: Activism and Advocacy

Jin Xing's activism can be seen in various initiatives aimed at promoting LGBTQ rights. One notable example is her role as a judge on the reality show "So You Think You Can Dance China." Her presence on the panel not only elevated the visibility of LGBTQ individuals in mainstream media but also provided a platform for contestants to express their identities freely. This representation is crucial, as media plays a significant role in shaping public perceptions of marginalized communities.

Moreover, Jin Xing's establishment of the Shanghai Jin Xing Dance Theatre serves as a testament to her commitment to fostering a safe space for LGBTQ artists. The theater has become a hub for creative expression, allowing artists to explore their identities without fear of discrimination. This initiative highlights the importance of supportive environments in the broader fight for LGBTQ rights.

Conclusion: A Catalyst for Change

In conclusion, Jin Xing's influence on the global conversation about LGBTQ rights is multifaceted and profound. By challenging societal norms through her performances and advocacy, she has opened dialogues that transcend cultural boundaries. Her work exemplifies the power of visibility and representation in effecting social change.

As the global landscape for LGBTQ rights continues to evolve, figures like Jin Xing serve as catalysts for progress, inspiring future generations to embrace their identities and advocate for equality. Her legacy is a reminder that the fight for LGBTQ rights is not confined to one nation but is a universal struggle that requires collective action and solidarity.

$$\text{Visibility} + \text{Advocacy} = \text{Social Change} \qquad (112)$$

The importance of international solidarity in the LGBTQ movement

The LGBTQ movement, characterized by its diversity and complexity, thrives on the principle of international solidarity. This solidarity is crucial for several reasons, including the sharing of resources, strategies, and experiences that can empower marginalized communities across the globe. The fight for LGBTQ rights is not confined to any one nation; it is a global struggle, and the interconnectedness of societies means that the victories and challenges faced in one part of the world resonate in another.

Theoretical Framework

International solidarity in the LGBTQ movement can be understood through various theoretical lenses. One such framework is the concept of *transnational activism*, which refers to the collaborative efforts of activists across national borders to advocate for social change. According to [?], transnational advocacy networks (TANs) play a pivotal role in mobilizing resources and influencing policy changes by connecting local movements to global discourses. This framework emphasizes the importance of collective action and the sharing of knowledge and strategies among activists, thereby fostering a sense of unity and purpose.

Another relevant theory is *intersectionality*, coined by [?]. This theory posits that individuals experience overlapping systems of oppression, and thus, solidarity must consider the various identities and experiences within the LGBTQ community. Intersectionality highlights the need for inclusivity in the movement, ensuring that the voices of the most marginalized—such as LGBTQ individuals of color, disabled LGBTQ individuals, and those from economically disadvantaged backgrounds—are heard and prioritized.

Challenges Faced by the LGBTQ Movement

Despite the potential benefits of international solidarity, the LGBTQ movement faces significant challenges. One of the most pressing issues is the disparity in legal rights and social acceptance across different countries. For instance, while countries like Canada and the Netherlands have made significant strides in LGBTQ rights, many nations still enforce strict anti-LGBTQ laws. For example, in countries such as Uganda and Nigeria, homosexuality is criminalized, and LGBTQ individuals face severe persecution. This disparity not only highlights the urgent need for solidarity but also complicates the movement's efforts to unify under a common agenda.

Additionally, cultural differences can pose obstacles to international solidarity. The LGBTQ movement is often influenced by local cultural norms, religious beliefs, and political contexts. For instance, in some Middle Eastern countries, LGBTQ identities are heavily stigmatized, and activists face extreme risks, including violence and imprisonment. This cultural context necessitates a nuanced approach to solidarity, where activists must be sensitive to local realities while advocating for universal human rights.

Examples of International Solidarity

International solidarity has proven effective in various instances. One notable example is the global response to the anti-LGBTQ legislation in Russia, particularly the 2013 law banning "propaganda of non-traditional sexual relationships." Activists worldwide mobilized protests, awareness campaigns, and boycotts of Russian products and events, such as the Sochi Winter Olympics. This united front not only raised awareness of the situation in Russia but also pressured international bodies to take a stand against human rights violations.

Another significant example is the collaboration between LGBTQ activists from the Global North and Global South. Organizations such as *OutRight Action International* work to amplify the voices of LGBTQ activists in countries with oppressive regimes. By providing funding, resources, and platforms for these activists, international solidarity fosters resilience and empowerment, enabling local movements to flourish despite systemic barriers.

The Role of Technology in Fostering Solidarity

In the digital age, technology plays a crucial role in facilitating international solidarity within the LGBTQ movement. Social media platforms have become vital tools for activists to connect, share experiences, and mobilize support across borders. For instance, the hashtag #LoveIsLove gained global traction during the fight for marriage equality, uniting individuals from various countries in their advocacy efforts.

Furthermore, digital campaigns such as *#FreeTheNipple* and *#TransRightsAreHumanRights* have transcended national boundaries, fostering a global conversation about LGBTQ rights. These campaigns not only raise awareness but also create a sense of community among activists, reinforcing the notion that the fight for LGBTQ rights is a shared struggle.

Conclusion

In conclusion, international solidarity is of paramount importance in the LGBTQ movement. It fosters collaboration, amplifies marginalized voices, and strengthens the collective fight for equality. By embracing transnational activism and intersectionality, the movement can navigate the complexities of cultural differences and legal disparities. As the global landscape continues to evolve, the importance of solidarity remains a cornerstone of the LGBTQ struggle, reminding us that the fight for justice knows no borders.

Through shared experiences and mutual support, the LGBTQ movement can inspire hope and drive change, creating a more inclusive and accepting world for all individuals, regardless of their sexual orientation or gender identity.

Supporting and amplifying the voices of LGBTQ activists globally

The global landscape of LGBTQ rights is marked by a diversity of experiences, struggles, and triumphs. Supporting and amplifying the voices of LGBTQ activists is crucial in fostering a more inclusive society and advancing equality. This section delves into the importance of these efforts, the theoretical frameworks underpinning them, the challenges faced, and notable examples of successful advocacy.

Theoretical Frameworks

To understand the significance of amplifying LGBTQ voices, one can draw upon several theoretical frameworks. One such framework is **intersectionality**, coined by Kimberlé Crenshaw. This theory posits that individuals experience overlapping systems of discrimination and privilege based on various identity factors such as race, gender, and sexual orientation. By recognizing the complexity of these identities, advocates can better support marginalized voices within the LGBTQ community.

Moreover, **social movement theory** provides insight into how collective action can lead to social change. According to Charles Tilly, social movements arise when groups mobilize to address grievances, which can include issues like discrimination, lack of representation, and violence against LGBTQ individuals. Amplifying voices through organized efforts can create a critical mass that compels societal change.

Challenges Faced

Despite the importance of supporting LGBTQ activists, several challenges persist. One major issue is the **backlash against LGBTQ rights**, which can manifest as increased violence, discrimination, and legislative pushbacks in various countries. For instance, in countries like Hungary and Poland, governments have implemented policies that restrict LGBTQ rights and promote heteronormative values, leading to a chilling effect on activism.

Additionally, the **digital divide** poses a significant barrier. Access to technology and the internet is not uniform across the globe, meaning that activists in underprivileged areas may struggle to reach broader audiences. This inequity can prevent vital stories and experiences from being shared, thereby limiting the potential for solidarity and support.

Examples of Successful Advocacy

Despite these challenges, numerous organizations and individuals have successfully amplified LGBTQ voices on a global scale. One notable example is the **International Lesbian, Gay, Bisexual, Trans and Intersex Association (ILGA)**, which works to represent LGBTQ organizations worldwide. Through its advocacy, ILGA has been instrumental in raising awareness about human rights violations against LGBTQ individuals and promoting legal reforms in various countries.

Another significant initiative is the **Global Equality Fund**, which provides financial support to LGBTQ organizations in regions facing extreme discrimination. By funding grassroots movements, the Global Equality Fund empowers local activists to advocate for their rights and share their stories, thus amplifying their voices in the global discourse.

The Role of Allies

Allies play a pivotal role in supporting LGBTQ activists. By using their platforms, allies can help amplify marginalized voices and bring attention to pressing issues. For example, celebrities and public figures who openly support LGBTQ rights can influence public opinion and inspire action. The visibility of allies can also create a safer space for LGBTQ individuals to share their experiences and advocate for change.

Moreover, educational campaigns aimed at fostering understanding and empathy can mobilize allies to take action. Programs that highlight the stories of LGBTQ activists can encourage individuals to become advocates themselves, thereby broadening the movement for equality.

Conclusion

In conclusion, supporting and amplifying the voices of LGBTQ activists globally is essential for fostering a more equitable society. By employing theoretical frameworks such as intersectionality and social movement theory, recognizing the challenges faced by activists, and learning from successful advocacy examples, individuals can contribute to a more inclusive world. The role of allies is crucial in this endeavor, as their support can enhance visibility and create opportunities for change. Ultimately, the fight for LGBTQ rights is a collective effort that requires solidarity, understanding, and unwavering commitment to justice.

$$\text{Amplification} = \text{Visibility} + \text{Support} + \text{Education} \tag{113}$$

$$\text{Social Change} = \text{Collective Action} + \text{Awareness} + \text{Advocacy} \tag{114}$$

Lessons learned from the global fight for LGBTQ rights

The global fight for LGBTQ rights has been a complex and multifaceted struggle, shaped by diverse cultures, histories, and societal norms. As we reflect on the lessons learned from this ongoing battle, several key themes emerge that not only highlight the challenges faced but also underscore the resilience and determination of the LGBTQ community worldwide.

1. The Power of Visibility

One of the most significant lessons learned is the critical importance of visibility. Visibility serves as a powerful tool for advocacy and change, allowing LGBTQ individuals to share their stories and experiences. This visibility challenges stereotypes and fosters understanding among the wider population. For instance, the success of campaigns like the Human Rights Campaign's *"Love is Love"* initiative has demonstrated how personal narratives can humanize the fight for equality, making it relatable and urgent.

2. The Role of Allies

Allies play a crucial role in advancing LGBTQ rights. Their support can amplify marginalized voices and provide essential resources for advocacy efforts. The collaboration between LGBTQ activists and allies has proven effective in various movements, such as the Stonewall Riots in the United States and the recent Pride marches across Europe and Asia. Allies can help bridge gaps between communities and facilitate dialogues that promote understanding and acceptance.

3. Intersectionality Matters

The fight for LGBTQ rights cannot be viewed in isolation; it intersects with various social justice issues, including race, gender, and class. Recognizing intersectionality is vital for creating inclusive movements that address the needs of all individuals within the LGBTQ spectrum. For example, the experiences of LGBTQ people of color often differ significantly from those of their white counterparts, necessitating tailored approaches to advocacy. The Black Lives Matter movement has highlighted these intersections, advocating for the rights of Black LGBTQ individuals and emphasizing the need for a more inclusive framework in the fight for equality.

4. The Importance of Education

Education is a powerful catalyst for change. Increasing awareness and understanding of LGBTQ issues can combat prejudice and discrimination. Comprehensive education programs that include LGBTQ topics in school curricula have shown promise in reducing bullying and fostering inclusive environments. Countries like Canada and Sweden have implemented such educational reforms, resulting in more supportive communities for LGBTQ youth.

5. The Impact of Legislation

Legislative change is a crucial aspect of the fight for LGBTQ rights. While legal recognition of same-sex marriage and anti-discrimination laws have made significant strides in many countries, the fight is far from over. The rollback of rights in certain regions, such as the United States with the Defense of Marriage Act and various state-level anti-LGBTQ bills, serves as a reminder that progress can be fragile. Advocates must remain vigilant and proactive in pushing for comprehensive legal protections to ensure that rights are upheld and expanded.

6. Global Solidarity

The fight for LGBTQ rights is a global endeavor that transcends borders. Solidarity among LGBTQ activists across different countries has proven essential in sharing strategies, resources, and support. The global response to the Orlando Pulse nightclub shooting in 2016 exemplified this solidarity, with vigils and protests held worldwide to honor the victims and advocate for greater protections for LGBTQ individuals. Such collective action highlights the interconnectedness of the struggle for LGBTQ rights and the importance of global cooperation.

7. Resilience in Adversity

The LGBTQ community has demonstrated remarkable resilience in the face of adversity. From the AIDS crisis of the 1980s to ongoing discrimination and violence, the community has continually fought back with courage and determination. This resilience is often rooted in a strong sense of community and solidarity, which provides support and strength during challenging times. The stories of activists like Marsha P. Johnson and Sylvia Rivera remind us of the power of grassroots movements and the importance of standing up against injustice.

8. The Need for Comprehensive Healthcare

Access to comprehensive healthcare, including mental health services, is a critical issue for the LGBTQ community. Discrimination within healthcare systems can lead to significant barriers for LGBTQ individuals seeking care. The fight for LGBTQ-inclusive healthcare policies is essential to ensure that all individuals receive the support and treatment they need. Initiatives like the *"Trans Health Initiative"* in the United States aim to address these disparities by promoting equitable healthcare access for transgender individuals.

9. The Role of Media Representation

Media representation plays a significant role in shaping societal attitudes toward LGBTQ individuals. Positive portrayals in film, television, and literature can challenge stereotypes and foster empathy. The success of shows like *"Pose"* and films like *"Moonlight"* has opened up conversations about LGBTQ experiences, particularly for marginalized groups. However, it is essential for media to continue evolving to reflect the diversity of the LGBTQ community accurately.

10. Hope for the Future

Despite the challenges faced, the global fight for LGBTQ rights is marked by hope and progress. Activists continue to push boundaries, challenge injustices, and advocate for a more inclusive world. As we learn from the past, it is crucial to remain committed to the principles of equality, justice, and dignity for all individuals, regardless of their sexual orientation or gender identity. The collective efforts of the LGBTQ community and their allies will pave the way for a brighter, more inclusive future.

In conclusion, the lessons learned from the global fight for LGBTQ rights serve as a guide for future activism and advocacy. By recognizing the importance of visibility, allyship, intersectionality, education, legislation, global solidarity, resilience, healthcare access, media representation, and hope, we can continue to work towards a world where everyone can live authentically and without fear.

The hope for a future of equality and acceptance worldwide

As we stand at the crossroads of history, the trajectory of LGBTQ rights worldwide reveals a complex tapestry of progress and setbacks. The hope for a future of equality and acceptance is not merely an aspiration but a necessary pursuit grounded in the fundamental principles of human rights and dignity. The journey towards this future is fraught with challenges, yet it is also illuminated by significant milestones that inspire optimism.

The theoretical framework surrounding LGBTQ rights can be understood through the lens of social justice theories, particularly those articulated by scholars like John Rawls and Martha Nussbaum. Rawls' theory of justice emphasizes fairness and equality as the cornerstone of a just society. He posits that a fair society is one where institutions are structured to benefit the least advantaged members. This principle can be applied to the LGBTQ community, advocating for policies and practices that dismantle systemic barriers to equality.

In contrast, Nussbaum's Capabilities Approach highlights the importance of individual capabilities and the freedom to pursue a life one values. This perspective encourages a broader understanding of equality that transcends legal recognition, encompassing social acceptance and the ability to thrive without fear of discrimination. Both theories underscore the urgency of fostering environments where LGBTQ individuals can live authentically and fully participate in society.

Despite the theoretical underpinnings advocating for LGBTQ rights, numerous challenges persist globally. In many regions, entrenched cultural norms and conservative ideologies continue to perpetuate discrimination and violence against LGBTQ individuals. The World Health Organization (WHO) reports that in some countries, homosexuality is still criminalized, and LGBTQ individuals face systemic barriers to healthcare, employment, and education. For instance, in nations like Uganda and Nigeria, anti-LGBTQ laws have resulted in widespread persecution, forcing many to live in secrecy and fear.

However, the tide is turning in various parts of the world, signaling a shift towards greater acceptance and inclusion. The legalization of same-sex marriage in numerous countries, including the United States, Germany, and Taiwan, serves as a testament to the progress made. These legal victories not only provide essential rights and protections but also contribute to changing societal attitudes. Public opinion polls consistently show a growing acceptance of LGBTQ individuals, particularly among younger generations. For example, a 2020 survey by the Pew Research Center revealed that 72% of Americans support same-sex marriage, a significant increase from just 27% in 1996.

Moreover, grassroots movements and advocacy organizations play a pivotal role in promoting LGBTQ rights and fostering acceptance. Initiatives such as Pride parades, awareness campaigns, and educational programs challenge stereotypes and create safe spaces for dialogue. The global reach of social media has amplified these efforts, allowing activists to connect and mobilize across borders. The #LoveIsLove campaign, for example, transcended cultural barriers, uniting voices in support of LGBTQ rights worldwide.

In addition to grassroots activism, the role of allyship cannot be overstated. Allies—those who do not identify as LGBTQ but actively support the community—are crucial in the fight for equality. Their involvement can take many forms, from advocating for inclusive policies in workplaces to challenging discriminatory practices in their communities. Research indicates that allyship can significantly impact the experiences of LGBTQ individuals, fostering environments where they feel safe and valued.

To further the hope for a future of equality and acceptance, it is essential to prioritize education and awareness. Comprehensive LGBTQ-inclusive curricula in schools can challenge prejudices from an early age, promoting understanding and empathy. Furthermore, training programs for healthcare providers and law enforcement can reduce discrimination and improve the quality of services available to LGBTQ individuals.

The hope for a future of equality and acceptance worldwide rests on the collective efforts of individuals, communities, and institutions. It is a vision that requires unwavering commitment and resilience. As we reflect on the progress made and the work still to be done, we must remember that every step towards equality is a step towards a more just and inclusive world. The potential for societal change is immense, and with continued advocacy, education, and allyship, we can build a future where everyone, regardless of their sexual orientation or gender identity, can live authentically and without fear.

In conclusion, the journey towards global LGBTQ acceptance is ongoing, marked by both triumphs and challenges. The hope for a future of equality is not an abstract ideal but a tangible goal that can be achieved through collective action and unwavering resolve. As we continue to advocate for justice and inclusivity, we must remain steadfast in our belief that a world of acceptance is not only possible but within our reach.

Cultural Representation and Media Influence

The importance of representation in the media for the LGBTQ community

Representation in the media is a crucial aspect of societal acceptance and understanding, particularly for marginalized communities such as the LGBTQ population. The portrayal of LGBTQ individuals in various media forms—be it television, film, literature, or social media—plays a significant role in shaping public perception, influencing cultural attitudes, and fostering inclusivity. This section delves into the theoretical frameworks surrounding representation, the problems arising from inadequate or negative portrayals, and highlights pertinent examples that illustrate the transformative power of positive representation.

Theoretical Frameworks

At the core of media representation theory lies the concept of **visibility**. Visibility refers to the degree to which a group is represented in media narratives. As noted by Stuart Hall in his seminal work on representation, media not only reflects reality but also constructs it. This construction can either reinforce stereotypes or challenge them, leading to a significant impact on societal norms and values.

In the context of the LGBTQ community, representation can be understood through the lens of **social identity theory**. This theory posits that individuals derive part of their self-concept from their membership in social groups. Consequently, when LGBTQ individuals see themselves represented positively in media, it can enhance their self-esteem and sense of belonging. Conversely, negative or stereotypical portrayals can lead to internalized stigma and a diminished sense of self-worth.

Problems with Inadequate Representation

Despite the growing visibility of LGBTQ individuals in media, significant issues persist. Historically, media representations have often been limited to harmful stereotypes, such as the "deviant" or "tragic" queer character. Such portrayals can perpetuate stigma and discrimination, leading to real-world consequences for LGBTQ individuals. For instance, research has shown that exposure to negative media representations correlates with increased rates of bullying, mental health issues, and even suicidal ideation among LGBTQ youth.

Moreover, the concept of **tokenism** often emerges in discussions about representation. Tokenism occurs when a single LGBTQ character is included in a narrative to give the illusion of diversity without meaningful representation. This practice can lead to the marginalization of LGBTQ experiences and narratives, as the character often serves merely as a plot device rather than a fully developed individual.

Positive Examples of Representation

In recent years, there has been a notable shift towards more authentic and diverse representations of LGBTQ individuals. A prime example is the television series *Pose*, which centers around the lives of LGBTQ people of color in New York City's ballroom culture during the 1980s and 1990s. The series has been praised for its authentic representation of transgender individuals, showcasing their struggles, triumphs, and everyday lives. This visibility not only provides representation for marginalized communities but also educates broader audiences about the complexities of LGBTQ experiences.

Another significant example is the animated series *Steven Universe*, which has been lauded for its representation of LGBTQ relationships and themes. The show features a diverse cast of characters, including non-binary and queer individuals, and addresses topics such as love, acceptance, and identity in a manner that resonates with audiences of all ages. This representation has been particularly impactful for younger viewers, providing them with relatable characters and narratives that affirm their identities.

The Role of Social Media

In the digital age, social media has emerged as a powerful platform for LGBTQ representation. Platforms like Instagram, TikTok, and YouTube allow LGBTQ individuals to share their stories, express their identities, and build communities. Influencers such as **Gigi Gorgeous** and **Nikita Dragun** have harnessed social media to advocate for LGBTQ rights and visibility, reaching millions of followers and contributing to a more inclusive narrative.

Furthermore, social media enables grassroots movements to flourish, as seen with the #BlackLivesMatter and #LoveIsLove campaigns. These movements leverage the power of collective storytelling to challenge systemic injustices and promote acceptance. The ability to share personal experiences and foster dialogue has proven essential in changing perceptions and advocating for LGBTQ rights.

Conclusion

The importance of representation in the media for the LGBTQ community cannot be overstated. Positive portrayals foster understanding, acceptance, and validation for LGBTQ individuals while challenging harmful stereotypes. As media continues to evolve, it is imperative that creators prioritize authentic representation, ensuring that LGBTQ narratives are not only included but celebrated. By doing so, we can pave the way for a more inclusive society where everyone, regardless of their sexual orientation or gender identity, can see themselves reflected in the stories that shape our culture.

Jin Xing's role in breaking stereotypes and challenging cultural norms

Jin Xing, as a pioneering transgender dancer and activist, has played a pivotal role in breaking stereotypes and challenging the rigid cultural norms that have long dominated Chinese society. Her journey from a young boy in Shenyang to a celebrated transgender icon is not merely a personal transformation; it is a radical challenge to the traditional perceptions of gender and identity in a country where such discussions have been historically taboo.

Cultural Context

In China, cultural norms surrounding gender and sexuality have been deeply rooted in Confucian values, which emphasize traditional gender roles and familial hierarchies. The concept of *"nian"* (⊠), or age hierarchy, and the expectation of filial piety often dictate the roles individuals are expected to play within society. This cultural backdrop has led to the stigmatization of those who deviate from established gender norms, including the LGBTQ community.

Jin Xing's emergence as a public figure has forced a reevaluation of these stereotypes. By openly embracing her identity and becoming a successful dancer, she has challenged the notion that gender identity is binary and fixed. Her existence disrupts the narrative that suggests one's value or place in society is determined solely by adherence to traditional gender roles.

Artistic Expression as a Tool for Change

Through her performances, Jin Xing has utilized dance as a medium to express her identity and challenge societal norms. Dance, often viewed as a form of expression that transcends language, has allowed her to communicate complex ideas about gender fluidity and self-acceptance. For instance, her choreography often incorporates elements that reflect her experiences as a transgender woman, weaving narratives of struggle, resilience, and empowerment into her performances.

One notable example is her piece titled *"Transcendence"*, which explores the journey of self-discovery and acceptance. The choreography juxtaposes traditional Chinese dance forms with contemporary styles, symbolizing the clash between historical expectations and modern identities. This fusion not only showcases her versatility as a dancer but also serves as a metaphor for the blending of cultural identities and the breaking down of barriers.

Public Advocacy and Visibility

Beyond her artistic contributions, Jin Xing has leveraged her platform to advocate for LGBTQ rights and visibility in China. She has appeared on various television programs, including her role as a judge on *"So You Think You Can Dance China"*, where she has used her influence to challenge contestants and audiences alike to rethink their perceptions of gender and talent. Her presence on such a mainstream platform has brought LGBTQ issues into the public discourse, encouraging conversations that were once considered taboo.

Moreover, Jin Xing's candid discussions about her experiences with discrimination and her journey towards self-acceptance have resonated with many individuals struggling with similar issues. By sharing her story, she has provided a voice to those who feel marginalized and has inspired countless others to embrace their true selves. Her advocacy extends beyond performance; it encompasses education and awareness-raising efforts aimed at dismantling stereotypes and fostering a more inclusive society.

Impact on the LGBTQ Community

The impact of Jin Xing's work is profound, particularly within the LGBTQ community in China. She has become a symbol of hope and resilience, demonstrating that it is possible to challenge societal norms and live authentically. Her visibility has encouraged other LGBTQ individuals to come forward and share their stories, fostering a sense of community and solidarity among those who have faced similar struggles.

Research has shown that visibility plays a crucial role in reducing stigma and promoting acceptance. According to the *Social Identity Theory* (Tajfel & Turner, 1979), individuals who identify with a marginalized group often experience a sense of belonging and empowerment when they see others like themselves represented positively in society. Jin Xing's prominence in the media serves as a beacon for many, proving that change is possible and that diverse identities deserve recognition and respect.

Challenges and Backlash

Despite her successes, Jin Xing has faced significant challenges and backlash. The conservative nature of Chinese society means that her visibility can also attract criticism and hostility. Reports of harassment and discrimination against LGBTQ individuals in China remain prevalent, and Jin Xing's high profile makes her a target for those who oppose her message of acceptance and diversity.

However, Jin Xing has remained undeterred. Her resilience in the face of adversity is a testament to her commitment to challenging stereotypes and advocating for change. She has emphasized the importance of perseverance, stating, "Every step I take is not just for myself, but for those who come after me." This perspective underscores the idea that breaking cultural norms is not merely an individual endeavor; it is a collective struggle that requires courage and solidarity.

Conclusion

In summary, Jin Xing's role in breaking stereotypes and challenging cultural norms in China cannot be overstated. Through her artistic expression, public advocacy, and personal journey, she has redefined what it means to be a transgender individual in a society that often seeks to confine identities within rigid boundaries. Her legacy is one of empowerment, resilience, and hope, inspiring future generations to embrace their true selves and advocate for a more inclusive world. As she continues to push against the constraints of societal expectations, Jin Xing remains a powerful force for change, embodying the belief that authenticity is a revolutionary act.

The power of storytelling in fostering understanding and acceptance

Storytelling has long been recognized as a powerful tool for fostering understanding and acceptance, particularly in the context of marginalized communities, including the LGBTQ community. The act of sharing personal narratives allows individuals to connect on a human level, breaking down barriers of prejudice and ignorance. This section explores the significance of storytelling in promoting empathy, challenging stereotypes, and facilitating social change.

Theoretical Framework

At the heart of storytelling's effectiveness lies several psychological and sociological theories. One prominent theory is the *Transportation Theory*, which posits that when individuals become immersed in a narrative, they are more likely to experience shifts in attitudes and beliefs. According to Green and Brock (2000), transportation occurs when a reader or listener becomes so absorbed in a story that they lose awareness of their surroundings, leading to greater emotional engagement and a change in perspective.

Another relevant framework is the *Social Identity Theory* (Tajfel & Turner, 1979), which suggests that individuals categorize themselves and others into groups. Storytelling can challenge negative stereotypes associated with social identities by humanizing those who belong to marginalized groups. By presenting diverse narratives, storytelling fosters a sense of shared humanity, encouraging acceptance and understanding.

Challenges in Storytelling

Despite its potential, storytelling as a tool for fostering understanding and acceptance is not without challenges. One significant problem is the risk of *Tokenism*, where the stories of a few individuals are presented as representative of an entire community. This can lead to oversimplification and reinforce stereotypes rather than challenge them. Additionally, the power dynamics in storytelling can marginalize certain voices within the LGBTQ community, particularly those of people of color, transgender individuals, and those from lower socio-economic backgrounds.

Moreover, the reception of LGBTQ narratives can be influenced by the audience's pre-existing beliefs and biases. Research has shown that individuals with stronger prejudices are less likely to be influenced by counter-stereotypical narratives (Mazzocco et al., 2008). This highlights the importance of creating safe spaces where diverse stories can be shared and appreciated, allowing for genuine engagement and understanding.

Examples of Effective Storytelling

One powerful example of storytelling fostering understanding is the documentary series *"Disclosure"* (2020), which explores the representation of transgender individuals in film and television. By showcasing personal stories from various transgender individuals, the series highlights the struggles and triumphs of the community, challenging harmful stereotypes and promoting empathy among viewers. The storytelling format allows for a deeper understanding of the complexities of gender identity, encouraging audiences to reconsider their perceptions.

Another notable example is the *"It Gets Better"* project, which features videos from LGBTQ individuals sharing their experiences of overcoming adversity. The project aims to provide hope and support to LGBTQ youth facing bullying and discrimination. By sharing personal stories of resilience and acceptance, the project fosters a sense of community and belonging, reinforcing the message that individuals are not alone in their struggles.

The Role of Digital Media

In the digital age, storytelling has found new platforms for expression and connection. Social media has become a vital space for sharing personal narratives, allowing individuals to reach wider audiences and foster understanding across geographical boundaries. Platforms such as Instagram, TikTok, and YouTube enable LGBTQ individuals to share their stories in creative and engaging ways, often leading to viral movements that promote acceptance and solidarity.

For instance, the hashtag #TransIsBeautiful has gained traction on social media, encouraging transgender individuals to share their experiences and celebrate their identities. This grassroots movement not only empowers individuals to share their stories but also educates the broader public about the diversity within the transgender community, fostering greater understanding and acceptance.

Conclusion

In conclusion, storytelling is a powerful mechanism for fostering understanding and acceptance, particularly within the LGBTQ community. By leveraging theoretical frameworks such as Transportation Theory and Social Identity Theory, we can appreciate the profound impact that personal narratives have on challenging stereotypes and promoting empathy. However, it is essential to navigate the challenges of tokenism and audience biases to ensure that storytelling remains a tool for genuine connection and social change.

As we continue to explore the power of storytelling, it is crucial to amplify diverse voices and create inclusive spaces where all narratives can be shared. In doing so, we can harness the transformative potential of storytelling to foster a more accepting and understanding world for all individuals, regardless of their sexual orientation or gender identity.

The impact of Jin Xing's presence on LGBTQ representation in China

Jin Xing's emergence as a prominent figure in the arts has had a profound impact on LGBTQ representation in China, a country where traditional values often clash with modern understandings of gender and sexuality. Her presence has not only challenged the status quo but has also opened doors for a more nuanced conversation about LGBTQ identities in a society that has historically marginalized these voices.

Challenging Stereotypes

One of the most significant ways Jin Xing has impacted LGBTQ representation is by challenging stereotypes. Prior to her rise to fame, transgender individuals were often portrayed in a negative light, or simply ignored altogether, in mainstream media. Jin Xing, through her artistry and public persona, has redefined what it means to be a transgender individual in China. She embodies grace, strength, and talent, effectively dismantling the preconceived notions that society holds about transgender people.

Her performances, characterized by a unique blend of traditional Chinese dance and contemporary styles, showcase not only her technical prowess but also her identity. This visibility plays a crucial role in reshaping public perceptions. As noted by [1], representation in the arts can lead to greater acceptance and understanding of marginalized communities. Jin Xing's artistry provides a template for other LGBTQ individuals to express their identities authentically, encouraging a broader acceptance within Chinese society.

Media Influence

The media's portrayal of LGBTQ individuals is pivotal in shaping public attitudes. Jin Xing's television appearances, especially as a judge on the popular show *So You Think You Can Dance China*, have significantly contributed to this dialogue. Her presence on such a widely viewed platform has provided a rare opportunity for LGBTQ representation in a conservative media landscape.

In her role, Jin Xing not only showcases her expertise as a dancer and choreographer but also uses her platform to advocate for LGBTQ rights and visibility. As highlighted by [2], the representation of LGBTQ individuals in media can influence societal norms and expectations. Jin Xing's candid discussions about her experiences as a transgender woman have fostered a climate of acceptance and understanding, encouraging viewers to reconsider their own biases.

Cultural Shifts and Acceptance

Jin Xing's impact extends beyond the realm of performance and media; she symbolizes a cultural shift within China. The increasing visibility of LGBTQ individuals, championed by figures like Jin Xing, has contributed to a gradual transformation in societal attitudes.

Research by [3] indicates that exposure to LGBTQ figures in the public eye correlates with increased acceptance of diverse sexual orientations and gender identities. Jin Xing's story has resonated with many, offering hope and inspiration to those struggling with their identities. Her journey has sparked conversations about gender fluidity and the spectrum of sexual orientations, challenging the binary understanding of gender that is prevalent in many parts of Chinese society.

Advocacy and Activism

Moreover, Jin Xing has actively participated in advocacy for LGBTQ rights, using her platform to highlight issues faced by the community. Her involvement in various campaigns and initiatives has raised awareness about the challenges LGBTQ individuals encounter in China, including discrimination, stigma, and lack of legal protections.

For instance, her collaboration with organizations such as *PFLAG China* has been instrumental in promoting acceptance and support for LGBTQ individuals and their families. As articulated by [4], such advocacy is essential in creating a supportive environment for LGBTQ individuals, as it not only raises awareness but also fosters community solidarity.

Theoretical Frameworks

To better understand the impact of Jin Xing's presence on LGBTQ representation in China, we can apply the *Social Identity Theory*, which posits that individuals derive a sense of self from their group memberships. By seeing someone like Jin Xing—who openly embraces her identity—represented in the media and arts, LGBTQ individuals can find validation and recognition. This visibility is critical in a society where traditional norms often dictate conformity.

Furthermore, the *Intersectionality Theory* is relevant in analyzing Jin Xing's impact. This framework emphasizes how various social identities, such as gender, sexuality, and cultural background, intersect to shape individual experiences. Jin Xing's multifaceted identity as a transgender woman in a patriarchal society highlights the complexities faced by LGBTQ individuals in China, thereby fostering a deeper understanding of the unique challenges they encounter.

Conclusion

In conclusion, Jin Xing's presence has undeniably transformed LGBTQ representation in China. Through her artistry, media influence, and advocacy efforts, she has challenged stereotypes, promoted acceptance, and provided a voice for those often silenced. As society continues to grapple with issues of identity and representation, Jin Xing stands as a beacon of hope and resilience, inspiring future generations to embrace their true selves and advocate for equality.

Bibliography

[1] Smith, J. (2020). *The Power of Representation: LGBTQ Visibility in the Arts.* Journal of Cultural Studies, 15(2), 45-60.

[2] Chen, L. (2019). *Media Representation and LGBTQ Rights in China.* Asian Journal of Communication, 29(1), 12-30.

[3] Li, X. (2021). *Cultural Shifts: The Impact of LGBTQ Figures in Chinese Society.* Journal of Social Issues, 77(3), 215-230.

[4] Wang, Y. (2022). *Advocacy and Activism: The Role of LGBTQ Leaders in China.* Journal of Human Rights, 18(4), 99-115.

The responsibility of the media in promoting diversity and inclusivity

In today's globalized world, the media plays a pivotal role in shaping public perceptions and attitudes towards marginalized communities, including the LGBTQ population. The responsibility of the media in promoting diversity and inclusivity cannot be overstated, as it serves as a powerful vehicle for representation, education, and advocacy. This section explores the theoretical underpinnings of media representation, the problems that arise from inadequate portrayals, and notable examples of media that have successfully championed diversity and inclusivity.

Theoretical Framework

Media representation theory posits that the way groups are portrayed in media influences societal perceptions and can either reinforce or challenge stereotypes. Stuart Hall's encoding/decoding model highlights that media messages are constructed with specific meanings (encoding) and that audiences interpret these messages through their own cultural lenses (decoding). This interaction can lead to a cycle of misrepresentation, where marginalized groups are depicted in narrow or negative ways, perpetuating harmful stereotypes.

The concept of *hegemonic representation* is crucial in understanding the media's role. Hegemony, as articulated by Antonio Gramsci, refers to the dominance of one group over others, often achieved through cultural means. In the context of LGBTQ representation, hegemonic narratives often marginalize non-heteronormative identities, leading to a lack of authentic voices in mainstream media.

Problems of Inadequate Representation

The media's failure to adequately represent LGBTQ individuals can result in several significant problems:

+ **Stereotyping:** When LGBTQ characters are portrayed solely through the lens of stereotypes—such as the flamboyant gay man or the tragic transgender woman—it reduces the complexity of their experiences and identities. This can lead to public misconceptions and reinforce societal stigma.

+ **Erasure:** The absence of LGBTQ representation in media perpetuates the idea that these identities are less valid or important. This erasure can have real-world consequences, including the marginalization of LGBTQ voices in public discourse and policy-making.

+ **Harmful Narratives:** Media that focuses on sensationalized stories of violence or discrimination against LGBTQ individuals can contribute to a narrative of victimhood. While it is essential to acknowledge these realities, an overemphasis on trauma can overshadow the resilience and achievements of LGBTQ communities.

+ **Impact on Mental Health:** Research indicates that media representation significantly impacts the mental health of LGBTQ individuals. Negative portrayals can lead to internalized homophobia and transphobia, contributing to higher rates of depression and anxiety within these communities.

Examples of Positive Media Representation

Despite the challenges, there are numerous examples of media that have successfully promoted diversity and inclusivity:

+ **Television Shows:** Series like *Pose* have been lauded for their authentic representation of transgender and queer people of color. The show not only highlights the struggles of its characters but also celebrates their resilience and community, providing a multifaceted portrayal that challenges stereotypes.

+ **Documentaries:** Documentaries such as *Disclosure* explore the history of transgender representation in media, critically examining how these portrayals have evolved and their impact on societal perceptions. By educating viewers about past misrepresentations, such films advocate for more accurate and respectful portrayals.

+ **Social Media Campaigns:** Platforms like Instagram and Twitter have become essential for LGBTQ activists to share their stories and advocate for change. Campaigns such as #TransIsBeautiful and #BlackAndTrans are examples of grassroots movements that leverage social media to promote inclusivity and challenge harmful narratives.

+ **Literature and Film:** Works like *Moonlight* and *The Miseducation of Cameron Post* offer nuanced portrayals of LGBTQ experiences, focusing on themes of identity, love, and belonging. These narratives not only entertain but also foster empathy and understanding among audiences.

The Role of Media Professionals

Media professionals have a crucial role to play in promoting diversity and inclusivity. This responsibility encompasses several key actions:

+ **Authentic Storytelling:** Media creators should prioritize authentic storytelling by involving LGBTQ individuals in the writing, directing, and production processes. This ensures that narratives are grounded in real experiences and perspectives.

+ **Challenging Stereotypes:** Media professionals should actively work to challenge and dismantle harmful stereotypes by creating complex, multidimensional characters that reflect the diversity within LGBTQ communities.

+ **Advocacy for Representation:** Journalists and media outlets should advocate for greater representation of LGBTQ voices in news coverage and feature stories. This includes highlighting the achievements of LGBTQ individuals and communities, rather than solely focusing on issues of victimization.

+ **Education and Awareness:** Media organizations should invest in training programs that educate staff about LGBTQ issues, fostering a culture of inclusivity and understanding within the workplace.

Conclusion

The media's responsibility in promoting diversity and inclusivity is paramount in shaping societal attitudes towards marginalized communities. By prioritizing authentic representation, challenging stereotypes, and advocating for LGBTQ voices, media professionals can foster a more inclusive environment that reflects the richness of human experience. As Jin Xing's story illustrates, the power of media to drive social change is immense; it can inspire acceptance, foster understanding, and ultimately pave the way for a more inclusive future. The call to action for media professionals is clear: embrace the responsibility to represent all voices, particularly those that have been historically marginalized, and work towards a media landscape that celebrates diversity in all its forms.

The role of media in shaping public opinion and cultural attitudes

The media plays a pivotal role in influencing public opinion and shaping cultural attitudes, particularly regarding marginalized communities such as the LGBTQ community. This section delves into how various forms of media, including television, film, print, and social media, contribute to the construction of societal norms and perceptions.

Theoretical Frameworks

To understand the media's impact on public opinion, several theoretical frameworks can be employed:

+ **Agenda-Setting Theory:** This theory posits that the media doesn't tell people what to think, but rather what to think about. By prioritizing certain issues, the media can influence the public's perception of their importance. For instance, when LGBTQ issues are prominently featured in news cycles, they become more salient in the public discourse, prompting discussions and potentially altering societal attitudes.

+ **Framing Theory:** This theory suggests that the way information is presented (framed) can significantly influence how audiences interpret it. For example, framing LGBTQ representation in terms of rights and equality can lead to more supportive attitudes compared to framing it as a deviant behavior. The choice of language, imagery, and context can either reinforce stereotypes or promote understanding.

+ **Cultivation Theory:** This theory posits that long-term exposure to media content can shape an individual's perceptions of reality. For instance, consistent portrayals of LGBTQ individuals in positive roles can lead to greater acceptance and normalization of LGBTQ identities in society.

Media Representation and Stereotypes

Media representation is crucial in combating stereotypes and fostering a more nuanced understanding of LGBTQ lives. Historically, LGBTQ individuals have been misrepresented or underrepresented in mainstream media, often portrayed through a lens of negativity or sensationalism. This lack of representation can perpetuate harmful stereotypes, leading to societal misconceptions.

For instance, a study by [?] found that LGBTQ characters in television shows often fall into archetypical roles—such as the flamboyant gay best friend or the tragic transgender figure—which can reinforce narrow understandings of LGBTQ identities. Conversely, shows like *Pose* and *Schitt's Creek* have been lauded for their multi-dimensional representations of LGBTQ characters, showcasing their complexities and humanity, thereby contributing to a shift in public perception.

The Power of Social Media

Social media has emerged as a powerful tool for shaping public opinion, particularly among younger generations. Platforms like Twitter, Instagram, and TikTok provide spaces for LGBTQ individuals to share their stories, advocate for rights, and connect with allies. These platforms democratize the narrative, allowing marginalized voices to be heard directly, bypassing traditional media gatekeepers.

Research by [?] highlights how social media allows for the construction of identity and community among LGBTQ individuals, fostering a sense of belonging and empowerment. Campaigns such as #LoveIsLove and #TransRightsAreHumanRights have gained traction, mobilizing support and raising awareness for LGBTQ issues globally. The viral nature of social media can amplify messages, creating a ripple effect that influences public opinion and cultural attitudes.

Challenges and Misrepresentation

Despite the potential for positive influence, media representation of LGBTQ individuals is not without challenges. Misrepresentation can still occur, particularly in mainstream media, where LGBTQ characters are often sidelined or their stories are told through a heteronormative lens. This can lead to a lack of authenticity in portrayals and a failure to address the real issues faced by the LGBTQ community.

Moreover, the rise of "performative allyship" on social media can sometimes overshadow genuine activism. Brands and influencers may adopt LGBTQ-friendly messaging during Pride Month without committing to substantive support for LGBTQ rights year-round, which can dilute the movement's impact and perpetuate a cycle of tokenism.

Case Studies

Several case studies illustrate the media's role in shaping public opinion and cultural attitudes towards the LGBTQ community:

- **"Will & Grace"**: This groundbreaking sitcom played a significant role in normalizing LGBTQ relationships in the late 1990s and early 2000s. The show's popularity contributed to a broader acceptance of gay culture in American society, demonstrating how positive representation can influence public attitudes.

- **"Orange Is the New Black"**: This series provided a platform for diverse LGBTQ narratives, particularly highlighting the experiences of transgender women of color. The show's success sparked discussions about intersectionality within the LGBTQ community and brought attention to issues of race and gender identity.

- **Social Media Campaigns**: The #BlackTransLivesMatter movement gained momentum through social media, highlighting the specific challenges faced by Black transgender individuals. The visibility of these issues on platforms like Twitter and Instagram has contributed to a broader conversation about intersectionality and the need for inclusive activism.

Conclusion

In conclusion, the media plays a crucial role in shaping public opinion and cultural attitudes towards the LGBTQ community. Through various theoretical lenses, we can see how representation, framing, and the rise of social media influence societal perceptions. While challenges remain, the potential for media to drive positive change and foster understanding is significant. As society continues to evolve, the responsibility lies with media creators and consumers alike to advocate for authentic representation and challenge harmful stereotypes, paving the way for a more inclusive future.

The need for accurate and positive portrayals of LGBTQ individuals

The representation of LGBTQ individuals in media has long been a contentious issue, with portrayals often oscillating between caricatures and stereotypes, which can perpetuate harmful misconceptions. Accurate and positive representations are crucial not only for the individuals they depict but also for society at large, as they contribute to a broader understanding and acceptance of diverse identities.

Theoretical Framework

One of the foundational theories in media representation is Stuart Hall's Encoding/Decoding model, which posits that media messages are encoded with specific meanings by their creators and decoded by audiences based on their own cultural contexts. This model emphasizes the active role of audiences in interpreting media, suggesting that positive representations can foster understanding and empathy, while negative portrayals can reinforce prejudice and discrimination.

Moreover, the Social Identity Theory (Tajfel and Turner, 1979) suggests that individuals derive part of their identity from the groups to which they belong. When LGBTQ individuals see themselves represented positively in media, it can enhance their self-esteem and sense of belonging. Conversely, negative portrayals can lead to internalized stigma and decreased self-worth.

Problems with Current Representations

Historically, LGBTQ individuals have been depicted in media through a narrow lens, often characterized by tropes such as the "tragic gay" or the "predatory lesbian." These portrayals can lead to a distorted understanding of LGBTQ lives, reducing complex identities to simplistic narratives. For example, the character of Jack McPhee in the television series *Dawson's Creek* was groundbreaking for its time, but it also fell into the trap of the "tragic gay" trope, where his storyline revolved around societal rejection and personal tragedy rather than the celebration of his identity.

Furthermore, the lack of intersectionality in LGBTQ portrayals exacerbates the problem. Media often fails to represent the diversity within the LGBTQ community, neglecting the experiences of people of color, transgender individuals, and those with disabilities. This lack of representation can lead to feelings of invisibility and alienation among marginalized groups within the LGBTQ spectrum.

Examples of Positive Representation

In recent years, there has been a noticeable shift towards more nuanced and positive portrayals of LGBTQ individuals in media. Shows like *Pose* and *Schitt's Creek* have received critical acclaim for their authentic representation of LGBTQ lives. *Pose*, for instance, features a predominantly transgender cast and addresses issues such as the AIDS crisis and the ballroom culture of the 1980s and 90s, highlighting both the struggles and resilience of the community.

Moreover, the character of David Rose in *Schitt's Creek* exemplifies a positive representation of pansexuality. The show portrays his relationships in a light-hearted yet respectful manner, emphasizing love and acceptance without resorting to stereotypes. This kind of representation allows audiences to see LGBTQ individuals as multi-dimensional characters, fostering empathy and understanding.

The Role of Media in Shaping Public Perception

The media plays a pivotal role in shaping public perceptions of LGBTQ individuals. Positive portrayals can challenge stereotypes and promote acceptance, while negative representations can reinforce prejudice. Research has shown that exposure to positive LGBTQ characters can lead to increased acceptance among viewers. A study conducted by the Gay and Lesbian Alliance Against Defamation (GLAAD) found that audiences who viewed positive LGBTQ characters were more likely to support LGBTQ rights and issues.

The Responsibility of Content Creators

Content creators have a responsibility to ensure that LGBTQ individuals are portrayed accurately and positively. This includes consulting with LGBTQ individuals during the writing and production process to ensure authenticity.

Furthermore, creators should strive to depict a wide range of experiences within the LGBTQ community, showcasing diverse identities, backgrounds, and stories.

In conclusion, the need for accurate and positive portrayals of LGBTQ individuals in media is critical for fostering understanding, acceptance, and representation. By challenging stereotypes and promoting diverse narratives, media can play a transformative role in shaping societal attitudes towards the LGBTQ community.

$$\text{Positive Representation} \rightarrow \text{Increased Acceptance} \qquad (115)$$

The potential for media to drive social change and progress

The media plays a crucial role in shaping societal perceptions and attitudes, particularly regarding marginalized communities such as the LGBTQ population. Through various forms of media, including television, film, social media, and print, narratives can be constructed that either reinforce stereotypes or challenge them, ultimately influencing public opinion and policy. The potential for media to drive social change and progress lies in its ability to amplify voices, create awareness, and foster empathy.

Theoretical Framework

To understand the media's impact on social change, we can refer to the **Framing Theory**, which posits that the way information is presented (or framed) significantly affects how audiences interpret it. Media framing can highlight specific aspects of a story while downplaying others, thus shaping public discourse. For instance, when LGBTQ individuals are framed as victims of discrimination, it can elicit sympathy and support for their rights. Conversely, when portrayed as deviant or problematic, it may reinforce prejudices and discrimination.

Another relevant theory is the **Agenda-Setting Theory**, which suggests that the media doesn't tell us what to think, but rather what to think about. By prioritizing certain issues, the media can influence the public agenda. For example, increased media coverage of LGBTQ rights can elevate the issue in the public consciousness, prompting discussions that may lead to policy changes.

Examples of Media Driving Change

One notable example of media's power to effect social change is the portrayal of LGBTQ characters in television and film. Shows like *Will & Grace* and *Pose* have not only entertained but also educated audiences about LGBTQ experiences, contributing to greater acceptance and understanding. Research indicates that exposure to LGBTQ characters in positive roles can reduce homophobia and increase support for LGBTQ rights.

Furthermore, social media platforms have emerged as powerful tools for advocacy. Campaigns such as #LoveIsLove and #TransRightsAreHumanRights have mobilized millions, creating solidarity and raising awareness about LGBTQ issues. These campaigns illustrate how social media can bypass traditional media gatekeepers, allowing marginalized voices to be heard directly.

Challenges and Limitations

Despite the potential for media to drive social change, significant challenges remain. One major issue is the prevalence of negative stereotypes and misrepresentations of LGBTQ individuals in mainstream media. Such portrayals can perpetuate stigma and discrimination, undermining the progress made by positive representations.

Additionally, access to media varies greatly across different regions, particularly in countries where LGBTQ rights are heavily restricted. In these contexts, state-controlled media may disseminate harmful narratives that hinder progress rather than promote it.

The Role of Activism and Advocacy

Activism plays a pivotal role in shaping media narratives. LGBTQ activists and organizations work tirelessly to hold media outlets accountable for their representations and to advocate for more inclusive and accurate portrayals. Initiatives like the **GLAAD Media Institute** focus on training media professionals to create content that reflects the diversity and complexity of LGBTQ lives.

Moreover, grassroots movements have successfully pressured networks and studios to diversify their storytelling. The demand for authentic representation has led to increased opportunities for LGBTQ writers, directors, and producers, further enhancing the quality and diversity of narratives presented to the public.

Conclusion

In conclusion, the potential for media to drive social change and progress is immense. By framing issues thoughtfully, setting agendas, and providing platforms for marginalized voices, media can foster understanding, empathy, and acceptance. However, it is essential to remain vigilant against negative portrayals and to advocate for inclusive representation. The ongoing struggle for LGBTQ rights is intrinsically linked to how media narratives are constructed and disseminated, making it imperative that we harness the power of media to create a more just and equitable society.

The importance of supporting LGBTQ-inclusive media and content

In recent years, the visibility of LGBTQ individuals in media has increased significantly, yet the representation remains fraught with challenges. Supporting LGBTQ-inclusive media and content is essential not only for fostering acceptance and understanding but also for empowering marginalized communities. This section delves into the theoretical frameworks, current problems, and notable examples that highlight the necessity of such support.

Theoretical Frameworks

The importance of media representation can be understood through several theoretical lenses, including Social Identity Theory and Cultivation Theory. Social Identity Theory posits that individuals derive part of their self-concept from their membership in social groups. For LGBTQ individuals, seeing themselves reflected positively in media can enhance self-esteem and foster a sense of belonging. Conversely, negative portrayals can contribute to internalized stigma and societal discrimination.

Cultivation Theory, developed by George Gerbner, suggests that long-term exposure to media content can shape an individual's perceptions of reality. In this context, consistent exposure to LGBTQ-inclusive narratives can challenge stereotypes and promote a more nuanced understanding of gender and sexuality. Thus, supporting media that portrays LGBTQ lives authentically is vital for societal progress.

Current Problems

Despite advancements, LGBTQ representation in media often falls short due to several persistent problems:

- **Stereotyping:** Many LGBTQ characters are relegated to stereotypes that do not reflect the diversity of the community. This can perpetuate harmful misconceptions and limit public understanding of LGBTQ experiences.

- **Underrepresentation:** LGBTQ individuals, particularly those from marginalized racial and ethnic backgrounds, are often underrepresented in mainstream media. This lack of visibility denies these individuals the opportunity to share their stories and experiences.

+ **Tokenism:** When LGBTQ characters are included, they are sometimes merely token figures, lacking depth and development. This can lead to a superficial understanding of LGBTQ issues and fails to engage audiences on a deeper level.

Examples of LGBTQ-Inclusive Media

Several media productions have successfully navigated these challenges, providing authentic representation and contributing to the broader conversation about LGBTQ rights.

+ **"Pose":** This groundbreaking television series showcases the lives of transgender women and the ballroom culture of New York City in the 1980s and 1990s. With a predominantly transgender cast, "Pose" not only provides visibility but also highlights the struggles and triumphs of its characters, fostering empathy and understanding among viewers.

+ **"Moonlight":** This Academy Award-winning film tells the coming-of-age story of a young Black man grappling with his identity and sexuality. "Moonlight" received critical acclaim for its nuanced portrayal of LGBTQ experiences, illustrating the intersectionality of race and sexuality.

+ **"Schitt's Creek":** This comedy series features a pansexual character, David, whose relationships are portrayed with humor and authenticity. The show has been praised for its positive representation of LGBTQ relationships, contributing to a more accepting cultural narrative.

The Role of Audiences and Activism

Supporting LGBTQ-inclusive media goes beyond individual consumption; it requires active engagement. Audiences can play a crucial role by:

+ **Advocacy:** Supporting LGBTQ-inclusive content through social media, petitions, and community discussions can amplify the voices of creators and demand better representation.

+ **Financial Support:** Choosing to watch, share, and promote LGBTQ-inclusive films, shows, and literature can help ensure their success and encourage further production of diverse content.

- **Education:** Engaging in discussions about the importance of representation can foster understanding within communities, helping to dismantle prejudices and misconceptions.

Conclusion

In conclusion, supporting LGBTQ-inclusive media and content is vital for promoting understanding, acceptance, and visibility. By addressing the challenges of representation and actively engaging in advocacy, audiences can contribute to a more inclusive media landscape. As Jin Xing's journey illustrates, representation matters; it has the power to inspire change, empower individuals, and foster a more accepting society. Therefore, the call to action is clear: support LGBTQ-inclusive media, not just as consumers, but as advocates for a more equitable world.

Jin Xing's role in reshaping cultural representation and media influence

Jin Xing, a prominent figure in the dance world and a groundbreaking transgender activist, has played a pivotal role in reshaping cultural representation and media influence in contemporary China. Her journey from a talented dancer in Shenyang to an international icon of LGBTQ advocacy illustrates the profound impact one individual can have on societal perceptions and media narratives surrounding gender and sexuality.

At the core of Jin Xing's influence is her ability to challenge entrenched stereotypes and cultural norms. In a society where traditional views on gender roles are deeply rooted, Jin Xing's visibility as a transgender woman defies the conventional expectations of femininity and masculinity. Her performances, which often blend classical Chinese dance with contemporary styles, serve as a powerful medium for expressing her identity and experiences. This fusion not only highlights her artistic versatility but also promotes a broader understanding of gender fluidity in a culture that has historically marginalized such expressions.

One of the theoretical frameworks that can be applied to understand Jin Xing's impact is Judith Butler's concept of gender performativity. Butler posits that gender is not a fixed attribute but rather a series of performances that individuals enact based on societal expectations. Jin Xing embodies this theory through her art, demonstrating that gender can be a dynamic and evolving construct. Her performances challenge audiences to reconsider their preconceived notions of gender, encouraging a more nuanced understanding of identity.

Moreover, Jin Xing's role in media extends beyond her performances. As a judge on the reality television show "So You Think You Can Dance China," she has brought LGBTQ representation into the mainstream media landscape. This platform has allowed her to advocate for acceptance and inclusivity, reaching millions of viewers who may have previously held narrow views of gender and sexuality. By occupying a position of authority in a widely watched program, Jin Xing not only normalizes the presence of transgender individuals in popular culture but also educates the public on the complexities of gender identity.

Despite her achievements, Jin Xing's journey has not been without challenges. The conservative nature of Chinese society often poses significant obstacles for LGBTQ representation in media. Many media outlets remain hesitant to portray LGBTQ individuals authentically, fearing backlash from traditionalist segments of the population. Jin Xing's visibility, therefore, is both a triumph and a battleground; her presence forces the media to confront its biases while simultaneously risking potential censorship and criticism.

The importance of representation in media cannot be overstated. Research has shown that positive portrayals of marginalized groups can lead to increased acceptance and understanding among the general public. For instance, a study conducted by the Williams Institute found that individuals who consume media featuring LGBTQ characters are more likely to support LGBTQ rights and policies. Jin Xing's role in reshaping cultural representation aligns with this finding, as her visibility has contributed to a gradual shift in societal attitudes toward the LGBTQ community in China.

In addition to her work in television, Jin Xing has utilized social media platforms to amplify her message. By sharing her experiences and insights online, she has connected with a global audience, fostering a sense of solidarity among LGBTQ individuals worldwide. Her candid discussions about the challenges of being a transgender woman in China resonate with many, inspiring individuals to embrace their identities and advocate for their rights.

Jin Xing's influence also extends to the realm of cultural exchange. Through international tours and collaborations, she serves as a cultural ambassador, bridging the gap between Eastern and Western perceptions of gender and sexuality. Her performances often incorporate elements of both cultures, showcasing the richness of diversity while advocating for universal acceptance. This cultural dialogue not only enriches the arts but also fosters greater understanding and empathy across borders.

In conclusion, Jin Xing's role in reshaping cultural representation and media influence is multifaceted and profound. Through her performances, television presence, and social media engagement, she challenges stereotypes, educates the public, and advocates for LGBTQ rights. As a symbol of resilience and authenticity, Jin Xing continues to inspire individuals to embrace their true selves and advocate for a more inclusive society. Her journey exemplifies the power of representation in effecting social change, highlighting the importance of visibility in the ongoing fight for equality and acceptance.

$$\text{Cultural Representation} = \text{Visibility} + \text{Authenticity} + \text{Advocacy} \qquad (116)$$

This equation underscores the components that contribute to effective cultural representation, illustrating how Jin Xing embodies these elements in her work. As society progresses toward greater inclusivity, Jin Xing's legacy will undoubtedly serve as a cornerstone for future generations of LGBTQ activists and artists, inspiring them to continue the fight for equality and representation in all aspects of life.

Inspiring Change: Lessons from Jin Xing's Journey

Overcoming adversity and embracing authenticity

Throughout her journey, Jin Xing has exemplified the profound strength that comes from overcoming adversity and embracing one's authentic self. Her story is not merely one of personal triumph; it serves as a beacon of hope for many who face similar challenges in their lives. This section delves into the theoretical frameworks surrounding authenticity, the specific adversities faced by Jin Xing, and the broader implications of her journey in the context of LGBTQ activism.

Theoretical Framework: Authenticity and Identity

Authenticity, in the context of identity, can be understood through the lens of existential philosophy and psychological theories. According to [?], authenticity involves the realization of one's true self, unmediated by societal expectations. This aligns with [?]'s humanistic psychology, which posits that authenticity is crucial for personal growth and self-actualization.

The process of embracing authenticity often requires individuals to confront and navigate various forms of adversity. According to [?], the development of identity is a lifelong process influenced by social interactions and cultural contexts. For many LGBTQ individuals, societal norms and expectations can create significant barriers to self-acceptance, leading to internal conflicts and struggles for validation.

Jin Xing's Adversities

Jin Xing's life was marked by numerous adversities that she had to overcome in her quest for authenticity. Growing up in Shenyang, China, she faced societal stigma and discrimination as a transgender individual. The cultural backdrop of China, where traditional gender roles are deeply ingrained, posed significant challenges for her.

One notable instance of adversity was the lack of acceptance from her peers and the broader community. Jin Xing faced bullying and social ostracism during her formative years, which could have deterred many from pursuing their passions. However, her determination to succeed in dance became a powerful outlet for her self-expression.

Moreover, the decision to undergo gender reassignment surgery was fraught with emotional and physical challenges. Jin Xing had to navigate not only the medical aspects of the procedure but also the societal backlash that often accompanies such a transformative choice. The psychological toll of being in a society that often vilifies non-conformity cannot be understated. As [?] suggests, stigma can lead to a "spoiled identity," which Jin Xing worked tirelessly to reclaim through her art and activism.

Embracing Authenticity through Dance

Dance became Jin Xing's sanctuary and a medium through which she could fully express her identity. Her early exposure to dance provided her with a sense of freedom and empowerment that was otherwise elusive. In her performances, Jin Xing infused her unique experiences and emotions, transforming her struggles into powerful artistic expressions.

The transformational power of dance is well-documented in therapeutic settings. According to [?], dance therapy can facilitate self-exploration and healing, making it an effective tool for individuals grappling with identity issues. For Jin Xing, dance was not just a career; it was a means of reclaiming her narrative and asserting her authenticity in a world that often sought to diminish her identity.

Through her choreography and performances, Jin Xing challenged traditional notions of gender and identity, pushing the boundaries of what was considered acceptable in the dance community. Her unique style, which blends classical and contemporary techniques, serves as a metaphor for her journey—one that embraces complexity and fluidity rather than rigid definitions.

The Impact of Jin Xing's Journey

Jin Xing's journey of overcoming adversity and embracing authenticity has had a profound impact on the LGBTQ community in China and beyond. Her visibility as a transgender artist challenges stereotypes and promotes a broader understanding of gender identity.

As an advocate for LGBTQ rights, Jin Xing has utilized her platform to foster discussions around acceptance and inclusivity. Her presence on television as a judge on "So You Think You Can Dance China" has been particularly significant. By occupying a space traditionally dominated by cisgender individuals, she has brought visibility to transgender issues, encouraging conversations about representation in the media.

Furthermore, Jin Xing's story resonates with many individuals who face similar struggles. Her ability to articulate her experiences of adversity and authenticity provides a roadmap for others navigating their own paths. As noted by [?], vulnerability can be a source of strength, and Jin Xing's willingness to share her journey has empowered countless individuals to embrace their true selves.

Conclusion: A Legacy of Resilience

In conclusion, Jin Xing's journey of overcoming adversity and embracing authenticity is a testament to the power of resilience. Her story underscores the importance of self-acceptance and the need for societal change in the face of discrimination and stigma. By embracing her true self, Jin Xing not only transformed her own life but also inspired a generation of activists and artists to challenge societal norms and advocate for LGBTQ rights.

As we reflect on her legacy, it is essential to recognize the ongoing struggles faced by many in the LGBTQ community. Jin Xing's journey serves as a reminder that the fight for authenticity and acceptance is far from over. Her impact continues to resonate, urging us all to embrace our true selves and advocate for a more inclusive world.

The power of visibility and personal stories in driving social change

In the realm of social movements, visibility plays a crucial role in shaping public perception and fostering empathy. The LGBTQ community, historically marginalized and often subjected to discrimination, has found empowerment through the visibility of its members. Personal stories serve as powerful tools for advocacy, as they humanize the experiences of individuals within the community, breaking down stereotypes and fostering understanding.

Visibility can be defined as the degree to which individuals or groups are seen, acknowledged, and represented in public discourse and media. In the context of LGBTQ rights, increased visibility has been instrumental in challenging societal norms and promoting acceptance. According to [?], visibility not only affirms identity but also serves as a catalyst for social change by allowing marginalized voices to be heard.

$$V = \frac{E}{R} \qquad\qquad (117)$$

Where:

- V represents visibility,

- E represents the engagement of the community,

- R represents the resistance from societal norms.

As visibility increases, so does engagement from both the LGBTQ community and allies, while resistance may decrease as public awareness grows. This equation illustrates the dynamic relationship between visibility and societal acceptance.

One of the most significant examples of the power of visibility can be seen in the media representations of LGBTQ individuals. The portrayal of characters in television shows and films has evolved over the years, moving from stereotypical depictions to more nuanced and authentic representations. Shows like *Will & Grace* and *Pose* have not only entertained audiences but also provided a platform for dialogue about LGBTQ issues, showcasing the complexities of identity and the struggles faced by individuals within the community.

Furthermore, personal narratives shared through social media platforms have amplified the voices of LGBTQ individuals, creating a sense of community and solidarity. The hashtag #WeAreHere, for instance, has been utilized by countless individuals to share their stories of resilience and triumph over adversity. These personal accounts not only validate the experiences of others but also encourage individuals to embrace their identities openly.

The impact of visibility extends beyond personal narratives; it also influences policy changes and societal attitudes. Research conducted by [?] indicates that increased representation of LGBTQ individuals in media correlates with greater public support for LGBTQ rights. The visibility of LGBTQ figures, such as Jin Xing, has been instrumental in promoting awareness and acceptance in conservative societies like China. Jin Xing's journey from a local dancer to an international icon exemplifies how personal stories can challenge cultural taboos and inspire change.

However, the journey toward visibility is not without its challenges. Many LGBTQ individuals face backlash and discrimination when they choose to come out or share their stories. This resistance can manifest in various forms, including social ostracism, workplace discrimination, and even violence. The fear of such repercussions often leads individuals to remain silent about their identities, perpetuating a cycle of invisibility.

To combat this, it is essential for allies and advocates to create safe spaces where LGBTQ individuals can share their stories without fear of judgment or retribution. Educational initiatives that promote understanding and empathy can further enhance visibility, as they encourage open dialogue about LGBTQ issues and challenge preconceived notions.

In conclusion, the power of visibility and personal stories in driving social change cannot be overstated. As individuals share their experiences, they not only validate their own identities but also contribute to a broader narrative that fosters acceptance and understanding. The journey toward equality is ongoing, and the collective visibility of the LGBTQ community remains a vital component in the fight for rights and recognition. By amplifying these voices and embracing personal stories, society can move closer to a future where everyone is free to live authentically and without fear.

Allies and support systems in the fight for LGBTQ rights

The fight for LGBTQ rights is not solely the responsibility of those who identify as part of the community; it requires the active participation and support of allies. Allies are individuals who do not identify as LGBTQ but who support and advocate for the rights and dignity of LGBTQ individuals. They play a crucial role in advancing equality and fostering an inclusive society. Understanding the dynamics of allyship and the importance of support systems is essential in the ongoing struggle for LGBTQ rights.

The Role of Allies

Allies serve as bridges between the LGBTQ community and the broader society. They help to amplify the voices of marginalized individuals and challenge discriminatory practices and attitudes. Allies can be found in various spheres, including family, friends, workplaces, and political spaces. Their involvement can significantly impact the visibility and acceptance of LGBTQ individuals.

One of the primary roles of allies is to educate themselves and others about LGBTQ issues. This education involves understanding the historical context of discrimination, the current challenges faced by the community, and the importance of intersectionality. Allies must also recognize their privilege and the ways in which it can be leveraged to support LGBTQ rights. For instance, a heterosexual individual in a workplace can advocate for inclusive policies that protect LGBTQ employees from discrimination.

Support Systems

Support systems are vital for the well-being of LGBTQ individuals. These systems can take many forms, including:

1. **Family Support**: Acceptance from family members can profoundly affect an LGBTQ individual's mental health and self-esteem. Families that embrace their LGBTQ members create safe spaces where individuals can express their identities without fear of rejection.

2. **Peer Support**: Friends and peers play a significant role in providing emotional support. LGBTQ individuals often find community in friendships that affirm their identities, allowing them to share experiences and challenges.

3. **Community Organizations**: Various non-profit organizations and advocacy groups offer resources, support, and safe spaces for LGBTQ individuals. Organizations such as The Trevor Project, Human Rights Campaign, and local LGBTQ centers provide critical services, including mental health support, legal assistance, and community-building activities.

4. **Educational Institutions**: Schools and universities can foster supportive environments through LGBTQ-inclusive policies, training for staff, and the establishment of LGBTQ student organizations. These institutions can serve as safe havens for LGBTQ youth, providing them with resources and community.

Challenges Faced by Allies

While allies play a crucial role in supporting LGBTQ rights, they also face challenges. These challenges can include backlash from peers or family members who hold discriminatory views. For example, an ally who speaks out against homophobic remarks at a family gathering may be met with resistance or hostility. This can create a tension between the desire to support LGBTQ rights and the fear of social repercussions.

Moreover, allies must be cautious not to overshadow the voices of LGBTQ individuals. It is essential for allies to listen actively and allow LGBTQ individuals to lead the conversation about their rights and experiences. The concept of "performative allyship" has emerged, describing situations where individuals claim to support LGBTQ rights without taking meaningful action. True allyship involves ongoing commitment, education, and action rather than mere token gestures.

Theoretical Frameworks

The dynamics of allyship can be understood through various theoretical frameworks, including:

1. **Social Identity Theory**: This theory posits that individuals derive a sense of identity from their group memberships. Allies must navigate their identities as supporters while recognizing the unique experiences of LGBTQ individuals. Understanding the intersectionality of identities—such as race, gender, and socioeconomic status—is crucial for effective allyship.

2. **Critical Theory**: This framework encourages a critical examination of societal structures and power dynamics. Allies are urged to confront systemic inequalities and advocate for structural changes that promote LGBTQ rights. This involves questioning societal norms and challenging discriminatory practices at institutional levels.

3. **Empowerment Theory**: Empowerment theory emphasizes the importance of enabling individuals to gain control over their lives and advocate for their rights. Allies can empower LGBTQ individuals by providing resources, support, and platforms to share their stories and experiences.

Examples of Effective Allyship

Several notable examples illustrate the impact of allyship in the fight for LGBTQ rights:

- **Corporate Allyship**: Many companies have adopted LGBTQ-inclusive policies and practices, demonstrating their commitment to equality. For instance, during Pride Month, numerous corporations publicly support LGBTQ rights through marketing campaigns and sponsorships, showcasing their solidarity with the community.

- **Political Advocacy**: Politicians and public figures who advocate for LGBTQ rights can influence public policy and societal attitudes. For example, former President Barack Obama's support for same-sex marriage and the repeal of

"Don't Ask, Don't Tell" marked significant milestones in the fight for LGBTQ rights in the United States.

- **Grassroots Movements**: Local community organizations often rely on allies to mobilize support for LGBTQ rights. Initiatives such as pride parades, awareness campaigns, and educational workshops thrive on the participation of allies who help to raise awareness and foster acceptance.

Conclusion

In conclusion, allies and support systems are indispensable in the fight for LGBTQ rights. They contribute to creating inclusive environments, advocating for policy changes, and amplifying the voices of marginalized individuals. By educating themselves, challenging discriminatory practices, and providing emotional support, allies play a pivotal role in advancing the cause of equality. However, true allyship requires ongoing commitment, self-reflection, and a willingness to confront one's own biases. As the LGBTQ movement continues to evolve, the importance of allies in fostering a more inclusive society cannot be overstated.

Empowering the next generation of LGBTQ activists

Empowering the next generation of LGBTQ activists is crucial for the continuation of the fight for equality and acceptance. As society evolves, so too do the challenges faced by LGBTQ individuals. This section explores the importance of mentorship, education, and visibility in fostering a new wave of activists who are equipped to challenge societal norms and advocate for their rights.

The Role of Mentorship

Mentorship plays a pivotal role in empowering young activists. Older activists, like Jin Xing, can provide invaluable guidance, sharing their experiences and insights into navigating the complexities of activism. Mentorship creates a supportive environment where young activists can learn from the successes and failures of those who came before them.

For instance, programs that connect established activists with youth can facilitate the transfer of knowledge and skills. These programs often focus on critical areas such as grassroots organizing, public speaking, and media engagement. By fostering these connections, we not only honor the legacy of past activists but also ensure that the next generation is prepared to take on the mantle of leadership.

Education as a Tool for Empowerment

Education is another powerful tool for empowering LGBTQ youth. Incorporating LGBTQ studies into school curriculums can help normalize discussions around gender and sexuality, fostering an inclusive environment. Studies have shown that inclusive education reduces bullying and discrimination, creating safer spaces for LGBTQ students.

Moreover, workshops and seminars that focus on LGBTQ history, rights, and current issues can inspire youth to engage in activism. By understanding the struggles and triumphs of previous generations, young activists can draw strength and motivation from their predecessors.

$$\text{Empowerment} = \text{Mentorship} + \text{Education} + \text{Visibility} \qquad (118)$$

This equation highlights the interconnectedness of these elements. When combined, they create a powerful framework for empowerment, enabling young activists to forge their paths in the ongoing struggle for equality.

Visibility and Representation

Visibility is crucial in empowering the next generation of LGBTQ activists. When young people see themselves represented in media, politics, and society, they are more likely to feel validated in their identities and inspired to advocate for change. Jin Xing's presence in the media has significantly impacted LGBTQ representation in China, demonstrating the power of visibility.

For example, the rise of social media platforms has allowed young activists to amplify their voices and share their stories. Platforms like Instagram and TikTok have become vital spaces for LGBTQ youth to express themselves, connect with others, and organize campaigns. By leveraging these platforms, young activists can reach wider audiences and foster community support.

Challenges Faced by Young Activists

Despite the progress made, young LGBTQ activists still face numerous challenges. Societal stigma, discrimination, and lack of resources can hinder their efforts. Many young activists grapple with internalized homophobia and fear of rejection, which can stifle their willingness to engage in activism.

Additionally, systemic barriers such as inadequate legal protections and hostile environments can create significant obstacles. For instance, in many countries, LGBTQ individuals lack basic rights, making it difficult for activists to push for change without facing severe repercussions.

Examples of Successful Youth Activism

Despite these challenges, there are numerous examples of successful youth activism that serve as inspiration. The Stonewall Riots, often considered the catalyst for the modern LGBTQ rights movement, were led by young individuals who bravely stood up against oppression. More recently, youth-led movements like the March for Our Lives have shown that young people can mobilize effectively for social change.

Organizations such as GLSEN (Gay, Lesbian & Straight Education Network) empower students to advocate for safer schools and inclusive policies. Their initiatives provide students with the tools and resources needed to effect change within their communities.

Conclusion

Empowering the next generation of LGBTQ activists is essential for the ongoing fight for equality. Through mentorship, education, and visibility, we can equip young activists with the knowledge and support they need to navigate the complexities of advocacy. By recognizing the challenges they face and celebrating their successes, we can ensure that the legacy of activism continues to thrive.

As Jin Xing's journey illustrates, the power of resilience, authenticity, and community can inspire a new generation to rise up and advocate for their rights. The future of the LGBTQ movement lies in the hands of these young activists, and it is our responsibility to empower them to create a more inclusive and accepting world.

Jin Xing's lasting impact on the LGBTQ movement and the world

Jin Xing's journey from the streets of Shenyang to the global stage is not just a personal triumph; it is a beacon of hope and resilience for the LGBTQ community worldwide. Her influence extends beyond the realm of dance and performance; it encapsulates a larger narrative of acceptance, visibility, and the relentless pursuit of equality. This section explores the multifaceted impact Jin Xing has had on the LGBTQ movement and the world at large.

Visibility and Representation

One of Jin Xing's most significant contributions to the LGBTQ movement is her unwavering commitment to visibility. In a society where LGBTQ identities are often marginalized or outright erased, Jin Xing's presence as a transgender woman in the public eye challenges the status quo. Her rise to fame has opened doors for conversations about gender identity and sexual orientation in China, a country where such discussions are frequently taboo.

The theory of *social representation* posits that visibility in media and culture can significantly influence societal attitudes towards marginalized groups. Jin Xing's performances and public appearances serve as a counter-narrative to the often negative portrayals of transgender individuals in media. By presenting herself as a successful artist, she disrupts stereotypes and fosters a more nuanced understanding of transgender lives.

Cultural Shift in Attitudes

Jin Xing's influence transcends individual representation; it has sparked a cultural shift in attitudes towards LGBTQ individuals in China and beyond. Her advocacy work and public persona have contributed to a gradual, albeit challenging, transformation in societal perceptions. The concept of *cultural hegemony* describes how dominant groups maintain power through cultural institutions, often marginalizing alternative narratives. Jin Xing's activism challenges this hegemony by asserting the validity of LGBTQ experiences and identities.

For example, her role as a judge on "So You Think You Can Dance China" not only showcased her talent but also provided a platform for LGBTQ contestants to shine. This visibility has encouraged a younger generation to embrace their identities, fostering a sense of community and belonging.

Advocacy and Activism

Jin Xing has utilized her platform to advocate for LGBTQ rights in China, becoming a voice for those who often feel voiceless. Her activism aligns with the *social movement theory*, which emphasizes the importance of collective action in creating social change. By participating in public discussions, interviews, and events, she has raised awareness about the challenges faced by LGBTQ individuals, including discrimination, mental health issues, and lack of legal protections.

An example of her advocacy can be seen in her participation in pride events and her outspoken support for LGBTQ rights on social media. This engagement not only amplifies the voices of LGBTQ individuals but also educates the broader public on the importance of acceptance and equality.

Global Influence and Intersectionality

Jin Xing's impact is not confined to China; it resonates globally. Her story has inspired LGBTQ activists around the world, illustrating the power of resilience and the importance of intersectionality within the movement. Intersectionality, as defined by Kimberlé Crenshaw, recognizes that individuals experience multiple, overlapping identities that shape their experiences of oppression and privilege.

Jin Xing's experiences as a transgender woman of color in a conservative society highlight the complexities of navigating multiple identities. Her success challenges the notion that one must conform to societal norms to achieve acceptance. This intersectional approach encourages a more inclusive LGBTQ movement that recognizes the diverse experiences of its members.

Educational Impact

Education plays a crucial role in Jin Xing's legacy. By sharing her story, she educates the public about the realities of being transgender in a society that often stigmatizes such identities. Her willingness to discuss her journey, including her struggles with acceptance and her experiences with discrimination, fosters empathy and understanding.

The *theory of social learning* suggests that individuals learn from observing others. Jin Xing's openness about her journey serves as a powerful educational tool, helping to dismantle prejudices and misconceptions about transgender people. Schools and organizations can draw on her narrative to create programs that promote inclusivity and understanding.

Legacy of Hope and Inspiration

Ultimately, Jin Xing's lasting impact on the LGBTQ movement and the world is one of hope and inspiration. Her life exemplifies the power of authenticity and the importance of living one's truth. As she continues to break barriers and challenge societal norms, she inspires countless individuals to embrace their identities and advocate for their rights.

In conclusion, Jin Xing's contributions to the LGBTQ movement are profound and far-reaching. Through her visibility, advocacy, and commitment to education, she has not only changed perceptions in China but has also inspired a global movement towards acceptance and equality. Her legacy serves as a reminder that the fight for LGBTQ rights is ongoing, but with figures like Jin Xing leading the way, there is hope for a brighter, more inclusive future.

Lessons learned from Jin Xing's journey of courage and resilience

Jin Xing's life story is an extraordinary testament to the power of courage and resilience in the face of adversity. Her journey, marked by personal and professional challenges, offers invaluable lessons that resonate far beyond the boundaries of her own experience. This section explores the key lessons learned from Jin Xing's journey, emphasizing the importance of self-acceptance, the role of community support, and the transformative power of authenticity.

The Importance of Self-Acceptance

At the heart of Jin Xing's journey is the profound lesson of self-acceptance. Embracing one's identity, especially in a society that often stigmatizes differences, is a crucial step toward personal liberation. Jin Xing's decision to transition and her subsequent journey towards self-acceptance illustrate the psychological theory of *self-actualization,* as proposed by Maslow (1943). This theory posits that individuals must first satisfy basic needs before they can pursue higher-level psychological needs, such as esteem and self-actualization.

$$\text{Self-Actualization} = \text{Realization of one's potential} + \text{Self-fulfillment} + \text{Seeking personal gro}$$
$$(119)$$

Jin Xing's experiences highlight that self-acceptance is not merely a personal journey but a societal one. Her courage to live authentically inspires others to confront their fears and embrace their true selves, fostering a sense of community among those who feel marginalized.

Resilience in the Face of Adversity

Jin Xing's life is a masterclass in resilience. Resilience, as defined by Rutter (1987), is the ability to withstand adversity and bounce back from difficult experiences. Throughout her career, Jin Xing faced numerous challenges, including discrimination, societal rejection, and personal struggles. Yet, her ability to persevere exemplifies the psychological concept of *grit*, which Duckworth et al. (2007) describe as passion and perseverance for long-term goals.

$$\text{Grit} = \text{Passion} + \text{Perseverance} \qquad (120)$$

Jin Xing's grit is evident in her unwavering commitment to her art and activism. Despite facing setbacks, she continued to push boundaries, proving that resilience can be cultivated through determination and a strong sense of purpose. Her journey encourages individuals to view challenges as opportunities for growth rather than insurmountable obstacles.

The Role of Community Support

Another crucial lesson from Jin Xing's journey is the significance of community support. Jin Xing's success was not solely the result of her individual efforts; it was also the outcome of a supportive network of friends, family, and allies. Social support theory, as articulated by Cohen and Wills (1985), emphasizes that social relationships can provide emotional, informational, and instrumental support, which is vital for coping with stress and adversity.

$$\text{Social Support} = \text{Emotional Support} + \text{Informational Support} + \text{Instrumental Support} \tag{121}$$

Jin Xing's story illustrates how community support can empower individuals to embrace their identities and overcome challenges. Her advocacy for LGBTQ rights has fostered a sense of solidarity within the community, highlighting the importance of collective action in the fight for equality. By sharing her experiences, she has encouraged others to seek and provide support, creating a ripple effect of resilience.

Transformative Power of Authenticity

Jin Xing's journey underscores the transformative power of authenticity. Living authentically allows individuals to connect more deeply with themselves and others, fostering genuine relationships and a sense of belonging. The concept of authenticity is central to existential psychology, which posits that individuals find meaning and fulfillment when they live in accordance with their true selves (Yalom, 1980).

$$\text{Authenticity} = \text{Self-Expression} + \text{Alignment with Values} + \text{Connection with Others} \tag{122}$$

Jin Xing's authenticity not only transformed her life but also inspired countless others to embrace their identities. By being true to herself, she has become a beacon of hope for those navigating their own journeys, demonstrating that authenticity can lead to empowerment and positive change.

Conclusion

In conclusion, Jin Xing's journey of courage and resilience offers profound lessons that resonate across cultures and communities. Her story emphasizes the importance of self-acceptance, resilience in the face of adversity, the role of community support, and the transformative power of authenticity. As we reflect on these lessons, we are reminded that the journey towards acceptance and equality is ongoing, and that each individual's story contributes to the collective narrative of resilience and hope within the LGBTQ movement. By embracing these lessons, we can foster a more inclusive and accepting world, where everyone has the opportunity to live authentically and without fear.

The importance of empathy and understanding in creating change

In the realm of social justice, empathy and understanding are not merely desirable traits; they are essential catalysts for meaningful change. Empathy, defined as the ability to understand and share the feelings of another, fosters a connection that transcends personal experiences and cultural barriers. Understanding, on the other hand, involves comprehending the complexities of another's situation, including the historical and societal contexts that shape their experiences. Together, these qualities create a fertile ground for dialogue, collaboration, and ultimately, transformation.

Theoretical Framework

Empathy is often discussed within the context of social psychology. The *Empathy-Altruism Hypothesis*, proposed by Batson et al. (1981), posits that when individuals feel empathy towards others, they are more likely to engage in altruistic behavior. This theory suggests that empathy can motivate individuals to act in support of those who are marginalized or oppressed. For instance, when individuals witness the struggles of the LGBTQ community through the lens of empathy, they may be inspired to advocate for their rights, challenge discriminatory practices, or support inclusive policies.

Understanding is equally vital in this context. The *Contact Hypothesis*, articulated by Allport (1954), posits that under appropriate conditions, interpersonal contact is one of the most effective ways to reduce prejudice between majority and minority group members. When individuals from different backgrounds engage in open dialogues, they can foster understanding that dismantles stereotypes and misconceptions. This process can lead to greater acceptance and support for marginalized communities, including the LGBTQ population.

Challenges to Empathy and Understanding

Despite the clear benefits of empathy and understanding, several challenges hinder their development in society. One significant barrier is the prevalence of *cognitive biases*, such as the in-group bias and confirmation bias. The in-group bias leads individuals to favor those who share similar backgrounds or beliefs, often resulting in a lack of empathy for those outside their group. Confirmation bias, on the other hand, causes individuals to seek out information that aligns with their existing beliefs while dismissing contradictory evidence. These biases can perpetuate misunderstanding and division, making it challenging to cultivate empathy across diverse communities.

Moreover, societal narratives and stereotypes can further complicate the process of understanding. For example, media portrayals of LGBTQ individuals often focus on sensationalized or negative aspects, reinforcing harmful stereotypes and fostering fear or aversion. When individuals are exposed to limited or biased representations, their capacity for empathy may be stifled, leading to a lack of understanding and support for LGBTQ rights.

Empathy in Action: Case Studies

To illustrate the transformative power of empathy and understanding, we can examine several case studies where these qualities have led to significant social change.

Case Study 1: The Trevor Project   The Trevor Project, an organization focused on crisis intervention and suicide prevention for LGBTQ youth, exemplifies the impact of empathy in action. By providing resources, support, and a listening ear to young individuals grappling with their identities, the organization fosters an environment of understanding and acceptance. The Trevor Project's initiatives not only offer immediate assistance but also promote broader societal change by educating the public about the challenges faced by LGBTQ youth. This empathetic approach has helped reduce stigma and increase support for LGBTQ individuals, ultimately saving lives.

Case Study 2: Marriage Equality Movement   The marriage equality movement in various countries demonstrates how empathy and understanding can shift public opinion and lead to legislative change. As LGBTQ individuals shared their personal stories and experiences of love and commitment, many individuals outside the community began to empathize with their struggles. This shift in perspective was pivotal in garnering support for marriage equality. For instance, in the United States, the landmark Supreme Court case Obergefell v. Hodges (2015) was influenced by the growing public understanding of LGBTQ relationships, leading to the legalization of same-sex marriage nationwide.

Strategies for Fostering Empathy and Understanding

To create a more inclusive society, it is crucial to implement strategies that promote empathy and understanding. Here are several approaches that can be adopted:

+ **Storytelling:** Sharing personal narratives can humanize experiences and foster empathy. Initiatives that encourage individuals to share their stories can bridge gaps between communities and promote understanding.

+ **Education:** Educational programs that include LGBTQ history, culture, and rights can enhance understanding and reduce prejudice. Schools and organizations should prioritize inclusive curricula that reflect diverse perspectives.

+ **Intergroup Dialogues:** Facilitating dialogues between diverse groups can promote understanding and empathy. These conversations should be structured to encourage active listening and respectful exchanges, allowing participants to explore their differences and commonalities.

+ **Media Representation:** Advocating for accurate and positive representations of LGBTQ individuals in media can challenge stereotypes and foster empathy. Media creators should be encouraged to tell authentic stories that reflect the diversity of the LGBTQ experience.

Conclusion

In conclusion, empathy and understanding are indispensable in the pursuit of social change, particularly for marginalized communities such as the LGBTQ population. By fostering these qualities, individuals can break down barriers, challenge biases, and promote inclusivity. As we reflect on the journey of activists like Jin Xing, it becomes evident that empathy and understanding are not just ideals to aspire to but essential tools for creating a more equitable and compassionate world. The call to action is clear: we must embrace empathy and understanding as the foundation of our efforts to drive meaningful change and build a society where everyone can live authentically and without fear.

Taking action and speaking up for LGBTQ rights

Taking action and speaking up for LGBTQ rights is not merely an act of advocacy; it is a fundamental responsibility that individuals, communities, and organizations must embrace to foster a society rooted in equality and acceptance. The journey towards LGBTQ rights involves understanding the historical context, recognizing ongoing challenges, and mobilizing collective efforts to enact change.

Historical Context

The struggle for LGBTQ rights has a long and complex history, marked by significant milestones and setbacks. The Stonewall Riots of 1969 in New York City, often heralded as a catalyst for the modern LGBTQ rights movement, exemplified the necessity for activism. This uprising against police brutality highlighted the urgent need for visibility and representation of LGBTQ individuals. As noted by historian David Carter in *Stonewall: The Riots That Sparked the Gay Revolution*, the events at Stonewall were pivotal in galvanizing a community that had long been marginalized and oppressed.

Understanding the Challenges

Despite the progress made in many parts of the world, LGBTQ individuals continue to face systemic discrimination, violence, and social stigma. According to the International Lesbian, Gay, Bisexual, Trans and Intersex Association (ILGA), in many countries, same-sex relationships are still criminalized, and LGBTQ individuals are subjected to human rights violations. The Global Acceptance Index, a measure of societal acceptance towards LGBTQ individuals, reveals that acceptance varies significantly across cultures and regions. In some areas, the index scores remain alarmingly low, reflecting deep-seated prejudices and societal norms that perpetuate discrimination.

Theoretical Frameworks

To effectively advocate for LGBTQ rights, it is essential to employ various theoretical frameworks that illuminate the complexities of identity and power dynamics. One such framework is Queer Theory, which challenges normative assumptions about gender and sexuality. As Judith Butler posits in *Gender Trouble*, gender is performative, suggesting that societal constructs can be deconstructed and redefined. This theoretical lens encourages activists to question established norms and advocate for a more inclusive understanding of identity.

Another relevant framework is Intersectionality, coined by Kimberlé Crenshaw, which emphasizes the interconnectedness of social identities and the unique experiences of individuals at the intersection of multiple marginalized identities. Understanding intersectionality allows advocates to recognize that LGBTQ individuals do not experience discrimination in isolation; rather, their experiences are shaped by race, class, gender, and other factors.

Mobilizing Collective Action

Collective action is a powerful tool for enacting change. Grassroots movements, advocacy organizations, and community coalitions play a vital role in amplifying LGBTQ voices and pushing for policy reforms. For instance, organizations such as the Human Rights Campaign (HRC) and GLAAD work tirelessly to promote legislative changes, raise awareness, and combat discrimination. Their campaigns often highlight the importance of allyship and encourage individuals to take an active role in supporting LGBTQ rights.

A notable example of successful collective action is the legalization of same-sex marriage in the United States. The tireless efforts of activists, coupled with public support, culminated in the landmark Supreme Court decision in *Obergefell v. Hodges* (2015), which recognized the constitutional right to marry for same-sex couples. This victory not only exemplified the power of collective advocacy but also served as a beacon of hope for LGBTQ individuals worldwide.

Strategies for Advocacy

To effectively take action and speak up for LGBTQ rights, individuals can employ various strategies:

- **Education and Awareness:** Raising awareness about LGBTQ issues and educating others about the challenges faced by the community is crucial. Hosting workshops, seminars, and discussions can foster understanding and empathy.

- **Engagement in Political Processes:** Advocating for policy changes at local, national, and international levels can create systemic change. This includes lobbying for anti-discrimination laws, supporting LGBTQ-inclusive policies, and voting for representatives who prioritize LGBTQ rights.

- **Utilizing Social Media:** Social media platforms serve as powerful tools for advocacy.   Campaigns   such   as   #LoveIsLove   and

#TransRightsAreHumanRights have gained traction, mobilizing support and raising awareness on a global scale. Sharing personal stories can humanize issues and foster connections.

- **Building Alliances:** Collaborating with other marginalized groups can strengthen advocacy efforts. Intersectional alliances can highlight the interconnectedness of struggles and promote a more inclusive approach to activism.

- **Creating Safe Spaces:** Establishing safe spaces for LGBTQ individuals fosters community support and resilience. These spaces can serve as havens for expression, healing, and empowerment.

The Role of Individuals

Every individual has the power to make a difference. Whether through small acts of kindness, advocacy, or simply standing up against discrimination, each action contributes to a larger movement for change. As activist Marsha P. Johnson famously stated, "No pride for some of us without liberation for all of us." This sentiment underscores the importance of solidarity and collective action in the fight for LGBTQ rights.

Conclusion

Taking action and speaking up for LGBTQ rights is an ongoing journey that requires commitment, courage, and collaboration. By understanding the historical context, recognizing challenges, employing theoretical frameworks, and mobilizing collective action, individuals can contribute to a more equitable and inclusive society. The fight for LGBTQ rights is not just a matter of legal recognition; it is a fundamental human rights issue that calls for the active participation of everyone. Together, we can pave the way for a future where all individuals can live authentically and without fear of discrimination.

$$R = \frac{C}{D} \tag{123}$$

Where R represents the rate of change in societal attitudes towards LGBTQ rights, C is the collective action taken, and D is the degree of discrimination present in society. This equation illustrates the need for sustained collective action to effect meaningful change in societal attitudes and reduce discrimination.

Celebrating diversity and fostering inclusivity in all aspects of life

Diversity is a multifaceted concept that encompasses a variety of dimensions, including but not limited to race, gender, sexual orientation, age, ability, and cultural background. Celebrating diversity means recognizing and valuing these differences as strengths rather than barriers. Inclusivity, on the other hand, refers to the practice of creating environments in which any individual or group can be and feel welcomed, respected, supported, and valued. Together, these principles form the foundation for a more equitable society.

Theoretical Frameworks

Theories of social justice and equity provide a framework for understanding the importance of diversity and inclusivity. One such theory is the **Intersectionality** framework developed by Kimberlé Crenshaw, which posits that individuals experience overlapping and interdependent systems of discrimination or disadvantage. This theory emphasizes the necessity of addressing multiple identities and the unique challenges faced by those at the intersections of various social categories.

Additionally, the **Social Identity Theory** (Tajfel & Turner, 1979) illustrates how individuals categorize themselves and others into groups, which can lead to in-group favoritism and out-group discrimination. To foster inclusivity, organizations and communities must actively work to dismantle these biases and create spaces that celebrate diverse identities.

Challenges to Diversity and Inclusivity

Despite the clear benefits of diversity and inclusivity, numerous challenges persist. Structural inequalities, such as systemic racism, sexism, and heteronormativity, create barriers that hinder the participation of marginalized groups in various aspects of life. For example, in the workplace, studies have shown that diverse teams outperform homogeneous teams in problem-solving and innovation. However, many organizations still struggle with unconscious biases that affect hiring and promotion practices, leading to a lack of representation in leadership roles.

Moreover, the cultural stigmas associated with LGBTQ identities often result in discrimination and exclusion. For instance, a survey conducted by the Human Rights Campaign found that nearly 50% of LGBTQ individuals reported experiencing discrimination in their workplaces. This not only impacts their mental health but also stifles their potential contributions to society.

Examples of Celebrating Diversity and Fostering Inclusivity

1. **Inclusive Education:** Schools that implement inclusive curricula that reflect diverse perspectives and histories can foster a sense of belonging among students from various backgrounds. For example, the integration of LGBTQ history into social studies classes can help normalize diverse identities and promote acceptance among students.

2. **Workplace Diversity Initiatives:** Companies that prioritize diversity and inclusivity can implement policies that promote equitable hiring practices, mentorship programs for underrepresented groups, and diversity training for employees. Google, for instance, has made significant strides in increasing the representation of women and minorities in tech through targeted recruitment and support programs.

3. **Community Engagement:** Local organizations can host events that celebrate cultural diversity, such as festivals, art exhibitions, and panel discussions. These events not only provide a platform for marginalized voices but also educate the broader community about the importance of inclusivity. The Pride Parade is a prime example of such an event, celebrating LGBTQ identities while advocating for equal rights.

4. **Media Representation:** The media plays a crucial role in shaping societal attitudes towards diversity. Positive representation of diverse characters in films, television shows, and literature can challenge stereotypes and foster empathy. Shows like *Pose* and *Schitt's Creek* have been praised for their authentic portrayal of LGBTQ characters, contributing to a broader understanding of diverse experiences.

Conclusion

Celebrating diversity and fostering inclusivity is not just a moral imperative; it is essential for the progress and well-being of society as a whole. By embracing diverse perspectives and creating inclusive environments, we can unlock the full potential of individuals and communities. As Jin Xing's journey exemplifies, the power of visibility and representation can inspire change and promote acceptance across all aspects of life.

In the words of Maya Angelou, "It is time for parents to teach young people early on that in diversity there is beauty and there is strength." By committing to celebrate diversity and foster inclusivity, we can collectively build a future where every individual is empowered to live authentically and without fear.

The call to use Jin Xing's story as a catalyst for positive change

Jin Xing's journey is not merely a tale of personal triumph; it is a powerful narrative that serves as a beacon of hope and a catalyst for positive change within the LGBTQ community and beyond. Her life exemplifies the profound impact that individual stories can have on societal attitudes and policies, particularly in conservative environments where LGBTQ identities are often marginalized. This section explores the theoretical frameworks surrounding narrative change, the societal problems that persist, and the ways in which Jin Xing's story can inspire action and advocacy.

Theoretical Frameworks of Narrative Change

The theory of narrative change posits that storytelling is a potent tool for reshaping public perception and fostering empathy. According to [?], narratives serve as a means of making complex social issues more relatable and accessible to a broader audience. Jin Xing's story, laden with personal struggles and triumphs, resonates deeply with individuals who may not share her experiences but can empathize with the universal themes of resilience, identity, and acceptance.

$$\text{Empathy} = \frac{\text{Personal Connection}}{\text{Cultural Barriers}} \tag{124}$$

In this equation, empathy increases as personal connections to a narrative rise, while cultural barriers diminish. Jin Xing's visibility as a transgender icon in China allows her to bridge these gaps, fostering understanding and acceptance among diverse audiences.

Societal Problems and Challenges

Despite the progress made in LGBTQ rights globally, significant challenges remain, particularly in countries with conservative cultural norms. In China, the stigma surrounding transgender individuals often leads to discrimination, mental health issues, and social exclusion [?]. Jin Xing's experiences highlight these systemic problems, making her story an essential part of the dialogue surrounding LGBTQ rights.

$$\text{Discrimination Index} = \frac{\text{Instances of Discrimination}}{\text{Total Population}} \tag{125}$$

This equation illustrates the pervasive nature of discrimination faced by LGBTQ individuals. By sharing her story, Jin Xing not only confronts these issues but also encourages others to do the same, fostering a collective movement towards change.

Examples of Positive Change through Storytelling

Jin Xing's narrative has already catalyzed change in various ways. For instance, her role as a judge on "So You Think You Can Dance China" has amplified LGBTQ visibility on national television, challenging stereotypes and encouraging acceptance. This visibility has inspired other LGBTQ individuals to embrace their identities and pursue their passions, demonstrating the ripple effect of her influence.

Furthermore, Jin Xing's advocacy work has sparked conversations around LGBTQ rights in China, leading to increased awareness and dialogue. Organizations focused on LGBTQ rights have utilized her story in campaigns aimed at reducing stigma and promoting inclusivity. The impact of her narrative extends beyond the arts, influencing policy discussions and encouraging lawmakers to consider the rights of marginalized communities.

Call to Action: Amplifying Jin Xing's Story

To harness the full potential of Jin Xing's story as a catalyst for positive change, it is crucial for individuals, organizations, and allies to actively engage in advocacy efforts. This can be achieved through:

- **Education and Awareness:** Utilizing Jin Xing's narrative in educational settings to foster understanding of LGBTQ issues and promote acceptance.

- **Community Engagement:** Encouraging local communities to host discussions and events that center around Jin Xing's story, creating safe spaces for dialogue and support.

- **Advocacy Campaigns:** Leveraging social media and public platforms to share Jin Xing's journey, highlighting the importance of LGBTQ rights and representation.

- **Support for LGBTQ Organizations:** Contributing to and collaborating with organizations that advocate for LGBTQ rights, ensuring that Jin Xing's message of resilience and acceptance reaches those who need it most.

Conclusion

Jin Xing's story is a testament to the power of resilience, self-acceptance, and the transformative nature of art. By using her narrative as a catalyst for positive change, we can challenge societal norms, foster empathy, and promote a more inclusive world. The call to action is clear: let us embrace Jin Xing's story, amplify her voice, and work collectively towards a future where everyone, regardless of their identity, can live authentically and without fear. The journey towards equality and acceptance is ongoing, and it is through the sharing of stories like Jin Xing's that we can inspire change and create a more just society for all.

A Call to Action

The importance of advocating for LGBTQ rights

Advocating for LGBTQ rights is not just a matter of promoting equality; it is a fundamental human rights issue that affects millions of individuals worldwide. The fight for LGBTQ rights is rooted in the principles of dignity, respect, and justice, which are essential to the fabric of any democratic society. This section will delve into the significance of advocacy, the challenges faced by the LGBTQ community, and the transformative power of collective action.

Theoretical Framework

At the heart of LGBTQ advocacy is the concept of social justice, which seeks to address inequalities and promote equitable treatment for all individuals, regardless of their sexual orientation or gender identity. Theories of justice, such as those proposed by John Rawls, emphasize fairness and the "veil of ignorance" as a means to establish a just society. According to Rawls, principles of justice should be determined without knowledge of one's own social status, ensuring that policies benefit the least advantaged members of society. This theoretical framework underscores the need for advocacy to dismantle systemic barriers that marginalize LGBTQ individuals.

Problems Faced by the LGBTQ Community

Despite significant progress in many regions, the LGBTQ community continues to face numerous challenges, including:

+ **Discrimination and Violence:** LGBTQ individuals often encounter discrimination in various settings, including workplaces, educational institutions, and healthcare facilities. According to the Human Rights Campaign, LGBTQ individuals are more likely to experience hate crimes, bullying, and harassment.

+ **Legal Inequality:** In many countries, LGBTQ individuals lack legal protections against discrimination. For example, same-sex marriage remains illegal in several nations, denying couples the rights and benefits afforded to heterosexual marriages.

+ **Mental Health Issues:** The stigma and discrimination faced by LGBTQ individuals can lead to significant mental health challenges, including depression, anxiety, and suicidal ideation. The Trevor Project reports that LGBTQ youth are more than twice as likely to experience mental health issues compared to their heterosexual peers.

Examples of Advocacy in Action

Advocacy efforts have played a crucial role in advancing LGBTQ rights globally. Notable examples include:

+ **The Stonewall Riots:** The 1969 Stonewall Riots in New York City are often cited as a catalyst for the modern LGBTQ rights movement. Following a police raid on the Stonewall Inn, patrons fought back, sparking protests and raising awareness about the injustices faced by the LGBTQ community.

+ **Marriage Equality Movements:** The push for marriage equality has seen significant victories, such as the landmark 2015 Supreme Court ruling in Obergefell v. Hodges, which legalized same-sex marriage across the United States. This case exemplifies how advocacy can lead to transformative legal change.

+ **International Advocacy:** Organizations like ILGA (International Lesbian, Gay, Bisexual, Trans and Intersex Association) work tirelessly to promote LGBTQ rights on a global scale. Their initiatives aim to influence policy changes and provide resources for local activists in countries where LGBTQ rights are severely restricted.

The Role of Allies in Advocacy

Allies play a vital role in advocating for LGBTQ rights. By using their privilege to amplify marginalized voices, allies can help challenge discriminatory practices and foster a culture of acceptance. The concept of allyship emphasizes the importance of listening, learning, and standing in solidarity with the LGBTQ community. Effective allyship involves:

- **Educating Oneself:** Allies must educate themselves about LGBTQ issues, including the history, struggles, and triumphs of the community. This knowledge equips allies to engage in meaningful conversations and challenge misconceptions.

- **Speaking Out:** Allies should use their platforms to advocate for LGBTQ rights, whether through social media, community organizing, or participation in protests. By speaking out against injustice, allies can help shift societal attitudes and promote acceptance.

- **Supporting LGBTQ Organizations:** Financial and volunteer support for LGBTQ organizations can significantly impact advocacy efforts. These organizations often rely on donations to fund programs, provide resources, and engage in lobbying efforts.

The Transformative Power of Collective Action

Collective action is a powerful tool for effecting change. When individuals come together to advocate for a common cause, they can amplify their voices and create a more significant impact. Historical movements, such as the civil rights movement and the women's suffrage movement, demonstrate the power of collective action in achieving social change.

In the context of LGBTQ advocacy, collective action can take various forms, including:

- **Protests and Marches:** Events like Pride parades and protests serve as visible demonstrations of solidarity and support for LGBTQ rights. These gatherings raise awareness and foster a sense of community among participants.

- **Petitions and Campaigns:** Grassroots campaigns that mobilize individuals to sign petitions or contact lawmakers can influence policy decisions and promote legislative changes.

+ **Social Media Activism:** The rise of social media has transformed the landscape of advocacy, allowing individuals to share their stories, connect with others, and mobilize support for LGBTQ rights on a global scale.

Conclusion

The importance of advocating for LGBTQ rights cannot be overstated. It is a moral imperative that calls for collective action, solidarity, and unwavering commitment to justice. As we continue to confront the challenges faced by the LGBTQ community, it is essential to recognize that advocacy is not merely an act of charity; it is a fundamental responsibility of every individual who believes in equality and human rights. By standing together, we can forge a path toward a more inclusive and accepting world, where everyone can live authentically and without fear.

Ways individuals can support the LGBTQ community

Supporting the LGBTQ community is an essential aspect of fostering inclusivity, equality, and acceptance in society. Individuals can play a crucial role in this movement through various actions and initiatives. Below are several effective ways to support the LGBTQ community:

1. Educate Yourself and Others

Understanding the complexities of LGBTQ identities and issues is the first step towards effective advocacy. Individuals can:

+ Read books, articles, and research studies on LGBTQ history, rights, and experiences.

+ Attend workshops, seminars, and lectures that focus on LGBTQ topics.

+ Engage in discussions with LGBTQ individuals to gain personal insights and perspectives.

+ Share knowledge with friends, family, and colleagues to raise awareness and foster understanding.

Education can dispel myths and misconceptions, leading to a more informed and supportive community.

2. Use Inclusive Language

Language plays a pivotal role in shaping perceptions and attitudes. To support the LGBTQ community, individuals should:

- Use gender-neutral terms and pronouns when unsure of someone's identity.

- Respect and use individuals' chosen names and pronouns consistently.

- Avoid derogatory language and slurs that perpetuate stigma and discrimination.

- Promote the use of inclusive language in workplaces, schools, and social settings.

Inclusive language fosters an environment of respect and acceptance.

3. Advocate for Policy Changes

Supporting LGBTQ rights at the policy level is vital for systemic change. Individuals can:

- Contact local representatives to advocate for LGBTQ-inclusive policies and legislation.

- Participate in campaigns and petitions that aim to protect LGBTQ rights.

- Attend town hall meetings and public forums to voice support for LGBTQ issues.

- Collaborate with organizations that focus on LGBTQ advocacy to amplify efforts.

Policy changes can lead to significant improvements in the lives of LGBTQ individuals, addressing issues such as discrimination, healthcare access, and marriage equality.

4. Support LGBTQ Organizations

Many organizations work tirelessly to promote LGBTQ rights and provide essential services. Individuals can:

- ✦ Donate to LGBTQ organizations that align with personal values and goals.

- ✦ Volunteer time and skills to support local LGBTQ initiatives.

- ✦ Attend fundraisers and events organized by LGBTQ groups.

- ✦ Promote LGBTQ organizations on social media to raise awareness and encourage support.

Supporting these organizations helps sustain their efforts and expands their reach.

5. Create Safe Spaces

Creating environments where LGBTQ individuals feel safe and accepted is crucial. Individuals can:

- ✦ Establish inclusive policies in workplaces, schools, and community centers.

- ✦ Organize events and activities that celebrate LGBTQ culture and history.

- ✦ Provide resources and support for LGBTQ individuals facing discrimination or harassment.

- ✦ Foster open discussions about LGBTQ issues to promote understanding and acceptance.

Safe spaces empower LGBTQ individuals to express themselves without fear of judgment or reprisal.

6. Be an Ally

Being an ally involves actively supporting and advocating for LGBTQ rights. Individuals can:

- ✦ Stand up against homophobia, transphobia, and discrimination in all forms.

- ✦ Listen to and amplify the voices of LGBTQ individuals in discussions and decision-making.

- Share personal stories and experiences to highlight the importance of allyship.

- Educate others about the significance of allyship and how to be an effective ally.

Allies play a vital role in challenging societal norms and promoting equality.

7. Celebrate LGBTQ Culture

Recognizing and celebrating LGBTQ culture is an essential aspect of support. Individuals can:

- Attend pride events, parades, and festivals to show solidarity with the LGBTQ community.

- Support LGBTQ artists, writers, and creators by purchasing their work and promoting their contributions.

- Participate in LGBTQ-themed events and discussions to foster cultural appreciation.

- Encourage representation of LGBTQ stories and experiences in media and arts.

Celebrating LGBTQ culture promotes visibility and appreciation of diverse identities.

8. Challenge Stereotypes and Discrimination

Individuals can actively challenge stereotypes and discriminatory behavior by:

- Speaking out against harmful stereotypes and assumptions about LGBTQ individuals.

- Engaging in conversations that challenge discriminatory remarks or behaviors.

- Promoting positive representations of LGBTQ individuals in media and public discourse.

- Supporting educational initiatives that address LGBTQ issues and promote acceptance.

Challenging stereotypes helps dismantle prejudice and fosters a more inclusive society.

9. Support LGBTQ Youth

LGBTQ youth often face unique challenges and vulnerabilities. Individuals can:

+ Mentor LGBTQ youth and provide guidance and support.

+ Advocate for LGBTQ-inclusive policies in schools to create safe environments.

+ Support organizations that focus on LGBTQ youth services and resources.

+ Raise awareness about the challenges faced by LGBTQ youth in communities.

Supporting LGBTQ youth is crucial for their development and well-being.

10. Stay Informed and Engaged

Finally, individuals should remain informed and engaged in LGBTQ issues by:

+ Following news and developments related to LGBTQ rights and advocacy.

+ Engaging with social media platforms that focus on LGBTQ issues and activism.

+ Participating in discussions and forums that address LGBTQ topics.

+ Continuously educating oneself about the evolving landscape of LGBTQ rights.

Staying informed allows individuals to be effective advocates and allies for the LGBTQ community.

In conclusion, supporting the LGBTQ community requires commitment, education, and active participation. By taking these steps, individuals can contribute to a more inclusive and equitable society for all.

Amplifying voices and stories of LGBTQ activists

In the ongoing struggle for LGBTQ rights, amplifying the voices and stories of activists is not merely a matter of representation; it is a fundamental necessity for fostering understanding, empathy, and societal change. The narratives of those who have fought for equality serve as powerful tools for education and advocacy, helping to dismantle stereotypes and challenge the status quo. This section explores the importance of amplifying these voices, the challenges faced in doing so, and the transformative impact it can have on communities and society at large.

The Importance of Amplification

The act of amplification involves not only sharing stories but also ensuring that these stories are heard in spaces where they can effect change. According to [1], storytelling is a powerful method for creating connections and fostering empathy. When individuals hear personal accounts of struggle and triumph, they are more likely to understand the complexities of LGBTQ experiences and the systemic injustices that persist.

Moreover, the amplification of LGBTQ voices serves to validate the experiences of marginalized individuals. As noted by [?], representation in media and public discourse can significantly influence self-acceptance and community solidarity. For instance, the visibility of LGBTQ activists like Jin Xing has inspired countless individuals in China and beyond to embrace their identities and advocate for their rights.

Challenges in Amplification

Despite the clear benefits of amplifying LGBTQ voices, several challenges persist. One significant barrier is the prevalence of censorship and discrimination, particularly in conservative societies. In many countries, LGBTQ narratives are often silenced, leading to a lack of visibility and understanding. As highlighted by [?], activists frequently face threats, harassment, and even violence when attempting to share their stories.

Additionally, there is a risk of tokenization, where LGBTQ individuals are invited to share their experiences but are not provided with the platform or support necessary to effect real change. This phenomenon can lead to a superficial understanding of LGBTQ issues, as the complexities of their struggles are often reduced to mere anecdotes. To combat this, it is essential to create spaces where LGBTQ activists can share their stories authentically and have their voices heard in meaningful ways.

Examples of Effective Amplification

Numerous initiatives have successfully amplified LGBTQ voices and stories, demonstrating the power of collective action and storytelling. For example, the *It Gets Better Project* is a notable campaign that encourages LGBTQ individuals to share their experiences and messages of hope. By leveraging social media platforms, the project has reached millions, providing a sense of community and belonging for those who may feel isolated.

Another impactful example is the *Transgender Day of Visibility*, which celebrates transgender individuals and their contributions to society. This event not only amplifies trans voices but also raises awareness about the challenges they face, fostering greater understanding and acceptance.

In literature, works like *The Miseducation of Cameron Post* by Emily M. Danforth provide poignant narratives that resonate with LGBTQ youth, offering relatable experiences that validate their feelings and identities. Such narratives contribute to a broader cultural understanding of LGBTQ issues and inspire activism.

The Role of Allies

Allies play a crucial role in amplifying LGBTQ voices. By using their platforms and privileges to elevate marginalized narratives, allies can help create a more inclusive environment. According to [?], allyship involves active listening, advocacy, and a commitment to challenging discriminatory practices. Allies can amplify LGBTQ voices by sharing their stories, advocating for policy changes, and supporting LGBTQ organizations.

Moreover, it is essential for allies to recognize the diversity within the LGBTQ community. Intersectionality, as described by [?], highlights how various forms of discrimination can overlap, affecting individuals in unique ways. By amplifying a range of voices—those of people of color, individuals with disabilities, and others within the LGBTQ spectrum—alliances can contribute to a more nuanced understanding of the challenges faced by the community.

Conclusion

Amplifying the voices and stories of LGBTQ activists is a vital aspect of the ongoing fight for equality and acceptance. By sharing their narratives, activists not only educate others but also foster a sense of community and solidarity among those who may feel marginalized or isolated. Despite the challenges of censorship, tokenization, and discrimination, successful initiatives and the role of allies demonstrate the transformative power of storytelling. As we continue to advocate for LGBTQ rights, it is imperative to prioritize the amplification of diverse voices, ensuring that all stories are heard, valued, and celebrated.

The role of education and awareness in fostering change

Education and awareness are pivotal in fostering change, particularly in the context of LGBTQ rights and representation. The process of educating individuals about LGBTQ issues not only informs but also transforms societal attitudes, leading to greater acceptance and understanding. This section explores the theoretical foundations, existing challenges, and practical examples of how education and awareness can catalyze significant social change.

Theoretical Foundations

The role of education in social change is well-documented in various sociological theories. One pertinent framework is the *Social Learning Theory*, proposed by Albert Bandura, which posits that people learn behaviors and norms through observation and imitation of others. This theory suggests that when individuals see positive representations of LGBTQ individuals in educational settings, media, and public discourse, they are more likely to adopt inclusive attitudes and behaviors.

Moreover, *Critical Pedagogy*, as articulated by Paulo Freire, emphasizes the importance of dialogue and critical consciousness in education. Freire argued that education should not merely be about the transmission of knowledge but should empower individuals to challenge oppressive structures. By integrating LGBTQ topics into educational curricula, educators can foster critical thinking and encourage students to question societal norms surrounding gender and sexuality.

Challenges in Education

Despite the transformative potential of education, several challenges persist in the realm of LGBTQ awareness. One significant barrier is the presence of *heteronormativity* in educational institutions, where heterosexuality is often viewed as the default or "normal" orientation. This bias can marginalize LGBTQ students and create an environment where they feel unsafe or unsupported.

Additionally, many educational systems lack comprehensive sex education that includes LGBTQ perspectives. According to a report by the *Human Rights Campaign*, only 17 states in the U.S. mandate that sex education be inclusive of LGBTQ topics. This gap in education can perpetuate misinformation and reinforce negative stereotypes about LGBTQ individuals.

Examples of Effective Educational Initiatives

Numerous initiatives across the globe demonstrate how education and awareness can effectively foster change. One noteworthy example is the *Safe Schools Program* in Australia, which aims to create supportive school environments for LGBTQ students. The program provides resources and training for educators to address bullying and discrimination while promoting inclusivity. Preliminary studies indicate that schools implementing the program have seen a significant decrease in bullying incidents and an increase in students' sense of belonging.

In the United States, the *GSA Network* (Gay-Straight Alliance) empowers students to create safe spaces in their schools. GSAs serve as a platform for students to discuss LGBTQ issues, advocate for policy changes, and engage in community outreach. Research has shown that schools with GSAs report lower rates of harassment and a more positive school climate.

Internationally, the *No Hate Speech Movement* initiated by the Council of Europe aims to combat hate speech and promote diversity through educational campaigns. This initiative encourages young people to engage in discussions about human rights and to challenge discriminatory narratives. By fostering awareness and understanding, such programs contribute to a more inclusive society.

The Role of Media and Technology

In addition to formal education, media and technology play a crucial role in raising awareness about LGBTQ issues. Social media platforms have become powerful tools for advocacy, enabling individuals to share their stories and connect with broader audiences. Campaigns such as *#LoveIsLove* have gained traction, promoting acceptance and visibility for LGBTQ relationships.

Furthermore, educational resources such as documentaries, podcasts, and online courses can supplement traditional education. For instance, the documentary *Disclosure* explores the representation of transgender individuals in film and television, highlighting the impact of media on public perceptions. By utilizing various media formats, educators can create engaging and informative content that resonates with diverse audiences.

Conclusion

The role of education and awareness in fostering change cannot be overstated. By challenging existing biases, promoting inclusivity, and providing accurate information about LGBTQ issues, education serves as a powerful catalyst for social transformation. While challenges remain, the success of various initiatives and the increasing visibility of LGBTQ individuals in media and society indicate that progress is possible. As we continue to advocate for LGBTQ rights, it is essential to prioritize education and awareness as fundamental components of our efforts. Only through informed dialogue and collective action can we hope to create a more inclusive and accepting world for all.

Jin Xing's challenge to readers: Stand up and be heard for equality

In a world where silence often reigns louder than words, Jin Xing stands as a beacon of courage, urging each of us to rise and amplify our voices in the pursuit of equality. Her journey, marked by resilience and tenacity, serves as a powerful reminder that advocacy for LGBTQ rights is not merely an act of defiance; it is a call to humanity. Jin's challenge to her readers is clear: **to stand up and be heard for equality.**

The Power of Individual Action

Every great movement begins with the actions of individuals who dare to challenge the status quo. Jin Xing's life exemplifies how one person's courage can inspire a collective uprising against oppression. The theory of *social change* posits that individual actions can lead to significant societal transformations. As articulated by sociologist Charles Tilly, social movements often emerge from the interplay of individual grievances and collective mobilization.

Jin's challenge invites readers to engage in their communities, to speak out against injustices, and to support marginalized voices. For example, participating in local LGBTQ advocacy groups, attending pride events, or simply educating oneself and others about LGBTQ issues can create ripples of change.

The Importance of Visibility

Visibility is a crucial component of Jin Xing's message. The more individuals share their stories and experiences, the more they contribute to a broader understanding of LGBTQ issues. This aligns with the *theory of visibility*, which suggests that representation in media and public life can significantly affect societal attitudes. When individuals see themselves reflected in the stories of others, it fosters a sense of belonging and validation.

Jin Xing's own visibility as a transgender icon in China has not only challenged stereotypes but has also empowered countless others to embrace their identities. Her presence in the media, as a dancer, choreographer, and television personality, has sparked conversations about gender and sexuality in a conservative society. This highlights the importance of being visible and vocal in advocating for equality.

Addressing Systemic Issues

While individual actions are vital, they must also be coupled with an understanding of the systemic issues that perpetuate inequality. Jin Xing's challenge calls for readers to examine the structures of power that marginalize LGBTQ individuals. This involves recognizing the intersectionality of oppression, as articulated by Kimberlé Crenshaw. The interplay of race, class, gender, and sexuality creates unique challenges for different individuals within the LGBTQ community.

For instance, the experiences of a transgender woman of color may differ significantly from those of a white gay man. Understanding these nuances is essential for effective advocacy. Readers are encouraged to educate themselves about the systemic barriers faced by LGBTQ individuals and to advocate for policy changes that promote equality.

Examples of Collective Action

Jin Xing's challenge is not merely theoretical; it is grounded in real-world examples of collective action that have led to meaningful change. The Stonewall Riots of 1969, often cited as the catalyst for the modern LGBTQ rights movement, exemplify how collective resistance can transform societal norms. The bravery of individuals who stood up against oppression during those riots ignited a global movement that continues to fight for equality today.

Similarly, the global response to the HIV/AIDS crisis in the 1980s and 1990s showcased the power of community organizing. Activists mobilized to demand access to treatment, funding for research, and an end to the stigma surrounding the disease. Their efforts not only saved lives but also shifted public perceptions of LGBTQ individuals.

Embracing Intersectionality

In answering Jin Xing's challenge, it is imperative to embrace an intersectional approach to advocacy. This means recognizing that the fight for LGBTQ rights is intertwined with other social justice movements, including those for racial equality, gender justice, and economic equity. The interconnectedness of these struggles is encapsulated in the concept of *intersectionality*, which posits that individuals experience multiple, overlapping identities that shape their experiences of oppression.

For example, the Black Lives Matter movement has highlighted the need to address violence against transgender individuals, particularly transgender women of color. By standing in solidarity with other marginalized communities, advocates can build a more inclusive movement that addresses the root causes of inequality.

The Call to Action

Ultimately, Jin Xing's challenge is a call to action for all readers to engage actively in the fight for equality. This can take many forms, from participating in protests and advocacy campaigns to engaging in conversations about LGBTQ rights in everyday life.

$$Change = Individual\ Action + Collective\ Mobilization \qquad (126)$$

This equation underscores the idea that while individual efforts are crucial, they must be part of a larger, collective movement to effect meaningful change.

Conclusion

In conclusion, Jin Xing's challenge to stand up and be heard for equality is not merely a rallying cry; it is a profound invitation to each of us to reflect on our roles in the ongoing struggle for justice. By embracing visibility, addressing systemic issues, and engaging in collective action, we can honor Jin's legacy and contribute to a future where everyone can live authentically and without fear. The journey toward equality is ongoing, and it requires the courage and commitment of individuals who are willing to stand up, speak out, and be heard.

The power of collective action in advancing LGBTQ rights

Collective action has emerged as a powerful catalyst for advancing LGBTQ rights across the globe. The notion of collective action is rooted in social movement theory, which posits that individuals unite to achieve common goals that they cannot accomplish alone. This section explores the theoretical underpinnings of collective action, the challenges faced by LGBTQ movements, and prominent examples that illustrate the effectiveness of unified efforts.

Theoretical Framework

At the heart of collective action is the concept of social capital, defined by Pierre Bourdieu as the networks of relationships among people who live and work in a particular society, enabling that society to function effectively. In the context of LGBTQ rights, social capital manifests through networks of support, shared resources, and collective identity, which empower individuals to advocate for change.

The Resource Mobilization Theory (RMT) further elucidates how social movements, including those advocating for LGBTQ rights, mobilize resources—such as money, time, and manpower—to achieve their objectives. According to RMT, successful movements are characterized by their ability to organize and utilize these resources efficiently.

$$\text{Success} = f(\text{Resources, Organization, Strategy}) \qquad (127)$$

Here, *Success* denotes the effectiveness of a movement, which is a function of the resources available, the organization of the movement, and the strategies employed.

Challenges Faced by LGBTQ Movements

Despite the potential of collective action, LGBTQ movements often encounter significant obstacles. These challenges include:

+ **Internal Divisions:** Differences in identity, race, and socioeconomic status can lead to fragmentation within LGBTQ communities, complicating collective efforts.

+ **Opposition from Conservative Groups:** Many LGBTQ movements face backlash from conservative factions that seek to maintain traditional norms and values, often resulting in legislative and social pushback.

+ **Limited Resources:** Many LGBTQ organizations operate on limited budgets, which can hinder their ability to mobilize effectively and sustain long-term campaigns.

Examples of Collective Action

Despite these challenges, collective action has yielded significant victories for LGBTQ rights. Notable examples include:

+ **The Stonewall Riots (1969):** Often cited as the catalyst for the modern LGBTQ rights movement, the Stonewall Riots were a series of spontaneous demonstrations by the LGBTQ community in response to a police raid at the Stonewall Inn in New York City. This event galvanized the community and led to the formation of various advocacy groups, including the Gay Liberation Front.

- **The AIDS Coalition to Unleash Power (ACT UP):** Founded in 1987, ACT UP is a grassroots organization that emerged in response to the AIDS crisis. Through direct action and advocacy, ACT UP has significantly influenced public policy and increased awareness about HIV/AIDS, demonstrating the power of collective mobilization in addressing urgent health crises affecting the LGBTQ community.

- **The Marriage Equality Movement:** The fight for marriage equality in various countries, including the United States, exemplifies the effectiveness of collective action. Organizations such as the Human Rights Campaign and Freedom to Marry utilized grassroots organizing, legal challenges, and public campaigns to mobilize support, ultimately leading to landmark legal victories, including the Supreme Court's decision in Obergefell v. Hodges (2015).

The Role of Technology in Collective Action

In the digital age, technology has transformed the landscape of collective action. Social media platforms have become vital tools for mobilizing support, disseminating information, and fostering solidarity among LGBTQ activists. Hashtags such as #LoveIsLove and #BlackTransLivesMatter have transcended geographical boundaries, creating global movements that amplify marginalized voices and advocate for equality.

$$\text{Impact} = \text{Reach} \times \text{Engagement} \tag{128}$$

In this equation, *Impact* reflects the effectiveness of a campaign, which is determined by its *Reach* (the number of people exposed to the message) and *Engagement* (the level of interaction and participation).

Conclusion

The power of collective action in advancing LGBTQ rights cannot be overstated. By uniting individuals with shared experiences and goals, social movements have successfully challenged discriminatory practices, influenced public policy, and fostered greater acceptance and understanding of LGBTQ individuals. As the struggle for equality continues, it is imperative that activists harness the strengths of collective action, leverage technology, and build inclusive coalitions to create a more just and equitable society for all.

Creating safe spaces and supportive communities for LGBTQ individuals

Creating safe spaces for LGBTQ individuals is essential for fostering acceptance, understanding, and empowerment. These spaces provide environments where individuals can express their identities without fear of discrimination or violence, ultimately contributing to the mental and emotional well-being of LGBTQ individuals. The concept of safe spaces is rooted in the need for inclusivity and understanding, particularly in societies where LGBTQ identities are marginalized or stigmatized.

Theoretical Framework

The theoretical underpinnings of safe spaces can be linked to several key concepts in sociology and psychology. One such theory is *Social Identity Theory*, which posits that individuals derive part of their self-concept from their group memberships. In the context of LGBTQ individuals, belonging to a supportive community can enhance self-esteem and foster a sense of belonging. Moreover, *Intersectionality*, a framework developed by Kimberlé Crenshaw, emphasizes the importance of considering multiple identities, such as race, gender, and sexual orientation, in understanding the unique challenges faced by LGBTQ individuals. Safe spaces must therefore be inclusive and considerate of these intersecting identities.

Challenges Faced by LGBTQ Individuals

Despite the growing recognition of the need for safe spaces, LGBTQ individuals often encounter significant barriers. Discrimination, violence, and societal stigma can lead to feelings of isolation and marginalization. According to a report by the Human Rights Campaign (HRC), LGBTQ youth are more likely to experience bullying, homelessness, and mental health issues compared to their heterosexual peers. The lack of supportive environments exacerbates these challenges, making it imperative to create safe spaces that address these issues directly.

Examples of Safe Spaces

Several organizations and initiatives exemplify the creation of safe spaces for LGBTQ individuals. For instance, community centers such as the *LGBTQ Community Center* in New York City offer a range of services, including counseling, support groups, and educational workshops. These centers not only provide a physical space for LGBTQ individuals to gather but also foster a sense of community and belonging.

Another example is the establishment of *Safe Zone* programs in schools and universities. These programs train faculty and staff to create inclusive environments for LGBTQ students. By displaying Safe Zone stickers, educators signal their commitment to providing support and understanding, which can significantly impact the experiences of LGBTQ youth in educational settings.

The Role of Allies

Allies play a crucial role in creating safe spaces for LGBTQ individuals. An ally is someone who supports and advocates for the rights of LGBTQ individuals, often using their privilege to amplify marginalized voices. The concept of allyship is grounded in the idea of solidarity, where allies actively work to dismantle systems of oppression and discrimination. This can involve participating in LGBTQ events, educating themselves and others about LGBTQ issues, and challenging discriminatory behaviors and policies.

Strategies for Creating Safe Spaces

To effectively create safe spaces, several strategies can be employed:

1. **Education and Awareness**: Providing training and resources to individuals and organizations can foster understanding and reduce prejudice. Workshops on LGBTQ issues, inclusive language, and cultural competency can equip allies and community members with the tools necessary to support LGBTQ individuals.

2. **Policy Advocacy**: Advocating for inclusive policies at local, state, and national levels is essential for creating systemic change. This includes pushing for anti-discrimination laws, healthcare access, and protections for LGBTQ individuals in various sectors.

3. **Building Community**: Encouraging the formation of LGBTQ groups and networks can create a sense of belonging. Community events, social gatherings, and support groups can help individuals connect and share their experiences in a safe environment.

4. **Mental Health Support**: Providing access to mental health resources specifically tailored for LGBTQ individuals can address the unique challenges they face. This includes counseling services, peer support groups, and crisis intervention.

5. **Visibility and Representation**: Promoting LGBTQ visibility in media, politics, and public life can challenge stereotypes and foster acceptance. Representation matters; seeing LGBTQ individuals in various roles can inspire others and validate their identities.

Conclusion

Creating safe spaces and supportive communities for LGBTQ individuals is a vital component of fostering an inclusive society. By addressing the challenges faced by LGBTQ individuals and implementing effective strategies, we can cultivate environments where everyone can live authentically and without fear. The collective effort of individuals, organizations, and allies is essential in driving this change, ensuring that LGBTQ individuals not only survive but thrive in their communities.

$$\text{Safe Space} = \text{Inclusivity} + \text{Support} + \text{Empowerment} \tag{129}$$

This equation encapsulates the essence of a safe space, highlighting the need for inclusivity, support, and empowerment to create environments where LGBTQ individuals can flourish.

The responsibility of individuals to drive change in their own communities

In the quest for equality and acceptance, the responsibility of individuals to drive change in their own communities cannot be overstated. Each person possesses the potential to be an agent of transformation, and this section explores the theoretical underpinnings, challenges, and actionable steps that can empower individuals to effect meaningful change.

Theoretical Frameworks

The theory of social change posits that collective action can lead to significant societal transformations. According to *Mills' Sociological Imagination*, individuals must recognize the intersection between personal experiences and broader social structures. This awareness is crucial; it allows individuals to understand how their actions can contribute to systemic change. In essence, the sociological imagination enables individuals to see their role in a larger narrative, fostering a sense of responsibility towards their communities.

Moreover, *Collective Efficacy Theory* emphasizes the power of community cohesion and mutual trust in achieving shared goals. When individuals believe in their collective ability to enact change, they are more likely to take action. This theory underscores the importance of building supportive networks within communities, which can amplify the impact of individual efforts.

Challenges Faced by Individuals

Despite the potential for change, individuals often encounter significant challenges in their efforts to drive social transformation. One prevalent issue is *fear of backlash*. Many individuals hesitate to speak out or take action due to concerns about personal repercussions, such as social ostracism or even violence. This fear can be particularly pronounced in conservative communities where LGBTQ issues are stigmatized.

Additionally, the *bystander effect* can hinder individual action. This psychological phenomenon suggests that individuals are less likely to intervene in a situation when others are present, assuming someone else will take responsibility. This diffusion of responsibility can create a culture of inaction, perpetuating the status quo.

Actionable Steps for Individuals

To overcome these challenges, individuals can adopt several actionable strategies to drive change within their communities:

1. **Education and Awareness:** Knowledge is power. Individuals can educate themselves and others about LGBTQ issues, rights, and the importance of inclusivity. Hosting workshops, distributing informative materials, and utilizing social media platforms can help raise awareness and foster understanding.

2. **Advocacy and Allyship:** Individuals can become advocates for LGBTQ rights by supporting local organizations and initiatives. This could involve volunteering time, donating resources, or participating in campaigns that promote equality. Furthermore, being an ally means standing up for marginalized voices, amplifying their stories, and challenging discriminatory practices when encountered.

3. **Creating Safe Spaces:** Individuals can work towards creating inclusive environments where LGBTQ individuals feel safe and accepted. This could involve advocating for inclusive policies in schools, workplaces, and community organizations. For example, establishing gender-neutral

bathrooms or implementing anti-discrimination policies can significantly impact the well-being of LGBTQ individuals.

4. **Engagement in Dialogue:** Encouraging open conversations about LGBTQ issues can help dismantle stereotypes and foster empathy. Individuals can initiate discussions with friends, family, and community members, sharing personal stories and experiences that humanize the struggles faced by LGBTQ individuals.

5. **Mobilizing Resources:** Individuals can leverage their skills and resources to support LGBTQ initiatives. This could involve organizing fundraisers, art exhibitions, or cultural events that celebrate diversity and promote inclusivity. For instance, a community theater group could produce plays that highlight LGBTQ narratives, fostering dialogue and understanding.

6. **Participating in Local Politics:** Engaging in local governance and advocating for policy changes can have a profound impact. Individuals can attend town hall meetings, voice their concerns, and support candidates who prioritize LGBTQ rights. Grassroots movements often start at the local level, and individuals can play a crucial role in shaping policies that promote equality.

Examples of Successful Change Initiatives

Numerous individuals and grassroots movements have successfully driven change in their communities, serving as inspiration for others. For instance, the *It Gets Better Project*, initiated by Dan Savage and Terry Miller, began as a response to the bullying faced by LGBTQ youth. Through personal stories and videos, individuals shared their experiences, creating a powerful message of hope and resilience. This initiative has since grown into a global movement, demonstrating the impact of individual action on a larger scale.

Another example is the *Stonewall Riots*, which catalyzed the modern LGBTQ rights movement. The bravery of individuals who stood up against police harassment in 1969 sparked widespread activism and led to the formation of organizations advocating for LGBTQ rights. This historic event illustrates how individual courage can ignite collective action and drive societal change.

Conclusion

In conclusion, the responsibility of individuals to drive change in their communities is paramount in the ongoing struggle for LGBTQ rights. By leveraging their unique skills, fostering dialogue, and advocating for inclusivity, individuals can collectively contribute to a more equitable society. The path may be fraught with challenges, but the potential for transformation lies within each person. As Jin Xing's journey exemplifies, embracing one's identity and standing up for what is right can inspire others and create a ripple effect of positive change. The time for action is now; individuals must rise to the occasion and be the change they wish to see in their communities.

The potential for collective efforts to shape a more inclusive future

The quest for a more inclusive future hinges on the collective efforts of individuals, communities, and organizations working together towards common goals. This collaboration is essential in dismantling systemic barriers and fostering an environment where diversity is celebrated rather than merely tolerated.

Theoretical Framework

To understand the potential of collective efforts, we can draw on social movement theory, which posits that collective action is a crucial driver of social change. According to Tilly (2004), social movements arise when individuals come together to pursue shared interests, often in opposition to established norms and structures. This collective identity is fundamental in mobilizing resources, raising awareness, and influencing public policy.

The concept of *intersectionality*, introduced by Crenshaw (1989), further enriches our understanding of collective efforts. It emphasizes that individuals experience overlapping identities—such as race, gender, and sexual orientation—that shape their experiences of discrimination and privilege. Thus, inclusive movements must recognize and address these intersecting identities to create effective change.

Challenges to Collective Action

Despite the potential for collective efforts, several challenges can hinder progress. One significant barrier is the fragmentation within the LGBTQ community itself. Different subgroups may have varying priorities and experiences, leading to potential conflicts over representation and resource allocation. For instance, the needs of transgender individuals may differ from those of gay men or lesbians, creating tensions that can stall collective action.

Moreover, societal stigma and discrimination can discourage individuals from participating in collective efforts. Fear of backlash, isolation, or violence can inhibit engagement, particularly in conservative environments where LGBTQ identities are marginalized.

Examples of Successful Collective Action

Despite these challenges, there are numerous examples where collective efforts have led to significant advancements in LGBTQ rights and representation. One notable instance is the Stonewall Riots of 1969, which galvanized the LGBTQ community and sparked the modern LGBTQ rights movement. The collective uprising against police brutality and discrimination led to the establishment of Pride marches and various advocacy organizations, fundamentally shifting public perception and policy towards LGBTQ individuals.

Another example is the global response to the HIV/AIDS crisis in the 1980s and 1990s. Activist groups such as ACT UP (AIDS Coalition to Unleash Power) utilized collective action to demand government accountability, increased funding for research, and better access to treatment. Their efforts not only improved the lives of countless individuals but also highlighted the importance of grassroots activism in effecting change.

Strategies for Effective Collective Action

To harness the potential of collective efforts, several strategies can be employed:

1.   **Building Alliances**: Creating coalitions among diverse groups can amplify voices and create a united front. For example, alliances between LGBTQ organizations and other marginalized communities can foster solidarity and mutual support.

2.   **Education and Awareness**: Raising awareness about LGBTQ issues through education can empower individuals to engage in activism. Workshops, seminars, and community outreach programs can help demystify LGBTQ identities and foster understanding.

3.   **Utilizing Digital Platforms**: The rise of social media has transformed collective action by providing platforms for organizing, advocacy, and storytelling. Campaigns such as #BlackTransLivesMatter have successfully mobilized support and raised awareness about the specific issues faced by transgender individuals within the broader LGBTQ movement.

4.   **Creating Safe Spaces**: Establishing safe spaces for dialogue and expression is crucial for fostering community engagement. These spaces allow

individuals to share their experiences, build trust, and strategize for collective action without fear of judgment or retaliation.

5. **Advocating for Policy Change**: Collective efforts should also focus on influencing policy at local, national, and international levels. Engaging with policymakers, participating in lobbying efforts, and advocating for inclusive legislation can create systemic change that benefits the entire LGBTQ community.

Conclusion

The potential for collective efforts to shape a more inclusive future is immense. By recognizing the power of collaboration, understanding the complexities of identity, and employing strategic approaches, individuals and communities can work together to dismantle barriers and create a society where everyone can thrive. As we reflect on Jin Xing's journey and the ongoing fight for LGBTQ rights, it becomes clear that the future is not merely a result of individual actions but rather a tapestry woven from the collective struggles, triumphs, and dreams of many. The call to action is clear: together, we can forge a path toward a more inclusive and accepting world for all.

The hope for a world where everyone can live authentically and without fear

In our quest for a more inclusive society, the aspiration for a world where every individual can live authentically and without fear becomes paramount. This vision is not merely an idealistic dream; it is rooted in the fundamental principles of human rights, dignity, and respect. The journey towards this world is fraught with challenges, but it is also filled with hope, resilience, and the promise of change.

At the core of this hope lies the concept of authenticity, which can be defined as the alignment of one's actions, beliefs, and identity. As noted by [1], authenticity is essential for psychological well-being. It allows individuals to express their true selves, free from societal constraints and prejudices. However, the reality for many, particularly in marginalized communities, is that societal norms and expectations often impose barriers that inhibit this authenticity.

To illustrate this point, consider the case of LGBTQ individuals in various cultural contexts. In many societies, being true to oneself can lead to ostracism, discrimination, or even violence. According to the *International Lesbian, Gay, Bisexual, Trans and Intersex Association (ILGA)* report of 2021, more than 70 countries still criminalize same-sex relationships, and many individuals face significant risks when they choose to live openly. This presents a stark contrast to the ideal of a world where everyone can live authentically.

The theory of *intersectionality*, introduced by [2], provides a framework for understanding how various forms of discrimination overlap and compound the challenges faced by individuals in their pursuit of authenticity. For instance, a transgender person of color may experience discrimination not only due to their gender identity but also because of their race, leading to a unique set of challenges that must be addressed in the fight for equality.

In our pursuit of this hopeful vision, it is crucial to recognize the role of education and awareness in fostering understanding and acceptance. Programs that promote diversity, inclusion, and empathy can help dismantle the prejudices that create fear and inhibit authenticity. For example, initiatives in schools that educate students about LGBTQ issues have been shown to reduce bullying and improve the overall climate for acceptance [3].

Moreover, the media plays a pivotal role in shaping societal perceptions. Positive representation of LGBTQ individuals in film, television, and literature can challenge stereotypes and foster a more nuanced understanding of diverse identities. The success of shows like *Pose* and *Schitt's Creek* demonstrates the power of storytelling in humanizing experiences and promoting empathy.

Despite the progress made, significant barriers remain. The ongoing fight for legislative protections, such as anti-discrimination laws and marriage equality, is essential in creating a safe environment for all individuals to express their identities without fear. The *United Nations Free & Equal* campaign highlights the importance of legal frameworks that protect the rights of LGBTQ individuals, advocating for global standards that ensure everyone can live authentically.

Furthermore, community support systems are vital. Organizations that provide resources, advocacy, and safe spaces for LGBTQ individuals can empower them to embrace their identities. Initiatives like *The Trevor Project* offer crucial support to young LGBTQ individuals, helping them navigate the complexities of identity in a world that can often be hostile.

In conclusion, the hope for a world where everyone can live authentically and without fear is a collective aspiration that requires sustained effort, empathy, and advocacy. By addressing the systemic barriers that inhibit authenticity, promoting education and awareness, and fostering supportive communities, we can create a society that celebrates diversity and embraces the richness of human experience. As we move forward, let us hold onto this hope and work tirelessly towards a future where every individual can live their truth, free from fear and full of possibilities.

Bibliography

[1] Schmid, H. B. (2014). *Authenticity: A Philosophical Inquiry*. New York: Routledge.

[2] Crenshaw, K. (1989). Mapping the Margins: Intersectionality, Identity Politics, and Violence against Women of Color. *Stanford Law Review*, 43(6), 1241-1299.

[3] Espelage, D. L., & Holt, M. K. (2013). Bullying and Victimization during Early Adolescence: Peer Influence and Family Context. *Journal of Emotional Abuse*, 13(3), 244-261.

Index

-doubt, 25, 28, 59, 81, 107, 208

a, 1–37, 39–43, 46–79, 81–104,
106–110, 115–153,
155–199, 201–211,
213–227, 229–255,
257–266, 269–280,
282–285, 287–289, 291,
293–299, 301–307, 309,
310, 312–316, 319–322,
324–333, 335–338,
340–343, 345, 347, 348,
351, 353, 354
ability, 3, 5, 8, 25, 28, 31–33, 35, 39,
59, 64, 97, 99, 101, 103,
109, 118, 119, 121, 122,
125, 132, 134, 135, 137,
143, 160, 164, 165, 167,
171, 175, 176, 184, 188,
190, 209, 222, 232, 235,
247, 262, 279, 299, 303,
319, 325
absence, 28, 103, 177
academy, 18, 21, 24, 25, 27, 39, 207
acceptance, 4, 12–14, 16, 18, 20,
22–24, 27, 30, 31, 33–35,
39–41, 43, 47–49, 51, 52,
54–56, 58–67, 72, 73,

75–77, 79, 82, 83, 85,
87–92, 94–100, 102, 104,
106–110, 116, 117, 119,
121–126, 129–131, 133,
134, 138, 139, 141–144,
146–150, 152, 153, 157,
158, 160, 163–166, 169,
174, 178–181, 183, 185,
187, 189, 190, 192–197,
202–204, 208–210,
213–217, 219–221, 225,
226, 229, 230, 233–241,
243–250, 254, 255, 261,
263–267, 270, 272, 276,
278–280, 282–285, 287,
289, 294, 297, 299–301,
303–310, 312, 314–317,
319, 320, 322, 326–329,
331–333, 338, 339, 345,
346, 348
access, 12, 13, 28, 49, 62, 136, 137,
166, 175, 278, 300, 333
acclaim, 30, 34, 35, 87, 115, 124, 131
accolade, 39
account, 11, 224
achievement, 22, 97, 207
acknowledgment, 102
acquisition, 23

act, 14, 18, 47, 50, 55, 59, 65, 149,
    210, 285, 322, 332
action, 64, 65, 67, 117, 134, 165,
    178, 189, 193, 201, 208,
    225, 227, 271, 275, 277,
    280, 294, 303, 311,
    320–324, 327, 329, 331,
    332, 341–345, 351, 353
activism, 5, 9, 15, 17, 18, 33, 34, 40,
    41, 49, 51, 53, 61, 62, 85,
    87, 88, 91, 92, 94, 95, 99,
    101, 102, 108, 109, 123,
    131, 133, 142, 144, 150,
    160, 174, 179, 180, 183,
    184, 187, 191, 201–203,
    208, 215, 226, 227, 229,
    231, 232, 242–244, 247,
    249, 253, 254, 260, 261,
    263, 266–268, 270, 271,
    273, 278, 312–314
activist, 10, 16, 20, 24, 40, 43, 70, 86,
    89, 94, 98, 100, 109, 128,
    140, 142, 152, 163, 165,
    194, 244, 269, 283, 303
actualization, 18–20, 59
adaptability, 64, 122, 125
adaptation, 168
addition, 21, 40, 58, 95, 116, 126,
    141, 150, 166, 188, 196,
    210, 221, 243, 304
address, 12, 49, 65, 99, 110, 136,
    186, 189, 240, 242, 260,
    263, 276, 296, 342
adherence, 9, 46, 100, 283
admiration, 55, 96, 123, 208
adolescence, 4
adulthood, 7
advancement, 53, 259, 264
advent, 132

adversity, 3, 6, 9, 20, 30, 35, 49, 52,
    56, 58, 59, 64, 67, 75, 91,
    107, 109, 116, 121, 141,
    142, 144, 157, 158,
    160–162, 165, 167,
    169–171, 173, 175–178,
    181, 201, 202, 206, 209,
    211, 221, 232, 235, 236,
    277, 285, 306, 307, 316,
    319
advocacy, 4, 5, 10, 12, 13, 15, 29, 30,
    34, 35, 40, 41, 43, 49, 54,
    56, 58, 61, 62, 65, 67,
    73–75, 81–83, 85, 86, 88,
    91–93, 95, 97, 99, 104,
    106, 108–111, 115, 117,
    123–126, 130, 133–135,
    141, 147, 150, 151, 157,
    166–169, 174, 175, 177,
    178, 180, 182, 186–188,
    190, 191, 194–198, 204,
    206, 208–211, 215, 221,
    224–226, 231, 236, 238,
    240, 246–250, 253–255,
    260–263, 265, 266, 270,
    271, 274–276, 278, 280,
    284, 285, 289, 291, 303,
    308, 314–316, 322,
    327–329, 331, 332, 336,
    341–343, 352, 354
advocate, 18, 28, 34, 40, 43, 49, 53,
    61, 62, 64, 67, 70, 72–75,
    79, 90–92, 94, 98, 101,
    102, 106, 108, 110, 119,
    120, 123, 126, 127,
    129–134, 143, 150, 162,
    165, 166, 171, 173–175,
    178, 184, 186, 192, 194,
    196–199, 201, 204, 210,

214, 221, 227, 231, 232,
235, 236, 238, 241, 242,
247, 250, 254, 259, 263,
266, 271, 275, 277, 278,
280, 285, 289, 295, 297,
300, 304, 305, 307, 309,
310, 312–314, 316, 338,
341, 342, 344
aesthetic, 40
affinity, 206
affirmation, 23, 29, 51, 56, 59, 141
affront, 26
Africa, 258, 265–267
aftermath, 53, 55, 208
age, 1, 3, 5–9, 13, 18, 24, 121, 132,
137, 161, 188, 206, 240,
254, 280, 287, 325
agency, 224
agenda, 272
agent, 348
Ai Weiwei, 85
alienation, 298
allocation, 351
ally, 178, 310, 334, 347
allyship, 175, 227, 278, 280, 309,
311, 312, 331, 347
ambassador, 79, 129–131, 304
ambition, 196
amplification, 338
Angela Duckworth, 161
anticipation, 117
Antonio Gramsci, 246
anxiety, 28, 46, 52, 64, 95, 142, 143
appearance, 51
applause, 207
application, 85, 160, 257
appointment, 76
appreciation, 33, 119, 127, 128, 141,
335

apprehension, 125
approach, 9–11, 26, 37, 40, 49, 59,
81, 84, 85, 120, 127, 130,
143, 146, 149, 175, 180,
191, 196, 208, 237, 247,
255, 261–263, 272, 316,
320
appropriation, 127, 130, 136, 137
archive, 190
area, 95
arena, 33, 86
Argentina, 258, 265
array, 69
art, 1–3, 6, 7, 14, 16, 18, 20, 22, 24,
26, 29, 30, 32, 33, 35, 37,
40–43, 68, 72, 84–87, 89,
92–94, 109, 118–122,
125, 126, 129, 130, 132,
133, 135–137, 146, 159,
160, 165, 166, 184,
187–189, 197, 198, 201,
203, 204, 209, 214, 226,
227, 230, 231, 238, 270,
303, 329
artist, 1, 16, 22, 26, 36, 39, 40, 43,
58, 70, 73, 79, 82, 85, 94,
98, 119, 131, 132, 136,
146, 152, 165, 194, 195,
207, 307
artistry, 3, 6, 15, 33, 39, 85, 91, 94,
119, 120, 123, 130, 163,
165, 184, 188, 195, 203,
215, 224, 248, 288, 289
ascent, 31, 33
Asia, 124, 265, 268, 276
aspect, 58, 60, 109, 121, 216, 259,
277, 332, 335, 338
aspiration, 278, 353, 354
assistance, 57, 320

atmosphere, 25, 143

attachment, 9

attention, 15, 30, 32, 43, 82, 86, 140,
        166, 249, 263, 275

attribute, 235, 303

audience, 8, 42, 76, 79, 96, 120, 125,
        132, 134, 189, 226, 263,
        287, 304

Audre Lorde, 67, 261

authenticity, 5, 8, 18–20, 33, 35, 39,
        43, 47, 51–53, 65, 67, 73,
        76, 87, 88, 99, 116, 123,
        125, 131, 133, 137, 141,
        144, 150, 157, 160, 167,
        169, 181, 209, 210, 215,
        217–220, 225, 227, 236,
        244, 285, 296, 298,
        305–307, 314, 316, 317,
        319, 354

authority, 304

autobiography, 224

avenue, 55, 86

aversion, 320

awareness, 12, 28, 34, 61, 64, 65, 79,
        80, 85, 87, 91, 94–96, 101,
        103, 108, 110, 129, 130,
        169, 172, 175, 179,
        186–188, 196, 230,
        239–241, 243, 247, 249,
        250, 259–262, 266, 270,
        277, 280, 284, 289, 299,
        308, 328, 339–341, 354

awe, 8, 42

backdrop, 7, 17, 29, 39, 50, 73, 158,
        216, 306

background, 29, 101, 120, 129, 325

backing, 17, 168

backlash, 10, 30, 48, 53, 55, 62, 74,
        78, 82, 92, 95, 109,
        123–126, 150, 162, 164,
        183, 194, 208, 209, 214,
        221, 226, 236, 245, 247,
        263, 284, 304, 309, 310,
        352

bag, 53

balance, 13, 63, 119, 132, 208, 247

ballet, 7, 14, 15, 23, 25, 31

bar, 174

barrage, 97

barrier, 1, 19, 120, 136, 140, 351

battle, 27, 28, 45, 47, 57, 63, 106,
        213, 266, 276

battleground, 125, 304

beacon, 3, 5, 20, 22, 26, 37, 39, 41,
        47, 48, 54, 56, 58, 61, 65,
        67, 68, 70, 72, 73, 79, 88,
        90, 95, 97, 102, 107, 109,
        117, 122, 128, 133, 141,
        157, 163, 165, 169, 178,
        184, 185, 190, 193, 203,
        209, 214, 217, 221, 223,
        226, 229, 232, 233, 235,
        243, 245, 247, 262, 264,
        265, 289, 314, 327

beauty, 25, 238

beginning, 8, 70

behavior, 27, 48, 335

Beijing, 252

being, 16, 23, 24, 28, 29, 46, 48, 53,
        55, 58, 66, 73, 77, 80, 81,
        94, 96, 103, 119, 134,
        139–144, 147, 149, 166,
        175, 197, 209, 213, 222,
        223, 232, 235, 249, 304,
        310, 316, 326, 336, 341,
        346

belief, 6, 9, 10, 14, 18, 25, 46, 58, 64,
    84, 94, 116, 160–163, 165,
    197, 255, 280, 285
bell, 30, 230, 261
belonging, 16, 56, 93, 144, 175, 191,
    236–238, 301, 315
benefit, 16, 279
bias, 28
Bill C-16, 264
binary, 19, 47, 74, 102, 122, 143,
    158, 164, 193, 246, 283
biography, 210, 218
birth, 3, 5, 48
blend, 6, 33, 72, 86, 126, 130, 132,
    303
blending, 25, 35, 128, 136
body, 13, 39, 120
bond, 141, 142, 157
book, 190
boy, 109, 235, 283
brand, 189
bravery, 51, 53, 342
Brazil, 265
breaking, 84, 85, 94, 99, 179, 192,
    250, 283, 285, 308
breakthrough, 22, 29, 30, 32, 33, 35,
    39, 207, 210
breakup, 140
bridge, 22, 31, 33, 87, 115, 119,
    135–137, 225, 239, 247,
    276, 327
brilliance, 107
brutality, 352
buffer, 56, 57
build, 16, 56, 138, 143, 175, 214,
    280, 321, 343, 345
building, 4, 74, 116, 137, 139, 144,
    153, 175, 206, 263
bullying, 4, 146, 277, 306, 313

Butler, 122, 262, 303
Butoh, 128

call, 67, 165, 182, 201, 202, 227,
    294, 303, 321, 329, 343,
    353
calling, 2, 91
camaraderie, 207
Canada, 264, 267, 272, 277
canvas, 3
capacity, 19, 22, 64, 158, 180, 320
capital, 231, 343
care, 12, 189
career, 2–5, 8, 15, 17–19, 24,
    28–33, 39, 41, 43, 48, 53,
    55, 57–59, 68, 81, 82, 85,
    86, 96, 100, 118, 126, 128,
    130–132, 138, 181, 202,
    208, 215, 216, 225, 226,
    244, 262
Carl Rogers', 59
case, 48, 59, 96, 141, 148, 168, 296,
    320
catalyst, 15, 21, 24, 51, 79, 98, 110,
    122, 133, 150, 155, 165,
    173, 197, 202, 236, 244,
    248, 277, 314, 327–329,
    340, 342, 343
cause, 95, 225, 312
celebration, 160, 162, 252
censorship, 73, 185, 245, 249, 304,
    338
center, 209, 220
century, 158, 260
challenge, 2, 5–8, 12, 15, 18, 29, 30,
    32, 33, 36, 37, 39, 41, 43,
    48, 49, 58, 59, 66, 68, 70,
    72, 74, 75, 82–86, 91, 95,
    100, 102, 108, 119,

126–129, 135–137, 142,
152, 163, 165, 182, 189,
198, 201, 210, 213, 217,
220, 221, 227, 231, 232,
240, 244, 245, 254, 261,
262, 270, 278, 280, 283,
284, 297, 299, 301, 303,
307, 309, 312, 316, 321,
329, 331, 335, 336,
341–343
champion, 107, 221
change, 13, 15, 18, 21, 22, 24, 29,
37, 40, 41, 43, 49, 52, 58,
62, 65, 67, 70, 72, 73, 75,
77, 79, 81, 83, 85, 89, 91,
94, 95, 97–99, 102, 104,
106, 108–111, 117, 122,
125–127, 130, 131, 133,
135, 150, 152, 163, 165,
169, 173–175, 179, 182,
184, 185, 187–194, 197,
198, 201–204, 206, 208,
209, 211, 213, 214, 221,
223, 230–232, 236, 238,
241, 244–251, 253, 255,
258, 259, 263, 265, 266,
268, 269, 271, 273, 275,
277, 280, 285, 287, 294,
297, 299, 300, 303, 305,
307, 309, 313, 314,
319–322, 326–329, 333,
336, 337, 339–344,
348–351, 353
chapter, 115
character, 6, 32
characteristic, 173
charge, 75, 187
charisma, 96, 100
charity, 332

chasm, 215
child, 1, 12, 55
childhood, 1, 3–7, 9, 206
China, 1–3, 5–13, 15, 17, 18, 20,
22, 26, 27, 29, 30, 34, 37,
39–41, 43, 45–55, 58–62,
64, 66, 68–70, 72–75,
77–82, 84–87, 90–98,
100–102, 104–110, 115,
117, 118, 123–126, 129,
130, 133, 137–139, 147,
149–151, 158, 160, 161,
163, 164, 166, 167, 174,
178, 179, 182–187, 194,
196–198, 202, 203, 206,
209, 210, 213, 214,
216–218, 220–226, 229,
231–233, 235, 236, 238,
242–253, 255, 262, 263,
269, 270, 284, 285,
287–289, 303, 304, 306,
307, 313, 315, 316, 327,
328, 341
choice, 2, 5, 17–20, 48, 55, 85, 138,
157, 162, 214
choreographer, 24, 26, 34, 37, 40,
60, 70, 72, 82, 89, 96, 118,
126, 128, 163, 231, 236,
341
choreography, 31, 32, 35, 36, 40, 41,
70–72, 84, 85, 91, 120,
121, 129, 131, 163, 188,
202, 283
chorus, 196
chronicle, 115, 167
circle, 151, 213
cisgender, 28
city, 1, 3, 13
clarity, 140

clash, 10, 12, 94, 183, 216, 229, 270, 287

class, 6, 49, 74, 101, 186, 222, 255, 263, 276, 323, 342

cognition, 13, 59

collaboration, 34, 85, 93, 120, 127, 128, 273, 276, 319, 324, 351, 353

colonialism, 127

color, 102, 260, 276, 298, 316, 342, 343

combat, 53, 277, 309, 337

combination, 7, 21, 134, 188, 189, 197

commentary, 85, 220, 233

commitment, 1, 5, 10, 14, 16, 18, 20, 23, 24, 26, 32, 35, 37, 40, 55, 59, 65, 68, 70, 72, 77, 79, 81, 84–88, 95, 116, 117, 119, 122, 125, 130, 138, 141, 142, 147, 149, 157, 163–165, 175, 181, 191, 195, 197, 199, 204, 209, 210, 219, 225, 226, 231, 232, 242, 244, 250, 271, 275, 280, 285, 311, 312, 314, 316, 324, 332, 336, 343

commodification, 127, 136

communication, 120, 127, 141, 143, 153, 155, 217

community, 4, 5, 7, 8, 10, 13, 15, 16, 18, 20, 24, 26–28, 30, 33–37, 39, 46–49, 56–58, 60–67, 69–74, 79, 82, 85–88, 90–93, 95–97, 101, 106, 108, 109, 115–117, 120–123, 125, 126, 128, 130–134, 136, 141–144, 148–150, 152, 153, 156–158, 160, 163–169, 172, 174, 175, 178, 182, 185–191, 195–198, 202, 204–206, 209, 213, 214, 216, 217, 225, 226, 230, 235–238, 242, 244, 245, 247, 249, 250, 253–255, 260, 261, 263, 265, 266, 269, 276–279, 282, 284, 285, 287, 289, 294, 296, 298, 299, 304, 306–310, 313–315, 317, 319, 327, 329, 331–333, 336, 338, 342, 351, 352

companionship, 57

company, 22, 68–70, 72, 82, 84, 93, 95, 178, 191, 195, 221

compassion, 214

competition, 4, 8, 16, 23, 76

complexity, 45, 78, 140, 215, 222, 266, 271

component, 26, 135, 169, 171, 175, 233, 309, 348

composer, 119

concept, 12, 18, 19, 42, 57, 62, 65, 74, 78, 102, 107, 109, 166, 175, 179, 204, 226, 229, 231, 246, 247, 301, 303, 311, 325, 331, 343, 346, 347

conclusion, 3, 5, 7, 8, 10, 15, 17, 18, 20, 22, 24, 29, 33, 35, 37, 39, 43, 47, 49, 52, 58, 60, 62, 65, 70, 72, 75, 79, 85, 88, 89, 92, 94, 95, 97, 99, 102, 104, 108, 110, 117, 122, 123, 125, 128, 130,

132, 135, 139, 140, 142,
147, 150, 151, 158, 160,
163, 165, 167, 169, 172,
175, 178, 180, 182, 184,
190, 192, 195, 197, 199,
201, 203, 206, 210, 213,
219, 221, 225, 227, 234,
236, 245, 248, 253, 255,
263, 269, 271, 273, 275,
278, 280, 287, 289, 296,
299, 300, 303, 304, 307,
309, 312, 316, 318, 321,
336, 343, 350, 354
conditioning, 25
conduit, 7, 127
confidence, 2, 4, 6, 16, 17, 64, 138,
161, 237
confine, 5, 6, 82, 213, 285
conflict, 29, 55, 59, 213
confluence, 215, 222
conformity, 9, 17, 46, 50, 55, 100,
150, 216, 235
confusion, 46, 213
connection, 4, 6, 13, 42, 60, 92, 121,
122, 127, 157, 159, 225,
287, 319
conservatism, 90, 123, 258
construct, 143, 169, 222, 303
construction, 294
consumption, 132, 302
contagion, 42
content, 73, 74, 122, 132, 301, 303
contestant, 76
context, 9, 23, 35, 47, 49, 55, 59, 60,
65, 74, 83, 87, 101, 127,
130, 136, 143, 146, 153,
173, 179, 193, 197, 216,
217, 219, 223, 248, 272,
285, 301, 310, 322, 324,

331, 339, 343
continuation, 126, 312
contrast, 4, 125, 279
control, 73, 253
controversy, 209, 210
conversation, 18, 98, 125, 150, 220,
243, 269–271, 287, 302,
311
cooperation, 277
core, 84, 98, 121, 141, 175, 213,
226, 303
cornerstone, 28, 31, 43, 142, 217,
254, 273, 279, 305
correlation, 87
counter, 90, 237, 238
counterbalance, 6
country, 10, 11, 22, 47, 97, 107, 109,
126, 129, 150, 226, 236,
244, 247, 251, 252, 265,
267, 283, 287, 315
couple, 141
courage, 3, 5, 18, 48, 55, 59, 63, 76,
92, 116, 133, 144, 157,
162, 190, 208, 209, 214,
215, 229, 235, 277, 285,
316, 318, 324, 343
coverage, 96, 207, 224
crackdown, 74, 253
crackdowns, 185
craft, 5, 18, 23, 25, 26, 32, 55, 81,
82, 216, 236
creation, 127, 166, 172
creativity, 6, 21, 26, 33, 35, 40, 68,
72, 83–86, 122, 127, 146,
147, 165, 188, 196
credibility, 95
criminalization, 267
crisis, 175, 277, 320
critic, 61, 230

criticism, 30, 51, 53, 95, 97, 119,
123, 125, 126, 158, 160,
208, 210, 242, 263, 284,
304
critique, 79, 124
crucible, 6, 21, 120
cry, 67, 343
culmination, 3, 5, 17, 35, 55, 207
cultivation, 52, 179
culture, 17, 46, 67, 78, 79, 84, 96,
121, 126–130, 135, 149,
157, 179, 189, 226, 230,
232, 235, 246–248, 251,
263, 270, 282, 303, 304,
331, 335
curiosity, 77
curricula, 187, 240, 254, 277, 280
curriculum, 23, 25
cycle, 28, 171, 177, 191, 309

dance, 1–10, 13–29, 31–37, 39–41,
43, 53, 55, 59, 61, 66,
68–72, 76–79, 81–86, 88,
91–100, 108, 116–119,
121, 122, 124–126, 128,
129, 131, 132, 134, 136,
144, 146, 156, 159,
161–164, 166, 170, 171,
174, 178, 179, 181, 183,
184, 187, 188, 191, 195,
202, 207, 209, 214, 216,
221, 223, 225, 226, 230,
231, 233, 235–237,
242–244, 248, 262, 270,
283, 303, 306, 314
dancer, 1, 5, 6, 10, 12, 15, 18, 20–28,
31, 33, 36, 37, 40, 48, 60,
70, 73, 79, 82, 89, 90, 96,
100, 109, 110, 115, 118,
122, 128, 133, 140, 163,
185, 201, 204, 209, 215,
225, 231, 236, 246, 262,
269, 283, 303, 341
dancing, 14
daughter, 4, 9, 157
death, 258
decision, 2, 5, 11, 14, 17, 18, 20, 27,
48, 50–52, 55, 59, 97, 138,
149, 157, 162, 168, 170,
181, 209, 214, 224, 226,
265
declaration, 3, 6, 14, 55, 214
deconstruction, 127
decrease, 308
decriminalization, 11, 105, 265
dedication, 2–4, 15, 21–23, 25, 26,
33, 39, 68, 70, 79, 84, 138,
141
defiance, 31, 42, 50, 65, 210
definition, 161, 235
demand, 123, 252, 260, 300
demographic, 77
demonstration, 235
denominator, 262
depression, 28, 46, 64, 95, 142
depth, 24, 32, 42, 84, 160, 213
desire, 2, 4, 13, 18, 55, 68, 84, 88, 98,
138, 140, 142, 210, 310
despair, 156, 181
destination, 182
detention, 249
determination, 1–7, 13, 15, 17–20,
28, 31, 33, 41, 64, 69, 81,
82, 91, 116, 117, 126, 140,
156–158, 160–163, 170,
174, 180, 206, 214, 216,
248, 250, 253, 255, 262,
276, 277, 306

devaluation, 48

development, 6, 9, 10, 16, 26, 87, 196, 336

deviation, 6, 7, 46, 47, 50, 55, 81, 96, 97, 213

dialogue, 32, 35, 40, 43, 52, 79, 83–85, 87, 90, 100, 110, 116, 119, 121–123, 126–129, 131, 133, 135–137, 141, 157, 164, 182, 184, 187, 189, 192, 194, 196, 197, 221, 225, 234, 236–238, 240, 247, 248, 261, 263, 270, 304, 309, 319, 328, 341, 351

dichotomy, 66, 71, 77, 126, 206, 210, 215, 247

difference, 3

diffusion, 184

dignity, 106, 225, 278, 309, 329, 353

director, 70, 72, 82

discipline, 1, 3, 4, 7, 9, 15, 21, 24, 26, 31

discomfort, 27, 96, 140

disconnect, 45

discourse, 30, 32, 34, 91, 102, 125, 129, 131, 166, 178, 189, 210, 230, 255, 269

discovery, 7, 13–15, 21, 52, 58–60, 65, 87, 88, 141, 144, 236

discrimination, 2, 4, 6, 10–12, 18, 20, 23, 24, 27–29, 32, 34, 46, 48, 49, 53, 55, 57, 59, 61, 62, 64, 66, 69, 74, 75, 80, 81, 87, 91, 95, 96, 99, 101, 104, 107, 109, 110, 116, 132, 138, 143, 145, 148, 150, 158, 161, 166, 170, 174, 175, 179, 181, 183, 186, 194, 195, 198, 203, 205, 207, 209, 210, 214, 216, 222, 226, 227, 230, 235, 241–245, 247, 249–252, 254, 255, 257, 258, 262, 264–267, 270, 271, 277, 279, 280, 284, 289, 300, 301, 306, 307, 309, 310, 313, 316, 323, 324, 327, 333, 338, 346, 347, 352

disdain, 55

dismantling, 92, 133, 204, 239, 284, 288, 351

disorder, 73, 90

disparity, 27, 49, 272

dissemination, 254

dissent, 245, 253

dissonance, 46, 215

diversity, 6, 24, 29, 40, 64, 69, 76, 91, 123, 126, 130, 131, 139, 141, 143, 151, 155, 179, 187, 195, 197, 205, 208, 220, 226, 227, 235, 236, 239, 240, 254, 255, 269, 271, 274, 284, 291–294, 298, 300, 304, 325, 326, 351, 354

document, 190

documentary, 34, 87

documentation, 190

dominance, 246

door, 97, 149

doubt, 25, 28, 56, 59, 81, 107, 208

dream, 165, 233, 353

drive, 17, 175, 188, 190, 193, 231, 251, 273, 294, 297, 299, 300, 321, 348–350

duality, 10, 98, 123, 129, 207

Duckworth, 161
dynamic, 12, 78, 132, 139, 195, 209, 303, 308

ear, 320
Eastern Europe, 267
education, 9, 10, 49, 62, 81, 87, 96, 97, 110, 169, 175, 187, 188, 192, 196, 197, 204, 206, 237–241, 244, 250, 255, 261, 266, 277, 278, 280, 284, 291, 310–314, 316, 336, 339–341, 354
educator, 84
effect, 53, 66, 77, 108, 157, 180, 191, 204, 220, 231, 247, 268, 270, 328, 337, 343, 348, 351
effectiveness, 343
efficacy, 161, 162, 171
effort, 161, 178, 204, 208, 263, 266, 275, 348, 354
El Salvador, 265
element, 8, 55
emblem, 97
embrace, 3, 5, 8, 10, 13, 15, 19–21, 23, 27, 29, 34, 39, 41, 43, 46, 48, 49, 59–62, 65–67, 70, 72, 73, 75, 76, 78, 79, 83, 84, 90–92, 94, 98, 100, 101, 104, 107–110, 120, 123, 126, 130, 131, 133, 138, 139, 142, 144, 146, 148, 150, 151, 157, 158, 162, 164–167, 172, 174, 178, 180, 182, 184, 188, 192, 197, 201, 204, 209, 226, 227, 235–238, 253, 254, 263, 271, 284, 285, 289, 294, 304, 305, 315, 316, 321, 322, 328, 329, 341
emergence, 5, 47, 60, 84, 90, 183, 220, 229, 233, 266, 283, 287
emotion, 3, 8, 20
empathy, 42, 80, 91, 119, 122, 129, 134, 135, 179, 187, 188, 203, 208, 219, 225, 230, 240, 248, 250, 270, 275, 280, 285, 287, 299, 300, 304, 307, 309, 316, 319–321, 327, 329, 336, 354
emphasis, 43, 69, 131
employment, 242, 249, 252
empower, 5, 10, 86, 91, 136, 158, 164, 171, 172, 192, 205, 229, 253, 271, 303, 314, 334, 344, 348
empowerment, 7, 21, 22, 43, 51, 54, 56, 59–61, 65–67, 82–84, 86, 90, 109, 121, 126, 134, 140, 142, 150, 171, 174, 175, 181, 188, 190, 191, 197, 215, 223, 235, 244, 283, 285, 306, 307, 313, 346, 348
encounter, 7, 45, 61, 80, 105, 123, 143, 150, 176, 226, 289, 344
encouragement, 6, 9, 10, 25, 56, 59, 64, 162
end, 3, 6, 23, 196
endeavor, 65, 75, 178, 199, 275, 277, 285
enforcement, 280
engage, 128, 132, 136, 138, 196,

224, 225, 240, 253, 313,
328, 341, 343
engagement, 122, 125, 189, 198,
238, 247, 302, 304, 308,
312, 315, 352
entertainment, 34, 94, 183, 185, 202
enthusiasm, 125
entry, 196
environment, 1, 4, 6, 7, 9, 10, 23–25,
27, 30, 46, 48, 58, 59, 68,
70, 72, 81, 84, 85, 90, 94,
96, 121, 127, 138, 139,
141–144, 146, 147, 149,
159, 166, 168, 172, 175,
178, 185, 187–189, 196,
207–209, 214, 219, 221,
224, 233, 238, 239, 253,
258, 294, 312, 313, 320,
333, 351
epicenter, 33
episode, 76
equality, 13, 29, 61, 62, 79, 88, 90,
94, 95, 99, 100, 102, 104,
106–108, 117, 126, 129,
130, 133–135, 167, 173,
174, 180, 186, 187, 189,
191, 193–197, 204, 210,
215, 221, 226, 227, 231,
232, 243–255, 257, 259,
260, 262–264, 266–269,
271, 273–276, 278–280,
289, 305, 309, 312–316,
319, 322, 329, 332, 333,
335, 336, 338, 341–343,
345, 348
equation, 9–13, 19, 23–27, 34, 47,
49, 60, 63–65, 81, 83,
86–88, 96, 117, 133–135,
142, 161, 164, 166, 168,

169, 176, 184, 187–190,
196–198, 211, 213, 215,
220, 246, 250, 262, 305,
308, 313, 327, 343, 348
erosion, 78
Erving Goffman's, 48
escape, 3, 6, 55
essence, 13, 60, 117, 142, 215, 246,
348
establishment, 43, 68, 69, 166, 171,
226, 271, 352
esteem, 9, 17, 46, 64, 143, 238, 301
ethnicity, 186
Europe, 118–120, 131, 134, 264,
276
evaluation, 26
event, 3
evolution, 33, 39, 70, 72, 88, 115,
120, 131, 216, 244
examination, 205
example, 8, 20, 36, 49, 59, 76, 85,
87, 91, 93, 95, 97, 99, 109,
118, 120, 121, 123, 126,
128, 133, 136, 140, 142,
143, 157, 160, 166, 168,
171, 174, 224, 225, 235,
240, 263, 270–272, 275,
276, 310, 313, 315, 320,
325, 341, 342
excellence, 5, 23, 25, 26, 33
exception, 26
exchange, 34, 37, 43, 69, 116, 117,
119, 125, 127–129,
131–133, 135, 184, 187,
188, 190, 203, 243, 248,
253, 263, 304
excitement, 117
execution, 266
exercise, 225

exhibit, 174

exist, 101, 131, 221, 245

existence, 5, 42, 48, 55, 207, 215,
216, 221, 283

expectation, 19, 48

experience, 3, 8, 12, 24, 28, 40–42,
51, 57, 60, 67, 76, 91, 126,
131, 138, 141, 142, 144,
161, 163, 180, 188, 189,
201, 213, 215, 216, 222,
236, 247, 249, 258, 294,
316, 317, 323, 354

exploration, 72, 85, 86, 148, 215

exposure, 1, 6–8, 13, 18, 82, 159,
179, 192, 301, 306

expression, 4, 7, 9, 13–15, 17, 18,
20, 22, 24, 25, 27, 29,
35–37, 39, 55, 66, 68–70,
76, 84, 85, 91, 92, 109,
119, 121, 126–128,
130–132, 136, 141, 146,
148, 160, 161, 163, 164,
181, 188, 190, 194, 204,
209, 214, 226, 236–238,
245, 252, 253, 263, 264,
271, 283, 285, 287, 306

extension, 27, 118

extremism, 258

eye, 48, 78, 90, 96, 209, 226, 314

fabric, 27, 35, 102, 246, 329

face, 3, 9, 20, 35, 48, 49, 57, 58, 60,
62, 64, 75, 87, 104, 107,
116, 121, 130–132,
140–147, 150, 158, 160,
162, 163, 165, 167, 171,
174, 175, 178, 186, 188,
194, 201, 210, 211, 221,
232, 236, 247–249, 253,
255, 258, 261, 264–267,
272, 277, 285, 307, 309,
310, 313, 314, 316, 319,
329, 336

factor, 58, 109

failure, 14, 292, 296

fairness, 242, 279

fame, 12, 32, 33, 35, 49, 87, 98, 100,
123, 194, 210, 288, 314

family, 1, 7, 12, 17, 25, 47, 53,
56–59, 64, 66, 73, 78, 92,
116, 137–139, 141–143,
147–153, 155, 157, 162,
208–210, 213, 214, 216,
225, 248, 310

father, 4, 9, 206

fatigue, 25

fear, 2, 9, 14, 25, 46, 52, 55, 67, 69,
92, 95, 120, 130, 140–142,
147, 197, 199, 205, 221,
227, 230, 233, 241, 251,
253, 255, 262, 269, 271,
278–280, 309, 310, 313,
319–321, 324, 329, 332,
334, 343, 346, 348, 353,
354

feature, 32, 34

feedback, 26, 76, 177

femininity, 21, 25, 36, 71, 109, 122,
303

feminist, 164

fervor, 19

festival, 39, 270

field, 26, 27, 36, 39, 40

fight, 13, 29, 54, 65, 67, 79, 83, 88,
94, 95, 97, 99, 102, 104,
106, 108, 117, 126, 130,
134, 135, 166, 167, 174,
179, 180, 184, 186,

193–195, 197, 199, 205,
210, 215, 221, 226,
231–233, 243, 244,
247–250, 254, 255, 259,
260, 262, 263, 266, 271,
273, 275–278, 305, 309,
311, 312, 314, 316, 324,
329, 338, 342, 343, 353
figure, 39, 40, 56, 60, 72, 77–79, 81,
84, 85, 90, 96, 99, 100,
106, 108, 115, 116, 118,
123, 128, 131–133, 140,
144, 149, 160, 178, 187,
193, 202, 210, 215, 218,
229, 231–233, 235, 236,
246–248, 263, 269, 283,
287, 303
film, 34, 294, 299
finding, 13, 116, 132, 137–139, 304
flair, 4, 15
floor, 8, 15, 40, 41, 77, 93, 231
flourish, 157, 175, 196, 219, 348
flow, 250
fluidity, 1, 4, 13, 20, 35, 74, 78, 109,
122, 131, 193, 229, 235,
246, 263, 283, 303
focus, 25, 87, 95, 175, 188, 189, 196,
225, 312, 313, 320
folk, 7
following, 9, 10, 19, 23, 27, 53, 64,
79, 123, 260
force, 2, 5, 6, 20, 85, 95, 99, 137,
175, 204, 285
forefront, 125, 219, 221, 230, 254,
259
foreshadowing, 1
form, 2, 4, 7, 14, 20, 24, 26, 32, 59,
84, 121, 139, 190, 283, 325
formation, 8, 148

foster, 22, 35, 53, 85, 123, 126, 130,
135–137, 140, 152, 175,
182, 187, 188, 209, 217,
226, 227, 240, 247, 249,
254, 261, 262, 269, 282,
287, 294, 297, 299–301,
303, 313, 319, 322, 329,
331, 338
foundation, 5, 6, 8, 14, 39, 41, 56,
86, 142, 153, 208, 214,
246, 321, 325
founder, 40, 185
fragmentation, 351
framework, 2, 11, 24, 64, 78, 95, 96,
225, 246, 254, 276, 279,
313, 323
framing, 78, 97, 224, 297, 300
France, 125
freedom, 4, 7, 13, 30, 55, 85, 91,
121, 245, 279, 306
friendship, 58
frustration, 181
fuel, 6, 30, 109, 243
fulfillment, 60, 65, 138, 149
function, 96, 176, 214, 343
funding, 69, 82
fundraising, 69
fusion, 25, 37, 40, 84, 91, 125, 128,
187, 303
future, 5, 6, 13, 17, 22, 24, 28, 29,
33, 35, 39, 41, 43, 49, 62,
70, 75, 78, 79, 83, 85–89,
92, 94, 106, 111, 115, 117,
120, 123, 130, 132, 133,
135, 150, 152, 165, 174,
175, 180, 185–193,
195–197, 199, 201,
204–206, 210, 215, 219,
221, 225, 227, 232, 235,

236, 244, 246, 250,
253–255, 262, 267, 269,
271, 278, 280, 285, 289,
294, 297, 305, 309, 314,
316, 324, 329, 343, 351,
353, 354

gain, 39, 83, 87, 193
gap, 8, 129, 225, 304
gathering, 310
gay, 174, 342, 351
Gay da Bahia, 265
gender, 1, 2, 4–7, 9, 11, 12, 17–20,
22, 24, 27–30, 32, 34, 36,
37, 39, 40, 45–55, 59–61,
63, 66, 71, 73–75, 77–79,
81, 83, 84, 87, 88, 90, 91,
94–102, 107–110, 115,
116, 119, 122–124, 126,
129, 131–133, 136–139,
141–143, 147, 149, 150,
157–164, 166, 168, 171,
174, 178–181, 183–185,
190, 191, 193–195, 198,
202, 203, 205, 206,
208–210, 213, 214, 216,
217, 220–222, 224, 226,
229, 232, 235–237, 241,
244, 246–250, 254, 255,
258, 261–265, 269, 270,
273, 276, 278, 280, 282,
283, 287, 301, 303, 304,
306, 307, 313, 315, 323,
325, 341, 342
generation, 40, 43, 70, 72, 79, 84, 86,
92, 99, 126, 134, 180, 186,
188, 196, 231, 245, 248,
255, 307, 312–315
George Gerbner, 301

Germany, 125
gesture, 210
girl, 20
glamour, 216
glimpse, 4
glitz, 216
globalization, 127, 251, 253, 254
globe, 70, 88, 132, 165, 257, 262,
266, 271, 343
goal, 161, 204, 280
government, 73, 74, 90, 210, 244,
245, 249, 253, 264, 270
grace, 1, 6, 7, 35, 130, 144, 288
Graham, 34, 128
greatness, 26
grip, 249
grit, 161
ground, 319
groundbreaking, 1, 3, 5, 7, 8, 15, 34,
37, 39, 59, 76, 78, 85, 90,
97, 118, 120, 124, 126,
137, 156, 160, 184, 190,
210, 213, 220, 236, 303
groundwork, 10, 17, 18, 47, 115,
174, 192
group, 19, 23, 235, 238, 246, 325
growth, 22, 25, 26, 58–60, 87, 88,
117, 140, 143, 144, 150,
163, 168, 170, 173
guidance, 134, 312
guide, 4, 144, 224, 278

hallmark, 6
hand, 53, 127, 161, 319, 325
happiness, 65
harassment, 48, 74, 249, 260, 284
harmony, 13
haven, 69, 141
head, 35, 101, 156, 160, 162, 197

healing, 14, 197

health, 11, 24, 28, 58, 64, 95, 101,
        141, 166, 175, 194, 197,
        222, 231, 242, 249

healthcare, 12, 13, 49, 61, 62, 205,
        252, 264, 278, 280, 333

heart, 68, 94, 109, 129, 150, 163,
        235, 262, 343

hegemony, 246

help, 87, 95, 121, 142, 175, 186,
        187, 197, 250, 254, 275,
        276, 309, 313, 331

Henri Tajfel, 19

heritage, 1, 7, 91, 101, 129

heteronormativity, 261, 325

hierarchy, 19, 47

highlight, 11, 13, 29, 47, 62, 76, 102,
        116, 139, 141, 183, 188,
        198, 209, 210, 226, 266,
        275, 276, 289, 301, 316

hinge, 103

hiring, 325

history, 198, 215, 216, 278, 313

hobby, 2, 4, 6, 17

home, 3, 6, 126

homelessness, 194, 249

hometown, 15

homophobia, 313

homosexuality, 11, 73, 90, 105, 247,
        252, 258, 261, 265, 272

honesty, 222–224

honor, 12, 40, 157, 199, 223–225,
        227, 277, 312, 343

hope, 3, 20, 22, 37, 39, 41, 47, 48,
        54, 56–58, 61, 65, 67, 70,
        73, 75, 79, 88–90, 95,
        97–99, 102, 106, 107, 109,
        117, 122, 126, 128, 130,
        133, 135, 141, 157, 163,
        165, 169, 174, 175, 178,
        182, 184, 185, 187, 190,
        193, 195, 203, 204, 206,
        209, 214, 217, 221, 223,
        226, 229, 232, 233, 235,
        236, 241, 243, 245, 247,
        248, 250, 253, 255,
        262–265, 273, 278, 280,
        284, 285, 289, 314, 316,
        319, 327, 341, 353, 354

horizon, 85

hostility, 6, 23, 96, 174, 210, 284,
        310

household, 1, 141

housing, 249, 252

hub, 271

humanity, 128

hurdle, 82

husband, 116, 141, 142, 208

hybridity, 39

icon, 2, 3, 5–8, 10, 15, 17, 20, 34, 47,
        58–60, 66, 73, 75, 83, 85,
        88, 90, 92, 93, 96, 97, 100,
        107–109, 115, 119, 120,
        122, 124, 125, 127, 129,
        133, 137, 141, 142, 156,
        160, 178, 185, 190, 201,
        209, 210, 213, 220, 223,
        225, 233, 235, 237, 238,
        244, 246, 262, 283, 303,
        327, 341

idea, 14, 59, 76, 87, 95, 109, 134,
        149, 168, 169, 222, 231,
        232, 243, 285, 343, 347

ideal, 280

ideation, 95

identity, 1–3, 5–21, 23–25, 27, 29,
        31, 32, 34–36, 39–41,

45–56, 58–61, 63, 66, 67,
72, 74–76, 78, 79, 82–88,
90, 91, 94–101, 104,
107–110, 115, 116, 119,
120, 122–124, 126,
129–133, 136–139,
141–144, 146–150, 152,
153, 156–164, 166–169,
174, 176, 178–181, 183,
190, 193–195, 198, 202,
206–210, 213, 214,
220–222, 224–226, 229,
232, 233, 235–237, 241,
244, 246–248, 252, 258,
262–265, 270, 273, 278,
280, 282, 283, 287, 289,
303, 304, 306, 307, 315,
329, 344, 351, 353
ideology, 135
ignorance, 285
illustration, 107, 172
image, 77, 140, 215
imbalance, 128
impact, 10, 17, 20, 22, 24, 26, 28,
30, 33, 36, 37, 40, 43, 46,
47, 49, 58, 60–62, 67, 69,
72, 76, 79, 82, 83, 87–89,
91–95, 97–102, 107–110,
115, 117, 119, 122, 123,
125, 129–135, 143, 147,
150, 158, 160, 163, 166,
167, 173, 176–180, 184,
187–190, 192, 210,
213–215, 221, 225, 226,
230, 231, 235, 238,
245–247, 252, 255, 260,
262, 263, 269, 270, 284,
287, 288, 294, 303, 307,
310, 311, 314–316, 320,
327, 328, 337
imperative, 104, 106, 145, 223, 241,
282, 301, 326, 332, 338,
345
implementation, 205
importance, 9, 20, 24–26, 29, 30, 33,
35, 37, 40, 43, 47, 49, 51,
52, 54–60, 62, 64–67, 72,
75–77, 79, 85, 87, 89, 97,
99, 102, 104, 106, 108,
110, 116, 117, 119, 121,
126–128, 130, 134,
139–144, 146, 148–150,
152, 153, 155, 157,
162–165, 167, 176, 178,
180, 184, 188, 189, 191,
195, 197, 203, 208, 209,
211, 213, 214, 217–219,
221, 224, 226, 231, 232,
234, 236, 244, 247, 250,
260, 261, 263, 264, 266,
271, 273, 274, 277–279,
282, 285, 301, 304, 305,
307, 309, 310, 312,
315–317, 319, 331, 332,
337, 341
imprisonment, 258, 261, 265, 266,
272
improvement, 26
improvisation, 36
inadequacy, 25, 59
inclusion, 102, 177, 247
inclusivity, 22, 24, 28, 33, 40, 43, 49,
58, 67, 69, 70, 74, 75, 82,
85, 86, 90, 94, 95, 99, 108,
119, 123, 125–127,
130–132, 136, 150, 163,
164, 178, 180, 184, 185,
188, 197, 198, 203–205,

210, 221, 226, 235, 237,
241, 242, 259, 263, 270,
280, 291–294, 304, 305,
321, 325, 326, 328, 332,
340, 346, 348, 351
incorporation, 36
increase, 13, 77, 87, 249, 320
incubator, 196
India, 265
individual, 2, 4, 6, 8–10, 12, 13, 15,
17, 18, 23, 27, 29, 32, 33,
41, 50, 57, 65, 67, 79, 84,
89, 90, 94, 111, 115, 116,
134, 135, 139, 141,
143–145, 153, 156, 158,
160, 161, 163, 168, 175,
178, 183, 192, 197, 205,
207, 215, 217, 223, 225,
226, 244, 246, 279, 285,
288, 301–303, 306, 310,
319, 325, 327, 332, 342,
343, 353, 354
individuality, 72, 84, 95, 141, 143,
146
Indonesia, 265
industry, 1, 2, 10, 27–29, 31–34, 39,
40, 53, 59, 77, 81,
131–133, 181, 183, 185,
189, 196, 207, 242
inequality, 10, 104, 110, 195, 342,
343
influence, 3, 6, 8–10, 14, 15, 34, 35,
37, 43, 79, 84, 85, 87,
90–92, 95, 99, 100, 108,
110, 111, 116–118, 123,
126, 128, 130–132, 143,
150–152, 177, 179, 180,
184–186, 190, 193, 203,
221, 226, 231, 235, 236,

246, 248, 253, 254, 263,
268, 270, 271, 275, 289,
296, 297, 303, 304, 314,
328
information, 240, 250, 259, 340
initiative, 22, 93, 226, 236, 242, 271
injustice, 175, 247, 277
innovation, 26, 68, 70, 72, 85, 92,
325
insight, 83, 193
inspiration, 7, 22, 26, 33, 39, 65, 70,
83, 85, 88, 97, 99, 102,
108, 116, 122, 127, 144,
160, 163, 165, 169, 171,
174, 184, 191–193, 197,
201, 203, 227, 235, 314,
316
instability, 82
installation, 85
instance, 34, 48, 61, 64, 74, 79, 80,
85, 86, 90, 96, 116,
119–122, 124–126, 128,
131, 132, 136, 139, 149,
157, 159, 166, 170, 174,
175, 181, 194, 196, 202,
209, 210, 225, 226, 230,
240, 242, 247, 254, 261,
263, 265, 270, 272, 283,
304, 306, 310, 312, 313,
328, 342, 351, 352
institution, 20, 40
integration, 31
integrity, 35, 132
intensity, 23, 215, 258
interaction, 127
interconnectedness, 37, 81, 85, 88,
110, 117, 143, 179, 191,
255, 271, 277, 313, 323
interculturalism, 127

interdependence, 220

interest, 15, 33

interplay, 6, 36, 52, 64, 72, 106, 132, 142, 251, 253, 257, 342

interpretation, 125, 149

intersect, 49, 74, 99, 101

intersection, 15, 18, 26, 33, 41, 49, 96, 109, 129, 133, 187, 189, 201, 209, 226, 258, 270, 323

intersectionality, 30, 74, 79, 101, 102, 179, 186, 191, 193, 222, 226, 247, 255, 257, 259, 260, 263, 269, 273, 275, 276, 278, 298, 310, 316, 323, 342

intervention, 175, 320

intimacy, 140

introduction, 3

introspection, 52, 55, 59, 63

investment, 82

invisibility, 100, 298, 309

invitation, 343

involvement, 61, 74, 91, 95, 186, 259, 289, 310

Iran, 258, 266

isolation, 28, 29, 46, 49, 50, 57, 66, 81, 139, 143, 147, 156, 213, 216, 276, 323, 352

issue, 12, 82, 127, 136, 150, 207, 297, 300, 324, 329

Jin, 1, 2, 5–10, 13–16, 18–20, 25, 26, 31–35, 47–49, 52–56, 81–83, 94–97, 137–139, 149, 150, 158–161, 163–165, 171, 246–248, 341, 343

Jin Xing, 1, 3–5, 10, 13, 15, 17, 18, 20, 22–24, 27–30, 33, 35, 37, 39–41, 43, 46–48, 50–54, 58–62, 64–66, 68, 69, 71–79, 83–88, 90–95, 97–102, 104, 106, 107, 109, 110, 115, 116, 119–123, 125–136, 139, 140, 142–147, 149, 150, 152, 153, 155–158, 160, 162, 164, 166, 169, 174, 176, 178, 180–185, 187–191, 195–198, 201, 202, 204, 206–210, 213–224, 226, 230–233, 235–238, 243–248, 253, 255, 262, 269–271, 283–285, 288, 289, 303–307, 312, 314, 316, 321, 327

Jin Xing's, 1, 3–13, 15, 17, 18, 20–24, 26–31, 33, 35–37, 39–41, 43, 45–53, 55–70, 72, 74–102, 107–110, 115–135, 137, 139–142, 145, 147–151, 153, 155–158, 160–163, 165–167, 169–175, 178–188, 190–199, 201–204, 207–211, 213–217, 220, 221, 224–227, 229, 231–238, 242–248, 254, 262–264, 270, 271, 283–285, 287–289, 294, 303–307, 313–318, 326–329, 341–343, 351, 353

John Rawls, 279

John Turner, 19

journey, 1, 2, 4–8, 10, 11, 13–15,
        17–22, 24–35, 37, 39–41,
        43, 45–47, 49–67, 69, 70,
        72–76, 79, 81, 83–89, 91,
        92, 94–97, 100, 102, 107,
        109, 110, 115–117, 120,
        122–126, 128–130, 132,
        133, 135, 137–145,
        148–150, 152, 153,
        155–158, 160, 162, 163,
        165–167, 169–175, 178,
        180, 182, 183, 185, 187,
        190, 192, 193, 195, 197,
        199, 201, 203, 204,
        208–210, 213–218, 220,
        221, 223–225, 227, 231,
        234–236, 244–248, 250,
        251, 253, 262, 263, 269,
        270, 278, 280, 283–285,
        303–305, 307, 309, 314,
        316–319, 321, 322, 324,
        326, 327, 329, 343, 351,
        353
joy, 6, 138, 149, 203
judge, 34, 40, 67, 76, 77, 82, 86, 90,
        94, 108, 110, 122, 126,
        160, 166, 179, 192, 210,
        226, 235, 247, 263, 271,
        304, 315, 328
judgment, 2, 55, 59, 141, 160, 162,
        197, 205, 309, 334
Judith Butler, 32, 109, 229
Judith Butler's, 78, 122, 220, 224,
        226, 235, 262, 303
juncture, 18, 185
justice, 61, 85, 102, 106, 108, 129,
        173, 191, 202, 204, 231,
        248, 250, 253, 255, 259,
        262, 273, 275, 276,

        278–280, 319, 329, 332,
        343
juxtaposition, 55

Kazuo Ohno, 128
Kimberlé Crenshaw, 74, 179, 222,
        257, 316, 323, 342
knowledge, 26, 188, 253, 312, 314

labor, 58
lack, 1, 2, 12, 27, 28, 48, 49, 61, 62,
        82, 90, 96, 136, 175, 242,
        249, 289, 295, 296, 298,
        306, 313, 320, 325
landmark, 265
landscape, 10, 11, 15, 27, 37, 41,
        47–49, 55, 68, 70, 72, 78,
        82, 85, 90, 92, 100, 106,
        123, 131, 132, 137, 151,
        179, 181, 183–185, 197,
        202, 204, 206, 222, 244,
        247, 248, 252, 253, 255,
        257, 260, 264, 265, 267,
        271, 273, 274, 294, 303,
        304
language, 6, 8, 13, 14, 18, 84,
        120–122, 127, 135, 283,
        333
Latin America, 258, 265
launch, 70
law, 249, 280
layer, 140
lead, 12, 46, 49, 58, 65, 74, 78, 86,
        95, 103, 109, 119,
        127–129, 136, 143, 145,
        148, 166, 174, 175, 182,
        214, 221, 223, 238, 247,
        253, 266, 296, 298, 304,
        311, 333, 337

leader, 40, 189

leadership, 40, 312, 325

leap, 14, 42

learning, 23, 206, 275, 331

legacy, 10, 18, 33, 35, 39–41, 43, 62, 65, 67, 70, 72, 79, 83, 84, 86, 88–90, 94, 100, 106–108, 111, 117, 119, 127, 130, 133, 135, 150, 160, 165, 167, 180, 183, 184, 190, 192, 197–199, 201, 204, 209, 213, 219–221, 226, 227, 231, 236, 242, 244, 260, 264, 271, 285, 305, 312, 314, 316, 343

legislation, 99, 194, 258, 278

legitimacy, 69, 150

lens, 9, 23, 48, 67, 97, 99, 108, 122, 224, 226, 246, 279, 295, 296

lesson, 8

level, 12, 23, 25, 40, 49, 76, 83, 84, 87, 157, 159, 224, 225, 247, 277, 285, 333

leverage, 132, 171, 188, 196, 247, 345

liberation, 59

life, 2, 3, 5–8, 13, 17, 18, 21, 22, 24, 26, 29, 34, 47, 48, 51, 52, 54, 57–60, 63, 65, 67, 73, 84, 96, 97, 99, 100, 107, 110, 116, 134, 139, 141, 142, 144, 147, 150–153, 155, 157, 158, 160, 161, 163, 166, 167, 169, 181, 182, 207, 209–211, 213–217, 221, 223, 225–227, 244, 265, 279, 305–307, 316, 325–327, 343

lifeline, 4, 6, 17, 55

light, 8, 34, 87, 90, 130, 236, 288

limelight, 60, 98

limit, 74, 136, 209

limitation, 19

list, 105, 248, 264

listen, 311

listening, 320, 331

literature, 109, 240

London, 118

loop, 177

loss, 64

love, 1, 2, 4, 14, 55–59, 64, 66, 88, 98, 116, 117, 119, 122, 137–142, 144, 147–153, 155, 157, 158, 162, 193, 206, 208, 209, 213, 214, 216, 217, 230

luck, 33

luminary, 79, 183

mainstream, 34, 53, 78, 90, 96, 110, 160, 179, 192, 202, 210, 230, 235, 238, 246, 263, 271, 288, 295, 296, 300, 304

making, 29, 53, 83, 129, 145, 186, 189, 197, 202, 235, 267, 301, 313

Malaysia, 265

male, 9, 27, 46, 122

man, 342

manifestation, 68, 214

mantle, 312

marginalization, 100, 216, 246, 258, 270

mark, 36, 37, 70, 108, 147, 184, 190, 197, 244

marriage, 73, 90, 141, 210, 249, 258, 265, 267, 268, 277, 333

Marsha P. Johnson, 260, 277

Martha Graham, 34, 128

Martha Nussbaum, 279

masculinity, 36, 71, 109, 122, 303

Maslow, 19

matter, 161, 217, 324, 329, 336

meaning, 127, 136

means, 5–7, 13, 15, 18, 22, 43, 59, 66, 79, 85, 92, 110, 146, 150, 160, 229, 236, 247, 271, 284, 285, 288, 325

mechanism, 128, 287

media, 12, 13, 34, 40, 48, 53, 60, 66, 73, 74, 78, 79, 83, 87, 89–91, 94, 96, 98, 100, 102, 108, 109, 121–123, 125, 126, 132, 133, 140, 150, 160, 162, 166, 179, 180, 185, 188, 190, 192, 202, 207, 210, 214, 217, 220, 221, 224, 226, 230, 232, 235–238, 240, 246, 249, 253, 254, 259, 261, 263, 266, 271, 278, 282, 287–289, 291, 292, 294–297, 299–304, 312, 313, 315, 320, 341

medium, 2, 7, 29, 55, 70, 76, 84, 91, 120, 122, 163, 166, 181, 214, 230, 236, 283, 303, 306

member, 27, 141, 264

membership, 301

mentor, 79, 84, 134, 144, 145, 147, 247

mentoring, 145, 191

mentorship, 34, 79, 86, 134, 135, 142, 147, 188, 190, 191, 196, 197, 247, 312, 314

merit, 35

message, 22, 34, 121, 123, 127, 142, 165, 193, 203, 284, 304

microcosm, 13, 29, 236

mid, 138, 260

Middle Eastern, 272

midst, 27

milestone, 30, 43, 52, 70, 138, 224

milieu, 4

mind, 9, 13

mindset, 26

minefield, 210

minority, 24, 127, 261

mirror, 139

misinformation, 243

mission, 18, 68

misunderstanding, 48, 50, 97, 139

mix, 15, 162

mixture, 51

mobilization, 193, 247

model, 23, 64, 82, 91, 107, 108, 119, 149, 166, 184, 192

modeling, 62

modernity, 102

modernization, 251

moment, 6, 18, 20, 22–24, 29, 51, 52, 59, 68, 76, 82, 86, 97, 181, 207, 209

momentum, 18, 122, 260

morality, 78

mother, 4, 9, 138, 141, 142, 144, 147, 149–152

motherhood, 138, 210

motivation, 161, 171, 313

motor, 7

move, 74, 117, 219, 309, 354

movement, 1, 3, 4, 6–8, 13–15, 17, 18, 20, 21, 25, 31, 33, 35–37, 39, 43, 49, 55, 58, 59, 62, 67–70, 74, 75, 84, 85, 87, 88, 91, 98–100, 108–110, 115, 126, 130, 133–135, 167, 174, 178–180, 182, 193–195, 203, 210, 221, 232, 236, 244–249, 251, 253, 259–261, 263, 264, 268, 269, 271–273, 275, 276, 312, 314, 316, 319, 328, 332, 342, 343, 352

multitude, 259

music, 4, 29, 119, 146

myriad, 2, 18, 52, 81, 185, 196, 253

name, 1, 3, 6, 39, 92, 97, 209, 215

narrative, 1, 7, 13, 25, 30, 31, 33, 47, 57, 75, 79, 81, 90, 97–99, 109, 110, 115, 131, 134, 137, 139, 142, 150, 157, 163, 165, 167, 169, 183, 187, 196, 201, 209, 210, 214–216, 220, 223–226, 231, 235–238, 244, 246, 247, 253, 283, 295, 309, 314, 319, 327–329

nation, 216, 271

national, 73, 79, 82, 100, 116, 226, 247, 328

nature, 3, 11, 22, 27, 34, 76, 108, 142, 150, 180, 210, 214, 222, 227, 247, 284, 304, 327, 329

navigation, 11, 47

necessity, 24, 56, 63, 227, 301, 336

need, 12, 13, 24, 29, 35, 49, 54, 61, 62, 64, 69, 95, 99, 101, 102, 121, 123, 124, 127, 134, 140, 148, 166, 179, 180, 194, 197, 208, 209, 217, 221, 231, 263, 265, 270, 272, 276, 299, 307, 314, 342, 346, 348

negativity, 171, 295

negotiation, 143

neighboring, 268

Netherlands, 264, 272

network, 16, 143, 148, 176

New York City, 174, 260

newfound, 138, 140

news, 207

niche, 31

Nigeria, 258, 266, 272

nightclub, 277

non, 17, 50, 120, 122, 149, 150, 220, 229, 235, 240, 258, 263, 264

nonconformity, 4, 81, 174

norm, 50, 81, 96

normalization, 234

North America, 131

Norway, 264

notion, 14, 109, 122, 135, 208, 283, 316, 343

number, 252

numerator, 262

Nussbaum, 279

obstacle, 71, 249

occasion, 351

officer, 4, 9

Ohno, 128

on, 1–3, 5–8, 10, 12, 17, 18, 20, 21, 23, 25, 26, 28, 30, 32–37,

40, 43, 47, 49, 53, 55, 60,
62, 65–67, 69, 70, 74, 76,
78, 79, 82, 84–88, 90, 92,
94–96, 98, 100–104, 108,
115, 117–123, 125–135,
140–142, 147, 150, 151,
155, 156, 158–164, 166,
167, 174–180, 184,
187–190, 192, 196, 197,
199, 204, 206, 208, 210,
213–215, 220, 222,
224–227, 229, 232, 233,
235, 236, 238, 244–249,
253, 258, 260, 263, 265,
266, 268–271, 276, 280,
285, 287, 294, 303, 304,
307, 312–316, 319–321,
325, 327, 328, 337, 343,
351, 353
one, 5, 7, 20, 22, 26, 27, 33, 39, 47,
51–53, 58–60, 63, 64, 67,
72, 75, 76, 79, 81, 86, 88,
90, 98, 107–109, 111, 117,
120, 141, 146, 148, 157,
160, 165, 182, 185, 192,
205, 206, 209, 211, 215,
216, 220–222, 237, 246,
251, 271, 279, 283, 285,
303, 312, 316, 351
opening, 29, 149
openness, 123
opinion, 275, 294–296, 299
opportunity, 26, 39, 132, 190, 193,
195, 197, 205, 319
opposition, 174, 263
oppression, 74, 167, 174, 179, 222,
258, 260, 314, 316, 342,
347
optimism, 279

organization, 320
organizing, 260, 312
orientation, 36, 75, 88, 90, 94, 95,
109, 122, 129, 132, 147,
179, 180, 195, 230, 237,
241, 246, 254, 273, 278,
280, 282, 287, 315, 325
ostracism, 46, 146, 306, 309
ostracization, 80
other, 13, 24, 30, 67, 69, 93, 101,
126, 127, 141, 143, 146,
161, 164, 166, 186, 230,
242, 265, 284, 319, 323,
325, 328, 343
outlet, 7, 59, 159, 161, 306
outlook, 171
outreach, 87, 121, 236, 261
outside, 4, 6, 133
overshadowing, 128
overview, 257

pain, 64, 109, 159, 166, 214
pandemic, 194
panel, 271
parent, 142–144, 149, 150
parenthood, 116, 141, 143, 144, 149
parenting, 10, 143–145, 149
Paris, 39, 118, 270
part, 19, 65, 140, 144, 225, 254,
261, 271, 301, 309, 343
participate, 279
participation, 6–9, 15, 34, 98, 116,
129, 136, 160, 178, 179,
192, 210, 230, 232, 248,
252, 254, 263, 270, 309,
315, 324, 325, 336
partner, 138, 140, 153, 197
partnership, 34, 118, 126, 128, 141
passage, 264

passion, 1–3, 5, 6, 8, 13–15, 17–20, 26, 33, 43, 59, 61, 66, 69, 79, 96, 161, 174, 226

past, 84, 136, 205, 206, 278, 312

pastime, 7

path, 2, 5–7, 18, 25, 33, 35, 43, 47, 56, 58, 60, 63, 66, 88, 95, 130, 147, 156, 163, 183, 187, 206, 210, 216, 255, 268, 332, 351, 353

peer, 57, 146

people, 12, 60, 100, 175, 187, 192, 220, 232, 235, 260, 276, 288, 298, 313, 314, 343

perception, 46, 96, 107, 108, 143, 149, 150, 178, 179, 184, 220, 307, 352

perfection, 25

performance, 3, 4, 6, 8, 13, 15, 26, 28–30, 32–35, 39, 42, 55, 69, 76, 78, 81, 82, 86, 92, 96, 108, 118, 119, 122, 131, 132, 136, 179, 188, 189, 202, 207, 214, 226, 262, 270, 284, 288, 314

performativity, 32, 78, 122, 220, 224, 226, 235, 262, 303

performer, 60, 81, 122, 131, 178, 194

peril, 226

period, 7, 14, 17, 21

perpetuation, 13

persecution, 132, 194, 205, 258, 272

perseverance, 1, 4, 9, 20, 31, 79, 184, 216, 236, 285

persistence, 161

person, 153, 348, 351

persona, 52, 61, 66, 101, 107, 109, 140, 178, 215, 236, 246, 270, 288

personal, 5–7, 9–11, 15, 18–22, 25–27, 29, 30, 33, 36, 39–41, 43, 47, 48, 50, 52–54, 57–60, 63–65, 67, 75, 79, 81, 84, 87, 88, 91, 94, 97, 98, 101, 107, 109, 110, 115, 116, 123, 125, 131, 133, 137–142, 144, 147, 150, 155–158, 160, 162, 163, 165–175, 178, 182, 183, 196, 197, 201, 202, 209, 210, 213–216, 220–222, 224–226, 236, 244, 245, 283, 285, 287, 309, 314, 316, 319, 327

personality, 12, 48, 73, 89, 109, 236, 341

perspective, 76, 85, 129, 131, 191, 193, 225, 279, 285

phenomenon, 20, 22, 62, 126, 160, 175, 207, 215, 235, 337

philosophy, 84, 144, 196, 211

physicality, 35

picture, 264

piece, 34, 76, 85, 120, 126, 270

Pierre Bourdieu, 231, 343

piety, 73, 149, 248

pioneer, 84, 86, 183

pirouette, 14, 42

place, 5, 12, 17, 29, 32, 41, 67, 227, 283

planet, 189

platform, 8, 12, 15, 18, 22, 28, 34, 40, 61, 64, 66, 68, 69, 72, 76, 77, 79, 80, 82, 85, 91, 94, 98, 99, 101, 108, 110, 116, 117, 119, 122, 125, 126, 129, 131, 134, 136,

143, 150, 160, 162, 164,
166, 167, 171, 174, 178,
179, 185, 186, 189, 191,
194, 196, 198, 226, 235,
236, 242, 247, 252, 254,
263, 266, 271, 289, 304,
315, 337

play, 16, 49, 102, 132, 141, 150,
175–177, 187, 250, 261,
275, 276, 293, 299, 302,
309, 310, 312, 331, 332,
335, 347

point, 5, 32, 33, 55, 97, 174, 196,
214, 235, 260

police, 174, 260, 352

policy, 74, 175, 186, 193, 221, 245,
246, 259, 266, 267, 299,
312, 328, 333, 342, 345,
352

popularity, 123

population, 102, 204, 250, 291, 299,
304, 321

populism, 194

portrayal, 13, 48, 96, 207, 214, 225,
254

posit, 14, 221

position, 74, 189, 210, 304

possibility, 48, 217, 223

post, 52, 54, 214, 226

postmodernism, 39

potential, 1, 2, 4, 9, 10, 14, 19, 24,
25, 35, 49, 55, 58, 59, 86,
91, 92, 111, 117, 125–127,
131, 135–137, 139, 146,
152, 157, 187, 190, 203,
219, 223, 231, 232, 235,
240, 241, 251–253, 255,
262, 266, 268, 272, 280,
287, 296, 297, 299, 300,

304, 326, 328, 344, 348,
351–353

poverty, 49

power, 2, 3, 6–8, 13–15, 18, 22, 26,
29, 30, 33, 35, 37, 39, 40,
42, 47, 51, 55, 58, 61–64,
66, 70, 72, 73, 75, 79, 83,
85, 89, 92, 94, 98–100,
108–110, 116, 117, 120,
123, 125, 127, 128, 130,
133, 135–137, 139, 141,
142, 144, 157, 158, 162,
163, 165, 167, 169, 170,
174, 175, 178, 182, 184,
190, 195, 201, 203, 204,
209, 211, 214, 217, 218,
221, 223, 227, 232,
234–236, 244, 245, 248,
254, 255, 264, 266, 271,
277, 287, 294, 301, 303,
305, 307, 309, 313–317,
319, 320, 326, 329, 338,
342, 345, 353

practice, 25, 26, 325

precursor, 138

prejudice, 8, 23, 27, 28, 32, 39, 48,
62, 81, 96, 156, 158, 160,
161, 174, 227, 243, 277,
285, 335

preparation, 15

prerequisite, 11

presence, 12, 24, 34, 36, 40, 48, 53,
66, 76–79, 82, 87, 90, 94,
96, 98, 109, 119, 122, 126,
132, 133, 147, 149, 160,
176, 177, 179, 192, 210,
221, 226, 229, 235, 236,
246, 263, 271, 287, 289,
304, 313, 314, 341

present, 55, 84, 136, 223

presentation, 27

pressure, 2, 12, 17, 24, 25, 28, 50, 59, 66, 77, 138, 140, 146, 160, 202, 248, 253

prevalence, 300

prevention, 175, 320

pride, 91, 129, 191, 225, 247, 252, 254, 315, 341

principle, 163, 271, 279

print, 294, 299

privilege, 74, 101, 222, 247, 310, 316, 331, 347

prize, 15

problem, 146, 224, 298, 325

process, 11, 14, 23, 52, 58, 59, 63, 72, 172, 214, 232, 298, 320, 339

procreation, 73

product, 26, 83, 96, 190

production, 32, 84, 189, 298

professional, 10, 17, 18, 27, 28, 48, 53, 54, 81, 83, 88, 89, 96, 116, 144, 158, 207, 317

proficiency, 25, 120

profile, 284

profit, 127

program, 235, 263, 304

progress, 54, 90, 98, 104, 106, 117, 175, 185, 194, 196, 198, 206, 232, 247, 251–253, 257, 259, 263–268, 271, 277, 278, 280, 299–301, 313, 326, 329, 341, 351

prominence, 26, 33, 36, 39, 48, 49, 82, 96, 98, 116, 118, 235, 245, 246

promise, 117, 187, 206, 277, 353

promotion, 325

provide, 1, 39, 64, 68, 86, 106, 142, 144, 164, 178, 196, 197, 205, 237, 238, 240, 253, 257, 259, 266, 276, 295, 312, 334, 346

provider, 12

prowess, 24, 31, 33, 40, 84, 119, 160

psychologist, 161

psychology, 62, 64, 141

public, 2, 12, 28, 34, 48, 51–56, 60, 61, 66, 74, 77, 78, 80, 81, 83, 90, 91, 95, 96, 101, 102, 107–109, 116, 123, 124, 134, 140, 147, 149, 150, 160, 162, 171, 178, 179, 189, 208–210, 214, 215, 220, 226, 229, 230, 232, 236, 238, 240, 245, 246, 249, 253–255, 260–263, 270, 271, 275, 283, 285, 288, 291, 294–296, 299, 300, 304, 307, 308, 312, 314–316, 320, 345, 352

pulse, 13

purpose, 5, 58, 65

pursuit, 1, 5, 9, 18–20, 26, 72, 96, 106, 137, 139, 147, 160, 164, 183, 209, 217, 250, 254, 264, 278, 314, 321

push, 23, 26, 84, 86, 106, 118, 126, 128, 187, 205, 248, 278, 285, 313

pushback, 252

quality, 26, 76, 220, 262, 280, 300

queer, 74, 102, 164, 193

quest, 5, 52, 108, 126, 137, 169, 193, 202, 245, 248, 262, 266,

306, 348, 351, 353
quo, 29, 33, 37, 39, 41, 48, 70, 85,
    96, 98, 151, 160, 229, 232,
    245, 287, 314, 336

race, 30, 49, 74, 101, 102, 191, 222,
    255, 258, 261, 263, 276,
    323, 325, 342
racism, 102, 325
raid, 174
raise, 28, 34, 85, 91, 94, 103, 108,
    129, 149, 186, 259
range, 18, 103, 299
Rawls, 279
reach, 37, 59, 74, 90, 121, 122, 131,
    132, 188, 280, 287, 313,
    334
reaction, 48, 53, 54, 208, 209, 214
reality, 46, 48, 107, 160, 179, 197,
    271, 301, 304
realization, 5, 14, 18, 70
realm, 94, 100, 117, 118, 120, 126,
    129, 144, 147, 189, 215,
    217, 219, 223, 226, 288,
    304, 307, 314, 319
reassignment, 11, 20, 48, 51, 52, 55,
    59, 97, 109, 138, 157, 162,
    168, 171, 181, 209, 214,
    224
rebellion, 2, 14, 18, 55
reception, 125, 131
reclamation, 207
recognition, 11, 15, 16, 33–35, 39,
    40, 43, 61, 62, 102, 126,
    174, 187, 193, 210, 220,
    221, 245, 252, 254, 277,
    279, 309, 324
redefining, 37, 122, 149, 150, 220,
    229

reevaluation, 283
reference, 235
reflection, 14, 26, 54, 59, 115, 136,
    139, 197, 204, 208, 259,
    312
reform, 221, 245, 260
refuge, 57, 159
refusal, 20, 32
regimen, 23–25
region, 265–267
regression, 257
rejection, 9, 11, 12, 20, 46, 48, 52,
    55, 56, 64, 95, 109, 138,
    139, 147, 156, 158, 166,
    170, 181, 198, 206, 216,
    226, 245, 249, 262, 313
relation, 59
relationship, 9–12, 19, 23, 25, 116,
    140, 141, 149, 157, 308
relevance, 132
relief, 51
reluctance, 148, 161, 253
remembrance, 198
reminder, 20, 24, 26, 43, 47, 49, 52,
    55, 60, 62, 63, 72, 75, 90,
    91, 94, 95, 98, 108, 110,
    117, 126, 139, 142, 155,
    162, 165, 167, 180, 195,
    210, 213–215, 217, 219,
    221, 226, 232, 236, 245,
    248, 263, 266, 271, 277,
    316
removal, 74, 105
renaissance, 255
repeal, 205
repertoire, 126, 187
report, 64, 222, 265
representation, 2, 12, 13, 28, 30, 32,
    33, 35–37, 40, 41, 43, 47,

48, 53, 54, 60, 62, 67, 70,
72, 76–79, 83, 87–90, 92,
94, 98, 100, 102–104,
106–110, 119, 123–128,
130, 131, 133, 135, 136,
149, 151, 160, 164, 166,
178–180, 183–185, 194,
197, 201, 202, 204,
206–208, 210, 217–221,
225, 226, 234, 236, 246,
248–250, 253–255, 262,
263, 270, 271, 278, 282,
287–289, 291, 294–305,
313, 325, 326, 336, 339,
351, 352

representative, 254

reprisal, 334

reputation, 4, 34

research, 59, 121, 142, 143, 166, 179

resilience, 1, 3, 5–10, 13, 15, 18–20,
22, 24–26, 28, 29, 32–35,
39, 40, 43, 47, 49, 52, 54,
57–65, 67, 73, 75, 81, 83,
84, 86, 88, 89, 91, 92, 95,
97, 100, 106–111,
115–117, 119, 120, 122,
126, 129, 130, 133–135,
138–142, 144, 146, 147,
150, 152, 155–160,
164–178, 180–182, 184,
187, 188, 190, 193, 195,
196, 201–204, 209, 211,
213, 214, 216, 217, 219,
221, 224–227, 229, 230,
232, 235, 236, 238, 244,
245, 248, 250, 253, 255,
262, 264, 266, 276–278,
280, 283–285, 289, 304,
307, 314–316, 318, 319,

329, 353

resistance, 6, 71, 74, 78, 84, 95, 96,
124, 129, 131, 150, 160,
202, 221, 226, 236, 247,
249, 263, 308–310, 342

resolve, 161, 162, 280

resource, 190, 193, 247, 351

respect, 97, 121, 123, 127, 141, 149,
208, 225, 329, 333, 353

response, 74, 175, 277

responsibility, 132, 189, 226, 227,
291, 293, 294, 297, 298,
309, 314, 322, 332, 348,
350

result, 5, 33, 35, 46, 96, 128, 165,
248, 249, 292, 353

retribution, 221, 309

revelation, 221

revolution, 254

rhythm, 4, 13, 36

richness, 126, 226, 294, 304, 354

ridicule, 11

right, 65, 106, 351

ripple, 53, 66, 77, 108, 157, 180,
191, 204, 231, 268, 270,
328, 351

rise, 12, 26, 32, 33, 35, 36, 48, 49,
59, 82, 96, 98, 100, 109,
115, 118, 123, 132, 141,
185, 194, 246, 249, 254,
255, 288, 297, 313, 314,
327, 351

risk, 127, 136, 337

rivalry, 207

road, 232, 251, 253, 255

roadmap, 99, 107, 267

role, 4, 6, 8–10, 12, 14, 16, 17, 21,
22, 25, 28, 34, 36, 37, 39,
40, 48, 49, 56–62, 64, 66,

67, 75, 76, 78, 79, 82, 84,
86, 90, 91, 96, 97, 100,
102, 107–110, 118, 119,
121, 122, 125–127, 129,
131–134, 137, 138, 141,
142, 144, 145, 147–150,
157, 162, 166, 174–179,
183, 185–187, 192, 198,
204, 206, 210, 214, 216,
225, 226, 229–232, 235,
238–240, 246–248, 250,
254, 259, 261–263, 271,
275, 276, 283, 285, 291,
293, 294, 296, 299,
302–304, 307, 309, 310,
312, 315–317, 319, 328,
330–333, 335, 338, 340,
347
rollback, 277
room, 7, 46, 47, 55, 96, 213, 214
root, 254, 343
Russia, 194, 261

s, 1–37, 39–41, 43, 45–70, 72,
74–102, 107–111,
115–135, 137–142,
145–151, 153, 155–167,
169–175, 178–188,
190–199, 201–204,
207–211, 213–217,
220–227, 229, 231–238,
242–248, 253, 254,
262–264, 270–272, 279,
283–285, 287–289, 291,
292, 294, 296, 301,
303–307, 312–320,
326–329, 341–343, 351,
353
safety, 210

sanctuary, 2, 7, 15, 17, 55, 66, 93,
206, 214, 226, 306
Saudi Arabia, 258, 266
scale, 33, 60, 98, 104, 122, 126, 188
scene, 29, 69, 132
scholarship, 196
school, 277, 313
scope, 69
screen, 229
scrutiny, 30, 53, 96, 119, 140, 143,
160, 162, 171, 208, 210,
214, 221
section, 20, 22, 33, 47, 58, 65, 84, 97,
100, 104, 107, 133, 135,
142, 160, 173, 176, 178,
180, 185, 215, 217, 239,
251, 257, 260, 264, 267,
269, 274, 285, 291, 294,
301, 312, 314, 317, 327,
329, 336, 339, 343, 348
segment, 115
self, 1, 2, 4, 7–9, 13–15, 17–23, 25,
26, 28–30, 45–47, 51, 52,
54–56, 58–61, 63–68, 72,
76, 79, 81, 82, 87, 88, 95,
97, 99, 107, 109, 116, 121,
126, 130, 134, 138, 141,
143, 144, 146, 148, 157,
158, 160–163, 165, 171,
172, 181, 188, 190, 196,
202–204, 206, 208, 209,
213–215, 217, 219, 226,
235, 236, 238, 263, 283,
284, 301, 306, 307, 312,
317, 319, 329
sensationalism, 97, 130, 207, 223,
224, 295
sensationalist, 96
sense, 1, 4, 6, 7, 9, 13, 15, 16, 19–21,

23, 51, 55, 56, 59, 60, 67,
74, 92, 93, 121, 125, 134,
139, 140, 144, 175, 182,
191, 235–238, 254, 263,
277, 284, 301, 304, 306,
315, 338

sensitivity, 121, 122, 130

sequence, 29

series, 15, 29, 39, 87, 121, 125, 139,
188, 190, 216, 220, 224,
235, 303

set, 3, 8, 26, 29, 31, 87, 88, 121, 208

setting, 5, 140, 300

sex, 73, 90, 205, 249, 250, 254, 258,
265, 266, 268, 277

sexism, 325

sexuality, 19, 30, 47, 48, 61, 74, 77,
79, 83, 87, 91, 97, 100,
102, 107, 108, 116, 119,
122, 123, 126, 133, 136,
139, 147, 158, 164, 166,
178, 184, 191, 193, 198,
203, 214, 216, 217, 221,
222, 229, 232, 235, 244,
247–249, 258, 263, 287,
301, 303, 304, 313, 341,
342

Shanghai, 22, 40, 43, 68–70, 72, 82,
84, 93, 95, 171, 185, 191,
195, 226, 236, 242, 252,
271

share, 22, 53, 58, 69, 74, 85, 87, 91,
104, 120, 121, 126, 132,
133, 136, 143, 185, 188,
203, 205, 225, 227, 231,
237, 240, 249, 254, 259,
263, 275, 284, 287, 295,
309, 313, 319, 337

sharing, 20, 47, 53, 64, 79, 80, 95,

110, 120, 125, 126, 129,
142, 153, 157, 166, 169,
174, 190, 196, 209, 217,
218, 221, 224, 230, 237,
262, 271, 277, 284, 285,
287, 304, 312, 316, 327,
329, 338

Shenyang, 1, 3, 5, 7, 11, 13, 15, 17,
18, 20, 33, 35, 45, 54, 60,
66, 79, 97, 109, 115, 125,
133, 137, 158, 161, 201,
206, 213, 235, 244, 246,
262, 283, 303, 306, 314

shift, 18, 22, 33, 61, 62, 75, 77, 108,
123, 133, 150, 151, 179,
220, 221, 232, 240, 254,
255, 288, 304

show, 76–78, 90, 94, 160, 166, 210,
235, 271, 304

showcase, 6, 16, 28, 34, 40, 66, 68,
118, 132, 188

side, 141

significance, 14, 22, 39, 59, 64, 102,
109, 110, 127, 128, 130,
136, 160, 203, 217, 225,
246, 260, 285, 329

silence, 3, 6, 61, 178, 202, 248, 251

situation, 120, 265, 319

skepticism, 6, 18, 23, 28, 32, 69, 71,
96, 138, 209

skill, 23, 25, 180

society, 2, 4, 6, 8, 13–20, 22–24, 27,
29, 30, 34, 36, 39, 41, 47,
50, 52, 53, 55–63, 65–67,
69, 73, 75, 76, 78, 83, 90,
92, 94–97, 100–102, 104,
106, 109, 115, 130, 133,
134, 137–139, 141, 145,
149–151, 153, 156, 162,

164, 166, 167, 170–172,
174, 179, 180, 182, 187,
190, 192, 197–199, 202,
204–206, 208–211,
214–216, 219–221, 223,
225, 226, 229, 232–238,
241, 246, 247, 249–251,
253–255, 262, 263, 274,
275, 279, 282–285,
287–289, 297, 301,
303–305, 309, 312–314,
316, 321, 322, 324–326,
329, 332, 335–337, 341,
343, 345, 348, 351, 353,
354
socio, 1, 101
solace, 13, 17
solidarity, 20, 43, 92, 106, 130, 134,
135, 141, 167, 175, 184,
188, 196, 197, 205, 232,
236, 243, 250, 253, 255,
259, 263, 266, 271–273,
275, 277, 278, 284, 285,
287, 304, 331, 332, 338,
343, 347
solving, 325
soul, 84
source, 2, 4, 14, 19, 65, 117, 169,
171, 172, 174, 192, 227
South America, 121
space, 2, 6, 19, 30, 34, 36, 41, 43, 48,
58, 66, 68, 90, 95, 127,
141, 148, 157, 206, 207,
223, 236, 237, 242, 254,
271, 275, 287, 348
spark, 6
speaking, 28, 53, 61, 91, 123, 150,
208, 230, 247, 312, 322,
324

spectacle, 224
spectrum, 36, 102, 143, 255, 276,
298
sphere, 189
spirit, 1, 33, 49, 58, 70, 72, 100, 142,
152, 174, 225, 248, 262
spokesperson, 34
spontaneity, 36
spotlight, 3, 29, 207
stage, 2, 5, 34–36, 79, 90, 119, 120,
122, 125, 127–130, 132,
190, 220, 229, 246, 263,
314
stance, 270
stand, 67, 100, 157, 197, 201, 227,
278, 343
standing, 75, 146, 174, 211, 277,
331, 332, 343, 351
star, 3, 5
stardom, 8, 29, 216
state, 257, 259, 267, 277, 300
statement, 5, 6, 20, 29, 39, 82, 157,
162
status, 29, 33, 34, 37, 39–41, 48, 49,
70, 85, 96, 98, 101, 125,
151, 160, 229, 232, 245,
247, 258, 287, 314, 336
step, 63, 97, 117, 138, 199, 215, 241,
251, 280, 285, 332
stereotype, 149, 217
stigma, 4, 9, 11, 13, 14, 17, 20, 24,
46, 48, 49, 53, 55, 62, 64,
66, 73, 78, 80, 90, 96, 109,
138–140, 143, 145, 156,
174, 175, 178, 202, 213,
216, 222, 226, 235, 242,
248, 249, 251, 253, 254,
265, 266, 270, 289, 300,
301, 306, 307, 313, 320,

328, 352

stigmatization, 13, 104, 237

stone, 4

story, 1, 3, 5, 18, 20, 22, 24, 26, 29,
34, 41, 47, 49, 52–54, 58,
60, 61, 64–67, 75, 76, 80,
81, 83, 87, 88, 91, 97–99,
107–111, 116, 117, 120,
123, 125, 126, 129, 130,
132, 134, 135, 139, 141,
142, 144, 150, 152, 155,
157, 160, 162, 163,
165–167, 169, 174, 180,
184, 190, 192, 196, 198,
199, 203, 209, 210,
214–216, 219, 221,
223–227, 230–233, 235,
236, 244–246, 262, 263,
270, 284, 294, 307, 315,
316, 318, 319, 327–329

storytelling, 7, 25, 32, 70, 85, 87, 99,
120, 132, 135, 169,
217–220, 223, 237, 285,
287, 300, 338

strategy, 208

streaming, 34, 74

strength, 2, 7, 14, 19, 25, 65–67,
107, 110, 135, 139, 150,
157, 158, 160, 166, 171,
172, 196, 205, 236, 277,
288, 313

stress, 24, 165

stretching, 25

stride, 117

stroke, 33

structure, 143

struggle, 12, 13, 20, 24, 27, 46, 49,
51, 52, 54, 63, 75, 77–79,
82, 91, 93, 94, 97, 100,

104, 108, 123–126, 133,
137, 140, 160, 181, 193,
195, 204, 213, 215, 221,
225, 226, 230, 232, 233,
236, 243, 245, 246, 248,
250, 259, 262, 263,
265–267, 269, 271, 273,
276, 277, 283, 285, 300,
309, 313, 325, 336, 343,
345, 350

Stuart Hall, 107

student, 31

studio, 3, 13

study, 222, 304

style, 4, 21, 25, 35–37, 39, 82, 84,
91, 118, 131, 143

subject, 217

succeed, 2, 23, 171, 209, 306

success, 2, 6, 10, 16, 17, 19, 22, 24,
26, 33, 35, 40, 49, 55, 60,
61, 66, 69, 71–73, 78, 79,
81, 95, 97, 118, 119, 125,
126, 132, 142, 161,
163–166, 171, 236, 237,
244, 247, 254, 316, 340

suicide, 175, 320

suit, 189

suitability, 18

sum, 135

summary, 26, 40, 54, 120, 126, 155,
214, 244, 285

support, 1, 4, 6–10, 12, 14, 17–19,
25, 51, 53, 56–59, 64–67,
69, 74, 82, 95, 109, 134,
139, 141–144, 148, 149,
155, 162, 166, 168, 169,
172, 175–179, 182, 185,
194, 197, 205, 206,
208–210, 213–217, 231,

236, 247–250, 259, 265,
266, 273, 275–277, 301,
303, 304, 309–315, 317,
319, 320, 332, 333, 335,
337, 341, 343, 348

supporter, 95

surgery, 11, 20, 48, 51–55, 59, 97,
109, 138, 157, 162, 168,
171, 181, 208–210, 214,
224, 226, 258, 265

surrounding, 9, 11, 17, 20, 29, 47,
50, 58, 59, 62, 73, 96, 100,
109, 122, 129, 131, 133,
138, 145, 156, 157, 166,
178, 210, 215, 216, 220,
221, 224, 235–237, 243,
266, 269, 270, 279, 303,
327

survey, 166

sustainability, 189, 190

Sweden, 264, 277

sword, 17

Sylvia Rivera, 260, 277

symbol, 5, 47, 89, 98, 99, 126, 130,
135, 174, 236, 247, 248,
284, 304

symbolism, 35

synergy, 119, 161

system, 12, 59, 141, 142

taboo, 54, 97, 110, 235, 283, 315

Taiwan, 265, 268

takeaway, 64

tale, 1, 97, 183, 225, 327

talent, 1–7, 9, 14–18, 20, 22–24, 28,
29, 31, 33–35, 39–41, 66,
72, 78, 82, 90, 95, 96, 100,
108, 116, 118, 122, 161,
183, 191, 206, 207, 209,

214, 230, 236, 243, 247,
288, 315

Tan Dun, 119

tapestry, 1, 7, 15, 35, 57, 69, 89, 135,
201, 213, 216, 278, 353

target, 284

task, 82, 225

teacher, 9

teaching, 146

technique, 6, 21, 23, 25, 26, 188

technology, 121, 122, 132, 133, 188,
345

television, 12, 40, 48, 53, 73, 78, 79,
82, 86, 90, 94, 98, 100,
109, 110, 166, 226, 230,
235–237, 246, 249, 254,
294, 299, 304, 328, 341

tenacity, 115, 183, 216

tender, 3, 6

tenet, 110

tension, 10, 12, 30, 32, 78, 119, 157,
207, 210, 213, 310

term, 161, 301

terrain, 142

testament, 2, 3, 13, 18, 22, 26, 32,
33, 35, 40, 54, 58, 62, 64,
67, 70, 73, 83, 87, 92, 94,
100, 107, 116, 118, 120,
122, 125, 128, 133, 135,
139, 141, 150, 151, 158,
163, 165, 170, 174, 180,
184, 190, 192, 197, 201,
209, 211, 213, 217, 218,
221, 226, 227, 229, 235,
244, 245, 262, 271, 285,
307, 316, 329

the Middle East, 121, 124, 258, 266,
267

the United States, 134, 205, 276, 277

theater, 271

theatre, 40, 69, 70, 236

theme, 32, 47

theorist, 229

theory, 9, 18, 19, 23, 24, 48, 59, 65, 74, 78, 79, 107–109, 122, 127, 142, 143, 164, 169, 179, 193, 220, 222, 224, 226, 235, 238, 247, 257, 258, 262, 275, 279, 303, 343

therapy, 14

thought, 189

threat, 30, 202, 208, 221, 236

thrive, 28, 29, 107, 127, 178, 197, 209, 239, 279, 314, 348, 353

tightening, 253

time, 1, 6, 7, 13, 17, 23, 25, 27, 41, 46, 77, 121, 140, 207, 229, 251, 351

title, 39, 40

today, 3, 291, 342

token, 311

tokenism, 287

tokenization, 337, 338

toll, 12, 28, 81

tool, 15, 87, 94, 121, 125, 134, 146, 159, 169, 192, 204, 285, 287, 295, 313

tour, 118, 120, 121, 131

touring, 132

town, 97, 125, 244

traction, 193

tradition, 68, 78, 99

traditionalist, 304

trailblazer, 26, 35, 61, 70, 84, 94

training, 12, 15, 18, 21–26, 31, 34, 39, 82, 188, 207, 240, 253, 280

trait, 78, 158, 168, 180, 226

trajectory, 29, 131, 132, 185, 278

transfer, 188, 312

transformation, 1, 21, 22, 50, 59, 65, 76, 84, 109, 120, 129, 131, 138, 141, 147, 155, 169, 173, 182, 221, 232, 236, 253, 255, 283, 288, 319, 340, 348, 351

transgender, 2–4, 6, 8–13, 15–20, 22–24, 27–29, 32, 34, 36, 39, 45–53, 55–64, 66, 67, 71, 73, 78–82, 84, 85, 90, 92, 94, 96–98, 100, 107, 109, 110, 115, 116, 119, 120, 122–124, 126, 129, 131, 133, 134, 136–139, 142–145, 149–151, 153, 156–158, 160–162, 164, 166, 178, 179, 183, 185, 190, 192, 194, 201, 202, 209, 210, 213–218, 220, 222–226, 229, 233, 235, 237, 244–246, 260, 262, 263, 270, 283, 285, 288, 298, 303, 304, 306, 307, 314, 316, 327, 341, 342, 351

transition, 53, 54, 82, 86, 91, 97, 98, 140, 157, 162, 208, 214

transitioning, 52, 59, 140, 171

translation, 122

trauma, 165

triumph, 8, 18, 33, 39, 52, 79, 97, 115, 125, 160, 167, 183, 214, 220, 233, 244, 304,

314, 327
troupe, 3
trust, 153
truth, 14, 15, 67, 122, 157, 209, 211,
    213, 216–221, 226, 316,
    354
turmoil, 45, 174
turn, 11, 39, 47, 175, 246
turning, 5, 32, 33, 55, 64, 160, 171,
    174, 214, 260
Twyla Tharp, 126

Uganda, 194, 258, 261, 265, 272
uncertainty, 57, 157
underpinning, 274
understanding, 1, 12, 15, 22, 24, 27,
    33, 41, 42, 45, 47–49, 52,
    53, 57–60, 62, 63, 65, 67,
    72, 74, 78–80, 82, 83, 85,
    87–92, 96–100, 102, 104,
    116, 119–123, 125–130,
    133–141, 143, 148–150,
    152, 153, 155, 157, 158,
    163–166, 169, 172, 175,
    178, 179, 184, 187–189,
    191–195, 197, 208–210,
    214–217, 219, 221, 225,
    226, 230, 235–241, 243,
    246, 248, 250, 254, 258,
    261–263, 270, 275–277,
    279, 280, 282, 285, 287,
    294, 295, 297, 299–301,
    303, 304, 307–310, 313,
    316, 319–322, 324, 327,
    336, 337, 339, 342, 345,
    346, 353
unemployment, 194
uniqueness, 2
unit, 141

unity, 135
universality, 79, 98, 133
unveiling, 220
upbringing, 9, 10, 206
uplift, 142, 158, 171, 247
uprising, 260, 352
urgency, 279
Uruguay, 258
use, 15, 18, 30, 36, 122, 136, 167

validation, 55, 207, 263, 282
validity, 246
value, 9, 127, 146, 283
variance, 50
variety, 325
vehicle, 9, 18, 40, 89, 92, 125, 163,
    198, 230, 238, 291
venture, 68
versatility, 31, 303
version, 122, 247
victory, 22, 29, 161, 265
video, 122
view, 221, 236
viewership, 77
violence, 48, 55, 66, 80, 87, 99, 104,
    174, 186, 194, 249, 257,
    258, 261, 265–267, 272,
    277, 309, 342, 346, 352
visibility, 13, 18, 20, 22, 28, 30, 34,
    36, 40, 47, 49, 53, 54, 56,
    58, 60–62, 66, 67, 72–75,
    78, 81–83, 86, 87, 90, 92,
    94–98, 102, 104,
    106–110, 115, 117, 119,
    122–124, 126, 129, 133,
    135, 149, 151, 162, 164,
    166, 167, 178–180, 183,
    185, 187, 194–196, 201,
    203, 204, 211, 214, 215,

217, 220, 221, 225, 226,
229, 231–238, 244–249,
253–255, 262–264, 271,
275, 278, 284, 288, 301,
303–305, 307–310,
312–316, 326–328, 335,
341, 343

vision, 3, 68, 69, 71, 84, 85, 88, 116,
125, 131, 163–165, 185,
197, 205, 280, 353

visionary, 195

vocabulary, 36

voice, 5, 6, 8, 14, 15, 22, 31, 53, 58,
70, 85, 86, 99, 136, 214,
219, 232, 284, 289, 329

vulnerability, 52, 87, 140, 155, 224

wave, 84, 214, 312

way, 3, 6, 13–15, 41, 43, 50, 53, 57,
72, 75, 83, 90–92, 94, 97,
102, 117, 120, 122, 130,
152, 157, 165, 169, 183,
185, 191, 210, 221, 225,
230, 232, 235, 250, 255,
265, 269, 278, 282, 294,
297, 316, 324

wealth, 188

web, 49, 188

weight, 53, 203

well, 7, 15, 24, 28, 57, 58, 76, 125,
140–143, 147, 157, 166,
175, 197, 209, 222, 230,
231, 310, 326, 336, 346

West, 122, 123, 126

whole, 211, 326

willingness, 23, 72, 91, 312, 313, 316

woman, 4, 19, 23, 27, 28, 32, 34,
46–48, 53, 59, 63, 67, 71,
73, 81, 90, 96, 107, 126,

129, 133, 138, 139, 143,
149, 157, 164, 178, 185,
209, 214, 218, 222, 226,
237, 246, 262, 283, 303,
304, 314, 316, 342

word, 227

work, 1, 4, 9, 12, 14, 15, 17, 18, 26,
29, 30, 32, 33, 37, 39, 40,
53, 61, 62, 67, 69, 71, 72,
75, 84, 85, 88, 91, 92, 94,
95, 97, 100, 117–119,
124–128, 130–134, 136,
150, 157, 163–166, 175,
179, 180, 182, 184, 189,
190, 194, 201–204, 207,
210, 216, 218, 219, 221,
231, 236, 238, 246, 250,
254, 259, 261–263, 271,
278, 280, 284, 294, 304,
305, 328, 329, 334, 343,
347, 353, 354

workplace, 242, 309, 310, 325

workshop, 237

world, 2, 3, 5–8, 13–15, 17, 23–26,
28, 31, 36, 37, 39, 41, 43,
46, 47, 50, 52, 56, 59, 67,
70, 76, 79, 81, 83, 84,
86–88, 94, 96, 98, 104,
106, 111, 117–120, 123,
126, 128–130, 137, 142,
144, 147, 155, 159, 160,
165, 171, 180, 184,
192–195, 197, 201, 203,
204, 206, 209, 213, 215,
223, 225, 227, 233, 259,
261, 263, 264, 266, 269,
271, 273, 275, 278, 280,
285, 287, 291, 303,
314–316, 319, 321, 329,

332, 341, 342, 353, 354
worth, 10, 27, 47, 55, 157, 209
writing, 298

youth, 175, 196, 205, 243, 255, 277,
312–314, 320, 336

9 781779 695963